トリコ
劇場版

*Toriko: The Movie

Since this is the first film based on my work, I'm truly humbled but also looking forward to it! As the original creator, my only hand in it was the character design, but it would make me really happy if you readers went to see it. I'm thinking of going to see it at least 200 times, or maybe not, but either way, my heart's racing! See you at the movies!

(My current weight…68 kg!! Uh-oh!!)

—Mitsutoshi Shimabukuro, 2013

Mitsutoshi Shimabukuro made his debut in **Weekly Shonen Jump** in 1996. He is best known for **Seikimatsu Leader Den Takeshi!** for which he won the 46th Shogakukan Manga Award for children's manga in 2001. His current series, **Toriko**, began serialization in Japan in 2008.

TORIKO

TORIKO VOL. 25
SHONEN JUMP Manga Edition

STORY AND ART BY **MITSUTOSHI SHIMABUKURO**

Translation/Christine Dashiell
Weekly Shonen Jump Lettering/Erika Terriquez
Graphic Novel Touch-Up Art & Lettering/Elena Diaz
Design/Matt Hinrichs
Editor/Hope Donovan

Printed in Canada

Published by VIZ Media, LLC
P.O. Box 77010
San Francisco, CA 94107

10 9 8 7 6 5 4 3 2 1
First printing, December 2014

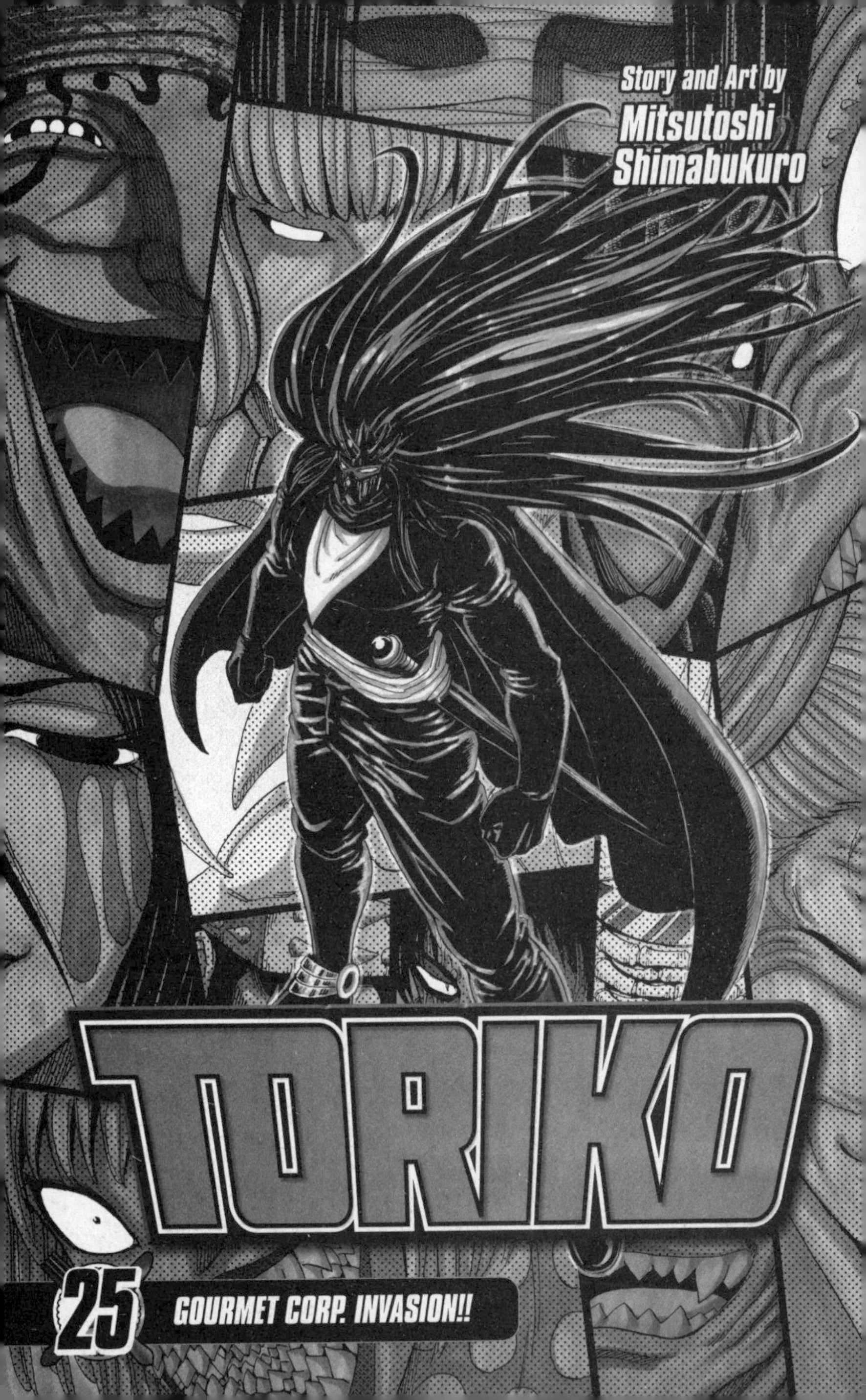
Story and Art by
Mitsutoshi Shimabukuro
TORIKO
25
GOURMET CORP. INVASION!!

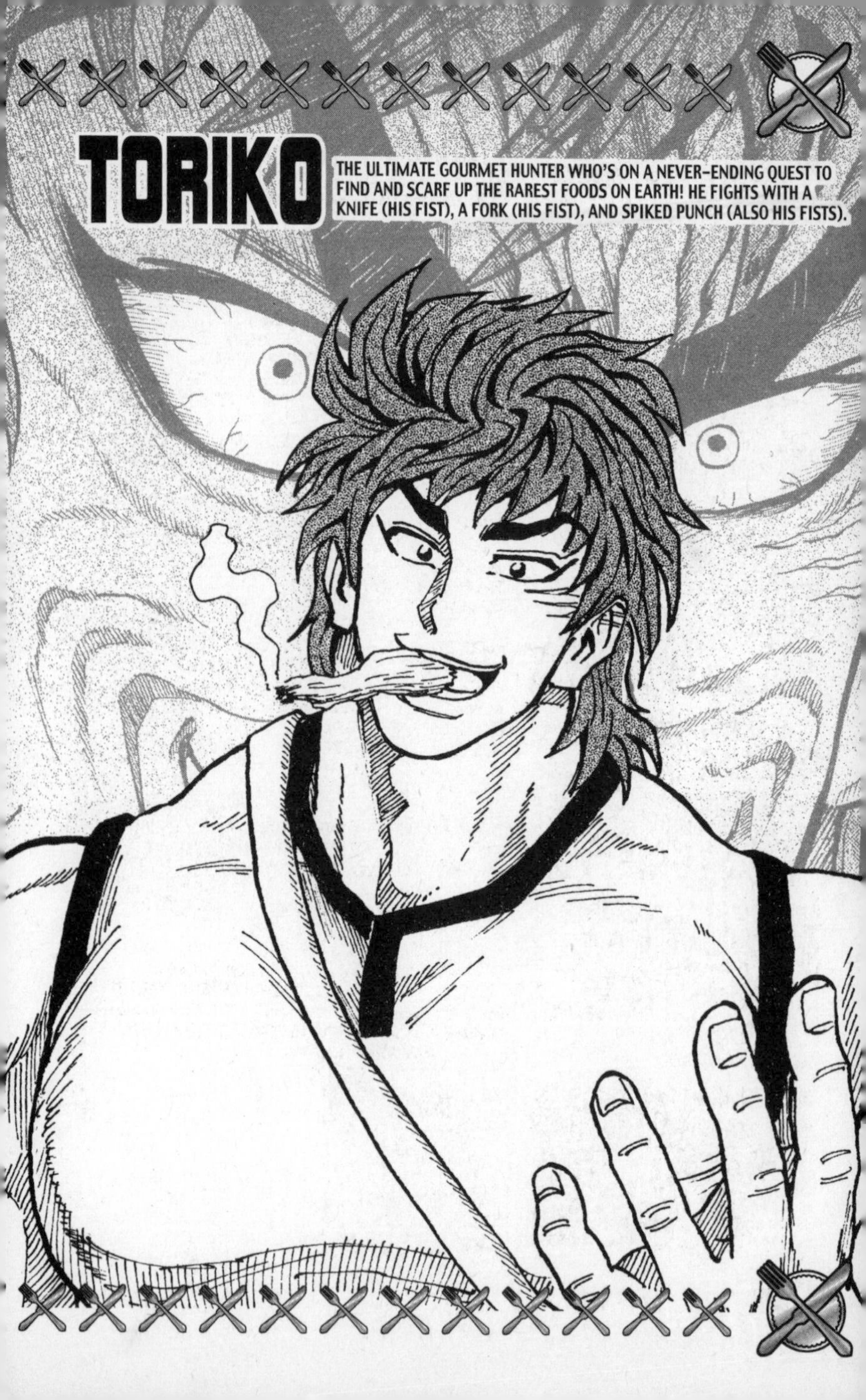
TORIKO
THE ULTIMATE GOURMET HUNTER WHO'S ON A NEVER-ENDING QUEST TO FIND AND SCARF UP THE RAREST FOODS ON EARTH! HE FIGHTS WITH A KNIFE (HIS FIST), A FORK (HIS FIST), AND SPIKED PUNCH (ALSO HIS FISTS).

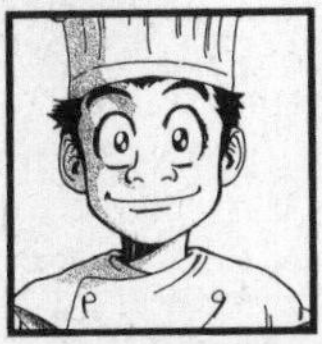

●KOMATSU
TALENTED IGO HOTEL CHEF AND TORIKO'S #1 FAN.

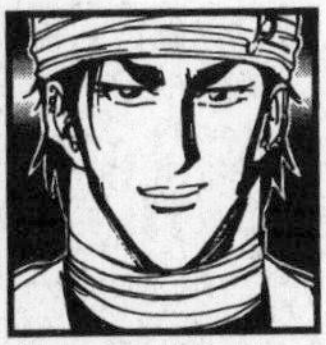

●COCO
ONE OF THE FOUR KINGS, THOUGH HE IS ALSO A FORTUNETELLER. SPECIAL ABILITY: POISON FLOWS IN HIS VEINS.

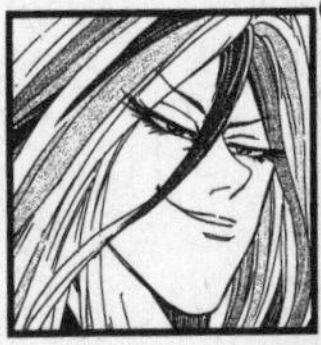

●SUNNY
A GOURMET HUNTER AND ONE OF THE FOUR KINGS. SENSORS IN HIS LONG HAIR ENABLE HIM TO "TASTE" THE WORLD. OBSESSED WITH ALL THAT IS BEAUTIFUL.

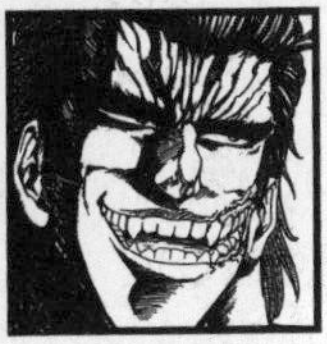

●ZEBRA
A GOURMET HUNTER AND ONE OF THE FOUR KINGS. A DANGEROUS INDIVIDUAL WITH SUPERHUMAN HEARING AND VOCAL POWERS.

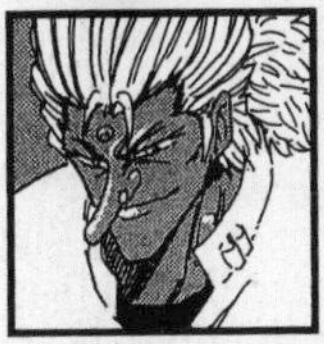

●BRUNCH
WORLD CHEF RANKING: #3. HEAD CHEF AT LEGENDARY "TENGU CASTLE."

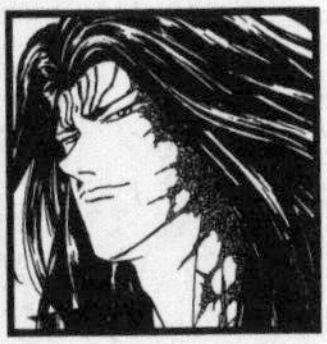

●STARJUN
ONE OF GOURMET CORP'S THREE VICE-CHEFS. WATCHFUL OF TORIKO'S GROWING POTENTIAL.

WHAT'S FOR DINNER

IT'S THE AGE OF GOURMET! KOMATSU, THE HEAD CHEF AT THE HOTEL OWNED BY THE IGO (INTERNATIONAL GOURMET ORGANIZATION), BECAME FAST FRIENDS WITH THE LEGENDARY GOURMET HUNTER TORIKO WHILE GATOR HUNTING. NOW KOMATSU ACCOMPANIES TORIKO ON HIS LIFELONG QUEST TO CREATE THE PERFECT FULL-COURSE MEAL. THROUGH THEIR ADVENTURES, THEY FIND THEMSELVES ENTANGLED IN THE IGO'S RIVALRY WITH THE NEFARIOUS GOURMET CORP. WITH TORIKO'S EVERY HUNT, THE INEVITABLE CLASH GROWS CLOSER!

GOURMET CORP. ASIDE, NOW THAT TORIKO AND KOMATSU ARE PARTNERS, THEY HAVE BEGUN TRAINING TO ENTER THE GOURMET WORLD BY COLLECTING FOODS FROM A TRAINING LIST PROVIDED BY IGO PRESIDENT ICHIRYU.

THEN ONE DAY, THE FOUR-BEASTS AWAKENS! THE FOUR KINGS POOL THEIR APPETITE TO DEFEAT THE FOUR-BEASTS. BUT THE REAL SAVIOR OF THE DAY IS KOMATSU, WHO CURES SCORES OF PEOPLE WITH HIS LIFESAVING MEDICIAL MOCHI. HIS FEAT IN SIMPLIFYING THE PREPARATION OF THE DETOXIFYING TREAT LIFTS HIM TO 88TH PLACE ON THE WORLD CHEF RANKING. BEING IN THE TOP 100 QUALIFIES HIM FOR THE COOKING FESTIVAL, A COOKING COMPETITION THAT HAPPENS ONCE EVERY FOUR YEARS.

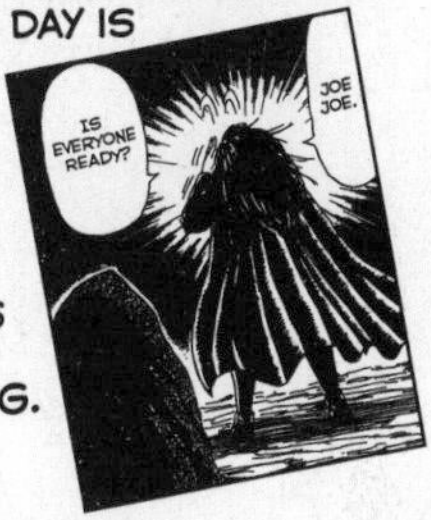

JOE JOE.
IS EVERYONE READY?

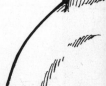

THE FESTIVAL BEGINS! KOMATSU IS OFF TO A LATE START, BUT LATECOMER BRUNCH PULLS HIM ALONG TO THE FINALS. THEN, UNEXPECTEDLY...

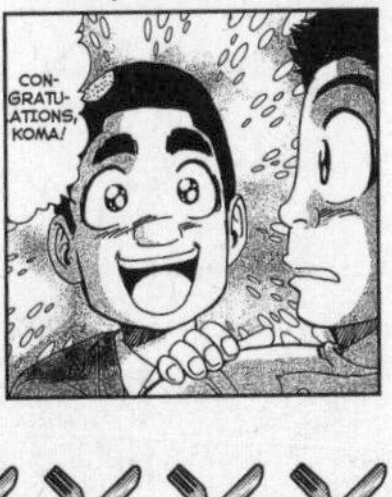

CON-GRATU-ATIONS, KOMA!

Contents

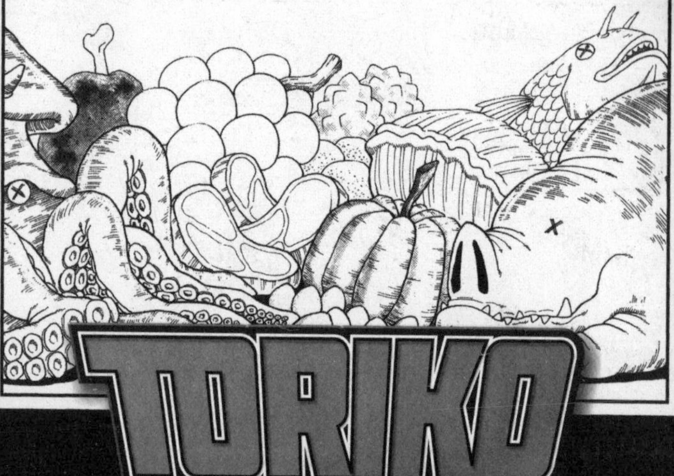

TORIKO

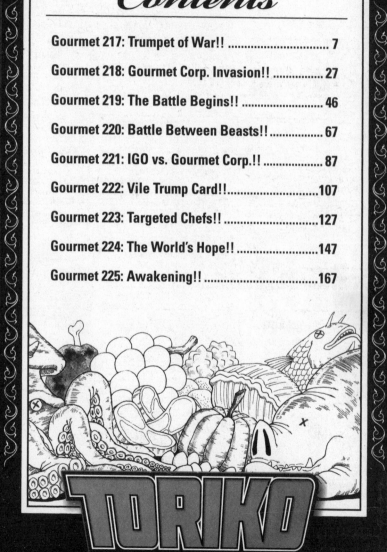

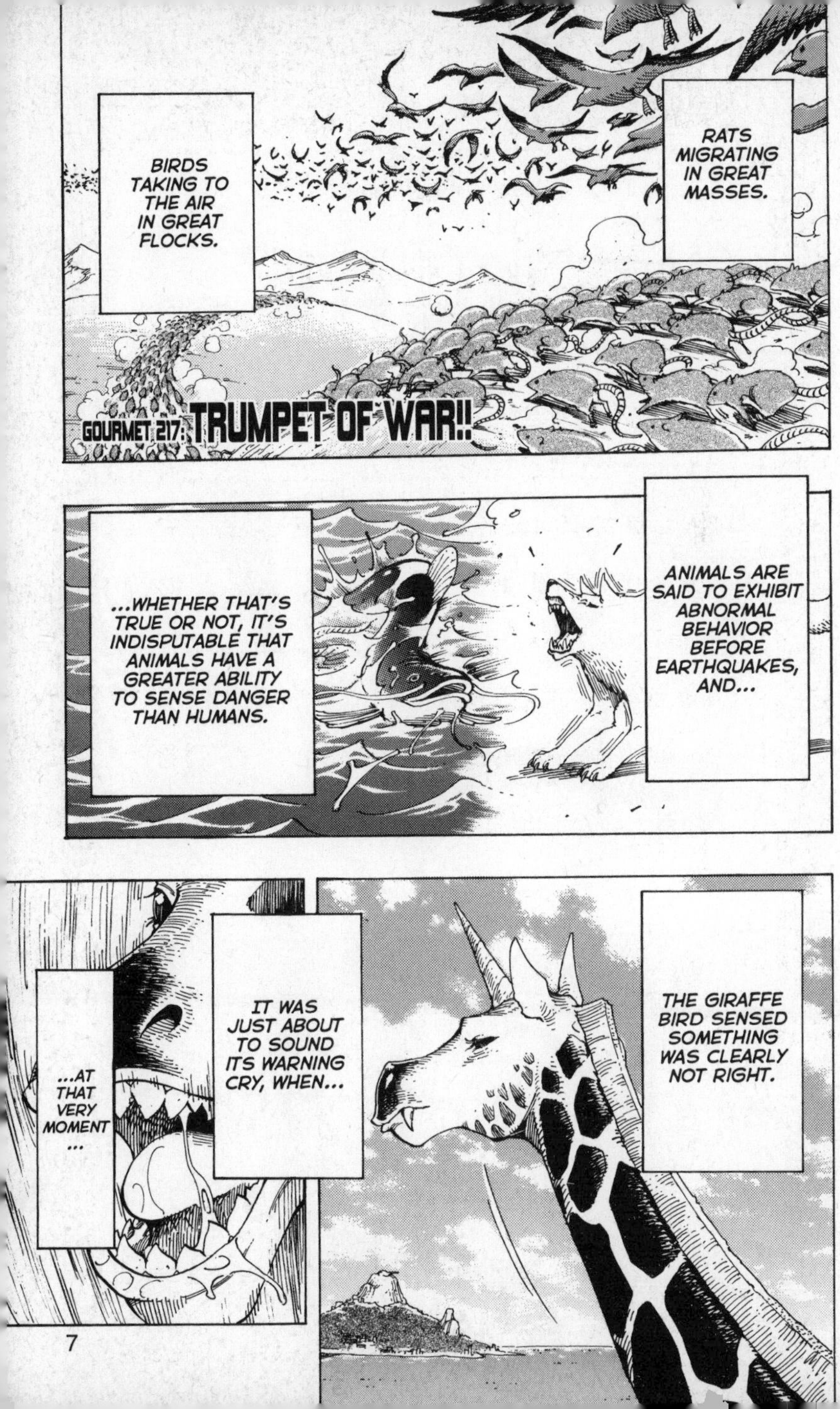
RATS MIGRATING IN GREAT MASSES.
BIRDS TAKING TO THE AIR IN GREAT FLOCKS.
GOURMET 217: TRUMPET OF WAR!!
ANIMALS ARE SAID TO EXHIBIT ABNORMAL BEHAVIOR BEFORE EARTHQUAKES, AND...
...WHETHER THAT'S TRUE OR NOT, IT'S INDISPUTABLE THAT ANIMALS HAVE A GREATER ABILITY TO SENSE DANGER THAN HUMANS.
THE GIRAFFE BIRD SENSED SOMETHING WAS CLEARLY NOT RIGHT.
IT WAS JUST ABOUT TO SOUND ITS WARNING CRY, WHEN...
...AT THAT VERY MOMENT...

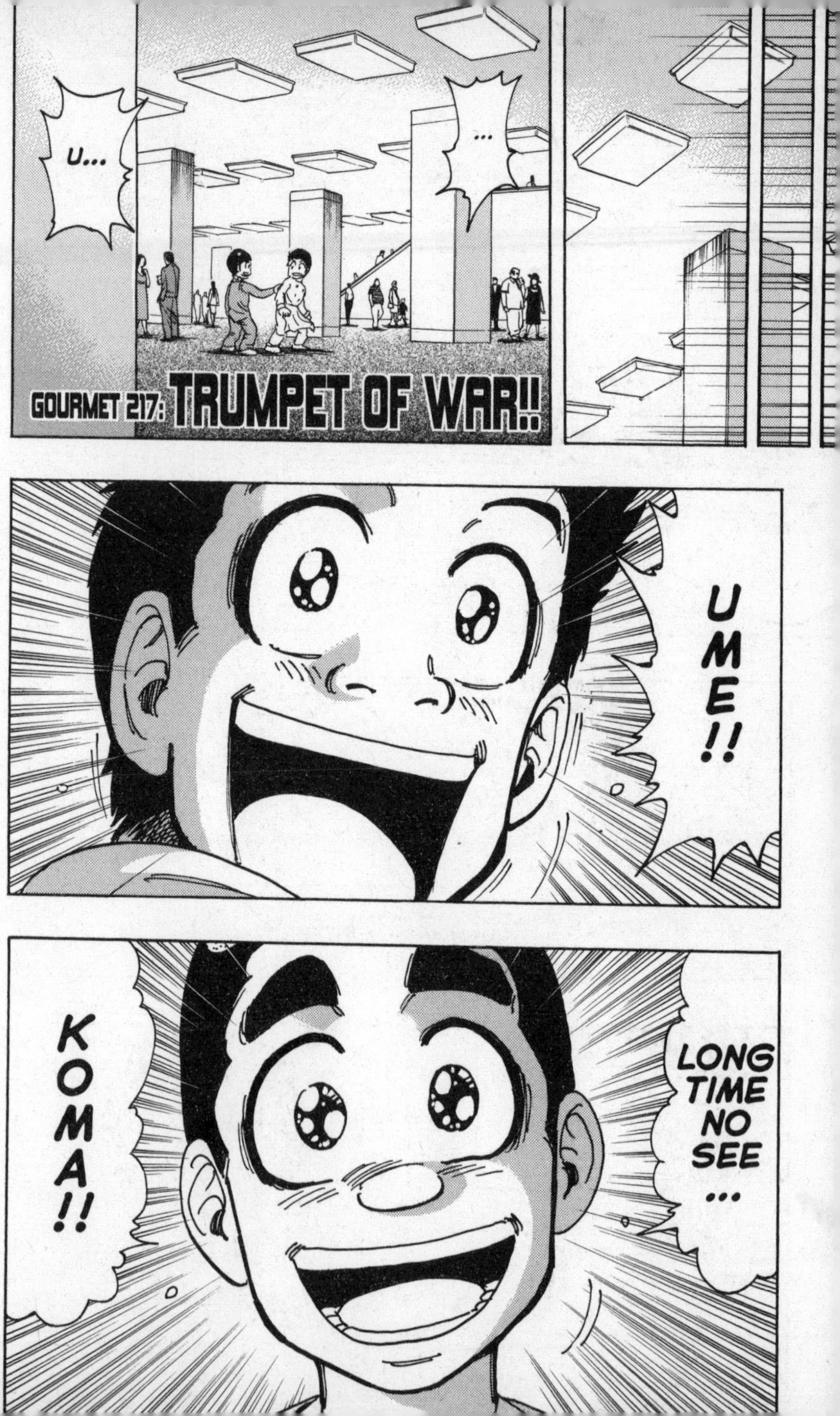
...
U...
GOURMET 217: TRUMPET OF WAR!!
UME!!
LONG TIME NO SEE...
KOMA!!

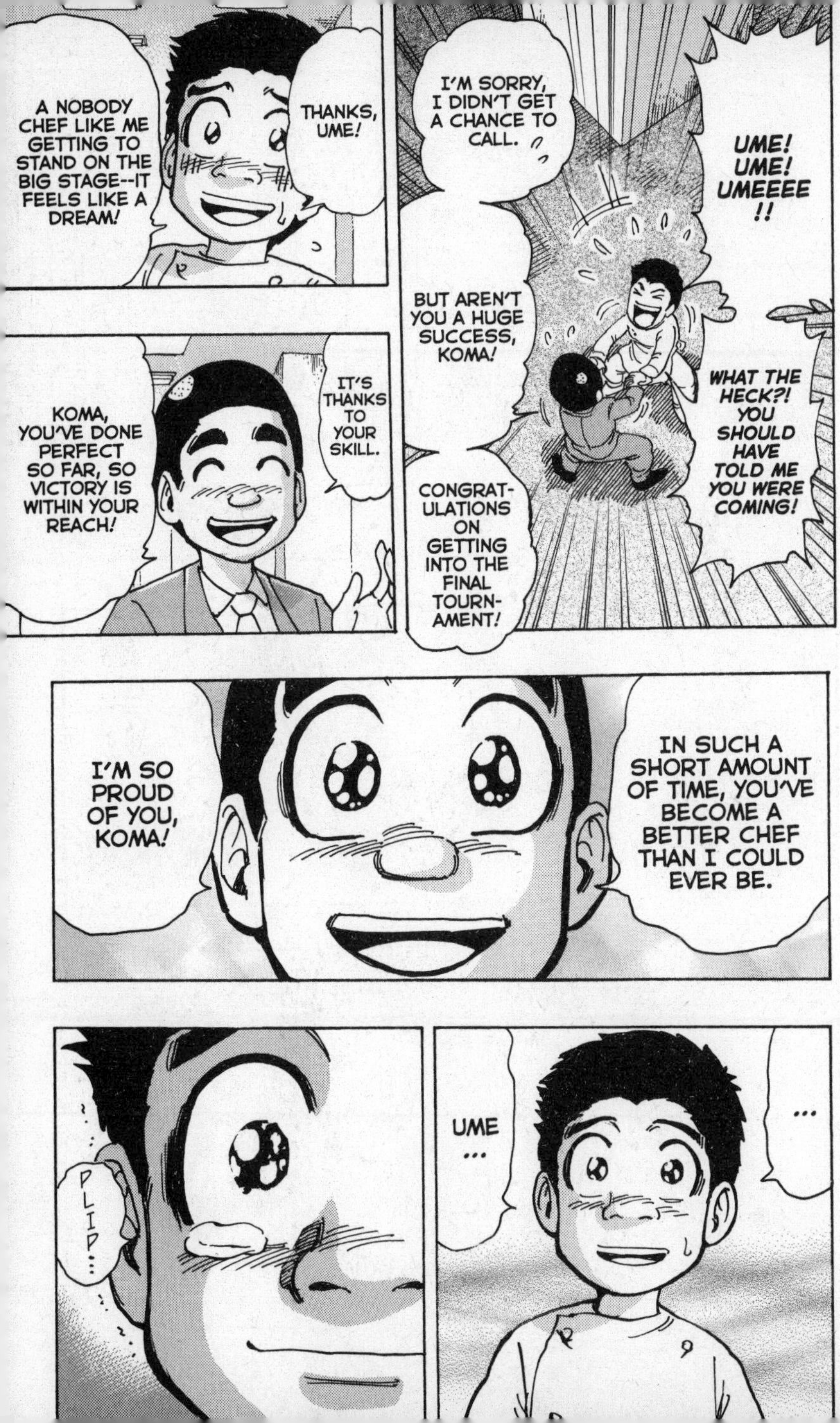
UME! UME! UMEEEE!!
WHAT THE HECK?! YOU SHOULD HAVE TOLD ME YOU WERE COMING!
I'M SORRY, I DIDN'T GET A CHANCE TO CALL.
BUT AREN'T YOU A HUGE SUCCESS, KOMA!
CONGRAT-ULATIONS ON GETTING INTO THE FINAL TOURN-AMENT!
THANKS, UME!
A NOBODY CHEF LIKE ME GETTING TO STAND ON THE BIG STAGE--IT FEELS LIKE A DREAM!
IT'S THANKS TO YOUR SKILL.
KOMA, YOU'VE DONE PERFECT SO FAR, SO VICTORY IS WITHIN YOUR REACH!
IN SUCH A SHORT AMOUNT OF TIME, YOU'VE BECOME A BETTER CHEF THAN I COULD EVER BE.
I'M SO PROUD OF YOU, KOMA!
...
UME ...
PLIP...

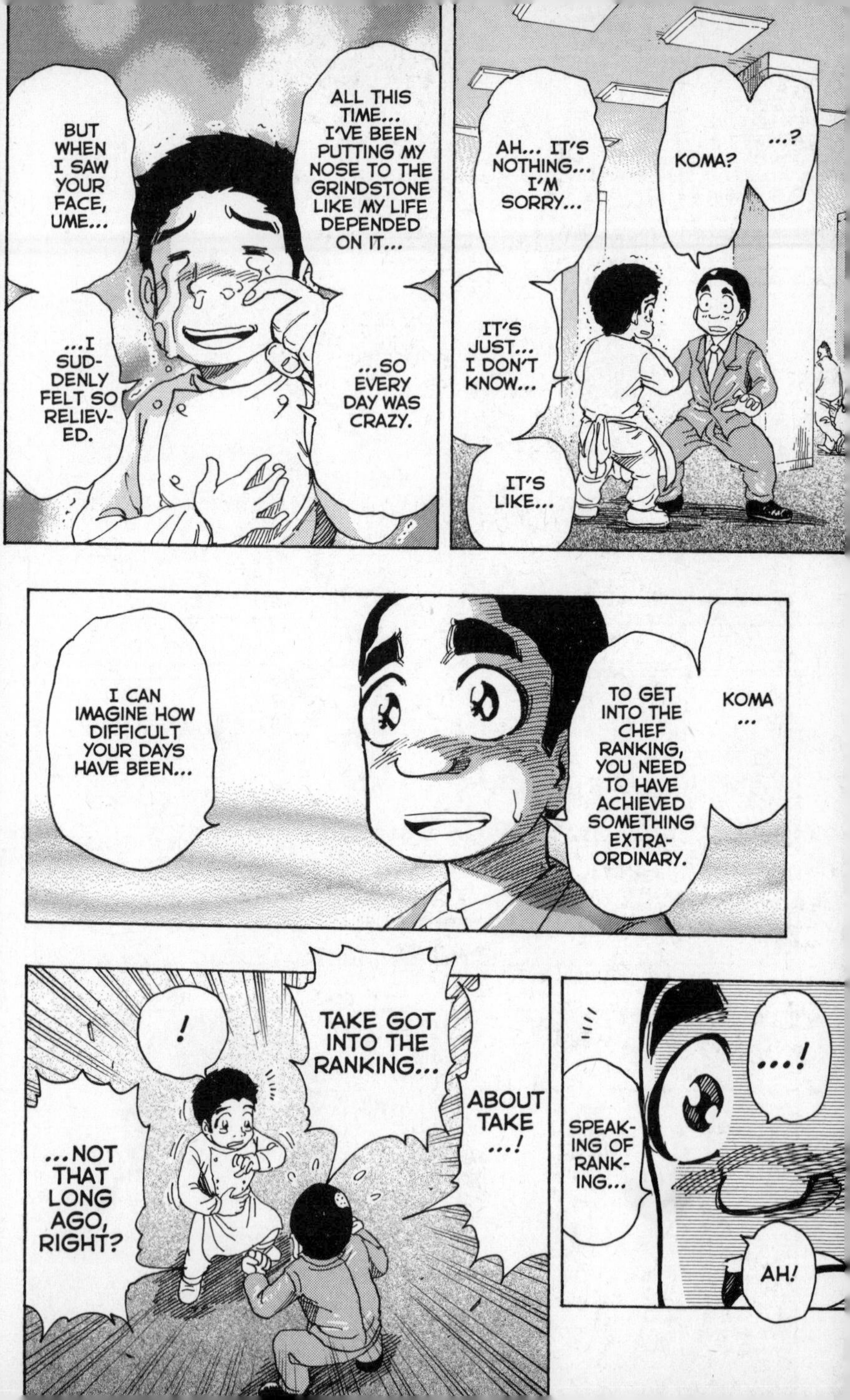
...?
KOMA?
AH... IT'S NOTHING... I'M SORRY...
IT'S JUST... I DON'T KNOW...
IT'S LIKE...
ALL THIS TIME... I'VE BEEN PUTTING MY NOSE TO THE GRINDSTONE LIKE MY LIFE DEPENDED ON IT...
BUT WHEN I SAW YOUR FACE, UME...
...SO EVERY DAY WAS CRAZY.
...I SUDDENLY FELT SO RELIEV-ED.
KOMA...
TO GET INTO THE CHEF RANKING, YOU NEED TO HAVE ACHIEVED SOMETHING EXTRA-ORDINARY.
I CAN IMAGINE HOW DIFFICULT YOUR DAYS HAVE BEEN...
...!
SPEAK-ING OF RANK-ING...
AH!
TAKE GOT INTO THE RANKING...
ABOUT TAKE...!
!
...NOT THAT LONG AGO, RIGHT?

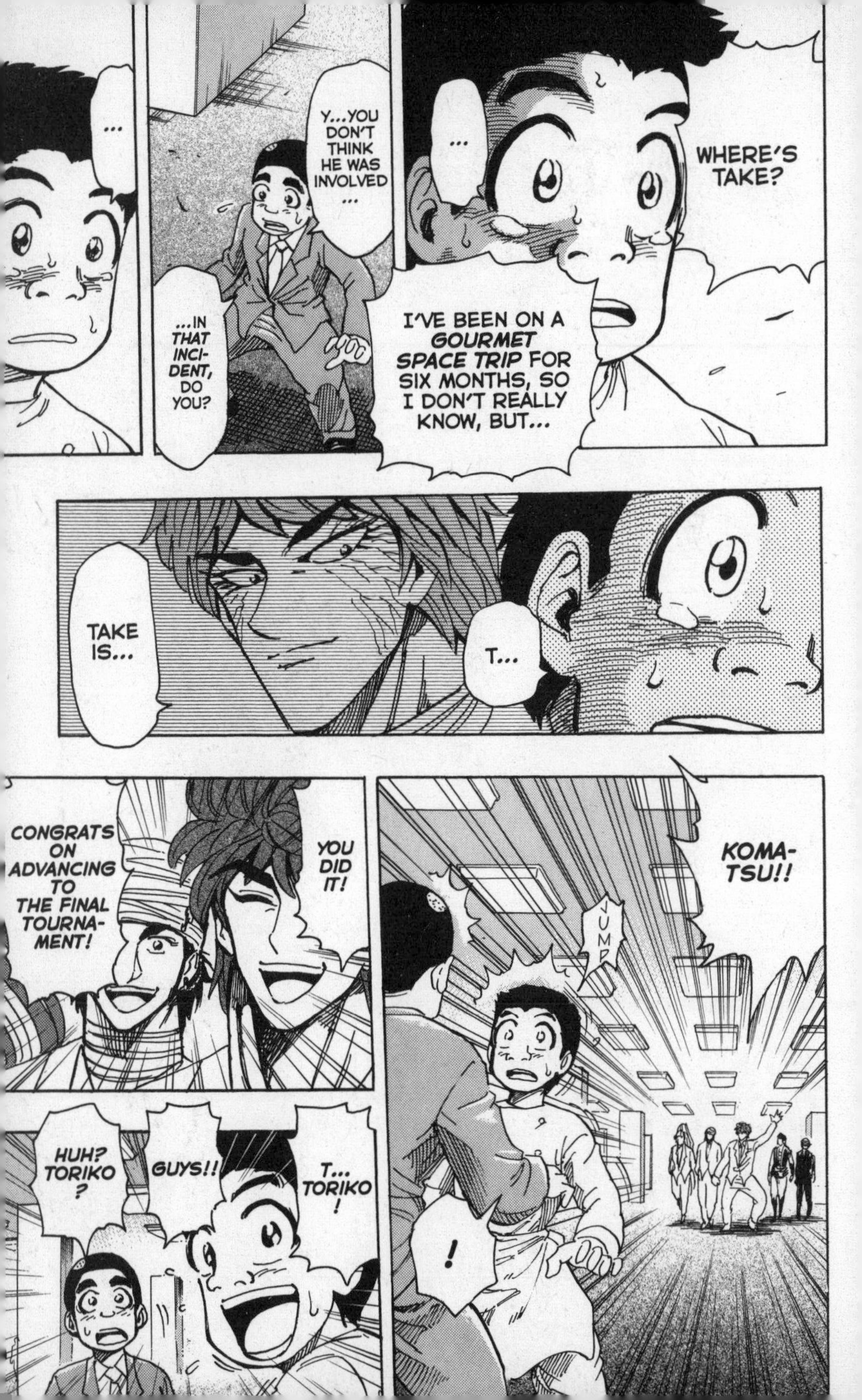
WHERE'S TAKE?
...
I'VE BEEN ON A *GOURMET SPACE TRIP* FOR SIX MONTHS, SO I DON'T REALLY KNOW, BUT...
Y...YOU DON'T THINK HE WAS INVOLVED...
...IN *THAT INCIDENT*, DO YOU?
...
T...
TAKE IS...
KOMATSU!!
JUMP
!
YOU DID IT!
CONGRATS ON ADVANCING TO THE FINAL TOURNAMENT!
T... TORIKO!
GUYS!!
HUH? TORIKO?

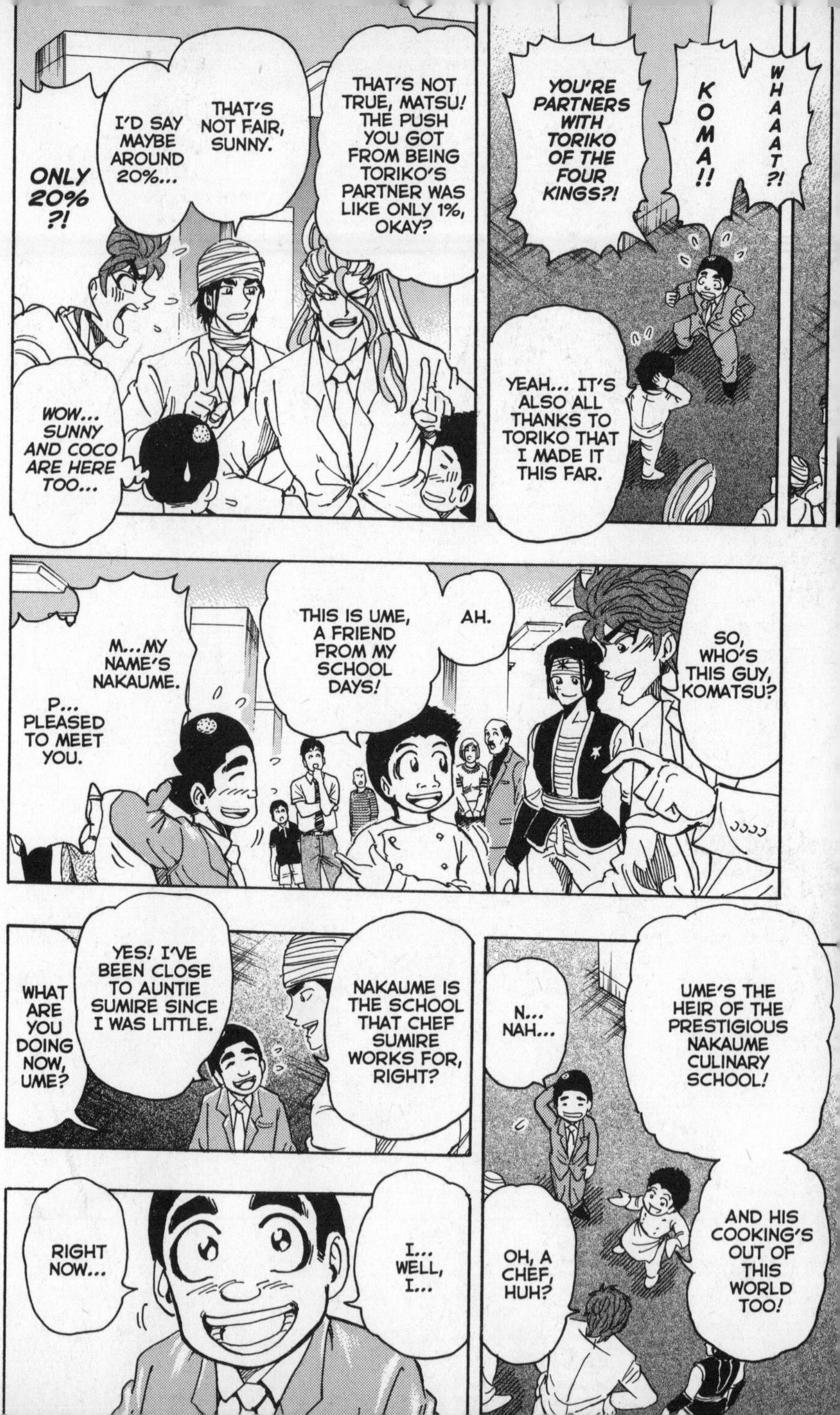
WHAAAAT?!
KOMA!!
YOU'RE PARTNERS WITH TORIKO OF THE FOUR KINGS?!
YEAH... IT'S ALSO ALL THANKS TO TORIKO THAT I MADE IT THIS FAR.
THAT'S NOT TRUE, MATSU! THE PUSH YOU GOT FROM BEING TORIKO'S PARTNER WAS LIKE ONLY 1%, OKAY?
THAT'S NOT FAIR, SUNNY.
I'D SAY MAYBE AROUND 20%...
ONLY 20%?!
WOW... SUNNY AND COCO ARE HERE TOO...
SO, WHO'S THIS GUY, KOMATSU?
AH.
THIS IS UME, A FRIEND FROM MY SCHOOL DAYS!
M...MY NAME'S NAKAUME.
P... PLEASED TO MEET YOU.
UME'S THE HEIR OF THE PRESTIGIOUS NAKAUME CULINARY SCHOOL!
N... NAH...
AND HIS COOKING'S OUT OF THIS WORLD TOO!
OH, A CHEF, HUH?
NAKAUME IS THE SCHOOL THAT CHEF SUMIRE WORKS FOR, RIGHT?
YES! I'VE BEEN CLOSE TO AUNTIE SUMIRE SINCE I WAS LITTLE.
WHAT ARE YOU DOING NOW, UME?
I... WELL, I...
RIGHT NOW...

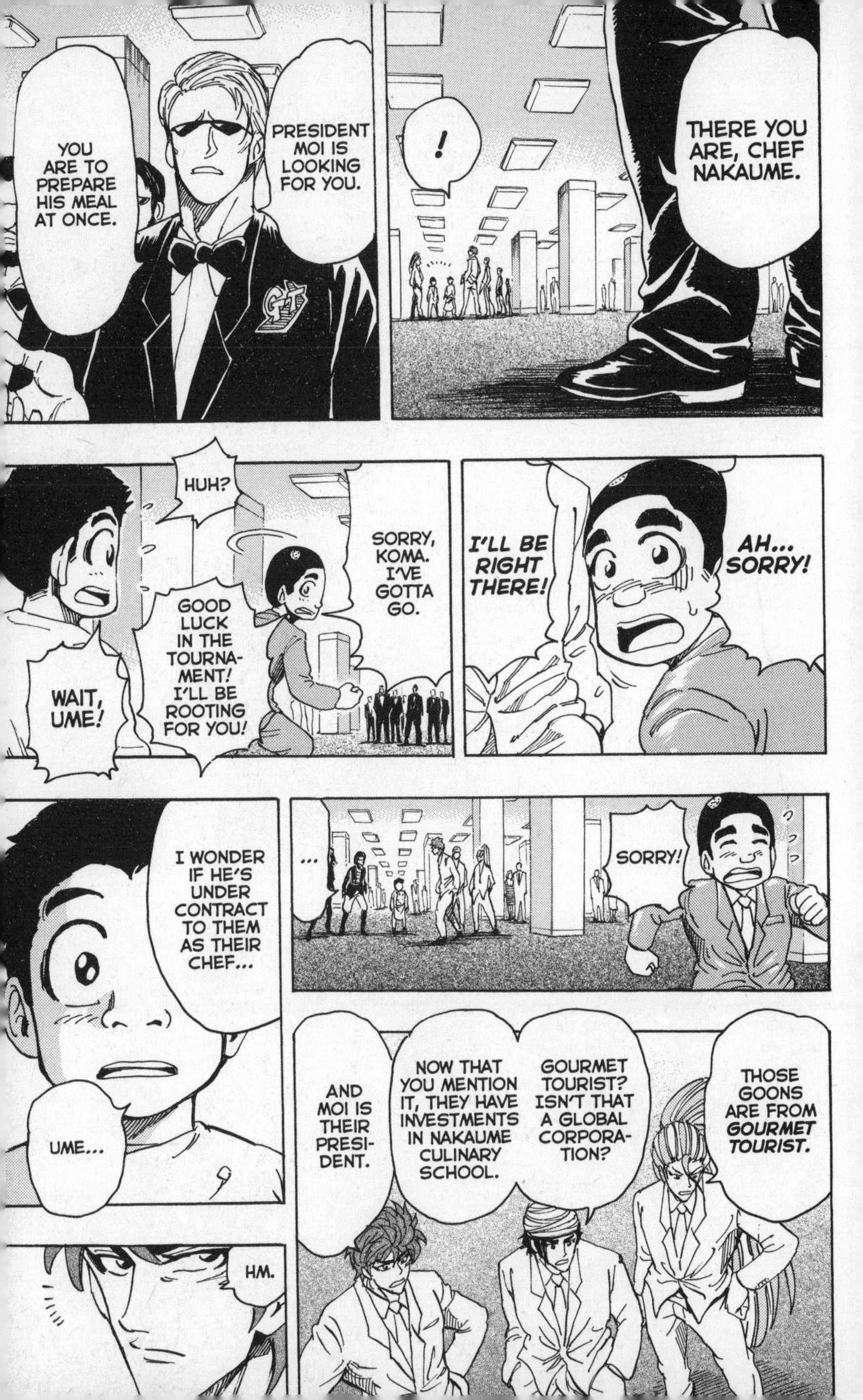
THERE YOU ARE, CHEF NAKAUME.
!
PRESIDENT MOI IS LOOKING FOR YOU.
YOU ARE TO PREPARE HIS MEAL AT ONCE.
AH... SORRY!
I'LL BE RIGHT THERE!
SORRY, KOMA. I'VE GOTTA GO.
HUH?
GOOD LUCK IN THE TOURNAMENT! I'LL BE ROOTING FOR YOU!
WAIT, UME!
SORRY!
...
THOSE GOONS ARE FROM GOURMET TOURIST.
GOURMET TOURIST? ISN'T THAT A GLOBAL CORPORATION?
NOW THAT YOU MENTION IT, THEY HAVE INVESTMENTS IN NAKAUME CULINARY SCHOOL.
AND MOI IS THEIR PRESIDENT.
I WONDER IF HE'S UNDER CONTRACT TO THEM AS THEIR CHEF...
UME...
HM.

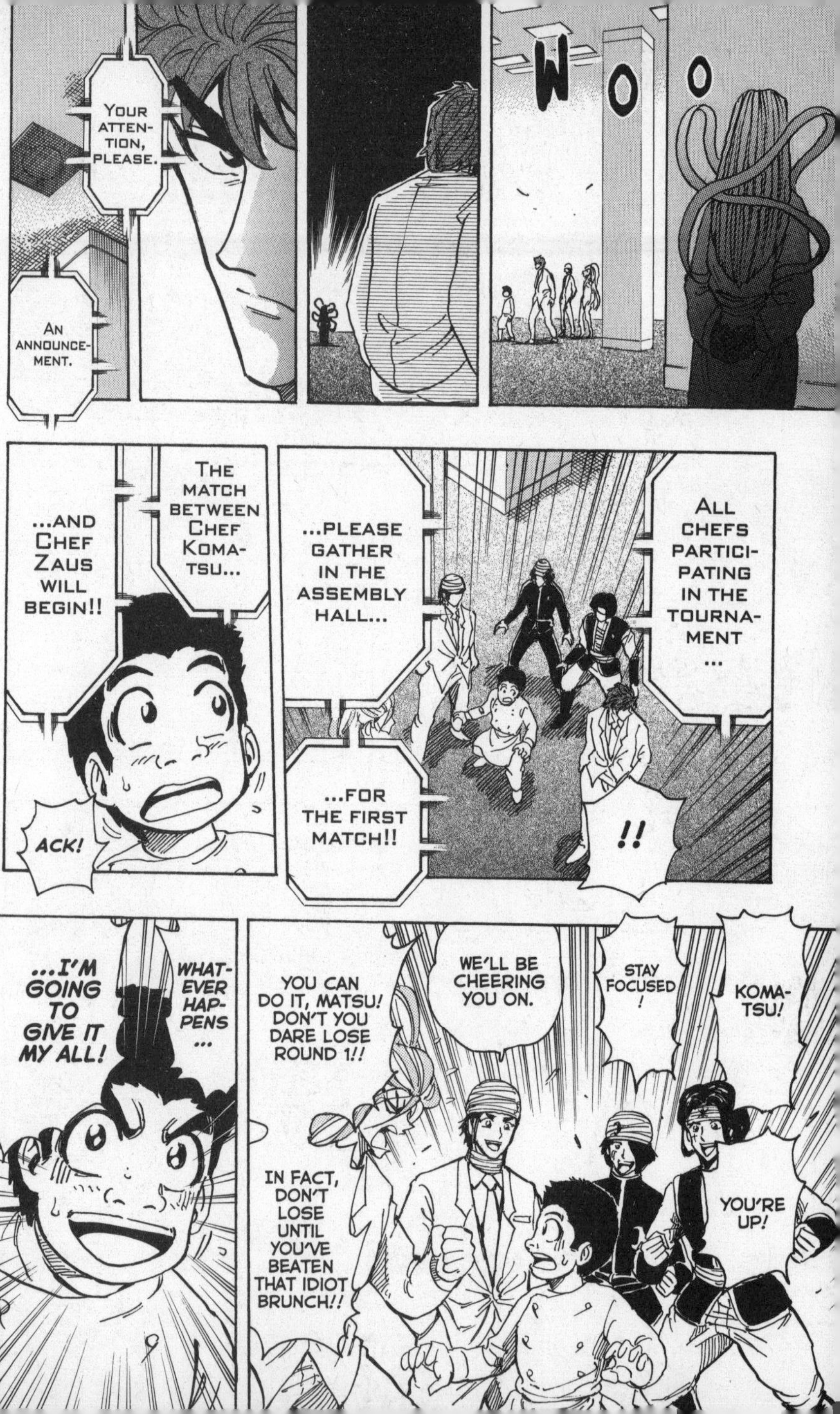
WOO
Your attention, please.
An announcement.
All chefs participating in the tournament...
...please gather in the assembly hall...
...for the first match!!
!!
The match between Chef Komatsu...
...and Chef Zaus will begin!!
ACK!
KOMATSU!
STAY FOCUSED!
WE'LL BE CHEERING YOU ON.
YOU CAN DO IT, MATSU! DON'T YOU DARE LOSE ROUND 1!!
YOU'RE UP!
IN FACT, DON'T LOSE UNTIL YOU'VE BEATEN THAT IDIOT BRUNCH!!
WHATEVER HAPPENS...
...I'M GOING TO GIVE IT MY ALL!

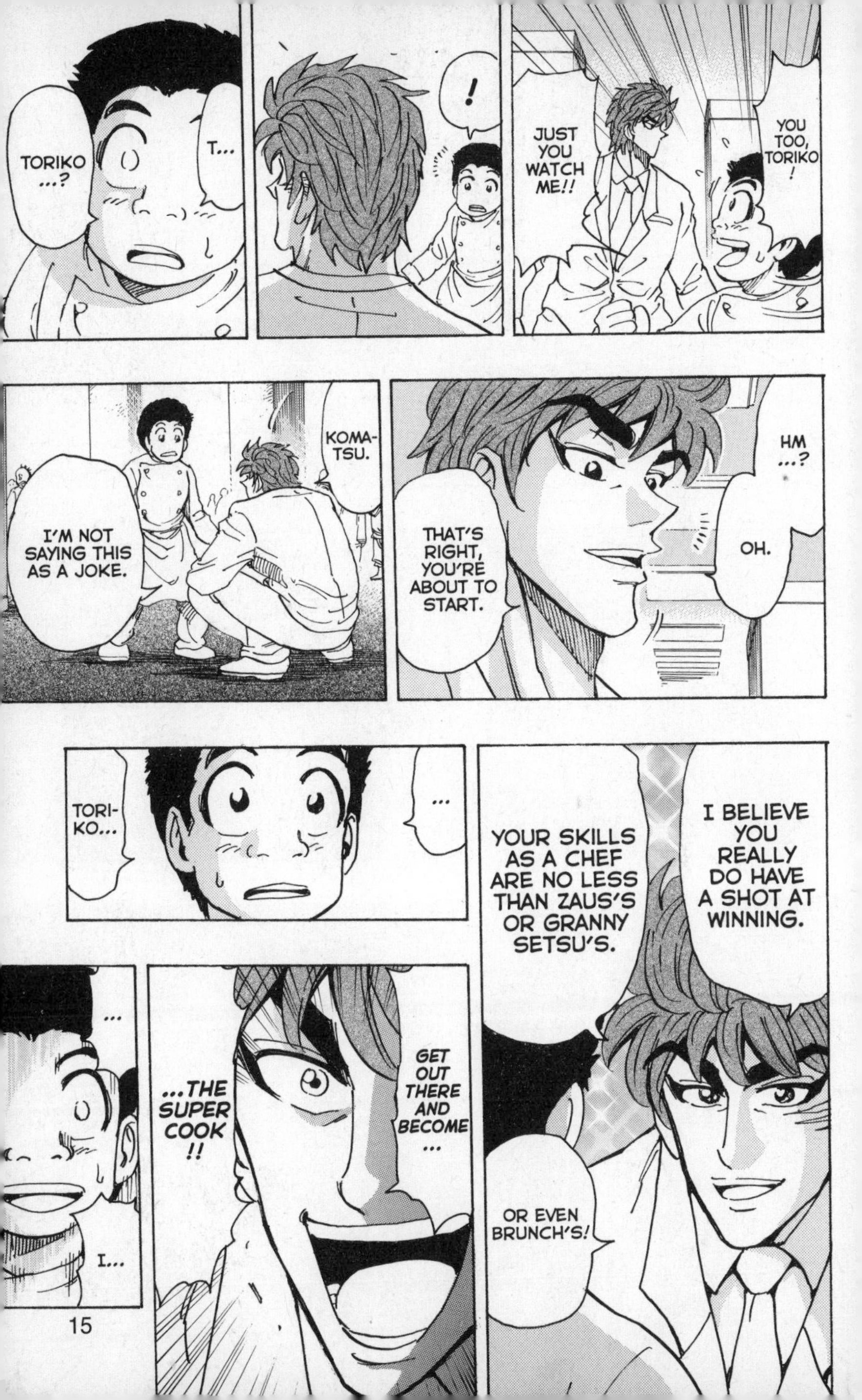
YOU TOO, TORIKO!
JUST YOU WATCH ME!!
!
T...
TORIKO...?
HM...?
OH.
THAT'S RIGHT, YOU'RE ABOUT TO START.
KOMA-TSU.
I'M NOT SAYING THIS AS A JOKE.
I BELIEVE YOU REALLY DO HAVE A SHOT AT WINNING.
YOUR SKILLS AS A CHEF ARE NO LESS THAN ZAUS'S OR GRANNY SETSU'S.
OR EVEN BRUNCH'S!
...
TORI-KO...
GET OUT THERE AND BECOME...
...THE SUPER COOK!!
...
I...

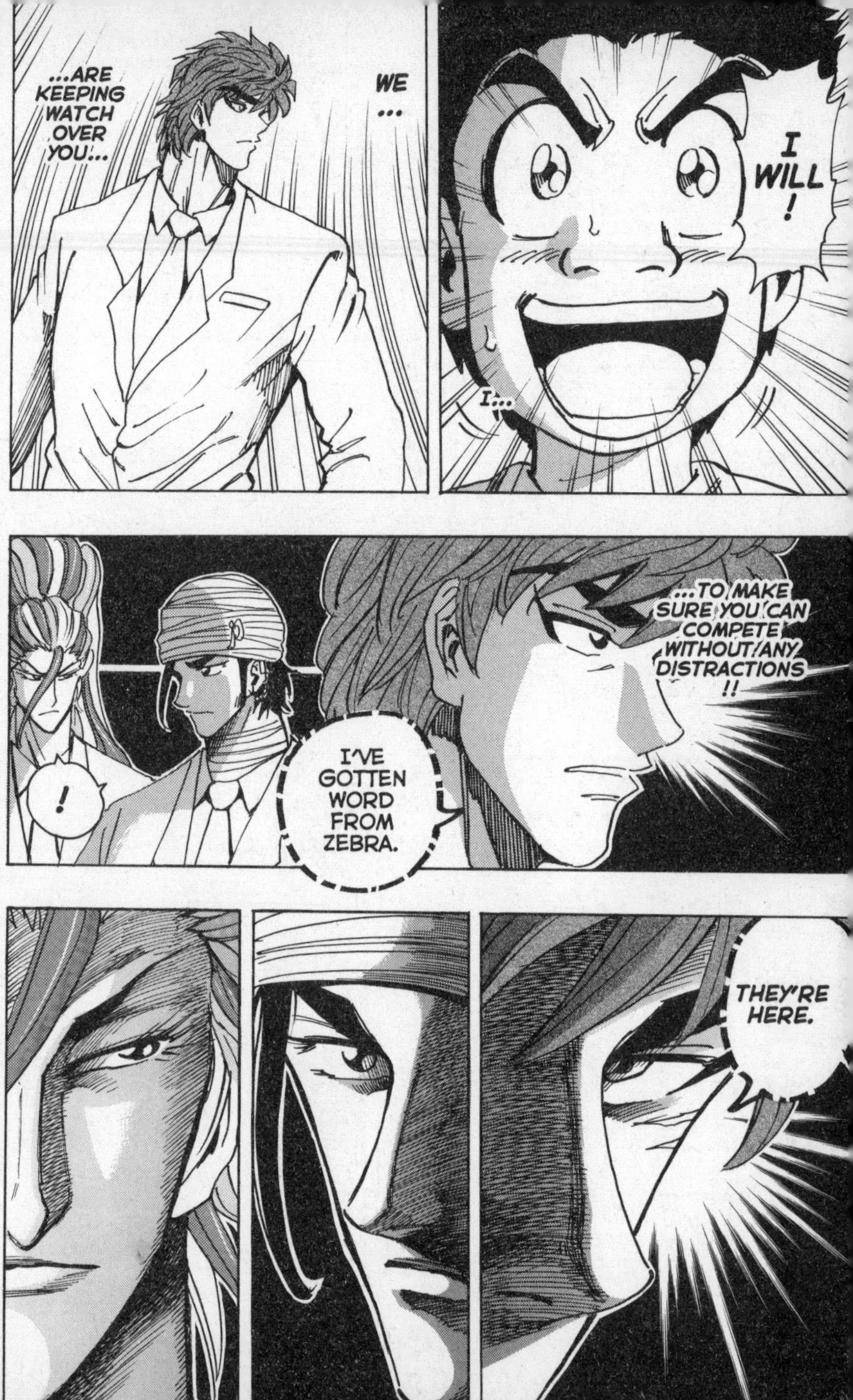
I...
I WILL!
WE...
...ARE KEEPING WATCH OVER YOU...
...TO MAKE SURE YOU CAN COMPETE WITHOUT ANY DISTRACTIONS!!
I'VE GOTTEN WORD FROM ZEBRA.
!
THEY'RE HERE.

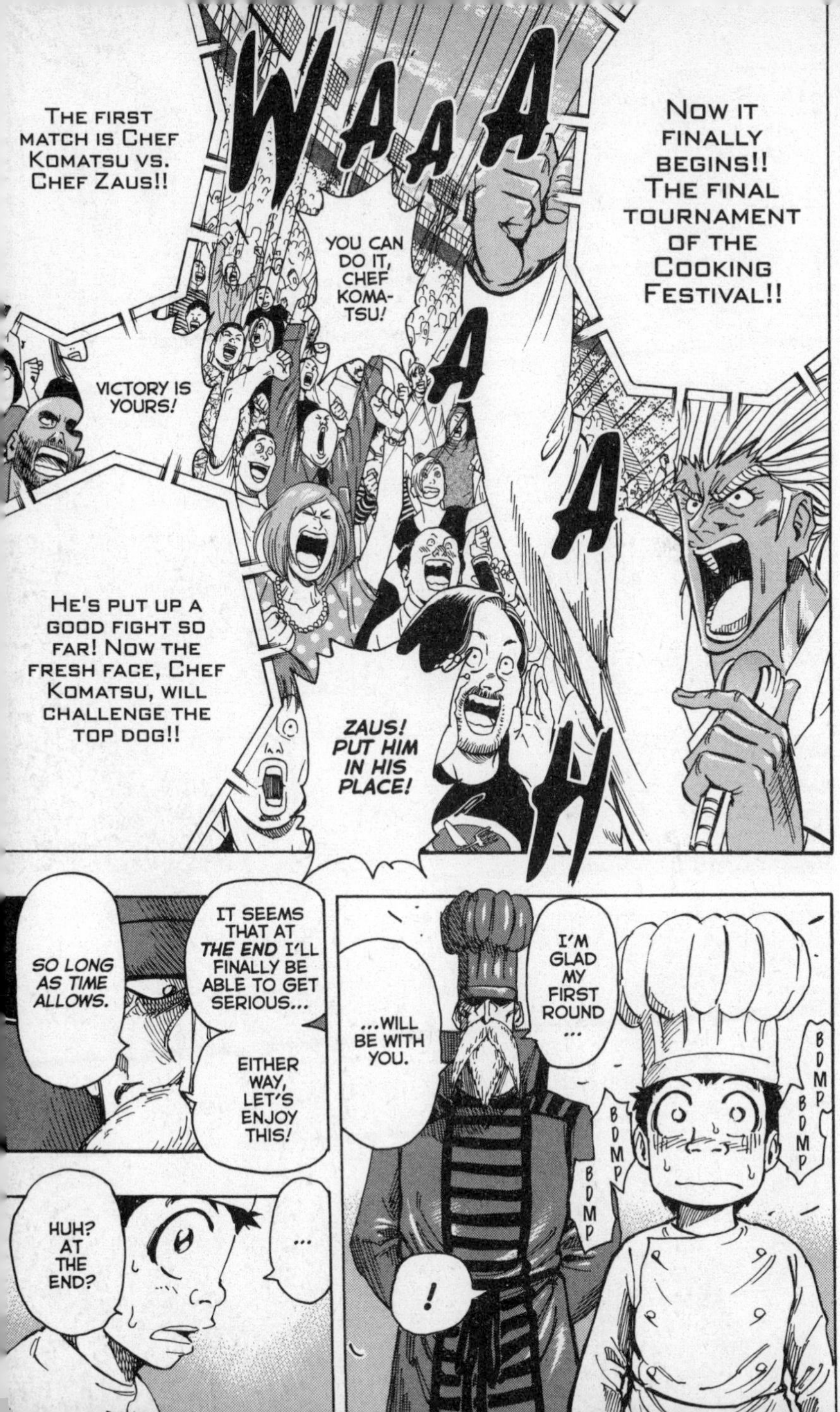
Now it finally begins!! The final tournament of the Cooking Festival!!
The first match is Chef Komatsu vs. Chef Zaus!!
WAAAAAH
You can do it, Chef Komatsu!
Victory is yours!
He's put up a good fight so far! Now the fresh face, Chef Komatsu, will challenge the top dog!!
Zaus! Put him in his place!
I'm glad my first round...
...will be with you.
BDMP BDMP
BDMP BDMP
!
It seems that at the end I'll finally be able to get serious...
So long as time allows.
Either way, let's enjoy this!
...
Huh? At the end?

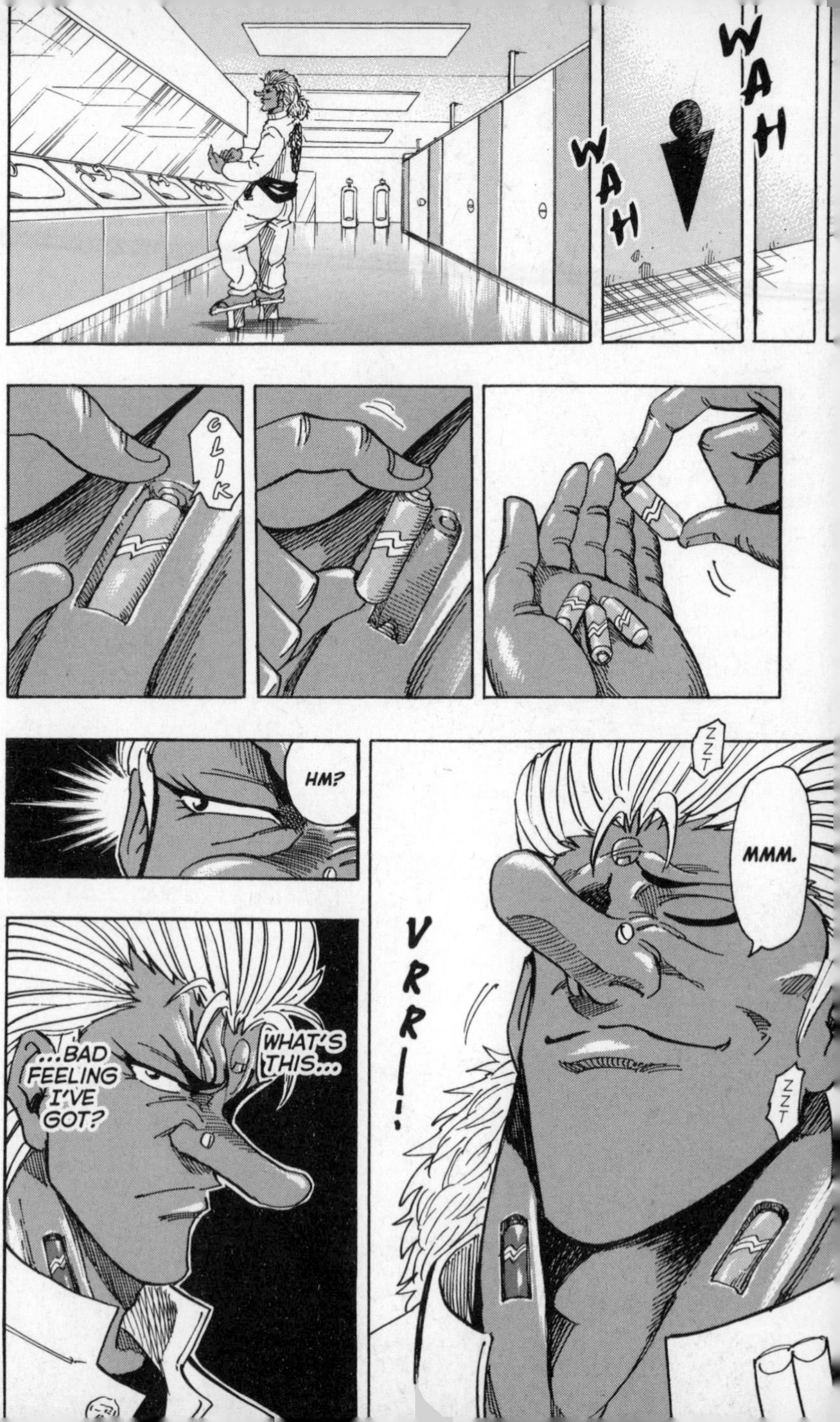
WAH
WAH
GLIK
ZZT
MMM.
VRRI!!
ZZT
HM?
WHAT'S THIS...
...BAD FEELING I'VE GOT?

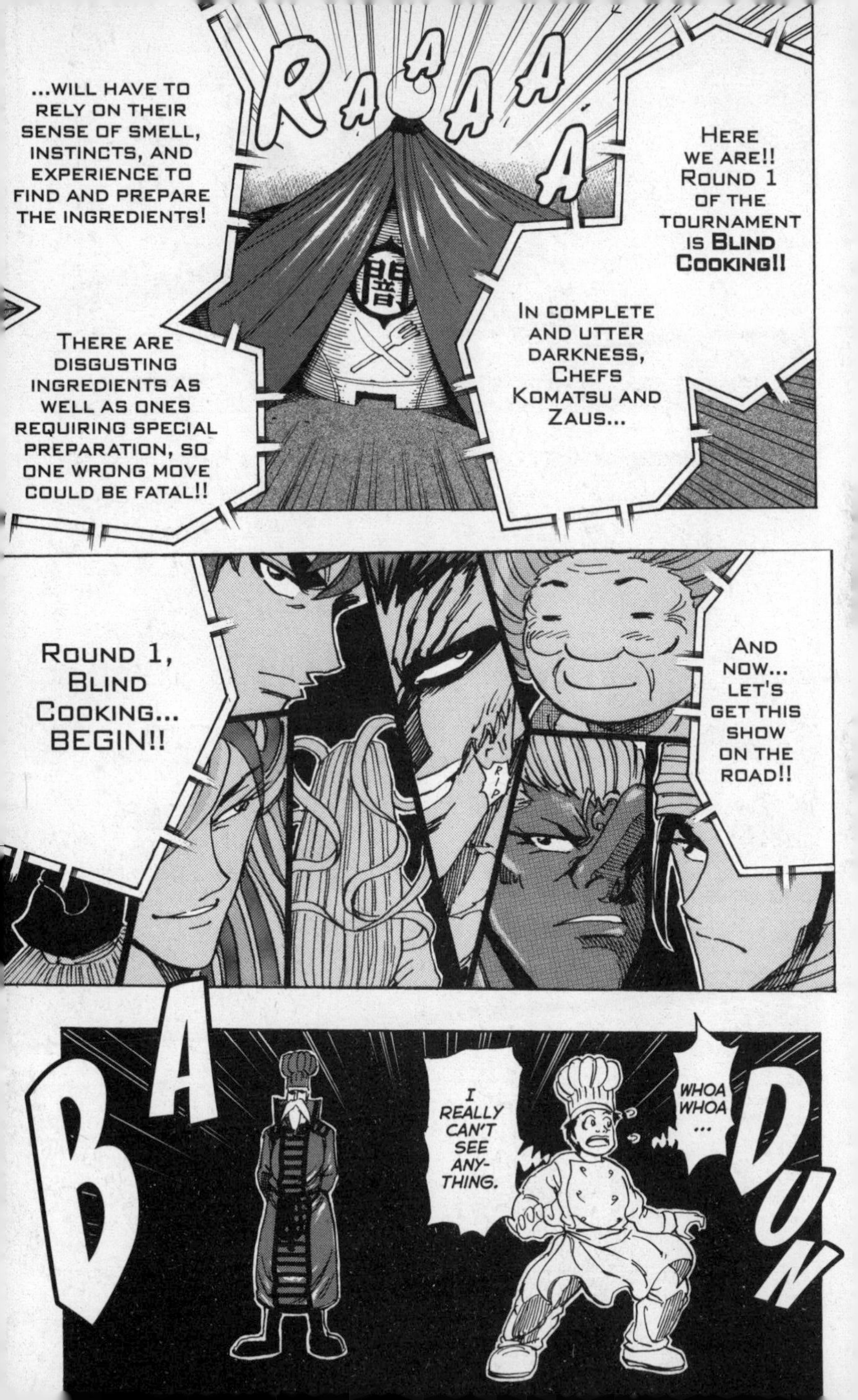
RAAAAAA
HERE WE ARE!! ROUND 1 OF THE TOURNAMENT IS BLIND COOKING!!
IN COMPLETE AND UTTER DARKNESS, CHEFS KOMATSU AND ZAUS...
...WILL HAVE TO RELY ON THEIR SENSE OF SMELL, INSTINCTS, AND EXPERIENCE TO FIND AND PREPARE THE INGREDIENTS!
THERE ARE DISGUSTING INGREDIENTS AS WELL AS ONES REQUIRING SPECIAL PREPARATION, SO ONE WRONG MOVE COULD BE FATAL!!
AND NOW... LET'S GET THIS SHOW ON THE ROAD!!
RIP
ROUND 1, BLIND COOKING... BEGIN!!
WHOA WHOA ...
I REALLY CAN'T SEE ANYTHING.
BADUN

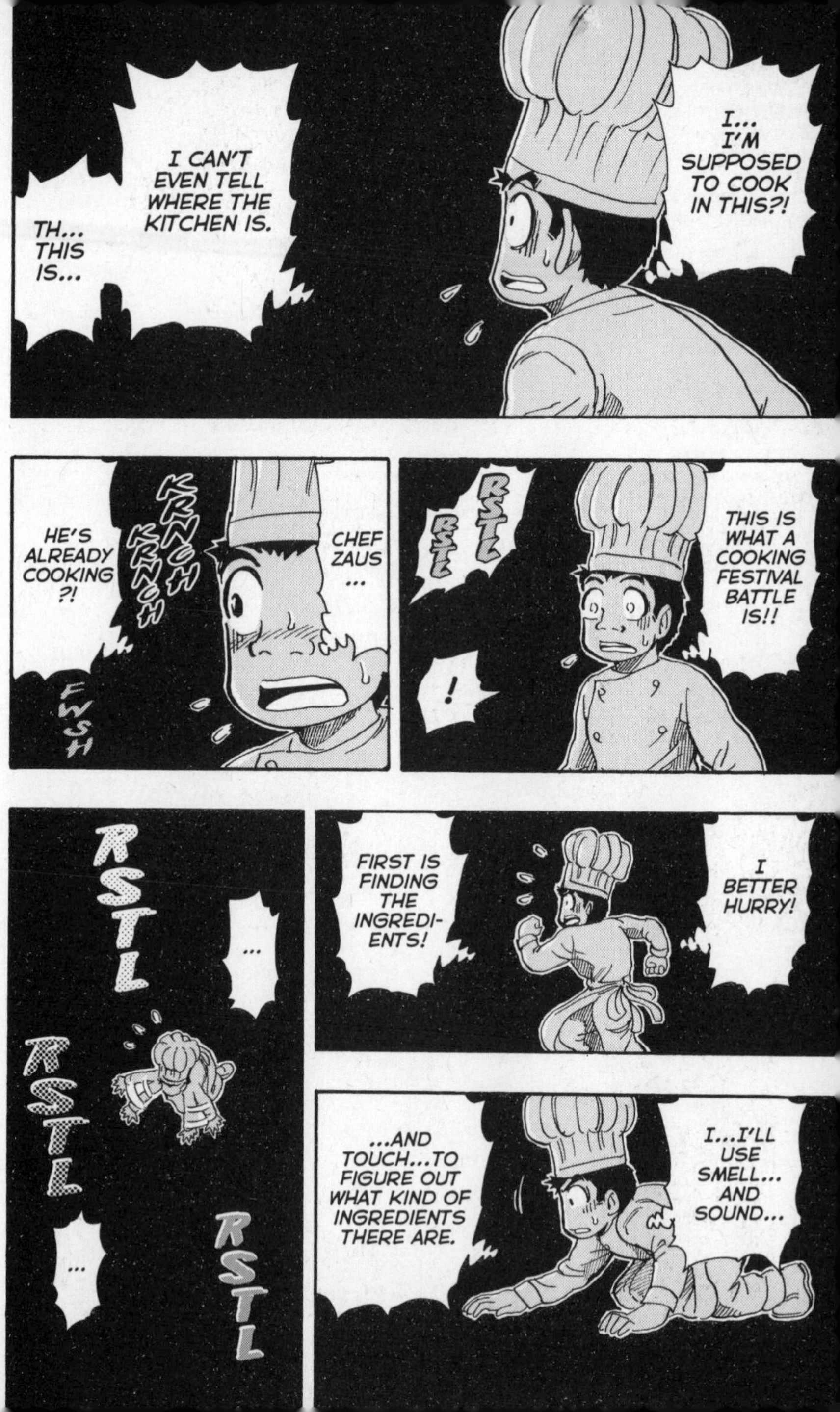
I... I'M SUPPOSED TO COOK IN THIS?!
I CAN'T EVEN TELL WHERE THE KITCHEN IS.
TH... THIS IS...
THIS IS WHAT A COOKING FESTIVAL BATTLE IS!!
RSTL
RSTL
!
CHEF ZAUS ...
KRNCH
KRNCH
HE'S ALREADY COOKING ?!
FWSH
I BETTER HURRY!
FIRST IS FINDING THE INGREDI- ENTS!
I...I'LL USE SMELL... AND SOUND...
...AND TOUCH...TO FIGURE OUT WHAT KIND OF INGREDIENTS THERE ARE.
RSTL
...
RSTL
RSTL
...

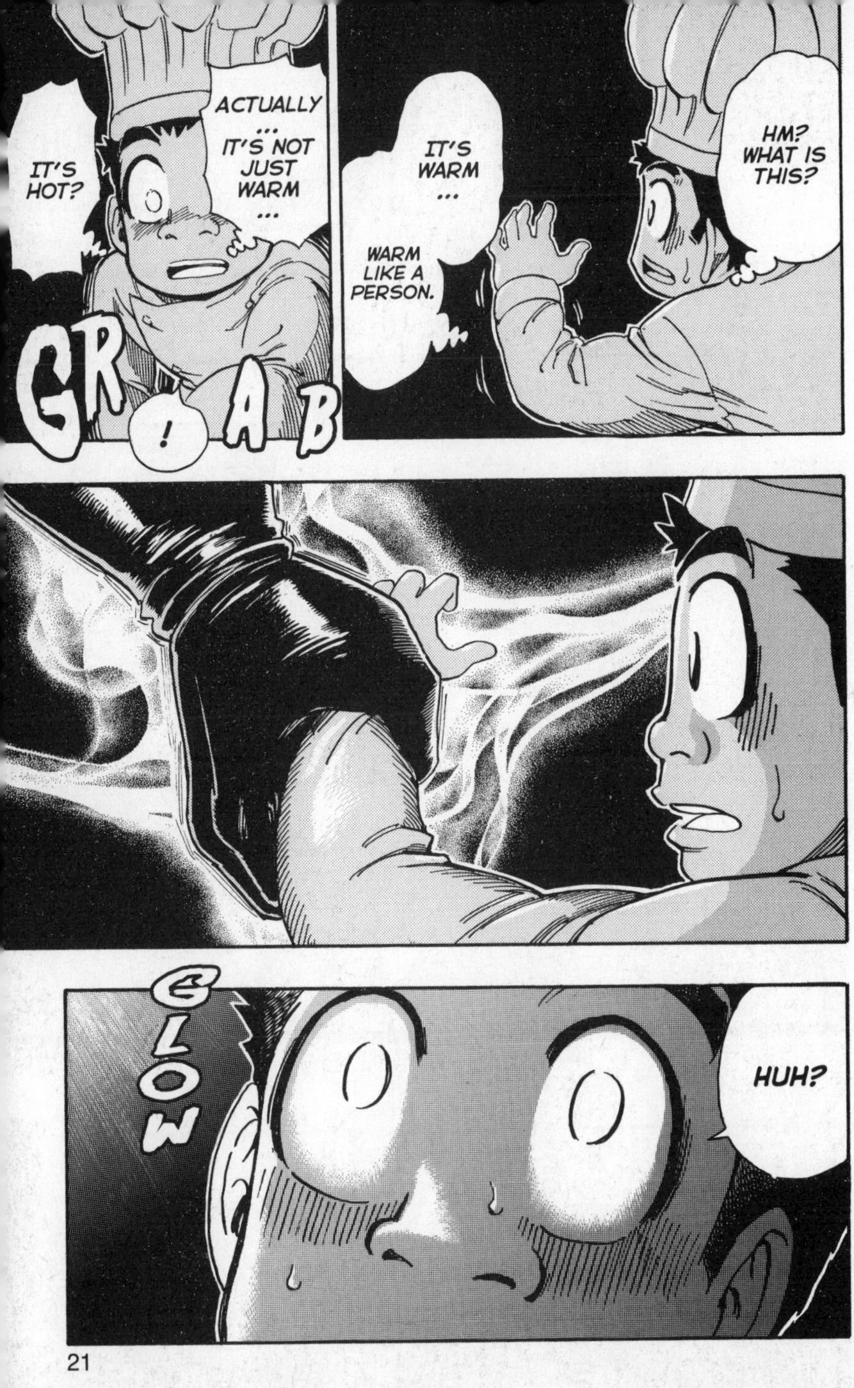
HM? WHAT IS THIS?
IT'S WARM ...
WARM LIKE A PERSON.
ACTUALLY ... IT'S NOT JUST WARM ...
IT'S HOT?
GRAB
!
HUH?
GLOW

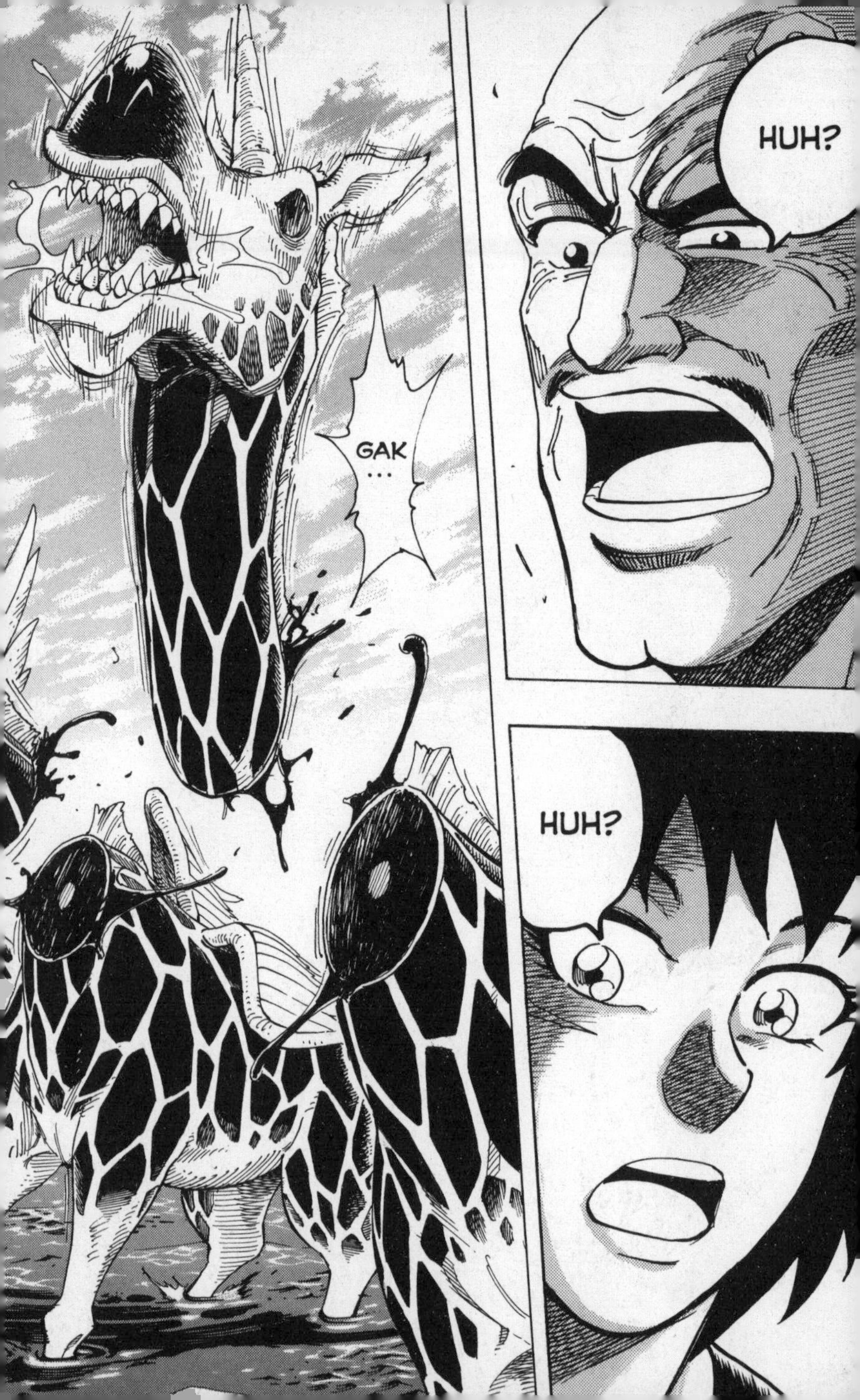
HUH?
HUH?
GAK...

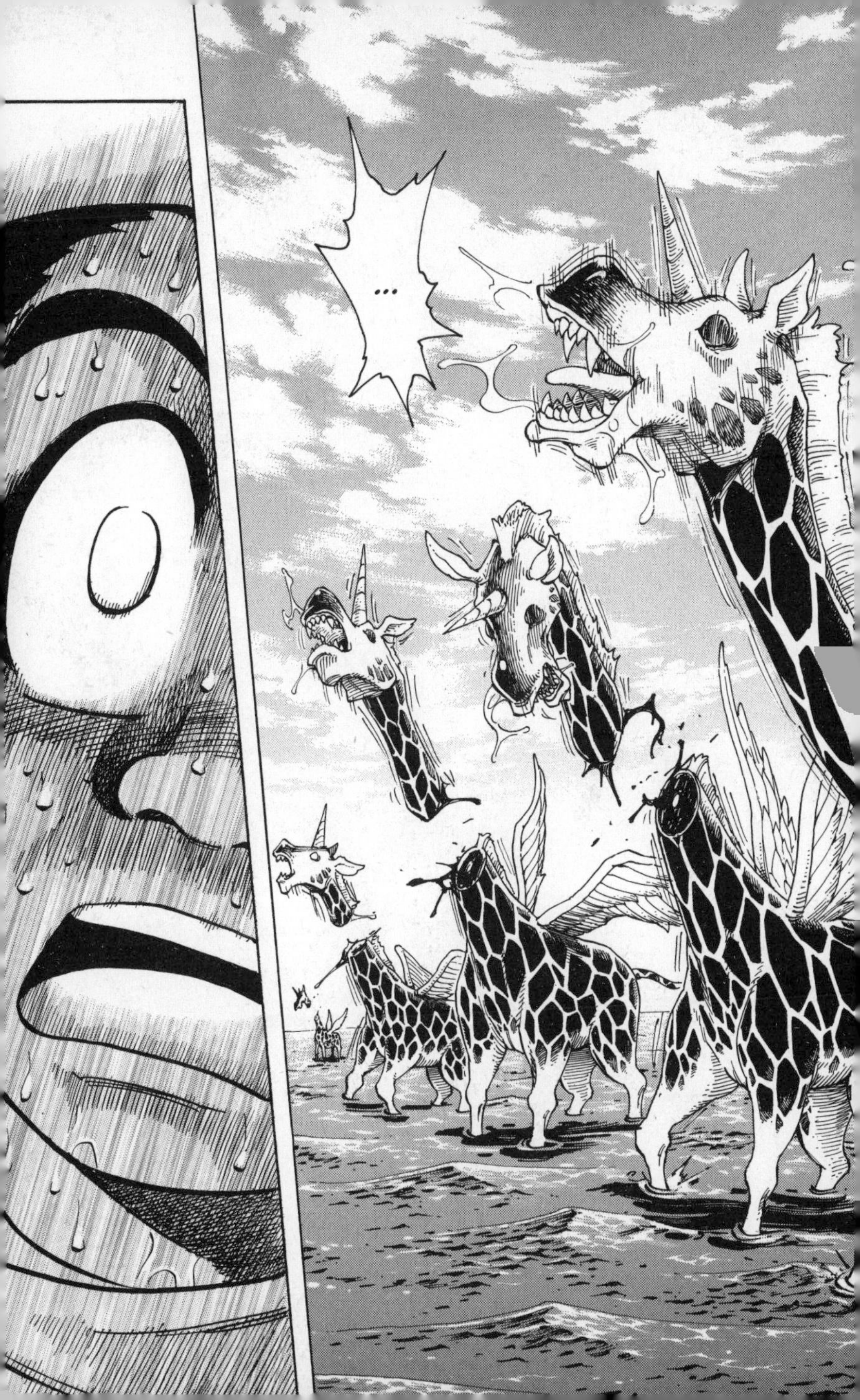
...

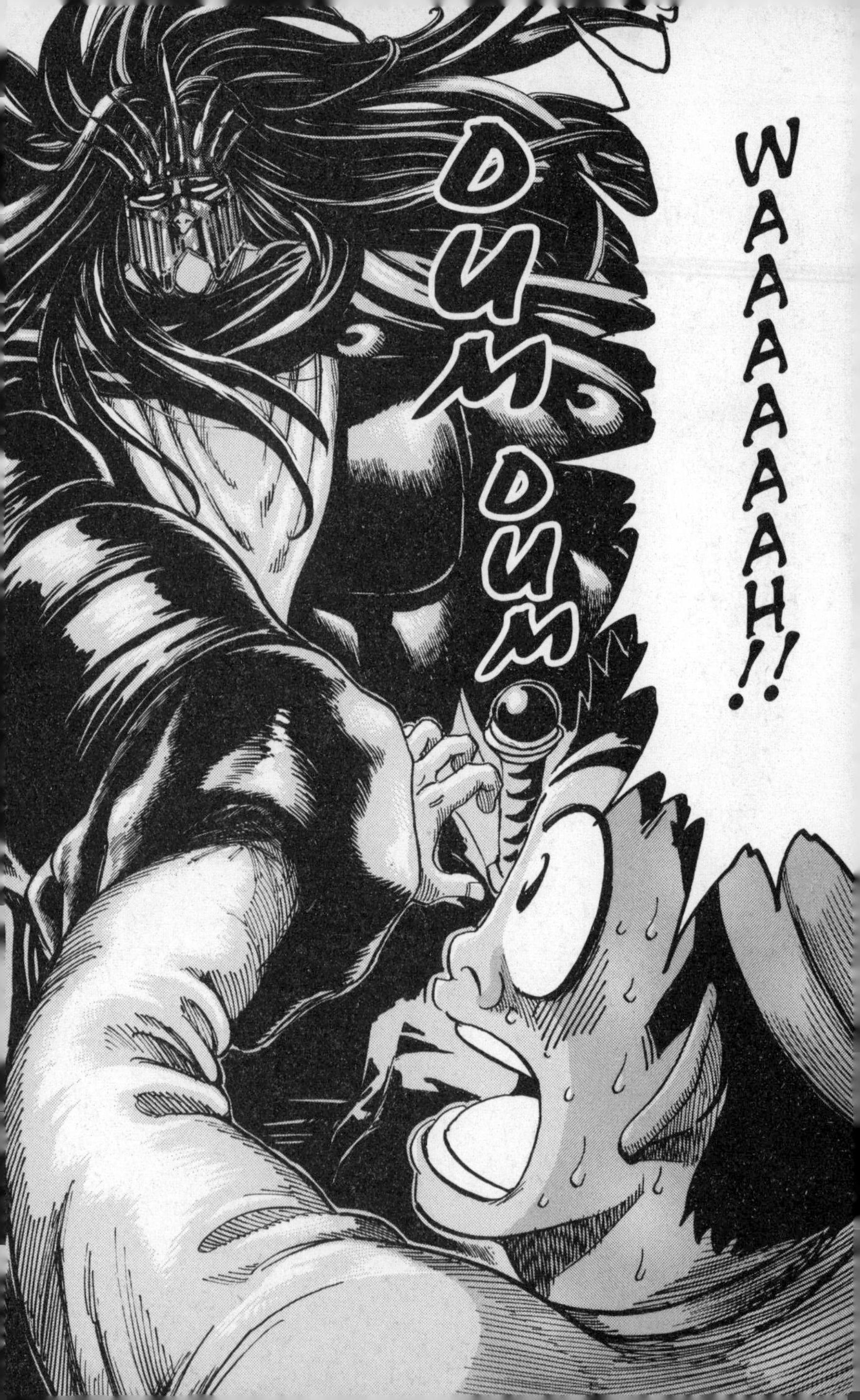
WAAAAAAH!!
DUM DUM

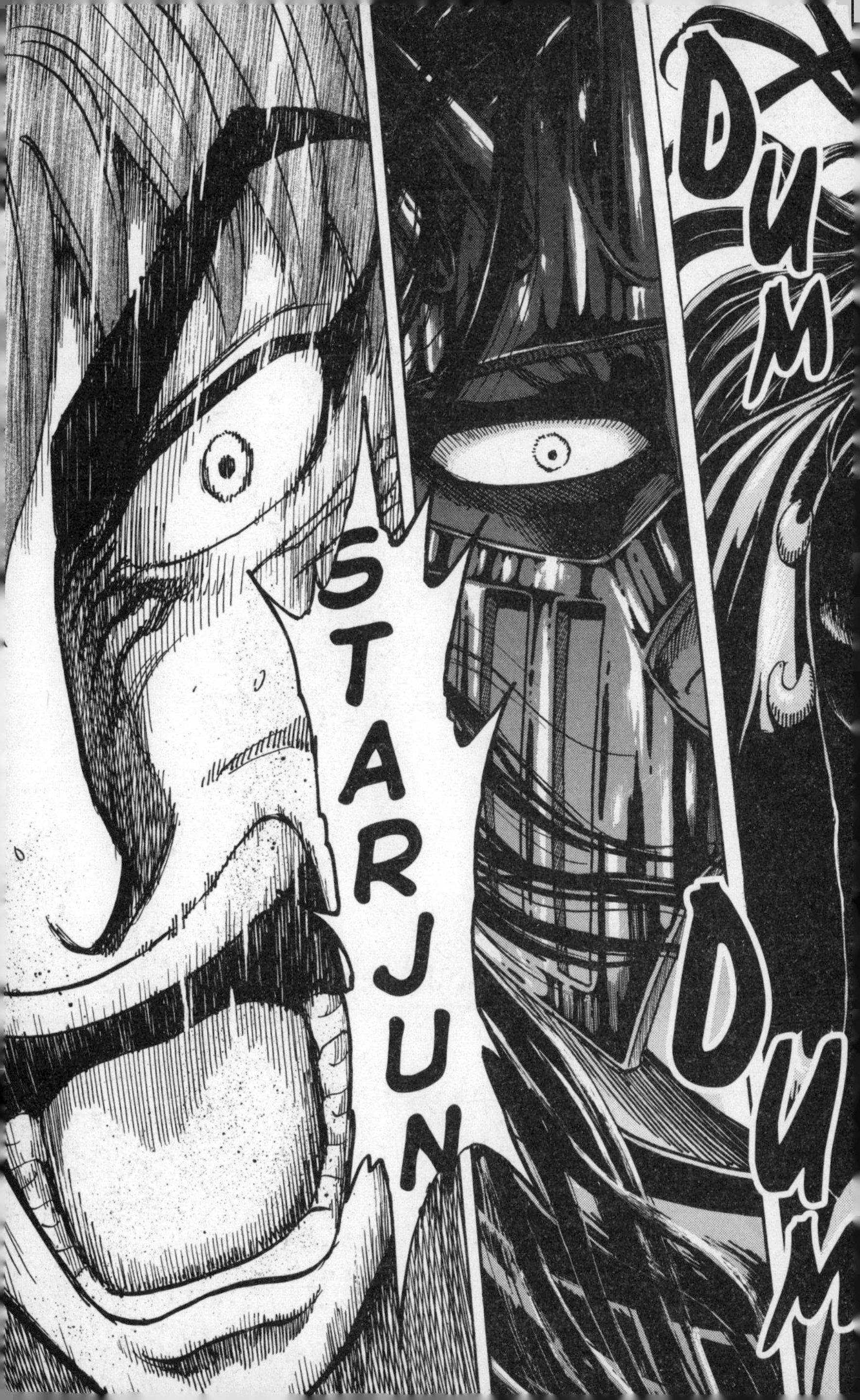
DUM
STARJUN
DUM

TORIKO

GOURMET CHECKLIST
Vol. 248

ROCKADILLO
(MAMMAL)

CAPTURE LEVEL: 25
HABITAT: ROCKY TERRAIN
LENGTH: 8 METERS
HEIGHT: 3 METERS
WEIGHT: 12 TONS
PRICE: 100 G / 7,000 YEN

HE'S GOT A MATCH WITH THE ROCKA-DILLO* FOR 70 POINTS!

SCALE

TALK ABOUT A CHIP ON YOUR SHOULDER—THE ROCKADILLO HAS A WHOLE BOULDER ON ITS BACK! IT'S ALSO GOT A ROCK ON THE TIP OF ITS TAIL. THE ROCKADILLO ATTACKS WITH THAT TEN-TON TAIL AS WELL AS ITS SHARP CLAWS. TO DEFEND, IT COILS INTO A BALL, PROTECTING ITS BODY WITH ITS TOUGH STONY SHELL. THIS CREATURE'S POWERFUL ATTACKS AND IMPENETRABLE DEFENSES GIVE IT ITS HIGH CAPTURE LEVEL. THE LARGER THE SPECIMEN, THE MORE DIFFICULT IT IS TO CAPTURE, BUT THE ROCKADILLO ALSO BECOMES TASTIER WITH AGE. MOST PEOPLE COOK IT BY GRILLING THE WHOLE THING AND THEN CRACKING ITS SHELL TO GET AT THE MEAT.

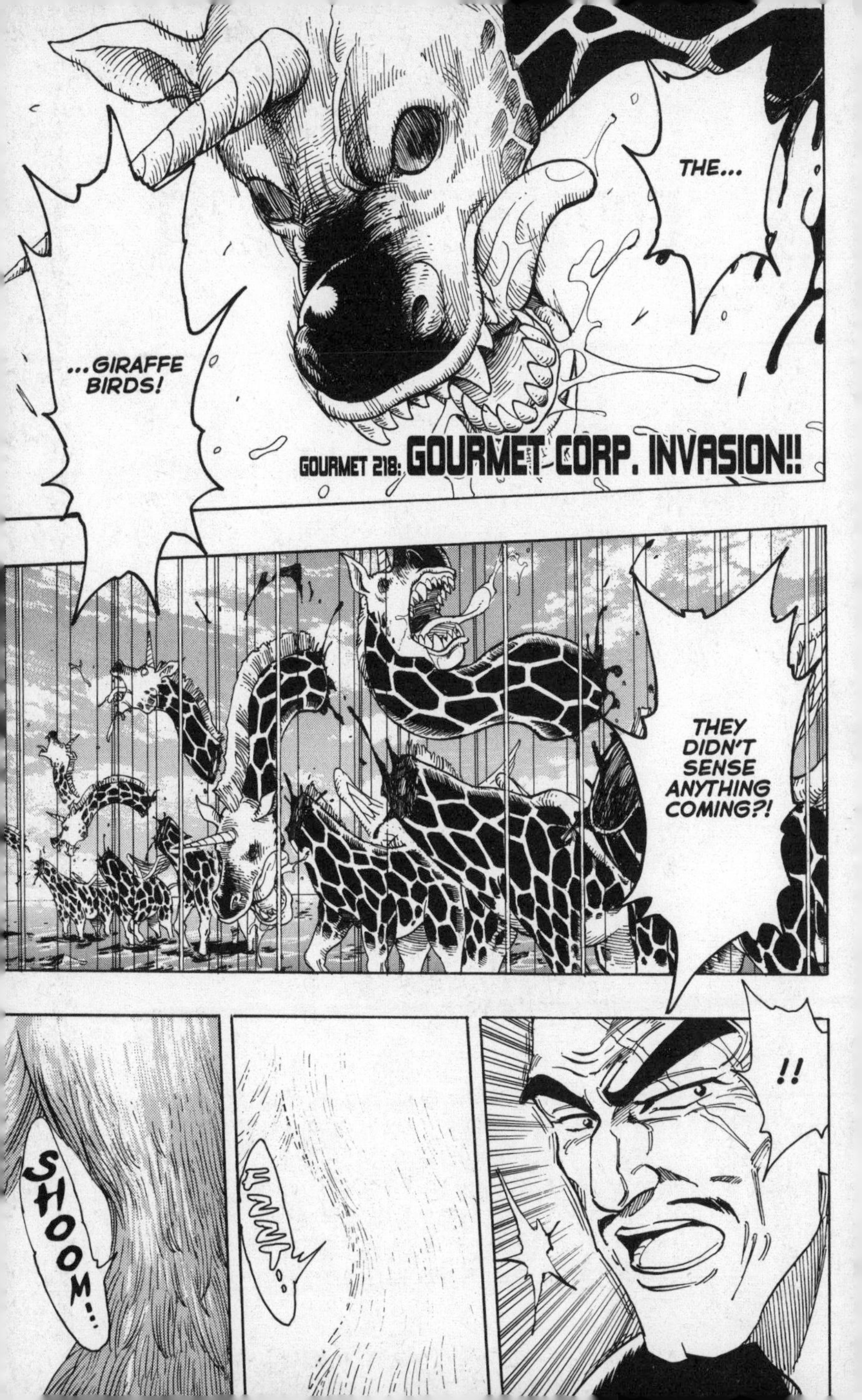
THE...
...GIRAFFE BIRDS!
GOURMET 218: GOURMET CORP. INVASION!!
THEY DIDN'T SENSE ANYTHING COMING?!
!!
FZZT..
SHOOM...

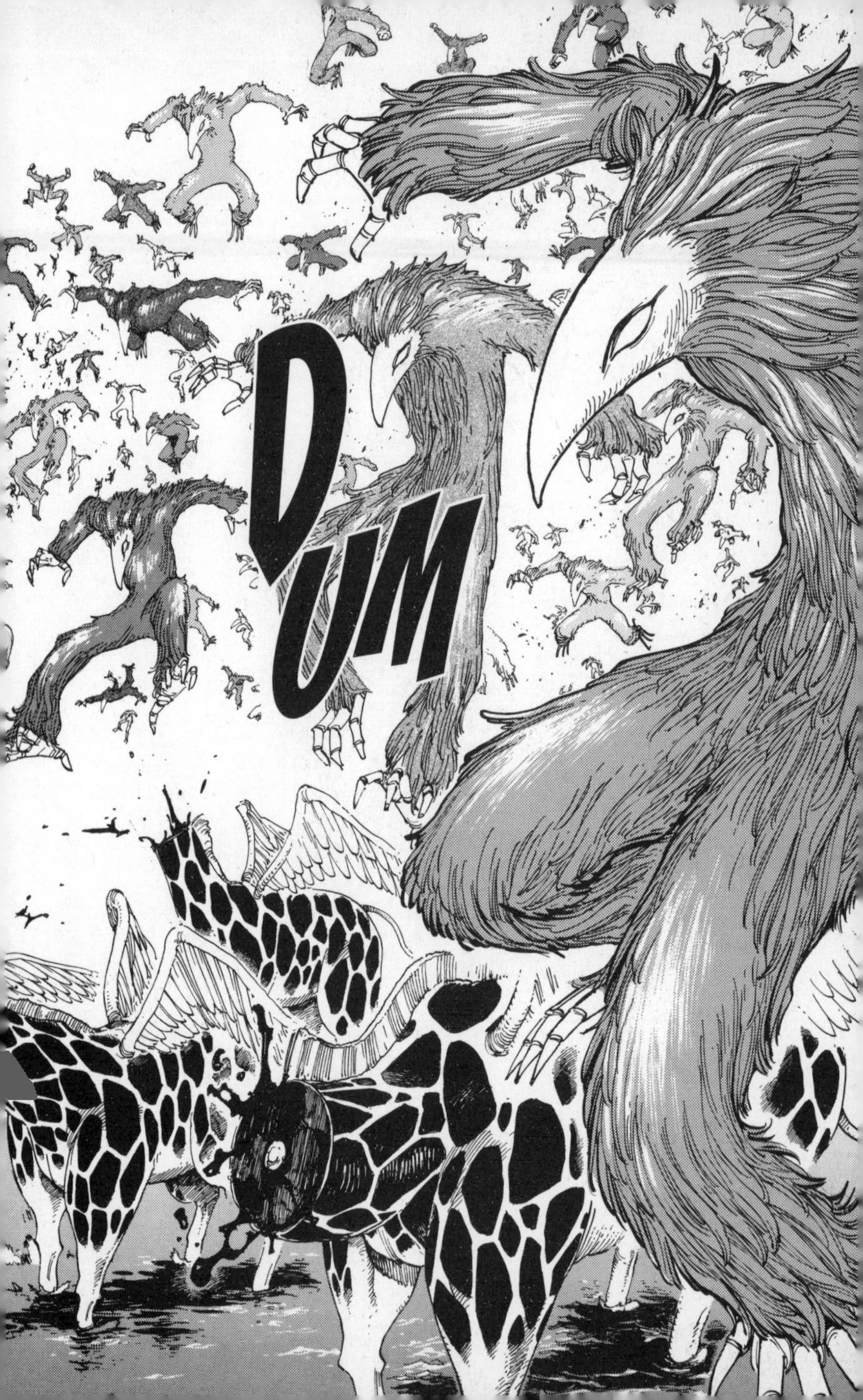
DUM

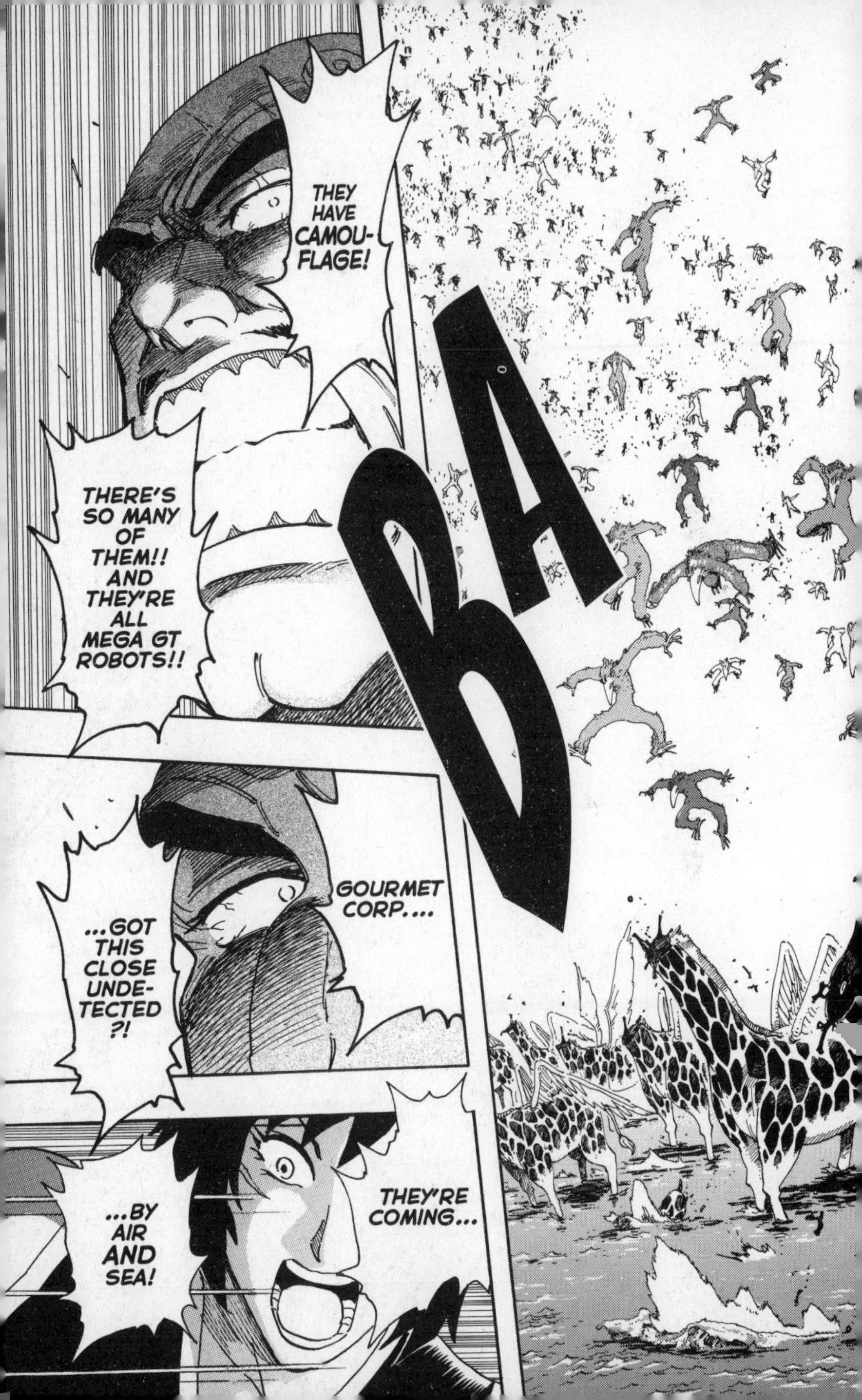
BA
THEY HAVE CAMOUFLAGE!
THERE'S SO MANY OF THEM!! AND THEY'RE ALL MEGA GT ROBOTS!!
GOURMET CORP....
...GOT THIS CLOSE UNDETECTED?!
THEY'RE COMING...
...BY AIR AND SEA!

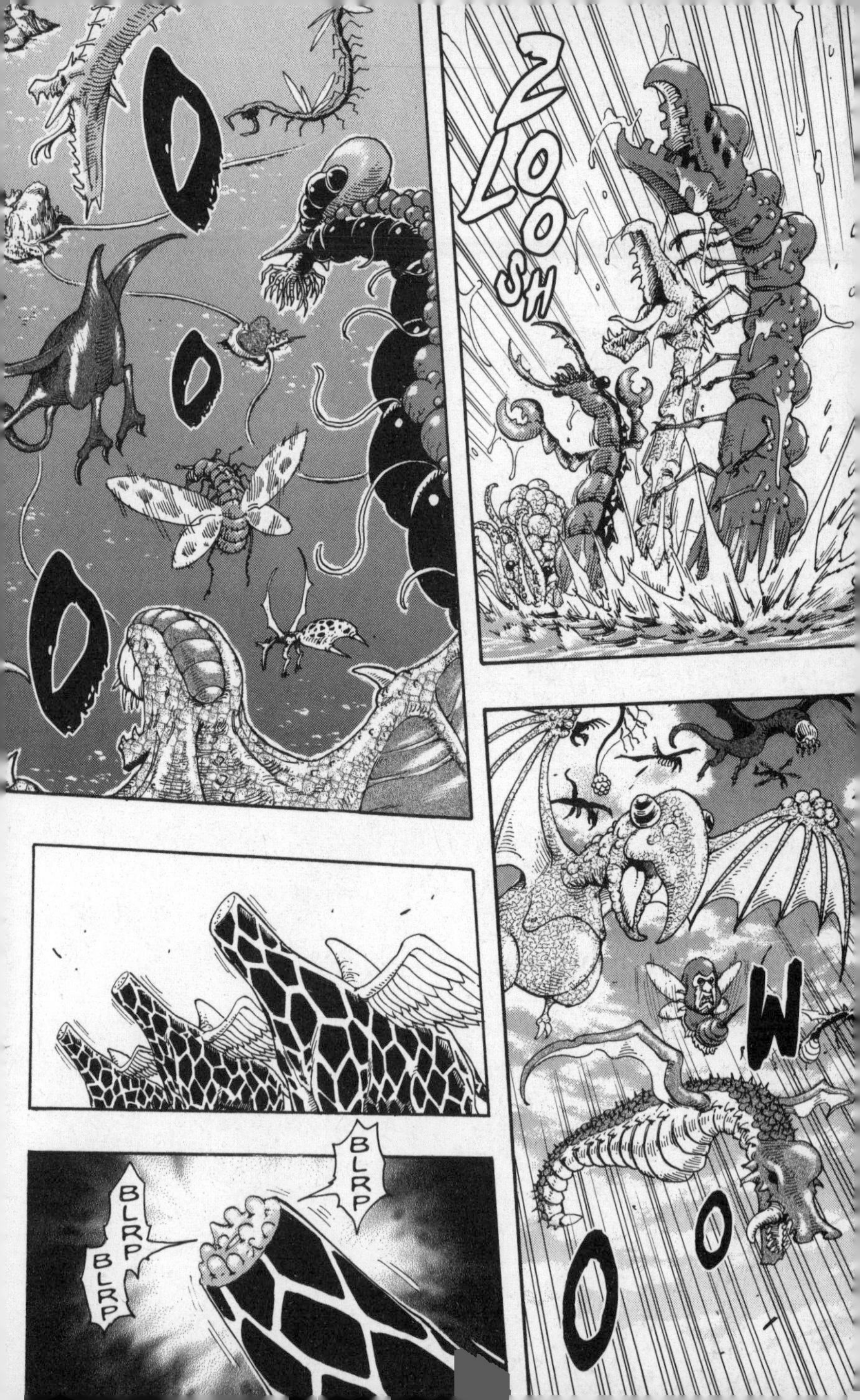
ZOOOSH
OOO
WOOO
BLRP
BLRP BLRP

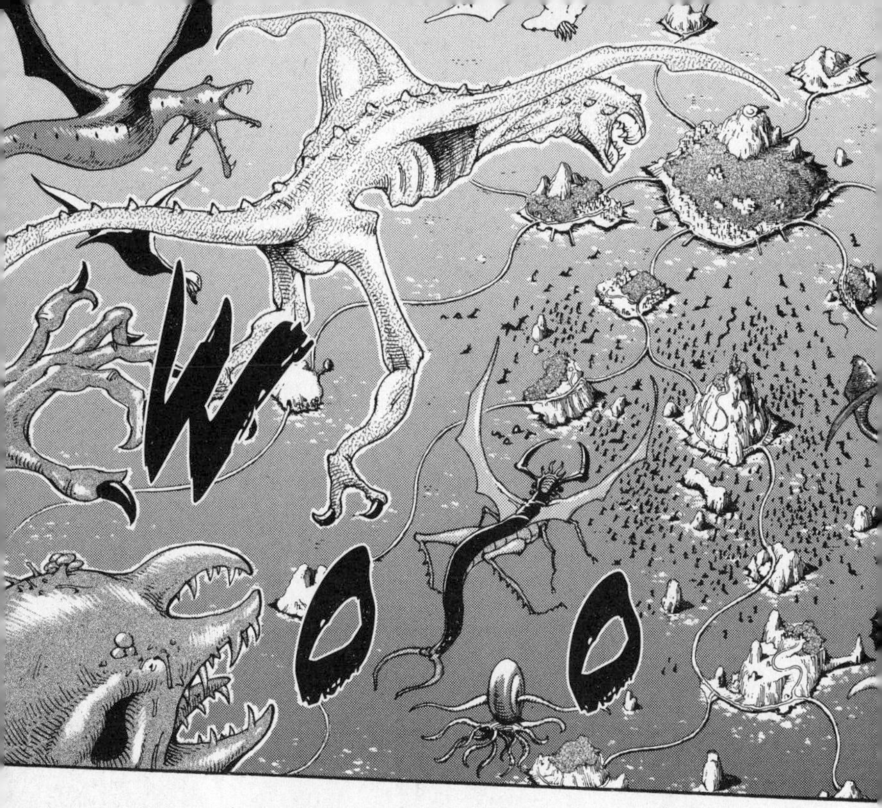
WOO
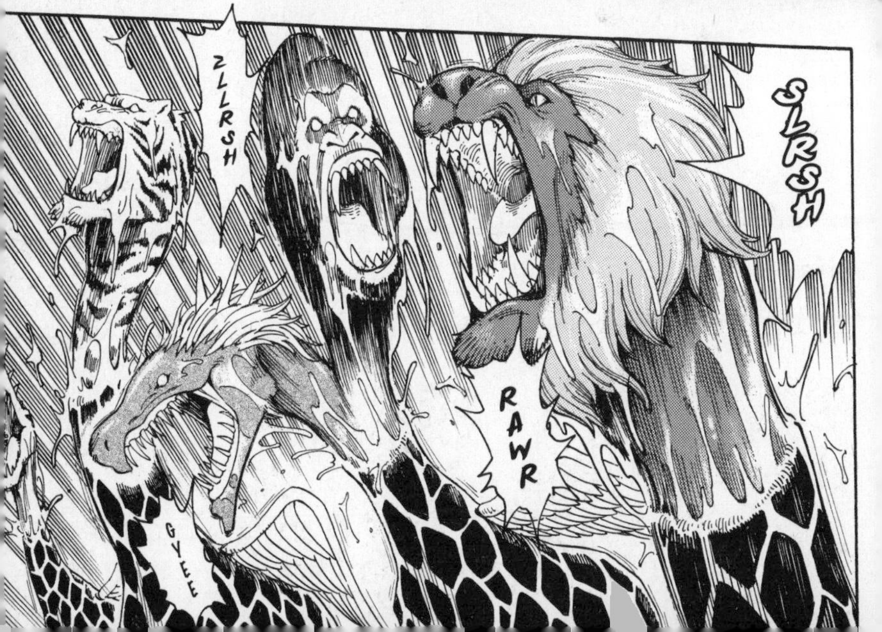
SLRSH
ZLLRSH
RAWR
GYEEE

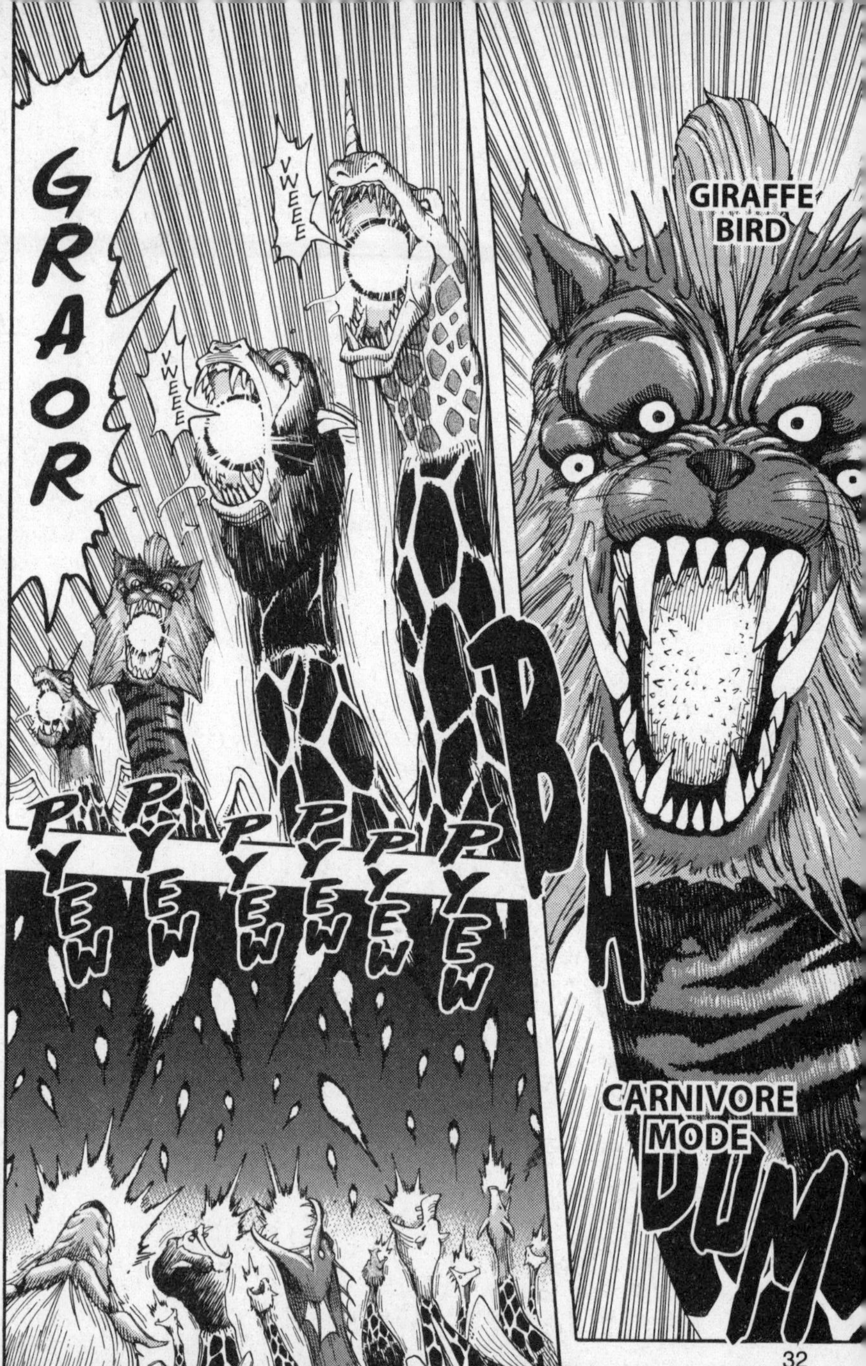
GIRAFFE BIRD
BA
CARNIVORE MODE
DUM
VWEEE
VWEEE
GRAOR
PYEW
PYEW
PYEW
PYEW
PYEW
PYEW

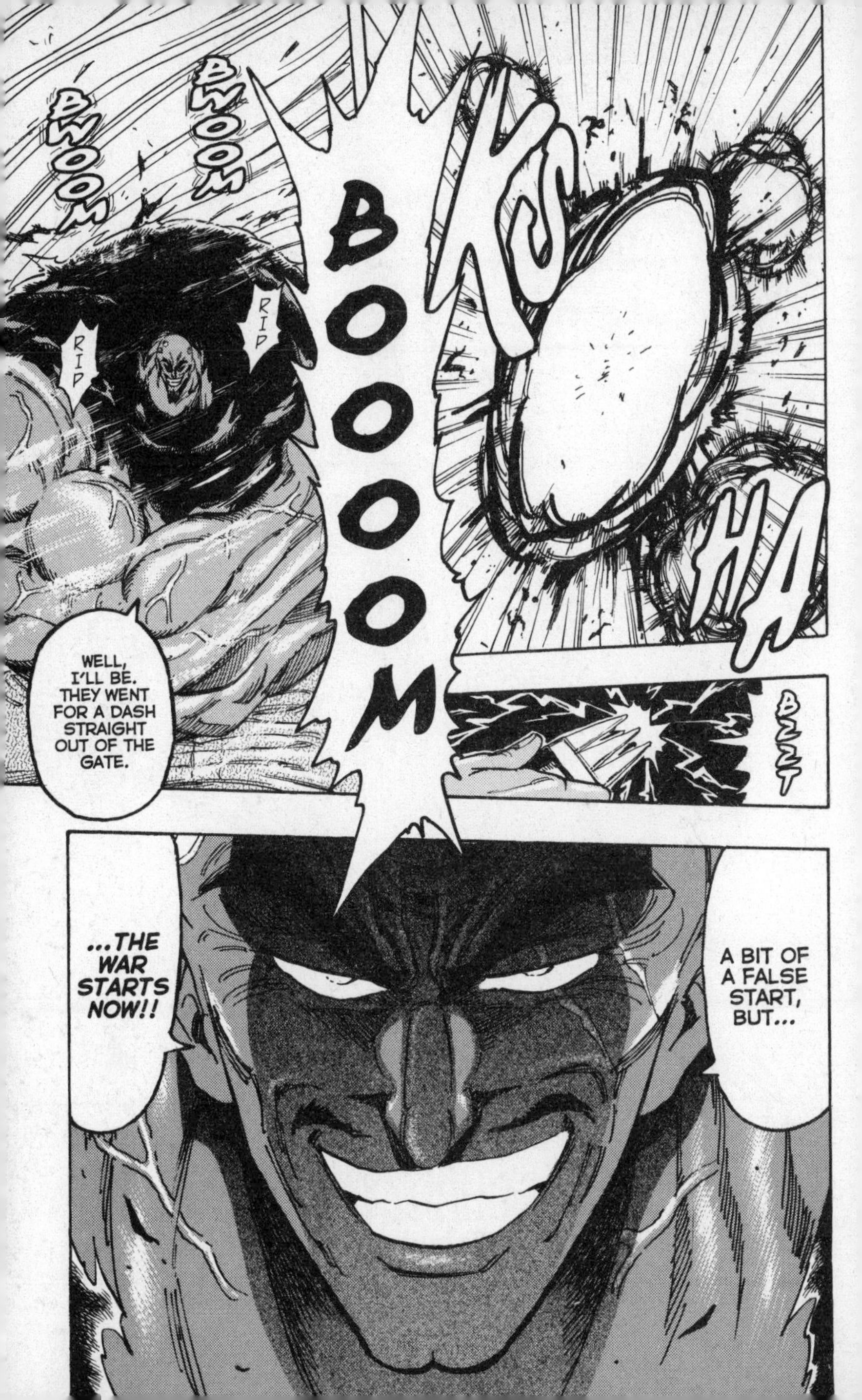
HA
BOOOOOM
BWOOM
BWOOM
RIP
RIP
WELL, I'LL BE. THEY WENT FOR A DASH STRAIGHT OUT OF THE GATE.
BZZT
A BIT OF A FALSE START, BUT...
...THE WAR STARTS NOW!!

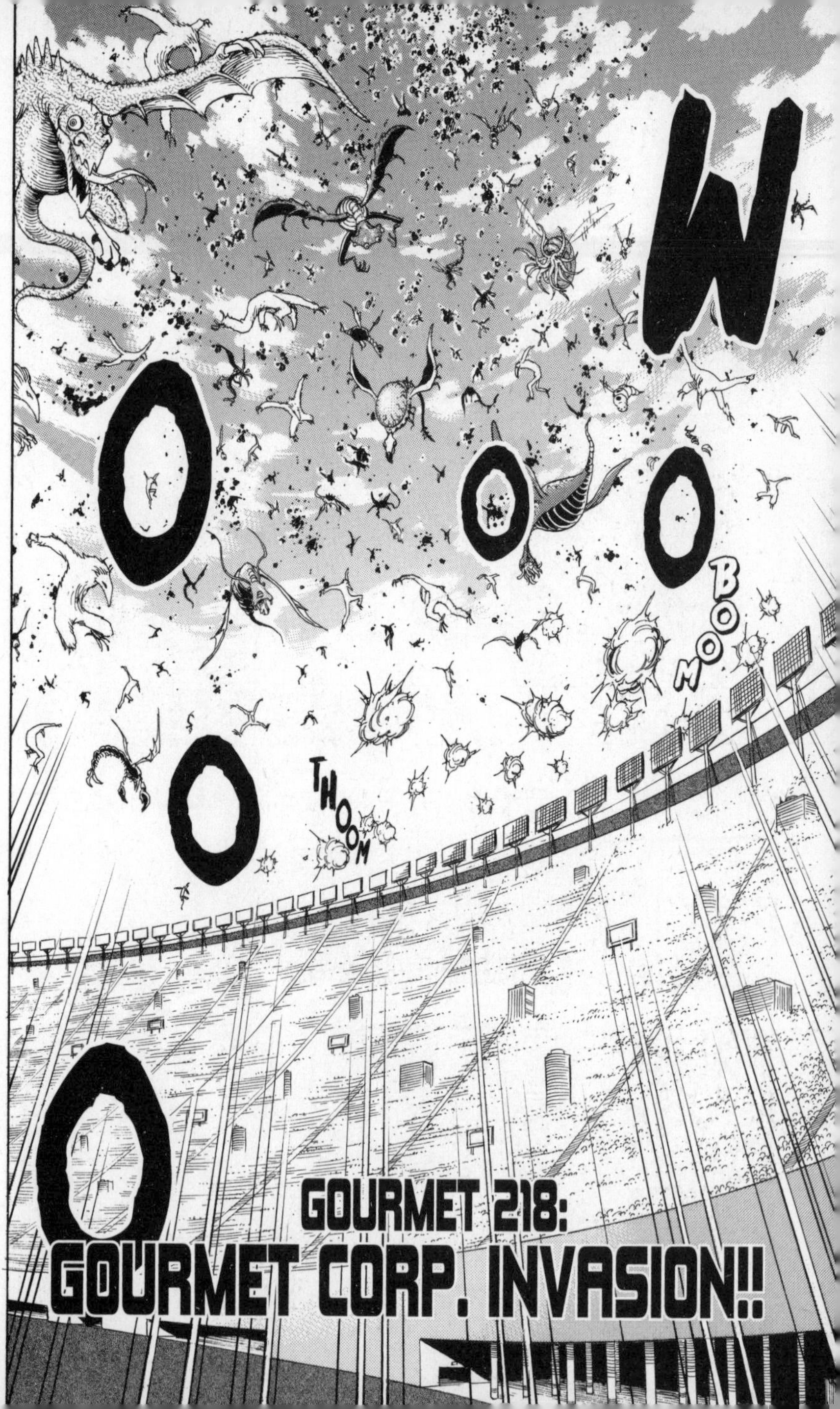
WOOOOO
BOOM
THOOM
GOURMET 218:
GOURMET CORP. INVASION!!

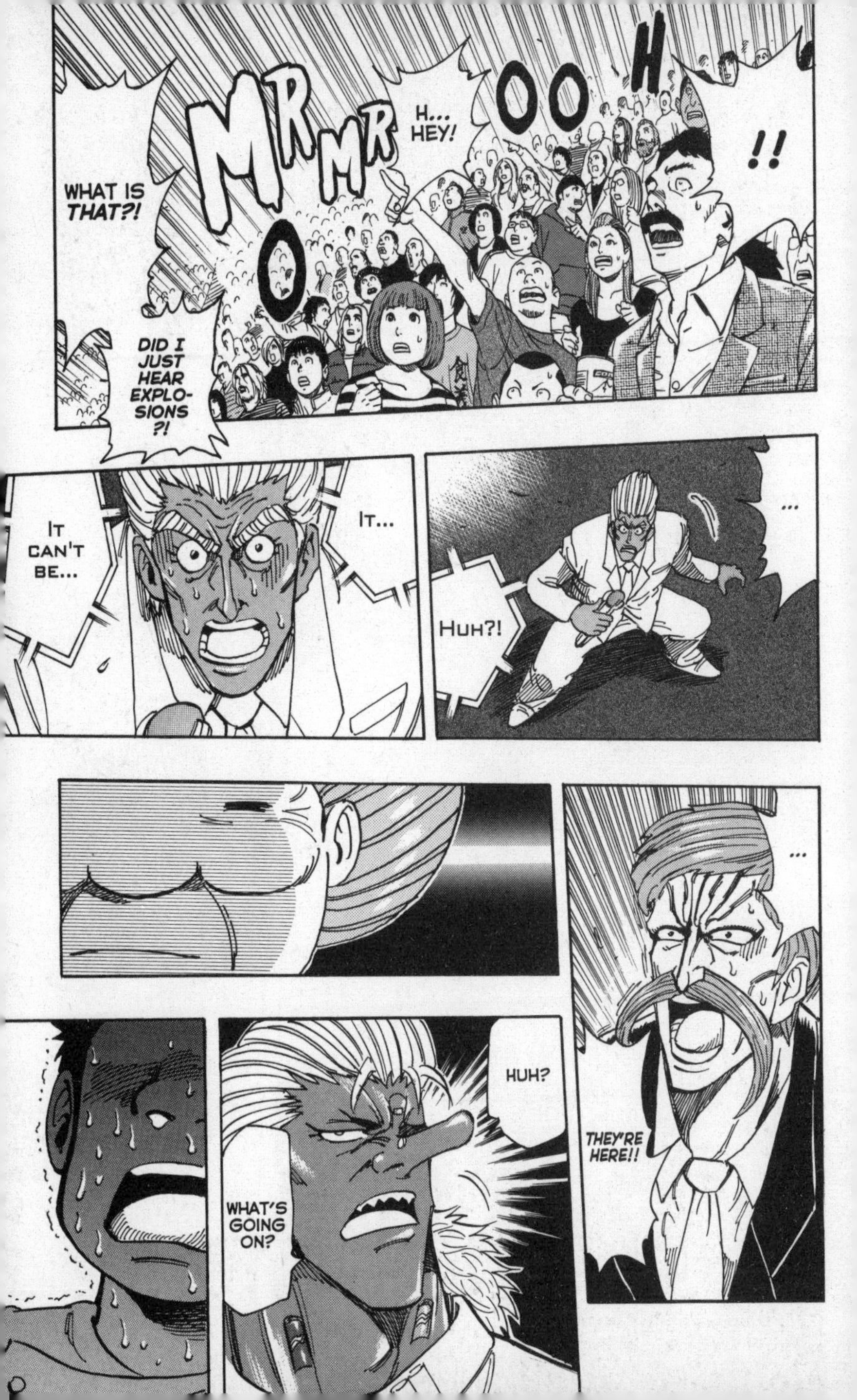
!!
MRMR OOOH
H... HEY!
WHAT IS THAT?!
DID I JUST HEAR EXPLOSIONS?!
...
HUH?!
IT...
IT CAN'T BE...
...
THEY'RE HERE!!
HUH?
WHAT'S GOING ON?

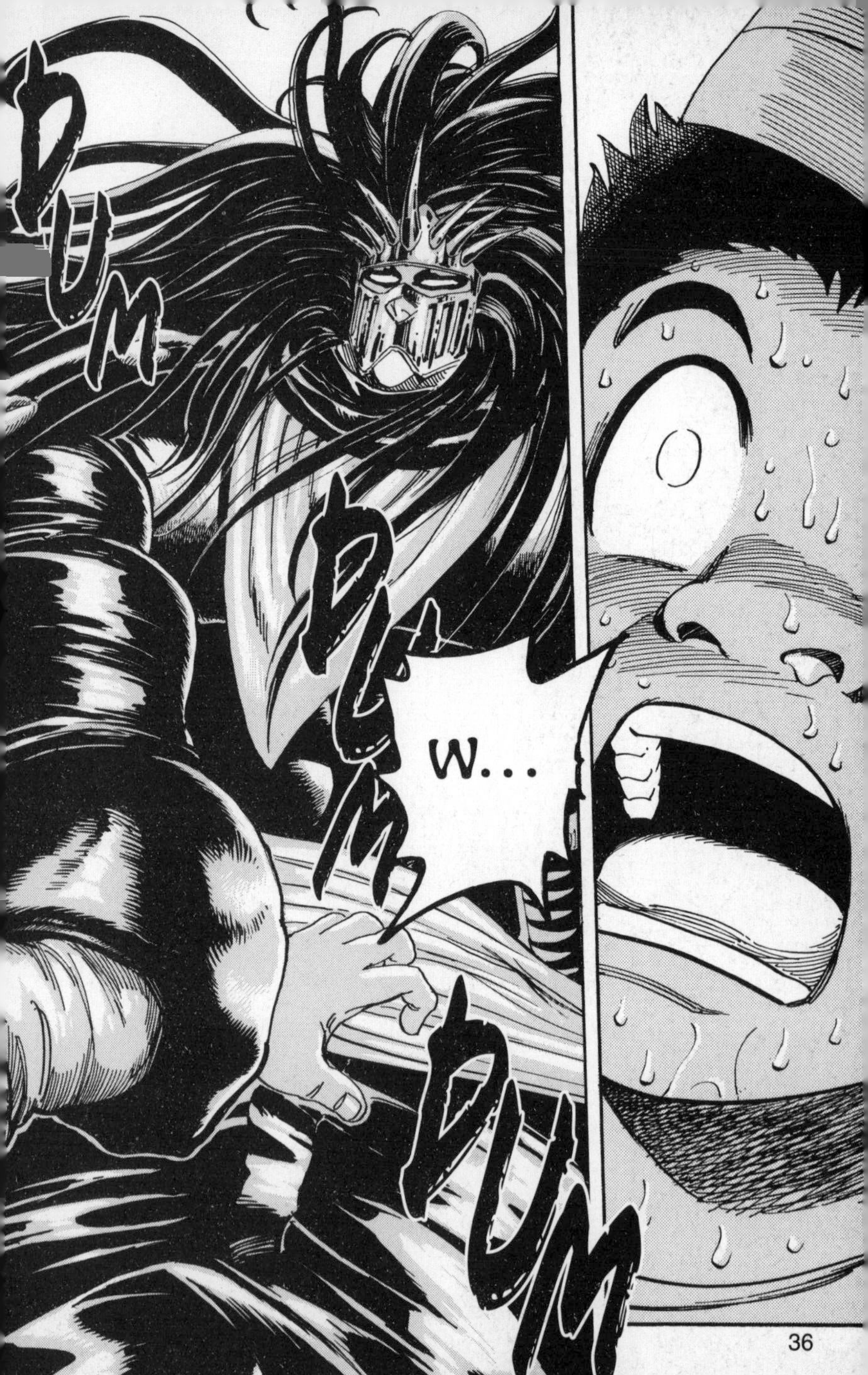
DUM DUM
W...
DUM
DUM

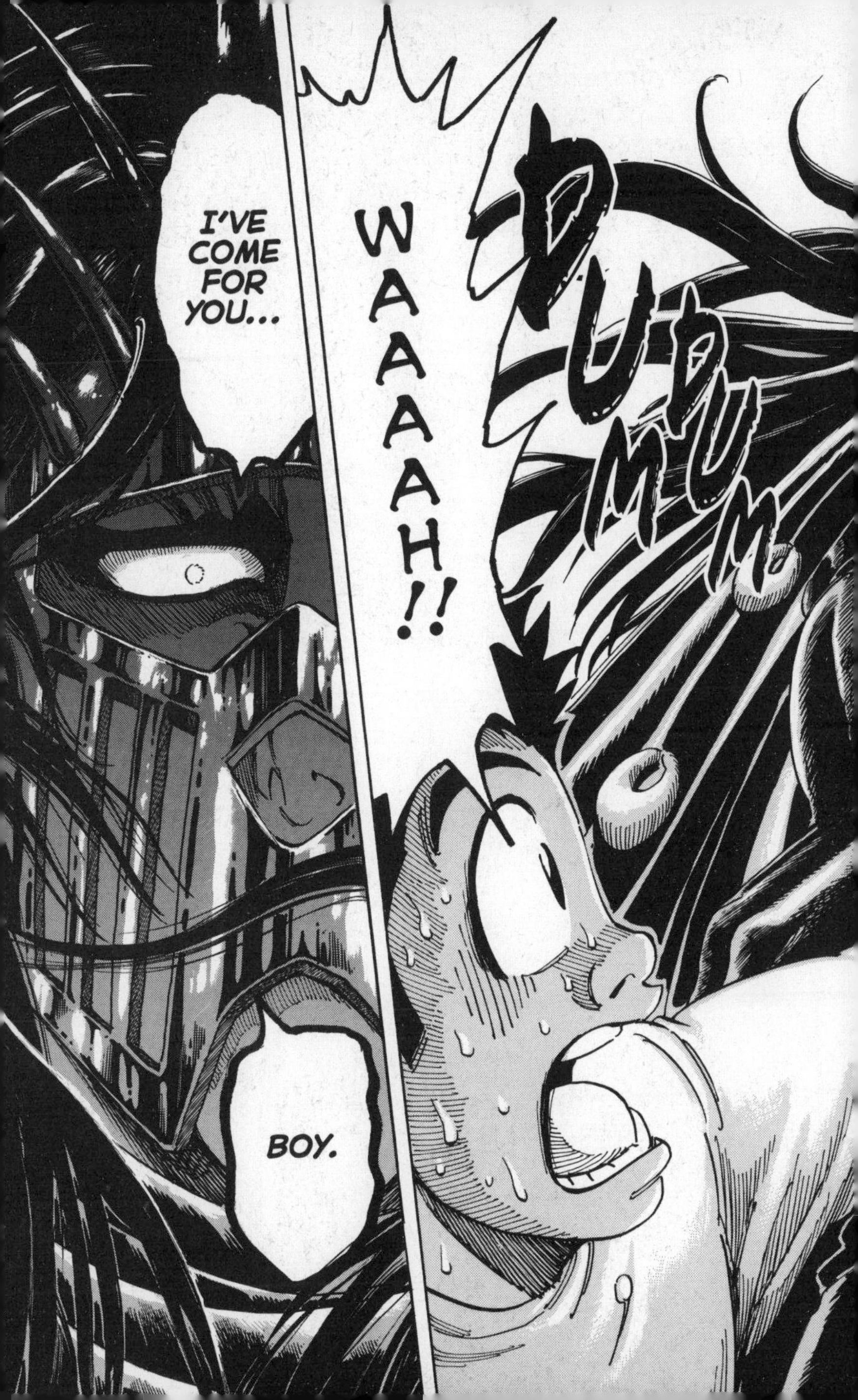
WAAAH!!
I'VE COME FOR YOU...
BOY.

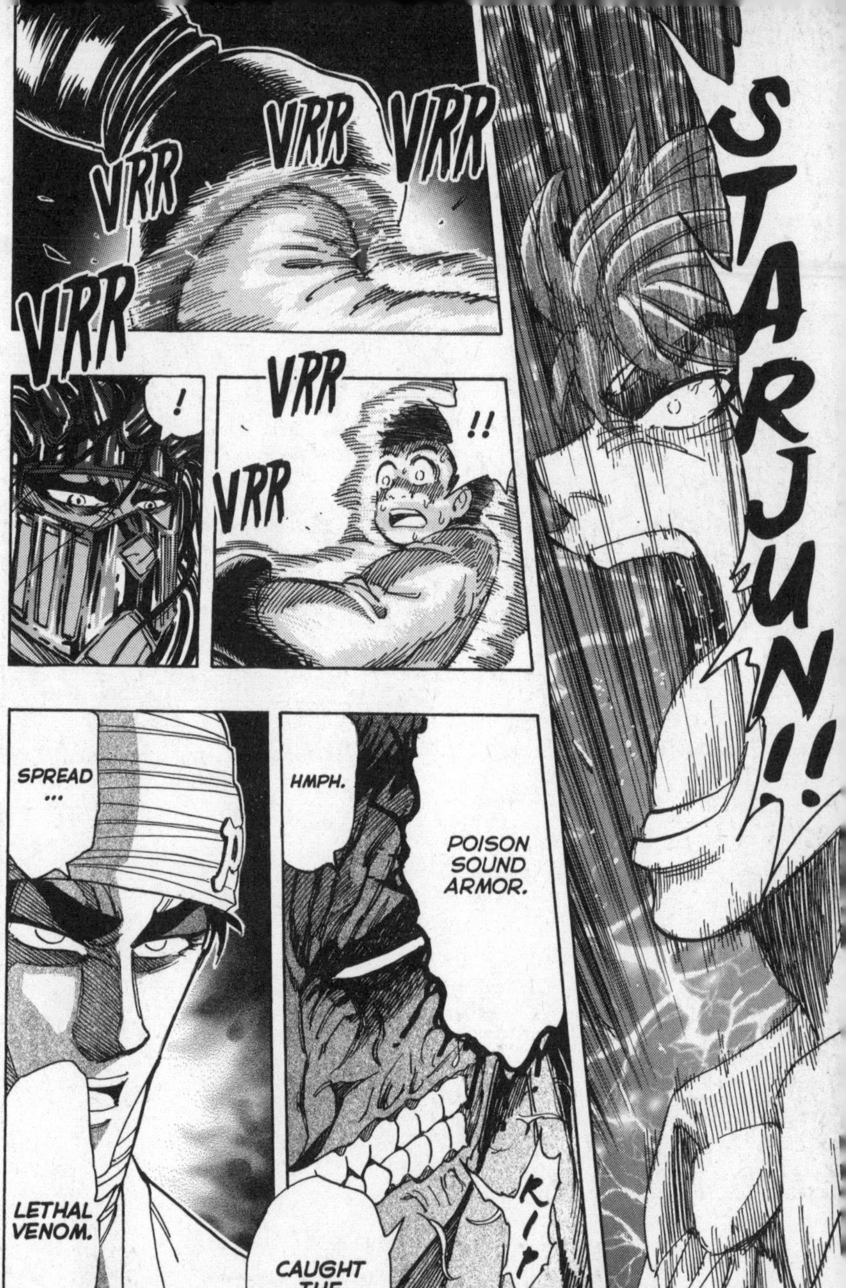
STARJUN!!
VRR
VRR
VRR
VRR
VRR
VRR
!!
!
HMPH.
POISON SOUND ARMOR.
CAUGHT THE MORON.
RIP
SPREAD...
LETHAL VENOM.

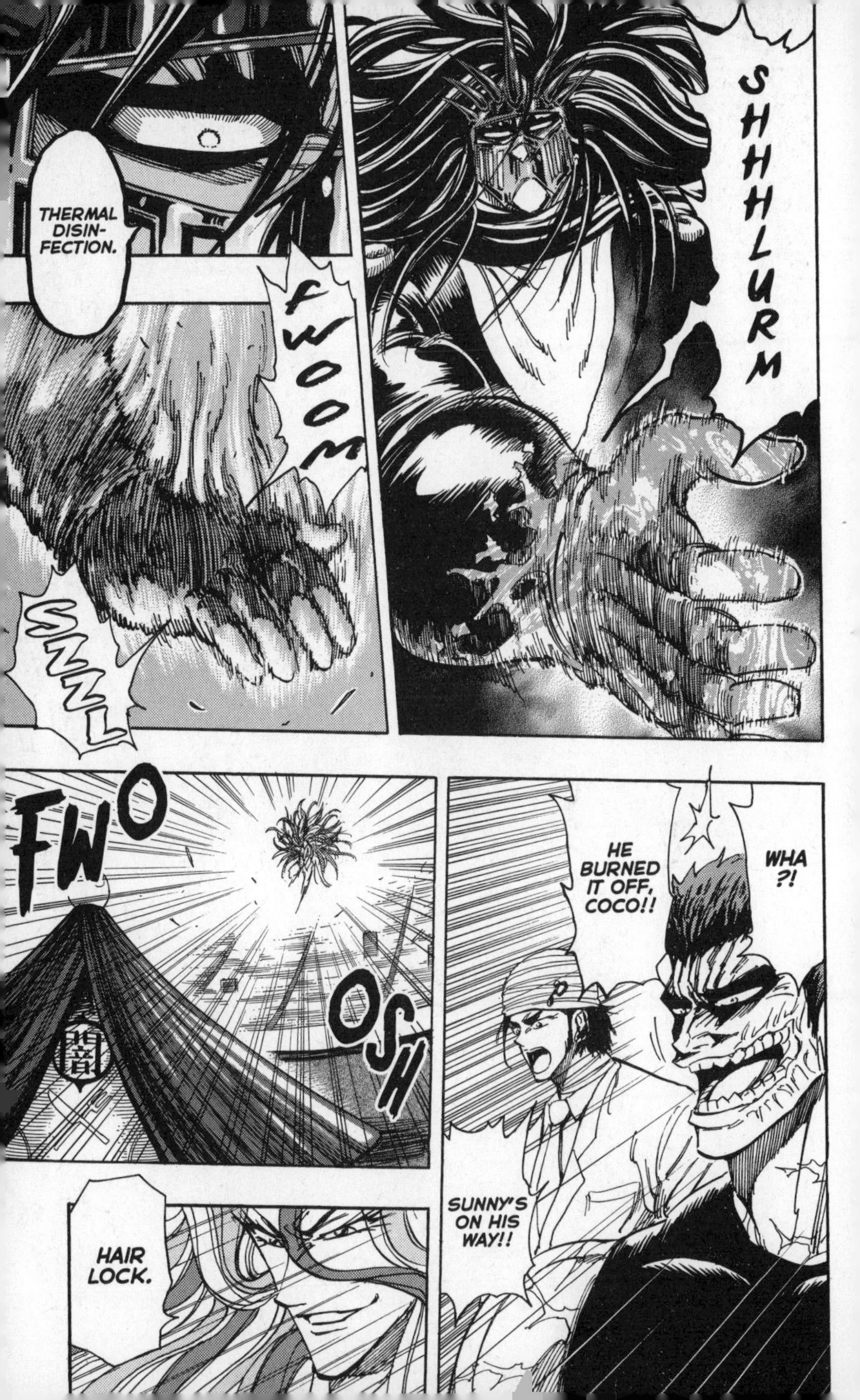

SHHHLURM
THERMAL DISIN-FECTION.
FWOOM
SIZZL
WHA ?!
HE BURNED IT OFF, COCO!!
SUNNY'S ON HIS WAY!!
FWOOSH
HAIR LOCK.

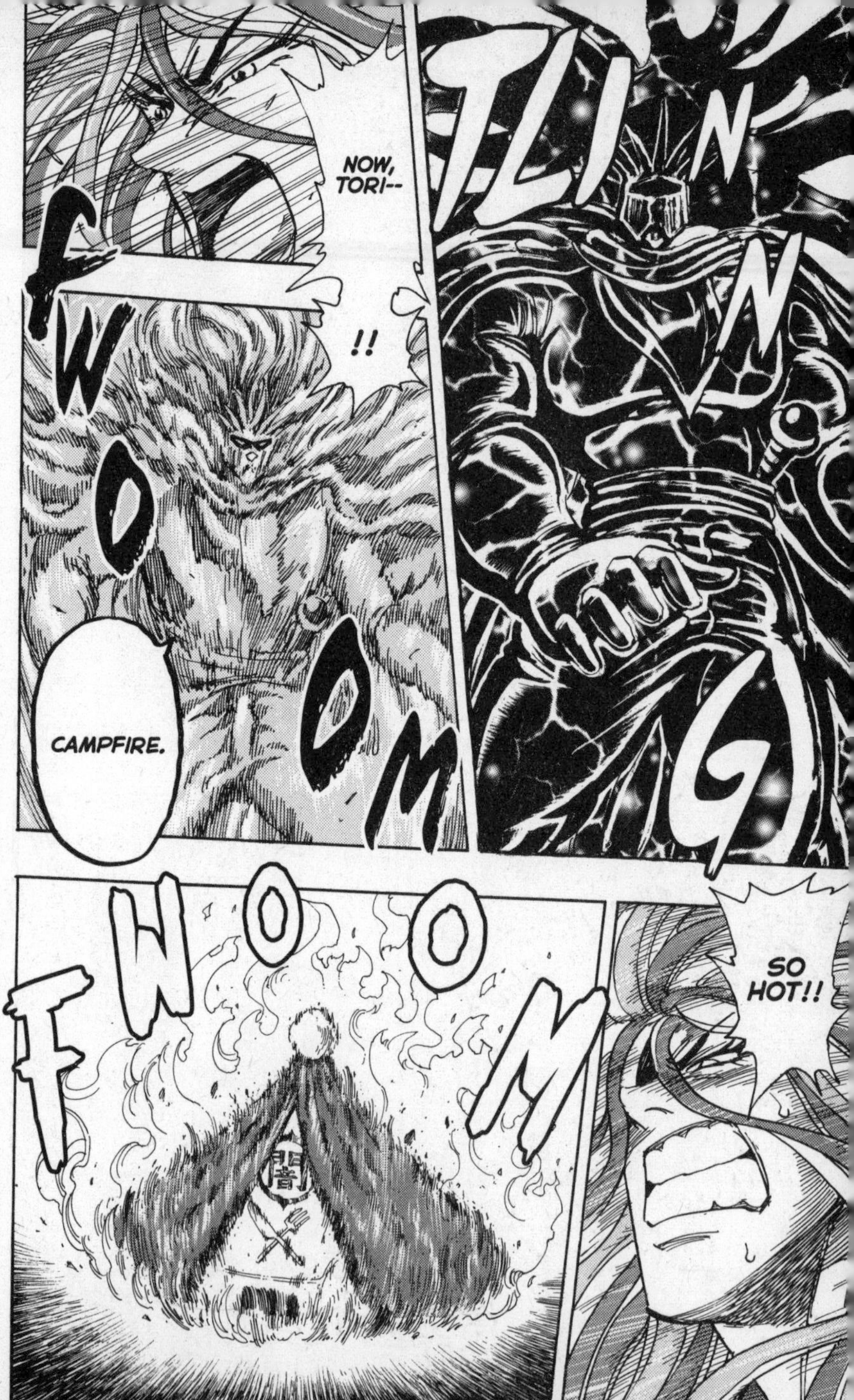

ZLINNG
NOW, TORI--
FWOOM
!!
CAMPFIRE.
SO HOT!!
FWOOM

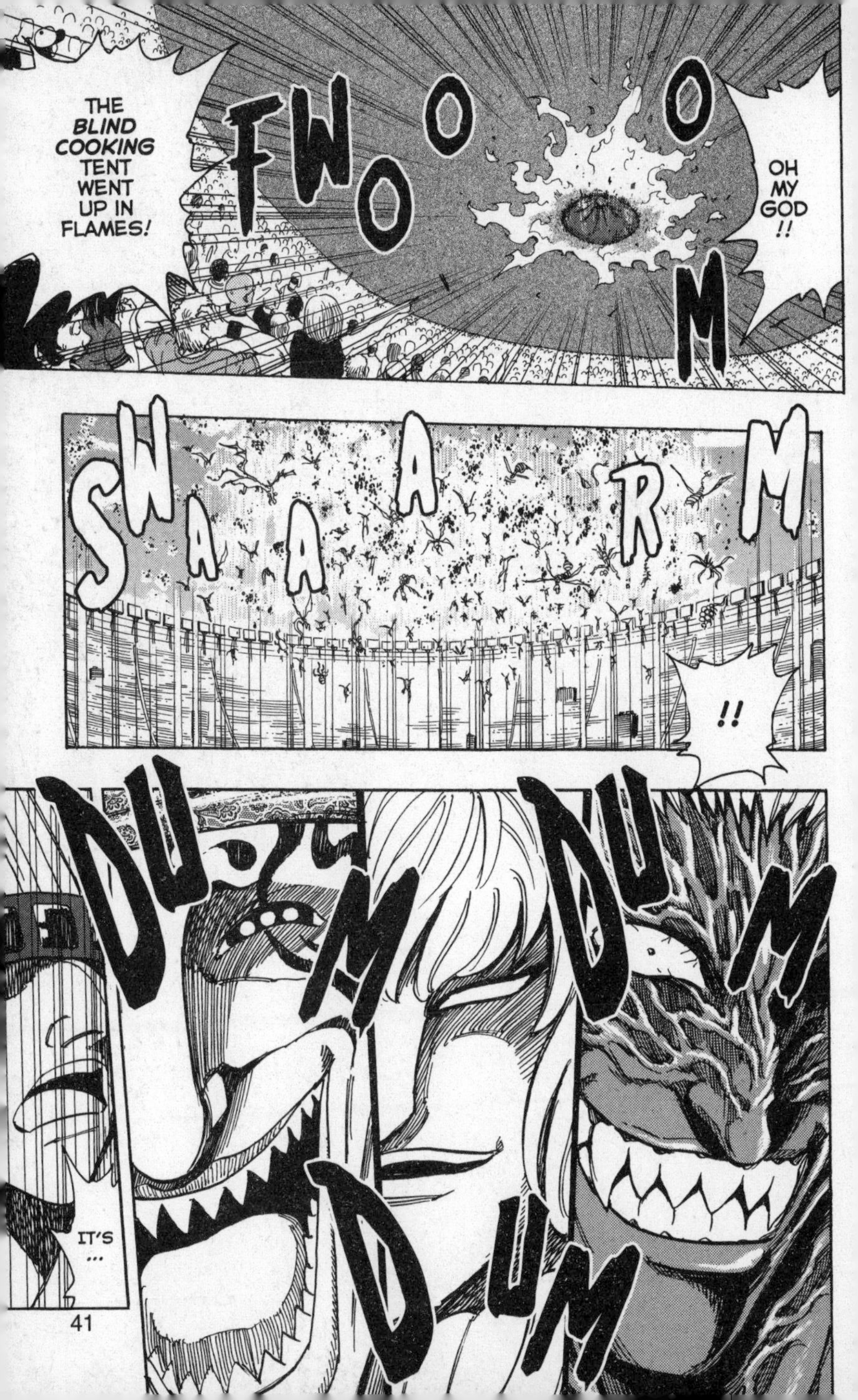
OH MY GOD !!
FWOOOOM
THE BLIND COOKING TENT WENT UP IN FLAMES!
SWAAARM
!!
DUM DUM
DUM DUM
IT'S ...

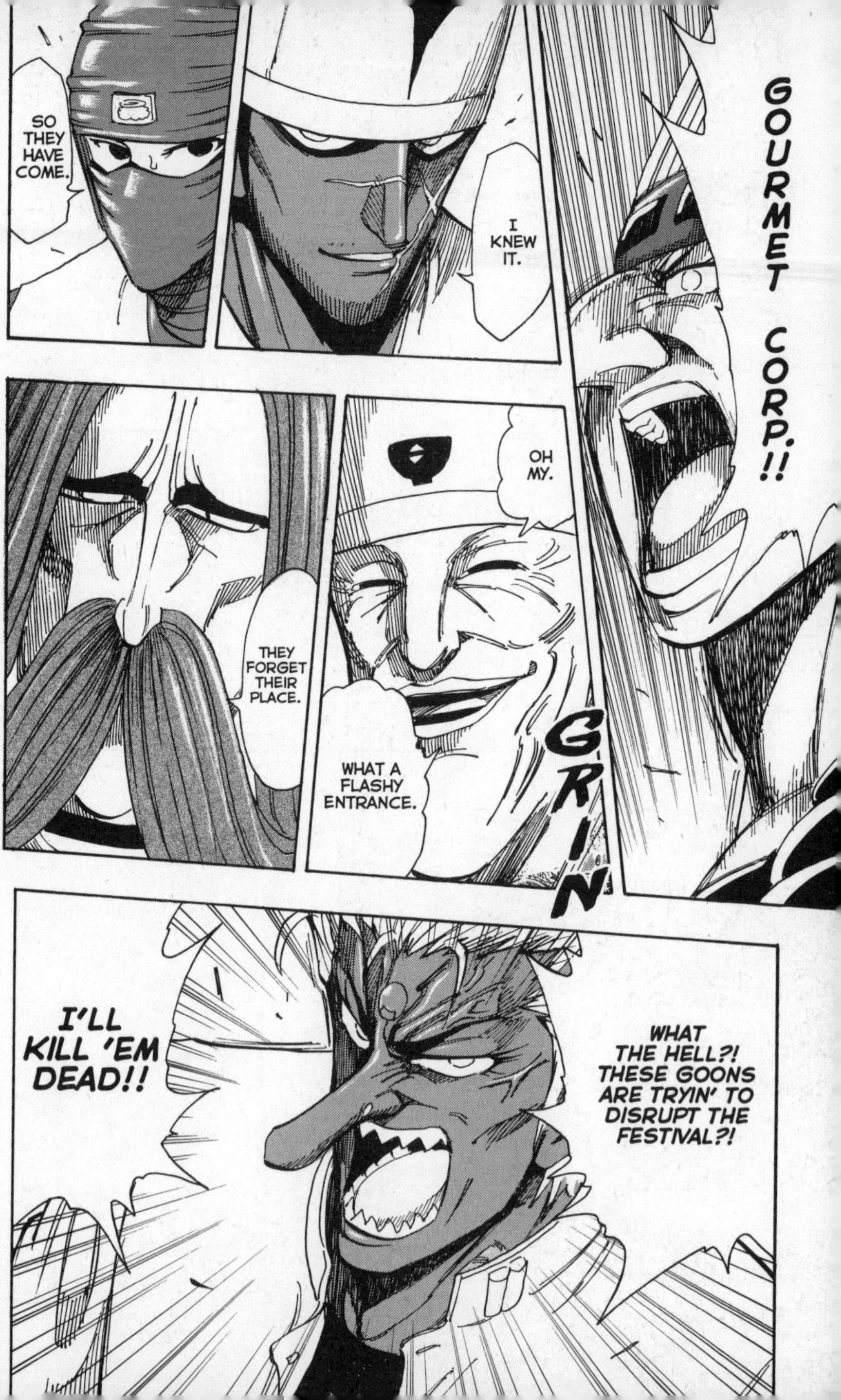
GOURMET CORP.!!
I KNEW IT.
SO THEY HAVE COME.
OH MY.
WHAT A FLASHY ENTRANCE.
GRIN
THEY FORGET THEIR PLACE.
WHAT THE HELL?! THESE GOONS ARE TRYIN' TO DISRUPT THE FESTIVAL?!
I'LL KILL 'EM DEAD!!

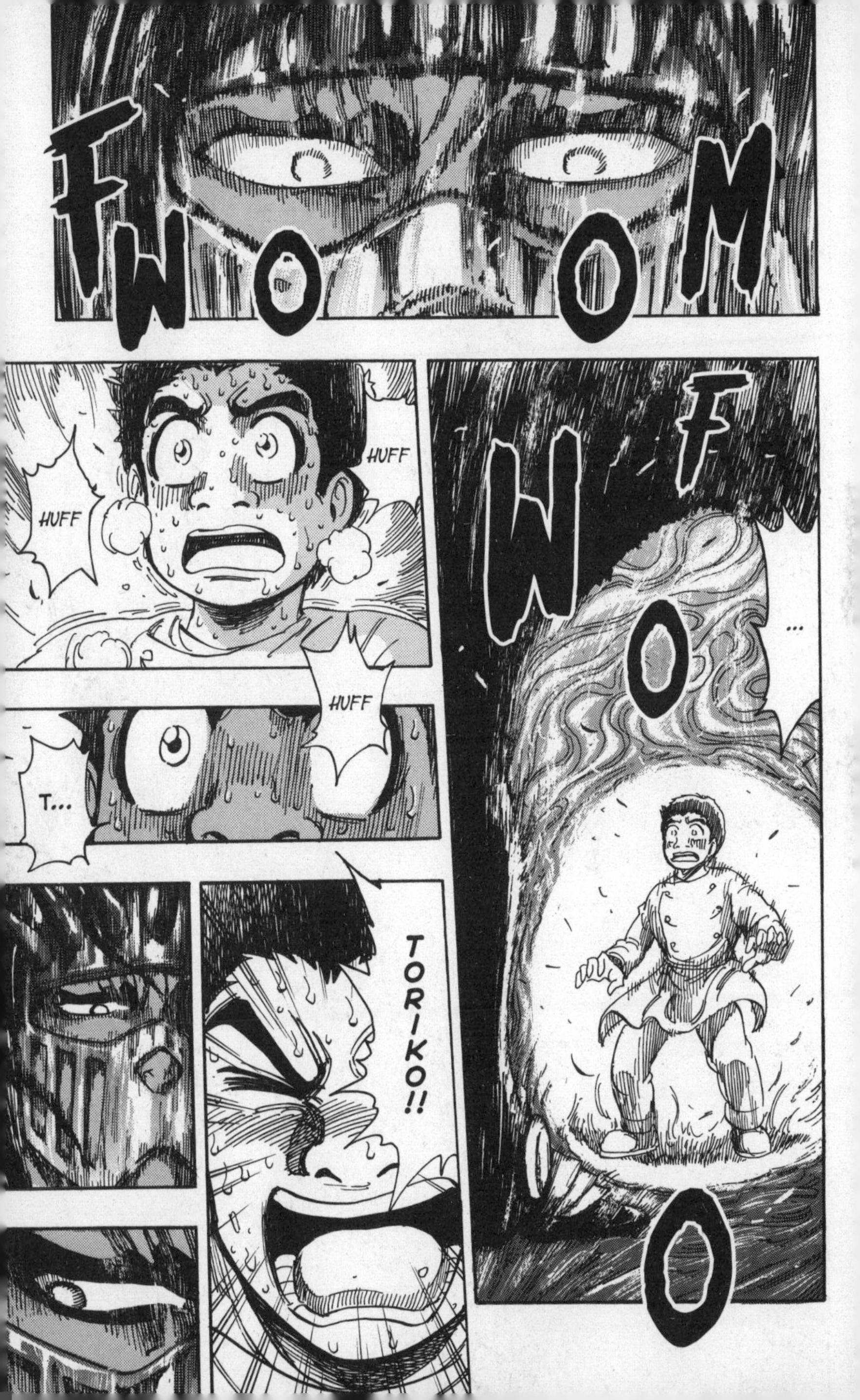
FWOOM
FWOO...
HUFF
HUFF
HUFF
T...
TORIKO!!

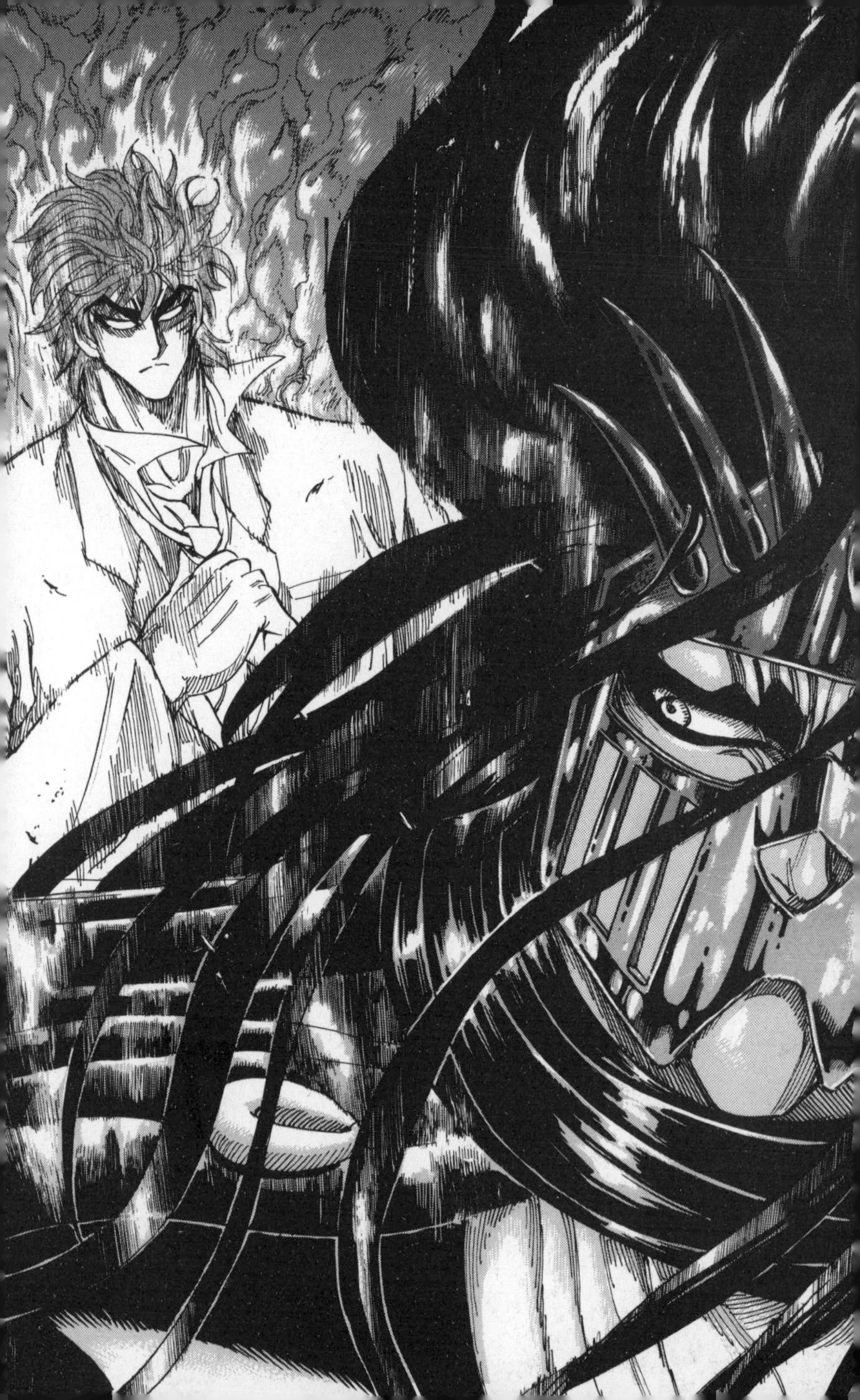

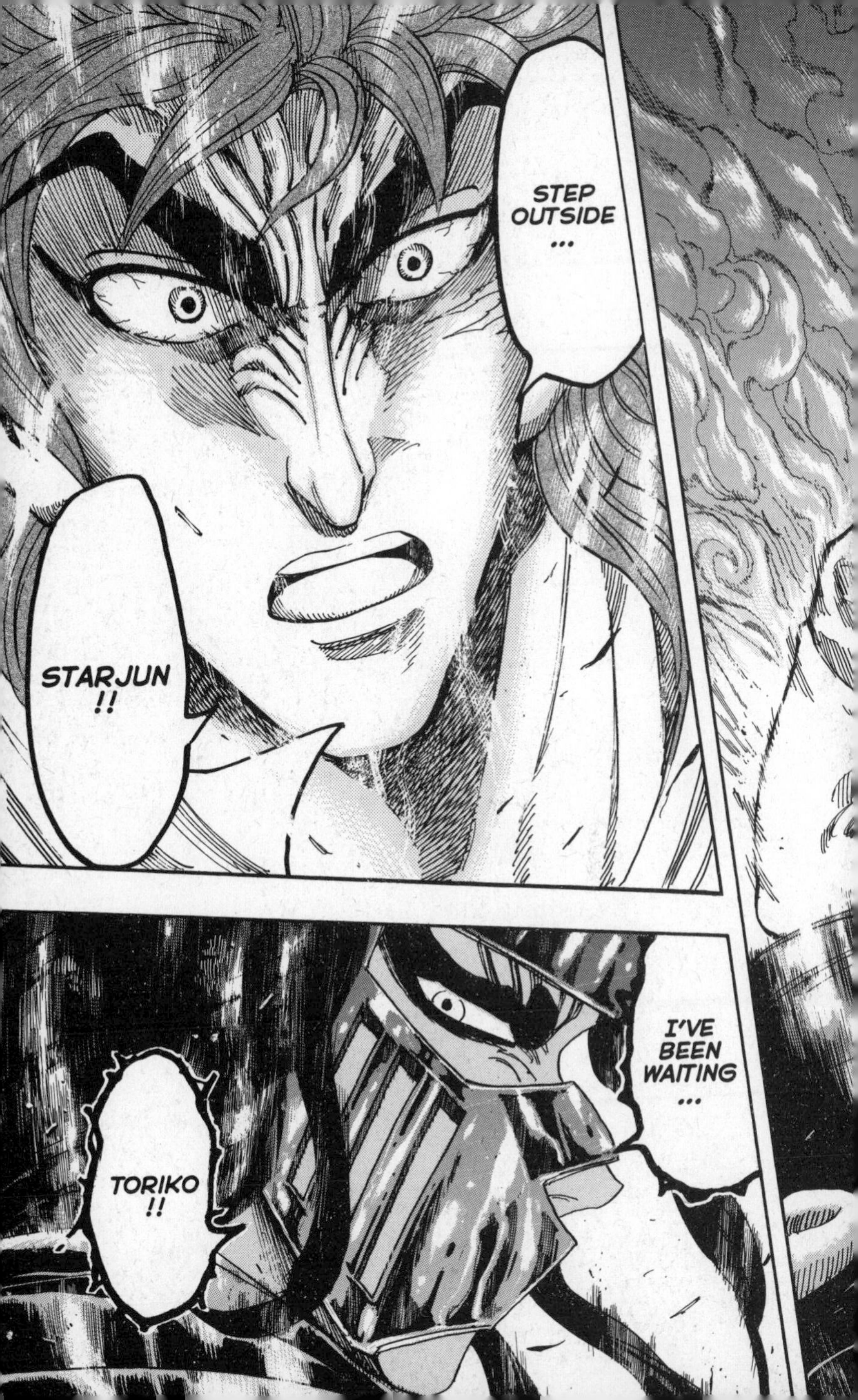
STEP OUTSIDE ...
STARJUN !!
I'VE BEEN WAITING ...
TORIKO !!

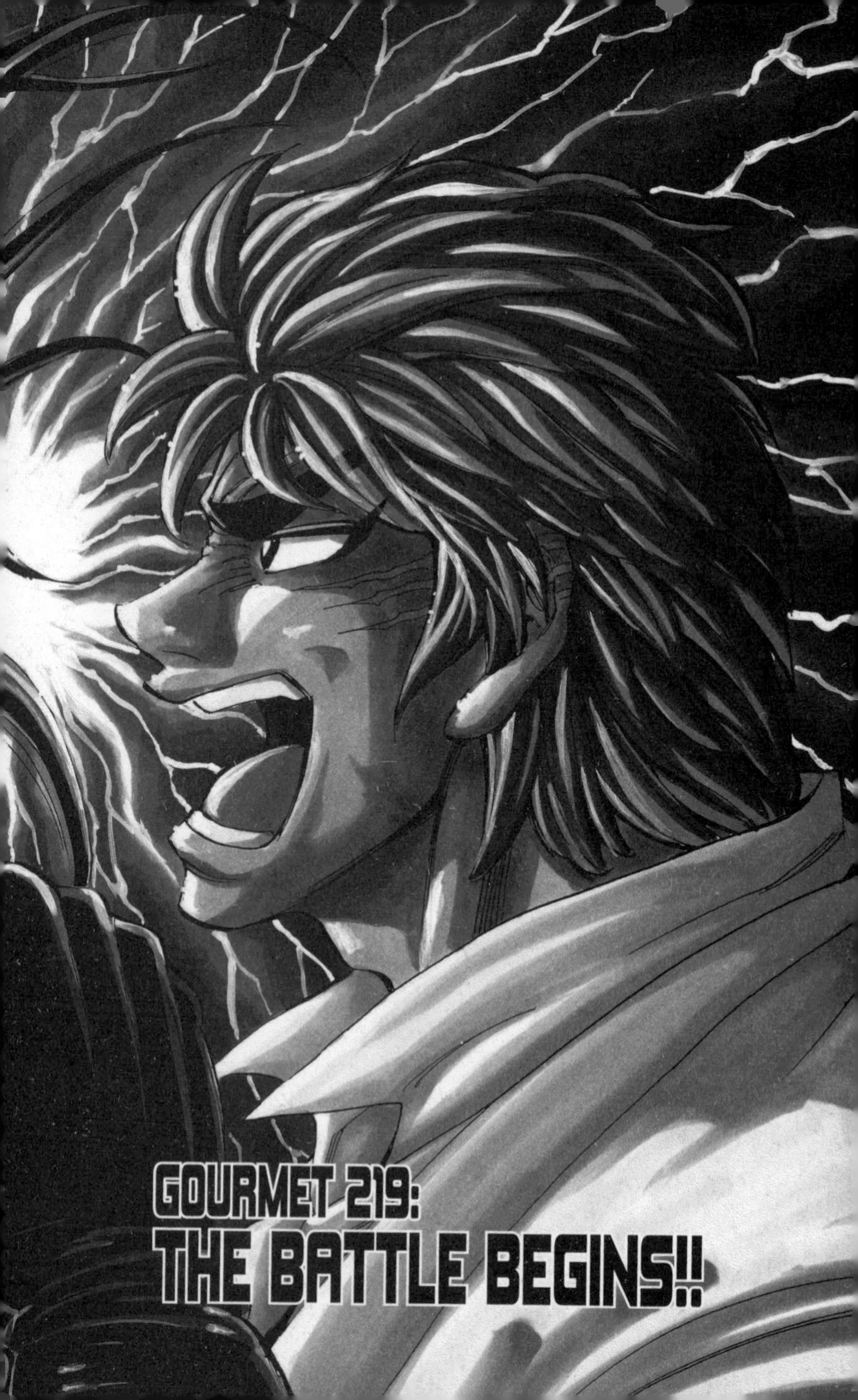
GOURMET 219:
THE BATTLE BEGINS!!

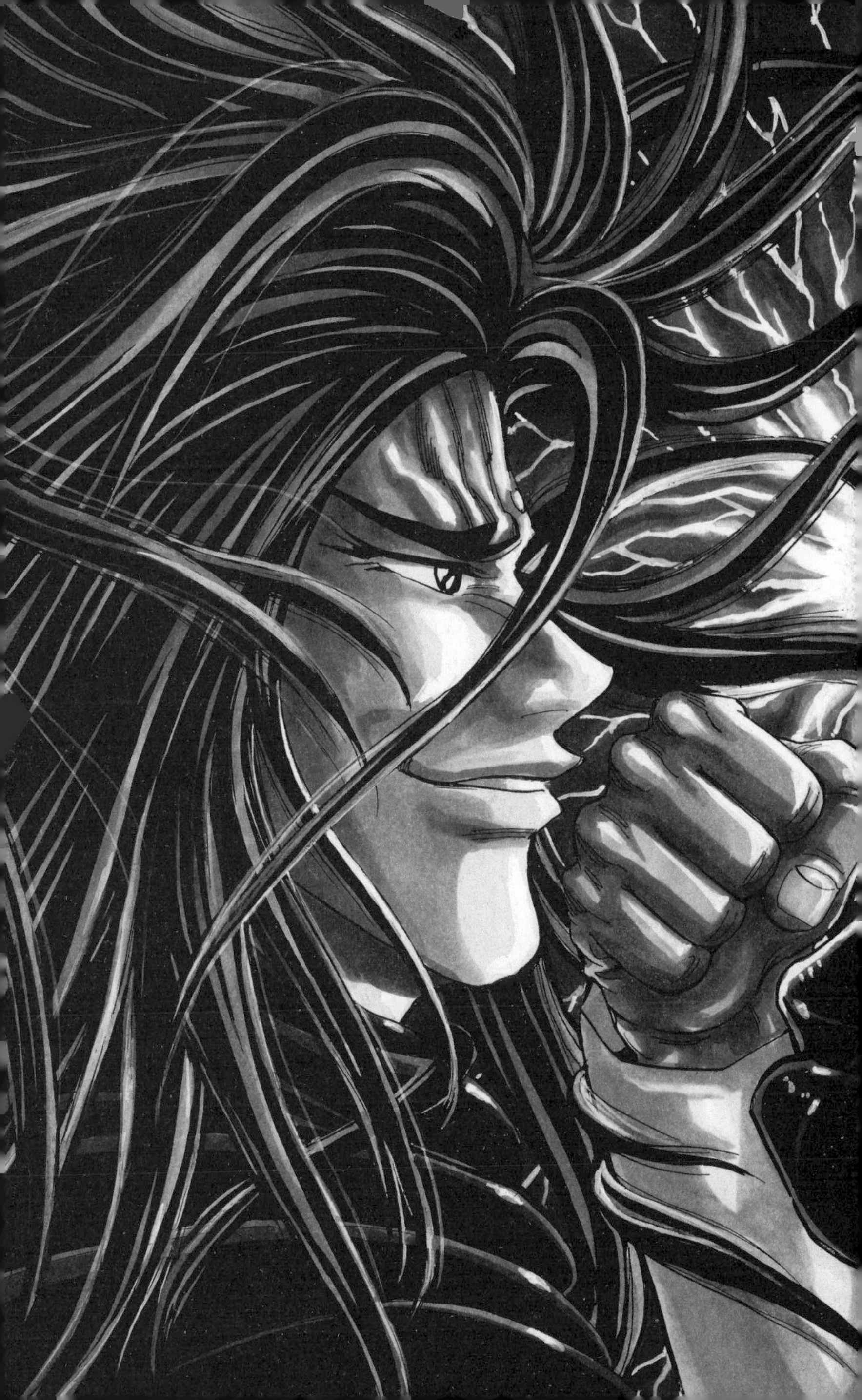

TORIKO

GOURMET CHECKLIST

Vol. 249

❯RIVER STYX POISON LIZARD❮
(REPTILE)

CAPTURE LEVEL: 21
HABITAT: RAIN FORESTS
LENGTH: 1 METER
HEIGHT: ---
WEIGHT: 20 KG
PRICE: 100 G / 10,000 YEN (MEAT);
      2.5 MILLION YEN (TAIL)

HIS NEXT MATCH IS THE RIVER STYX POISON LIZARD* AT 150 POINTS!!

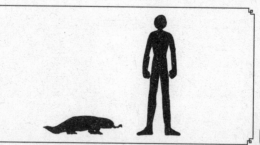

SCALE

ALSO CALLED THE RIVER STYX MONSTER, IT HAS AN AGGRESSIVE DISPOSITION AND ITS POISONOUS BITE WILL MELT THE SKIN RIGHT OFF YOUR BONES. AS ITS NAME SUGGESTS, THIS DANGEROUS CREATURE REQUIRING SPECIAL PREPARATION WILL SEND YOU ACROSS THE RIVER STYX. IT STORES ALL ITS NUTRIENTS IN ITS TAIL, ENABLING IT TO LIVE FOR TEN YEARS WITHOUT EATING A SINGLE THING. THE NUTRITIONAL VALUE OF ITS TAIL IS RIDICULOUSLY HIGH AND ALSO SERVES AS AN ANALEPTIC. IN THAT SENSE, THE RIVER STYX LIZARD IS BOTH LIFE AND DEATH ROLLED UP IN ONE.

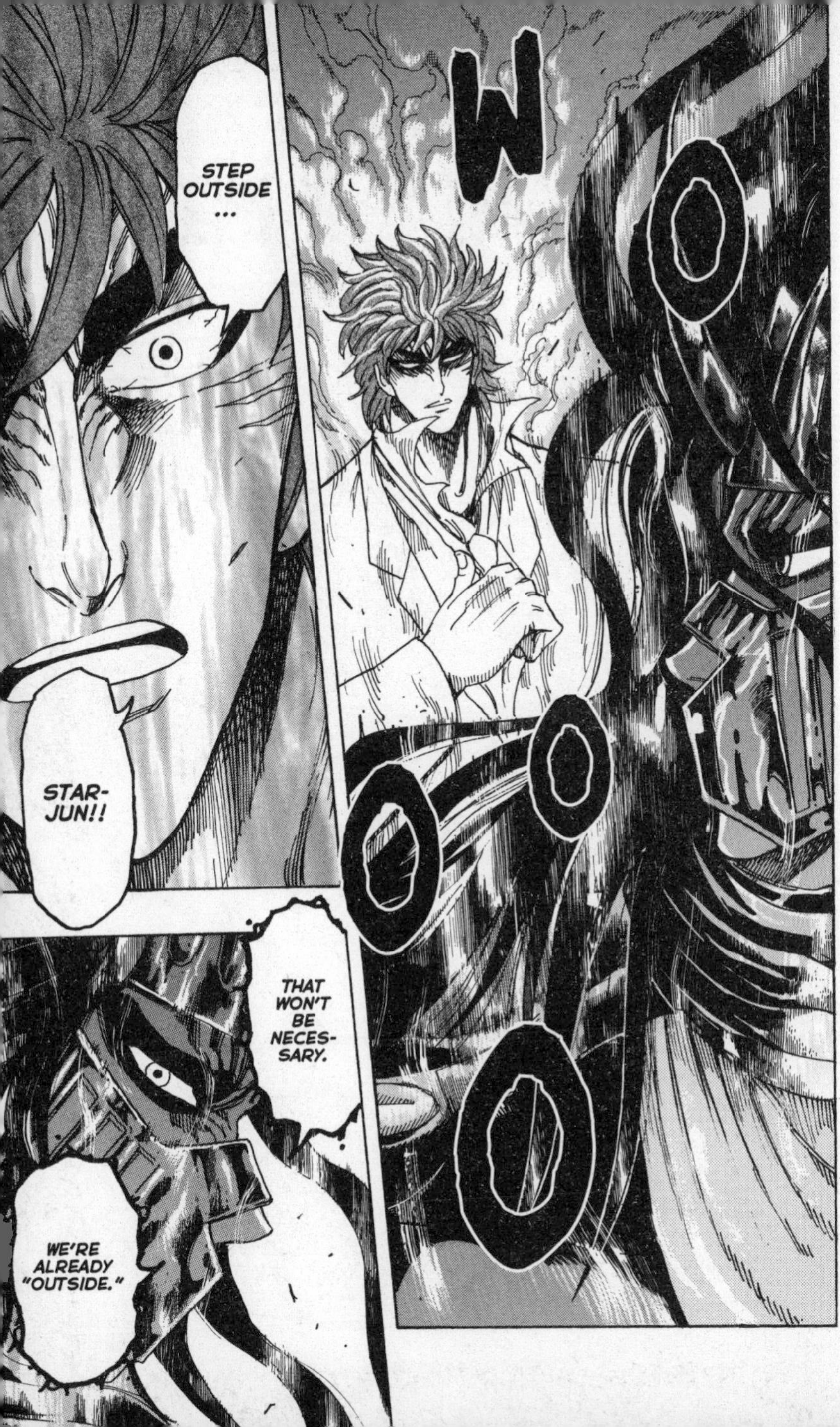
WOOOO
STEP OUTSIDE ...
STAR-JUN!!
THAT WON'T BE NECES-SARY.
WE'RE ALREADY "OUTSIDE."

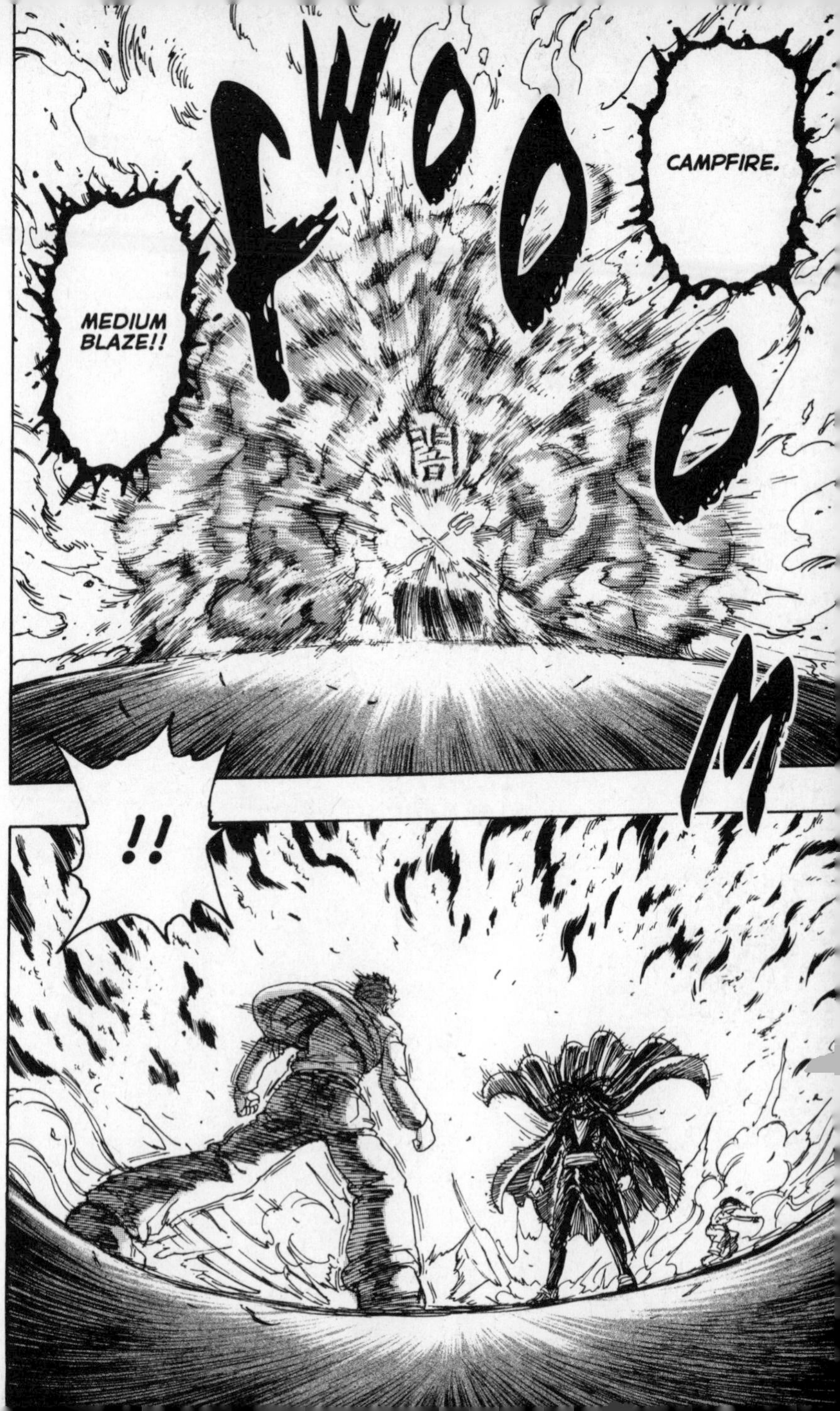

CAMPFIRE.
MEDIUM BLAZE!!
FWOOOOOM
!!

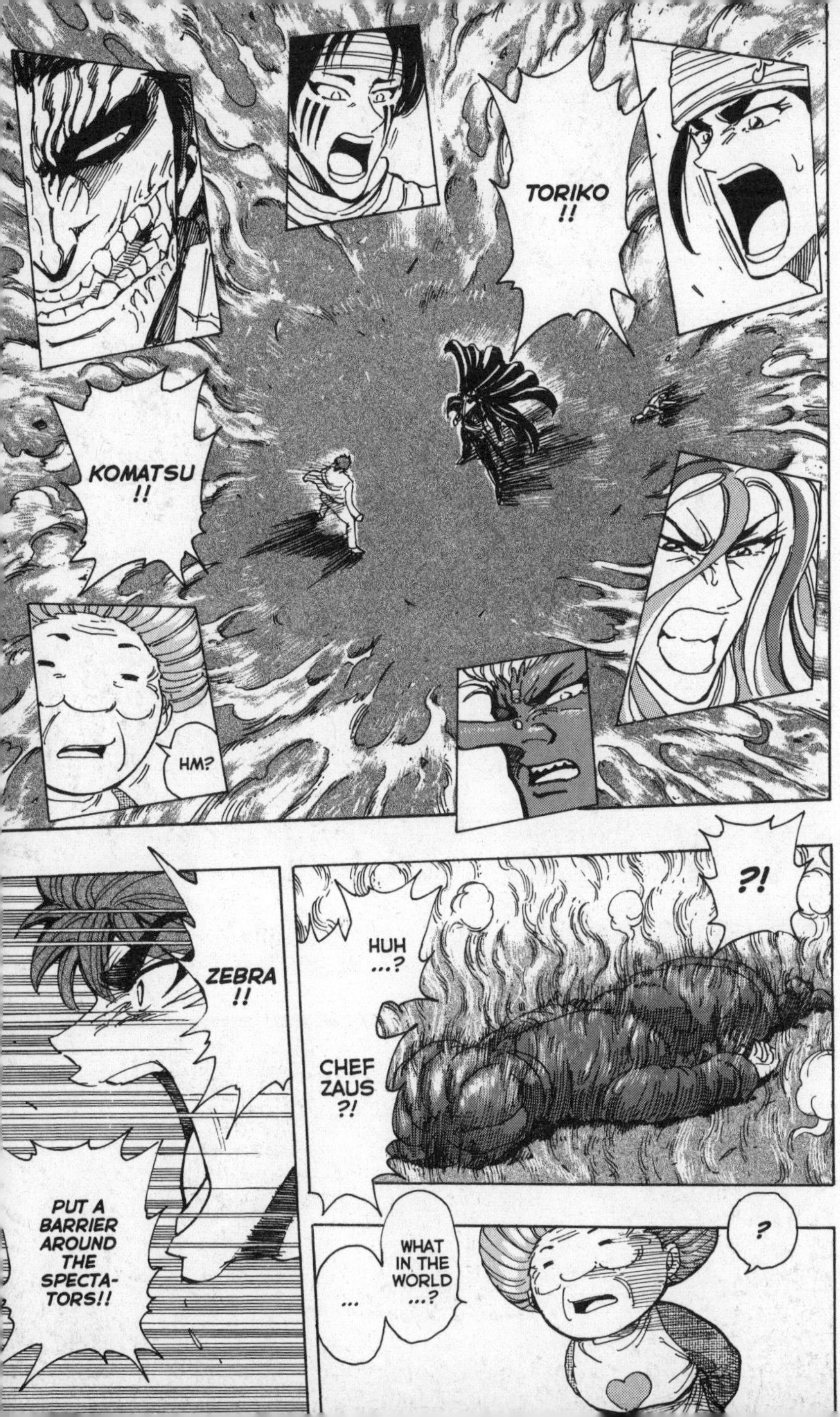
TORIKO !!
KOMATSU !!
HM?
?!
HUH ...?
CHEF ZAUS ?!
?
WHAT IN THE WORLD ...?
...
ZEBRA !!
PUT A BARRIER AROUND THE SPECTATORS!!

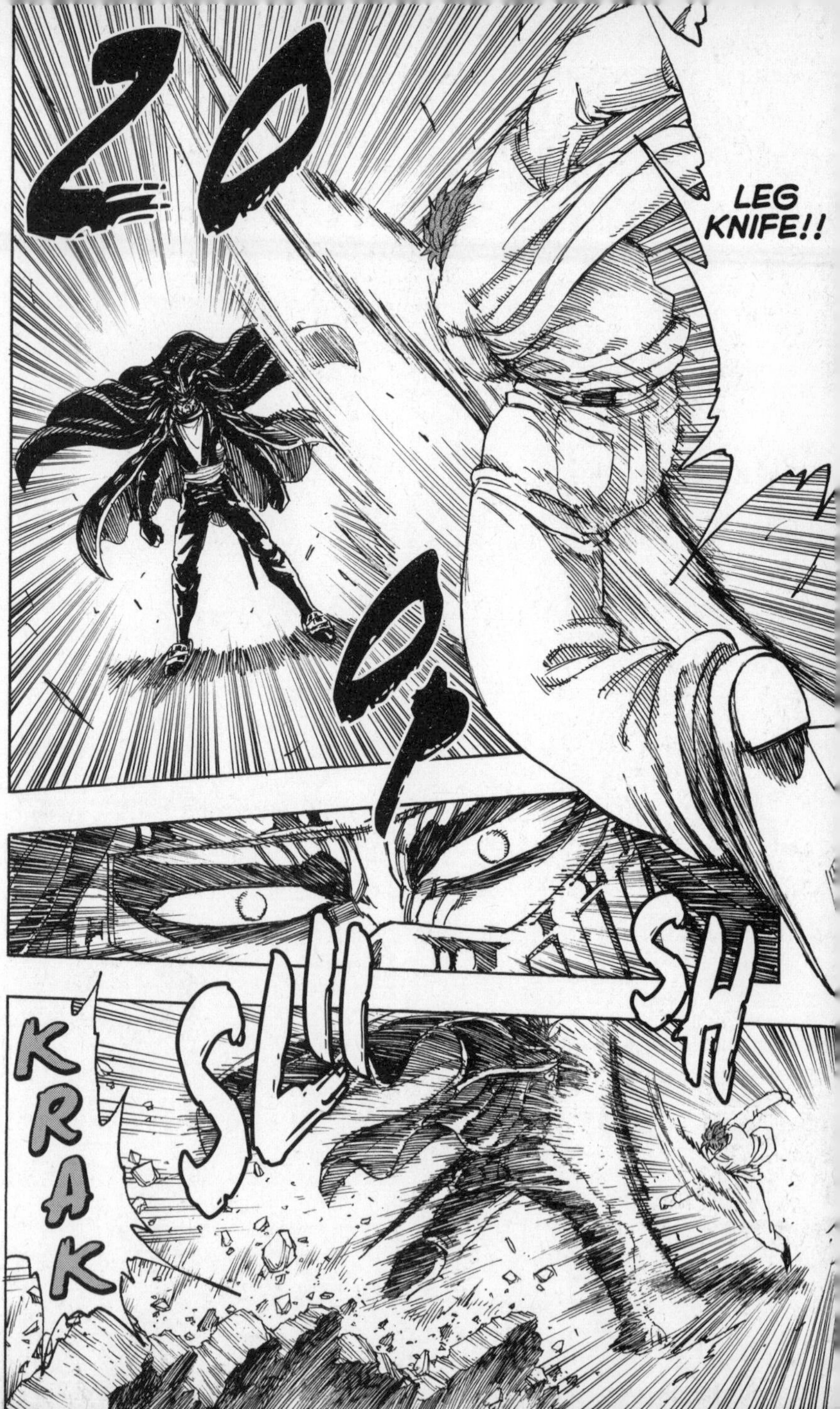
LEG KNIFE!!
KRAK

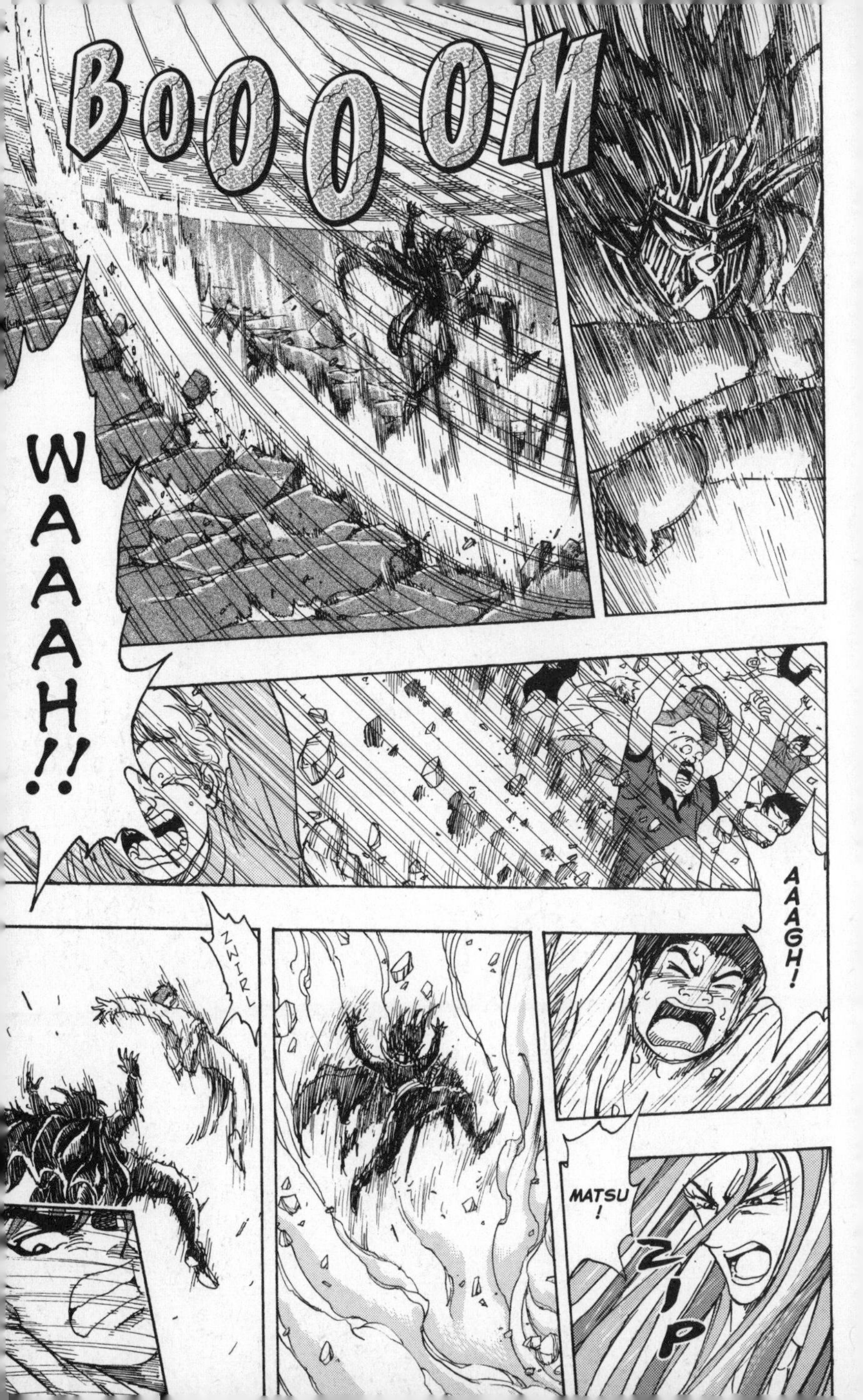
BOOOOM
WAAAH!!
AAAGH!
MATSU!
ZIP
ZWIRL

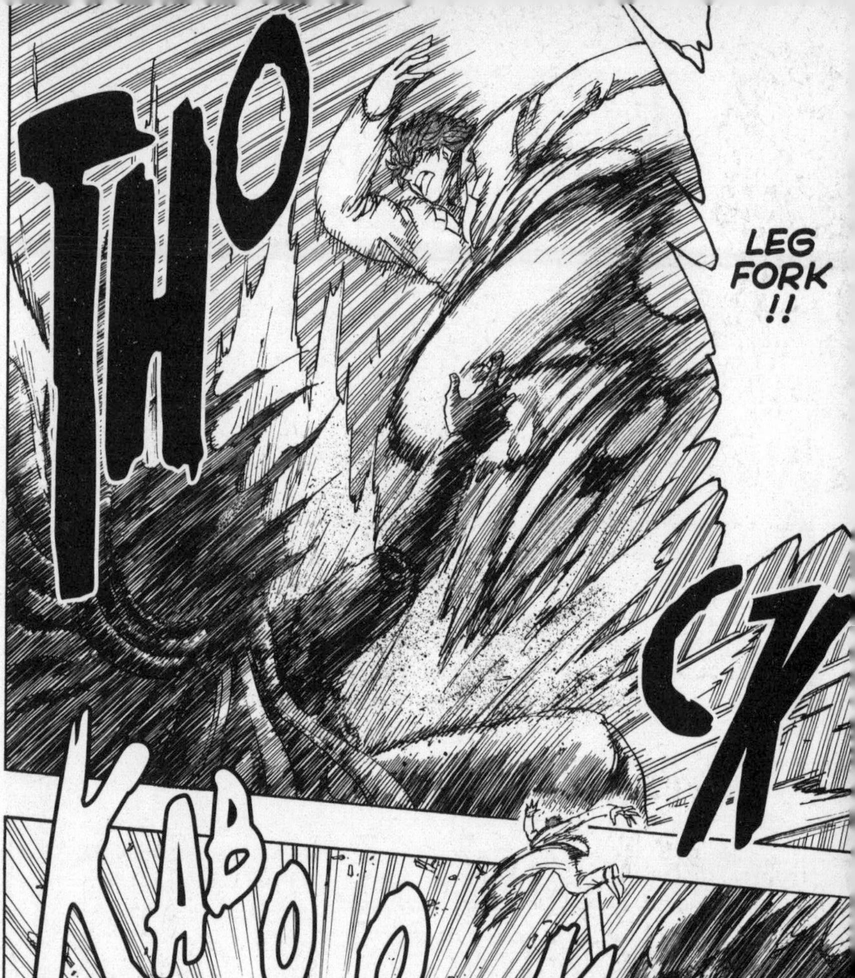
LEG FORK !!
THOCK
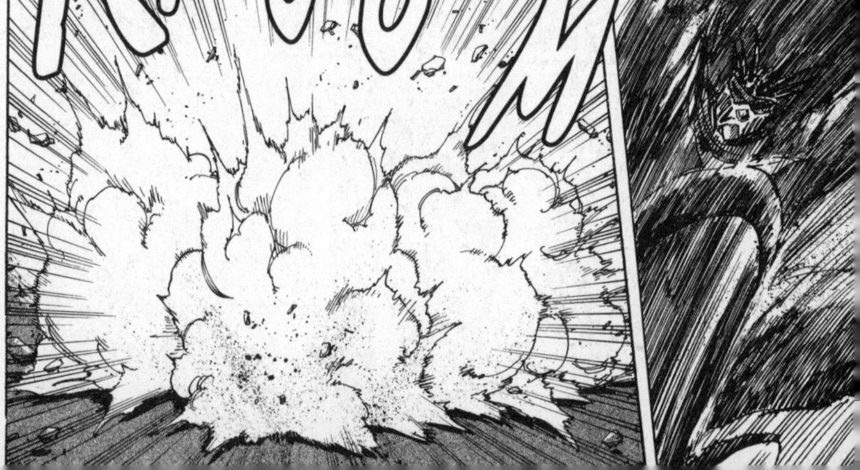
KABOOM

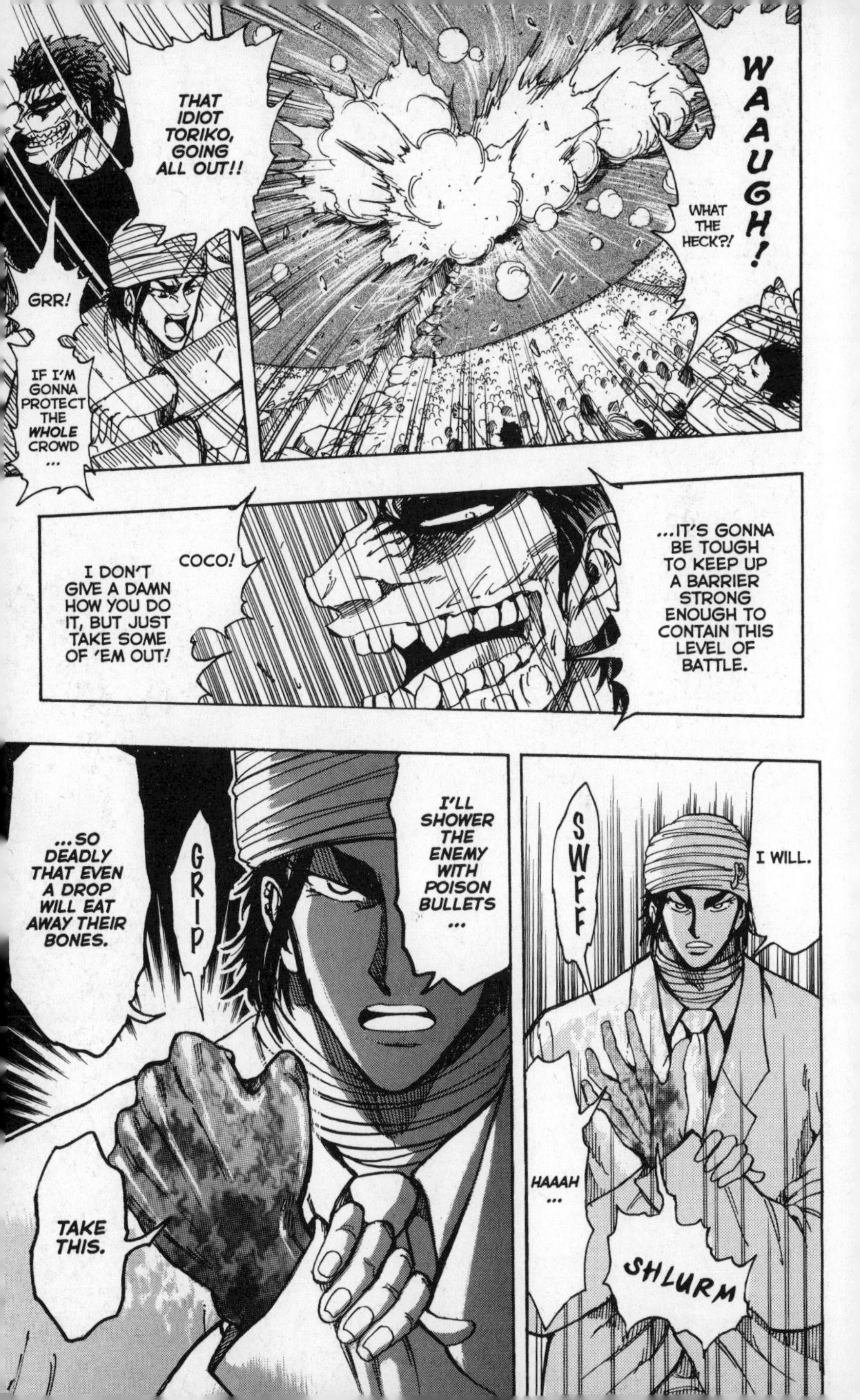
WAAUGH!
WHAT THE HECK?!
THAT IDIOT TORIKO, GOING ALL OUT!!
GRR!
IF I'M GONNA PROTECT THE *WHOLE* CROWD...
...IT'S GONNA BE TOUGH TO KEEP UP A BARRIER STRONG ENOUGH TO CONTAIN THIS LEVEL OF BATTLE.
COCO!
I DON'T GIVE A DAMN HOW YOU DO IT, BUT JUST TAKE SOME OF 'EM OUT!
I WILL.
SWFF
HAAAH...
SHLURM
I'LL SHOWER THE ENEMY WITH POISON BULLETS...
...SO DEADLY THAT EVEN A DROP WILL EAT AWAY THEIR BONES.
GRIP
TAKE THIS.

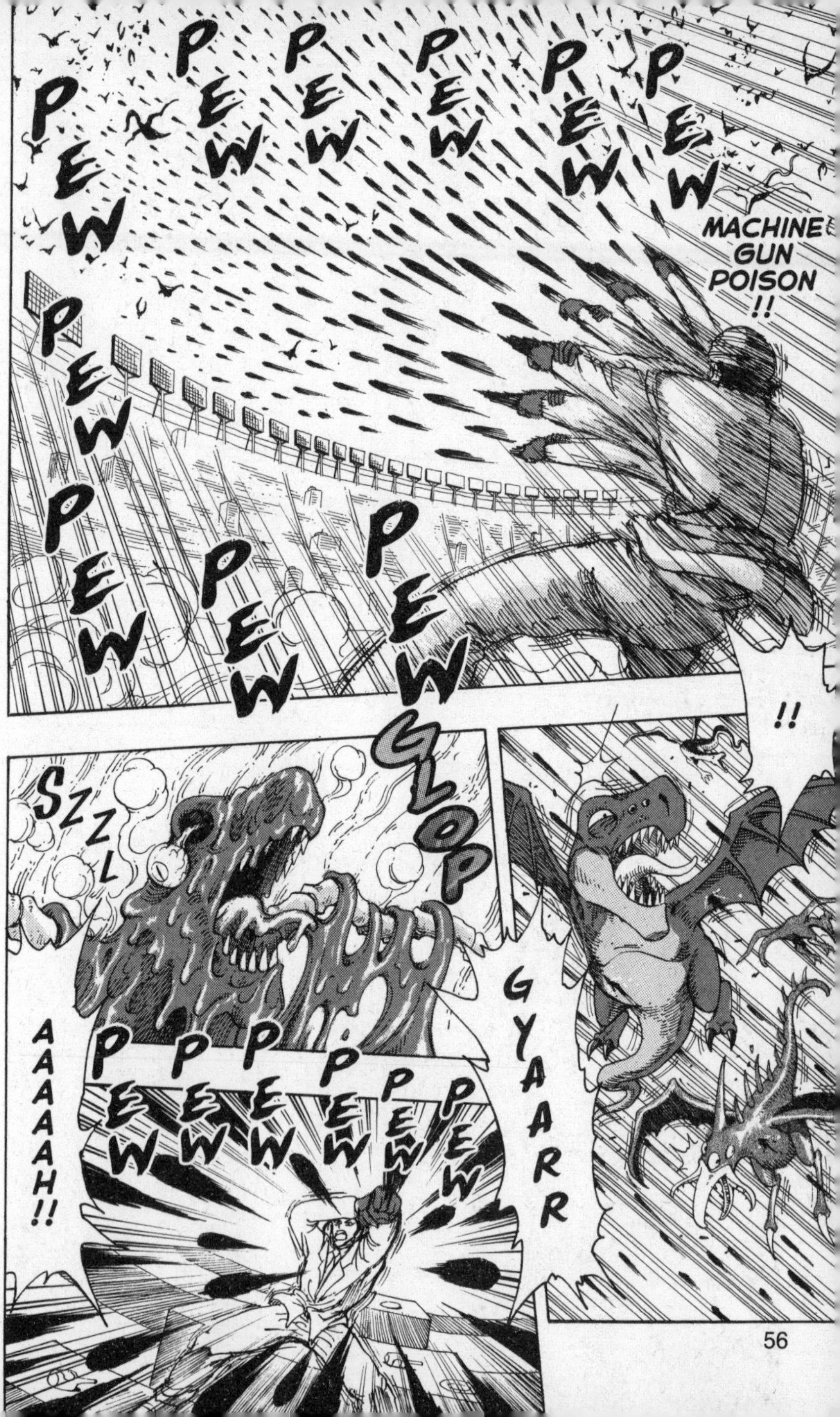

PEW PEW PEW PEW PEW PEW
MACHINE GUN POISON!!
PEW PEW PEW PEW
!!
GYAARR
GLOP
SZZL
PEW PEW PEW PEW PEW PEW PEW
AAAAAH!!

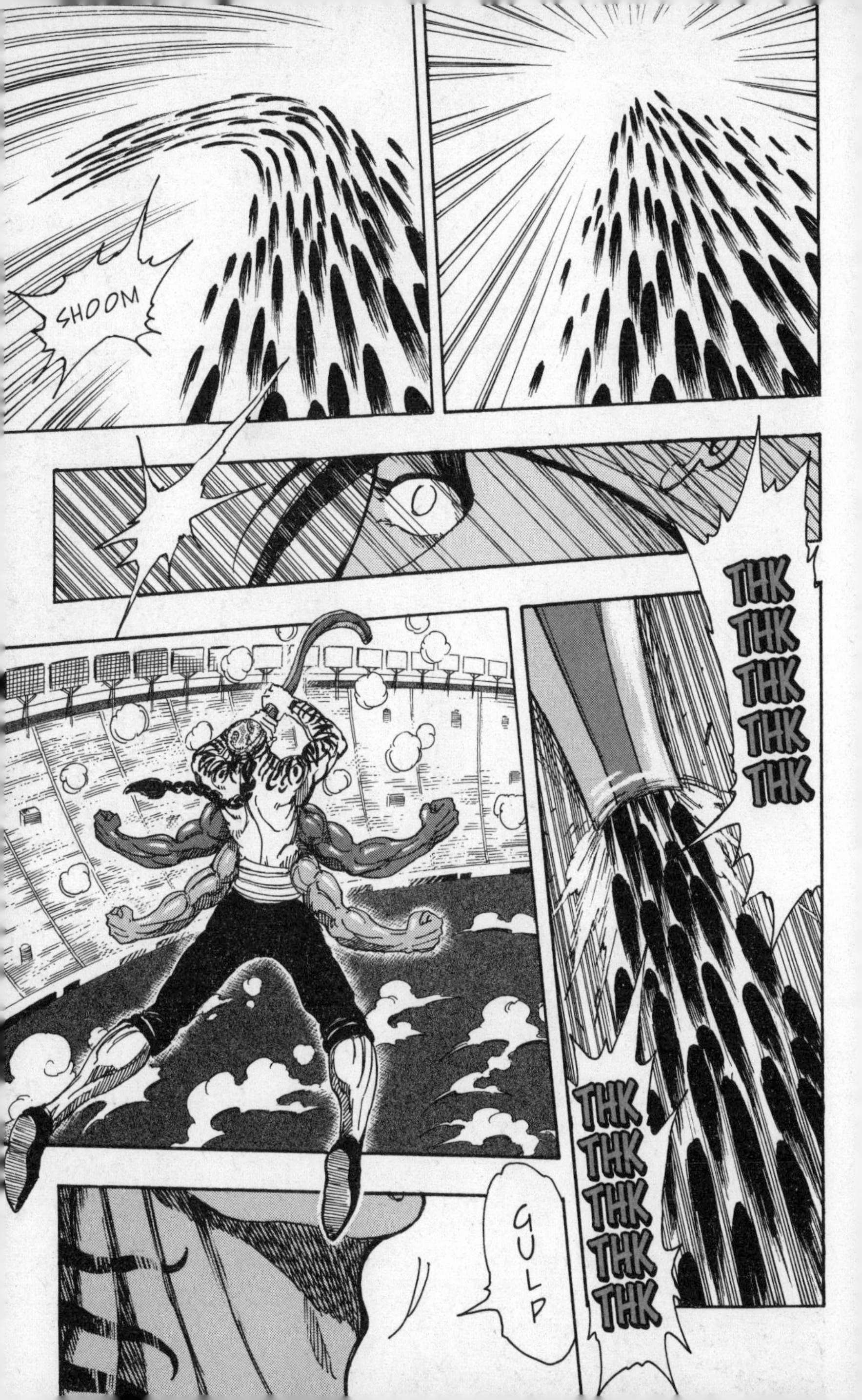
SHOOM
THK THK THK THK THK
THK THK THK THK THK
GULP

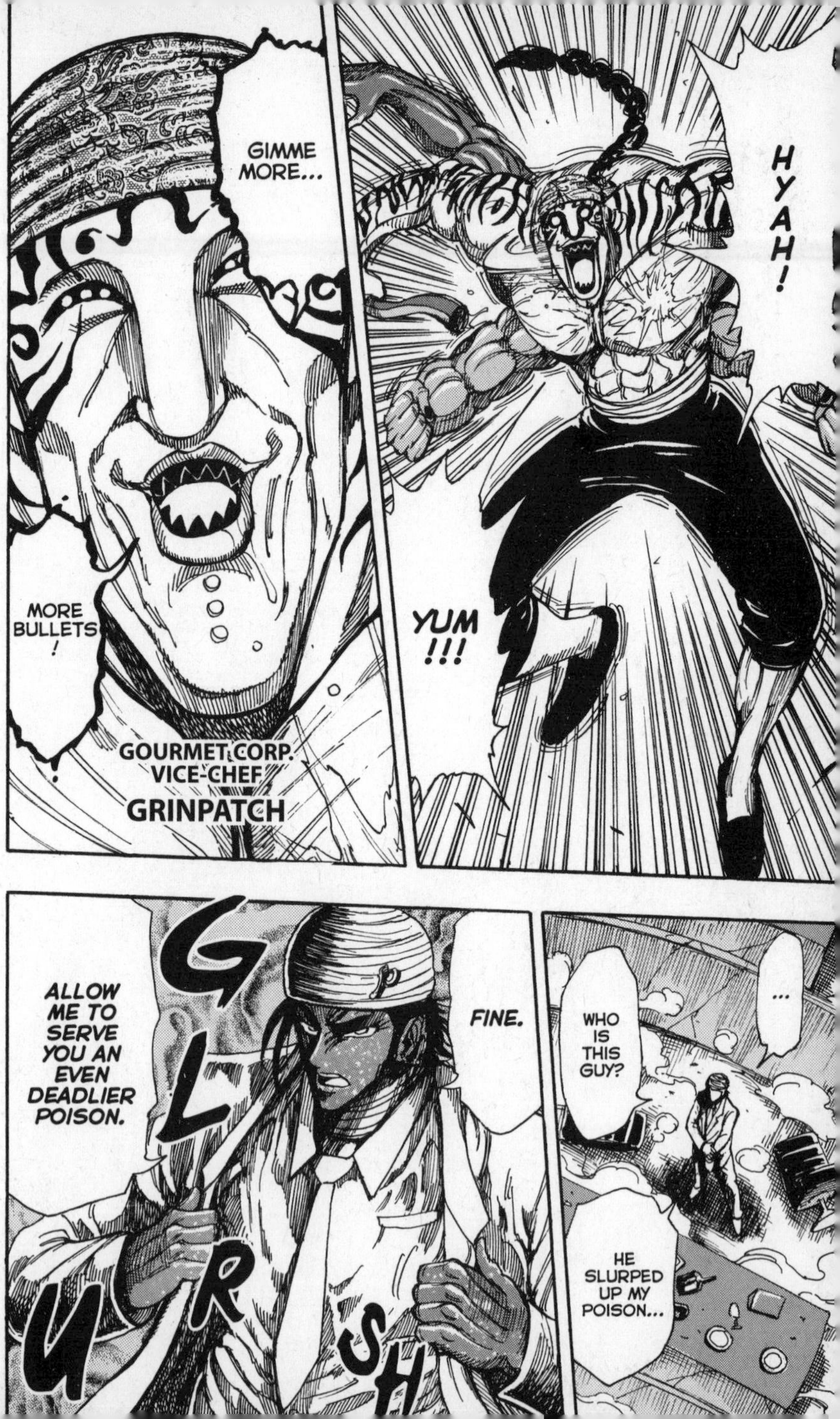
HYAH!
YUM!!!
GIMME MORE...
MORE BULLETS!
GOURMET CORP. VICE-CHEF
GRINPATCH
...
WHO IS THIS GUY?
HE SLURPED UP MY POISON...
FINE.
ALLOW ME TO SERVE YOU AN EVEN DEADLIER POISON.
GLURSH

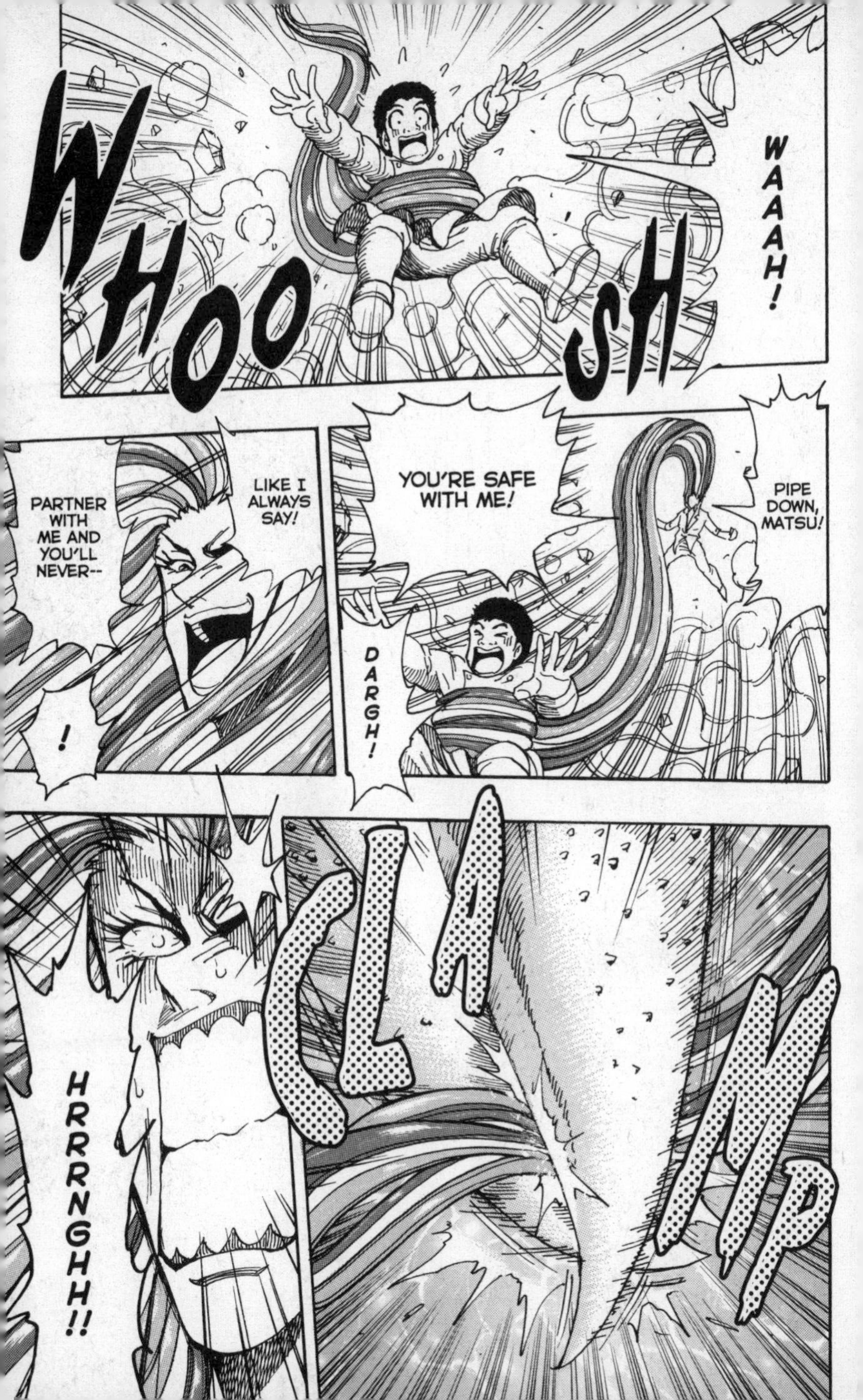
WAAAH!
WHOOSH
PIPE DOWN, MATSU!
YOU'RE SAFE WITH ME!
DARGH!
LIKE I ALWAYS SAY!
PARTNER WITH ME AND YOU'LL NEVER--
!
CLAMP
HRRRNGHH!!

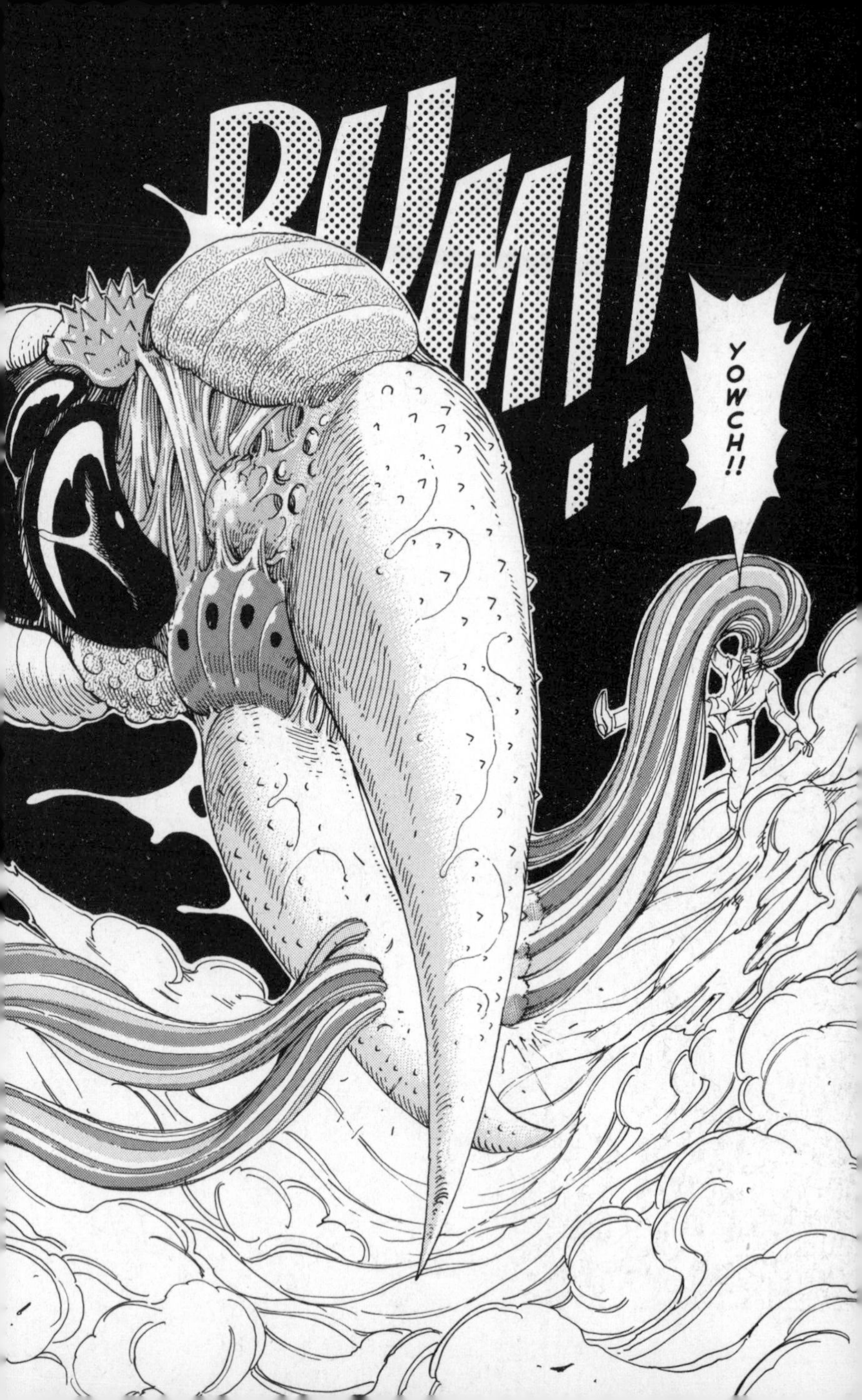
BUM!!
YOWCH!!

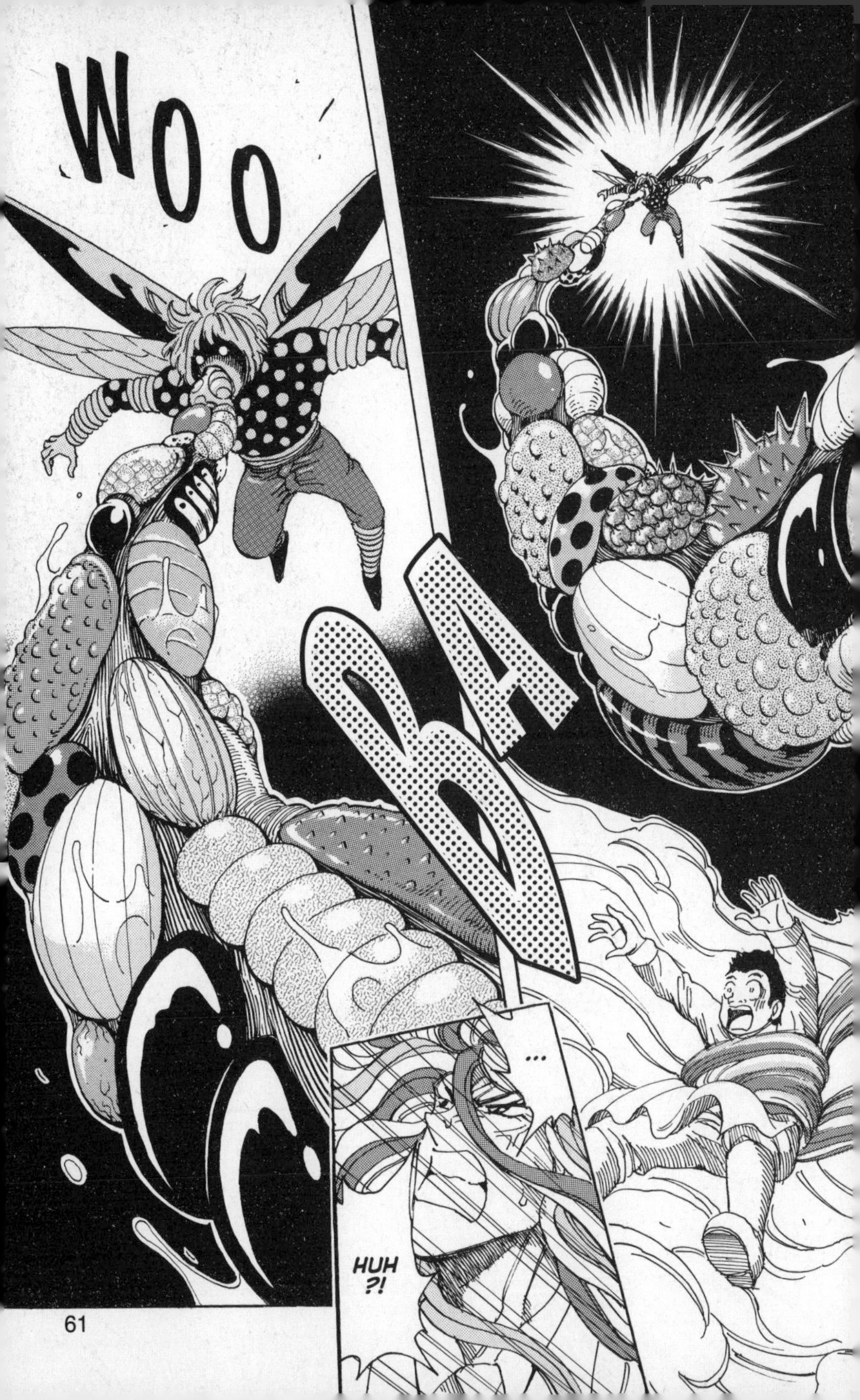
BA
WOO
...
HUH ?!

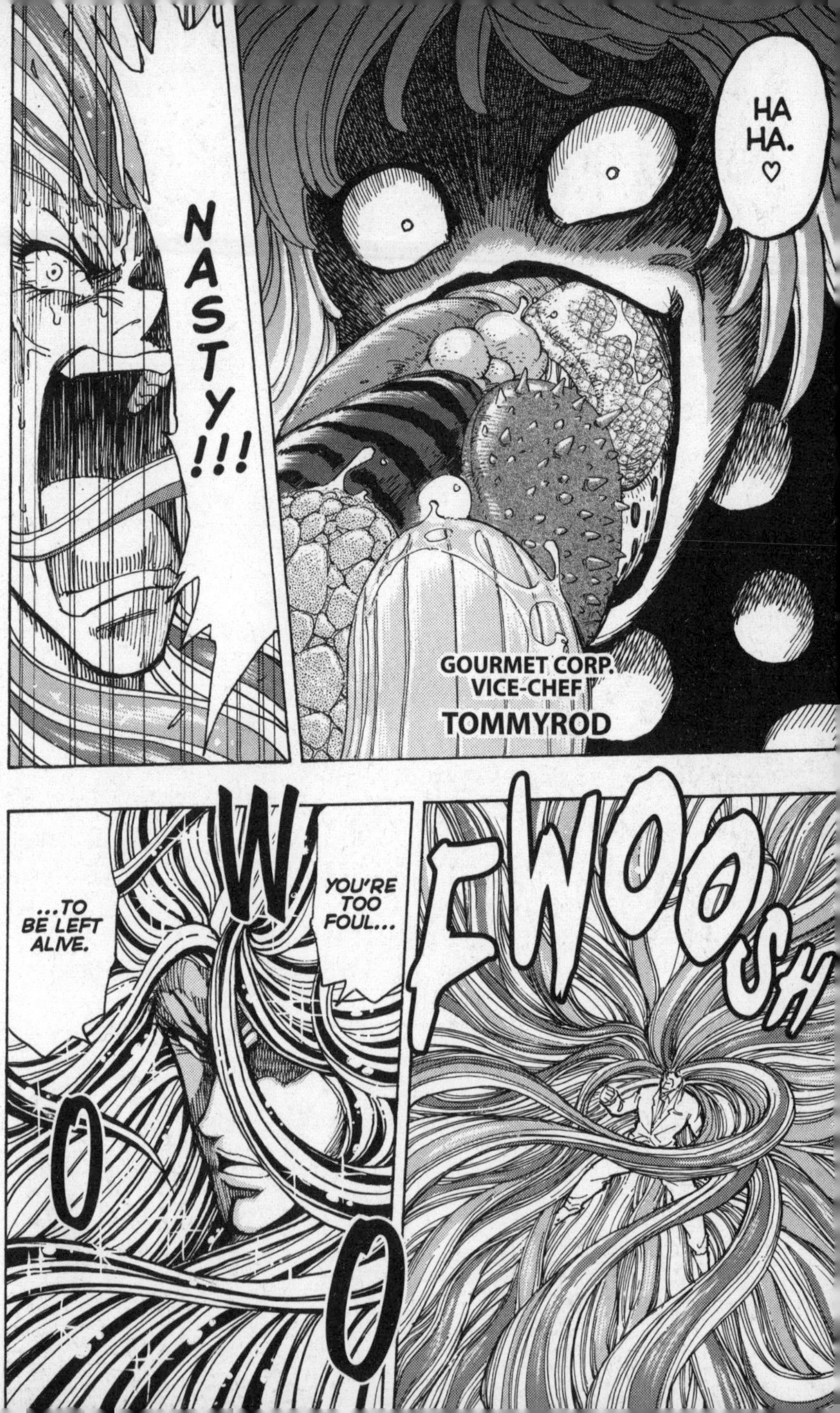
HA HA. ♡
GOURMET CORP. VICE-CHEF
TOMMYROD
NASTY!!!
FWOOSH
YOU'RE TOO FOUL...
...TO BE LEFT ALIVE.
WOOO

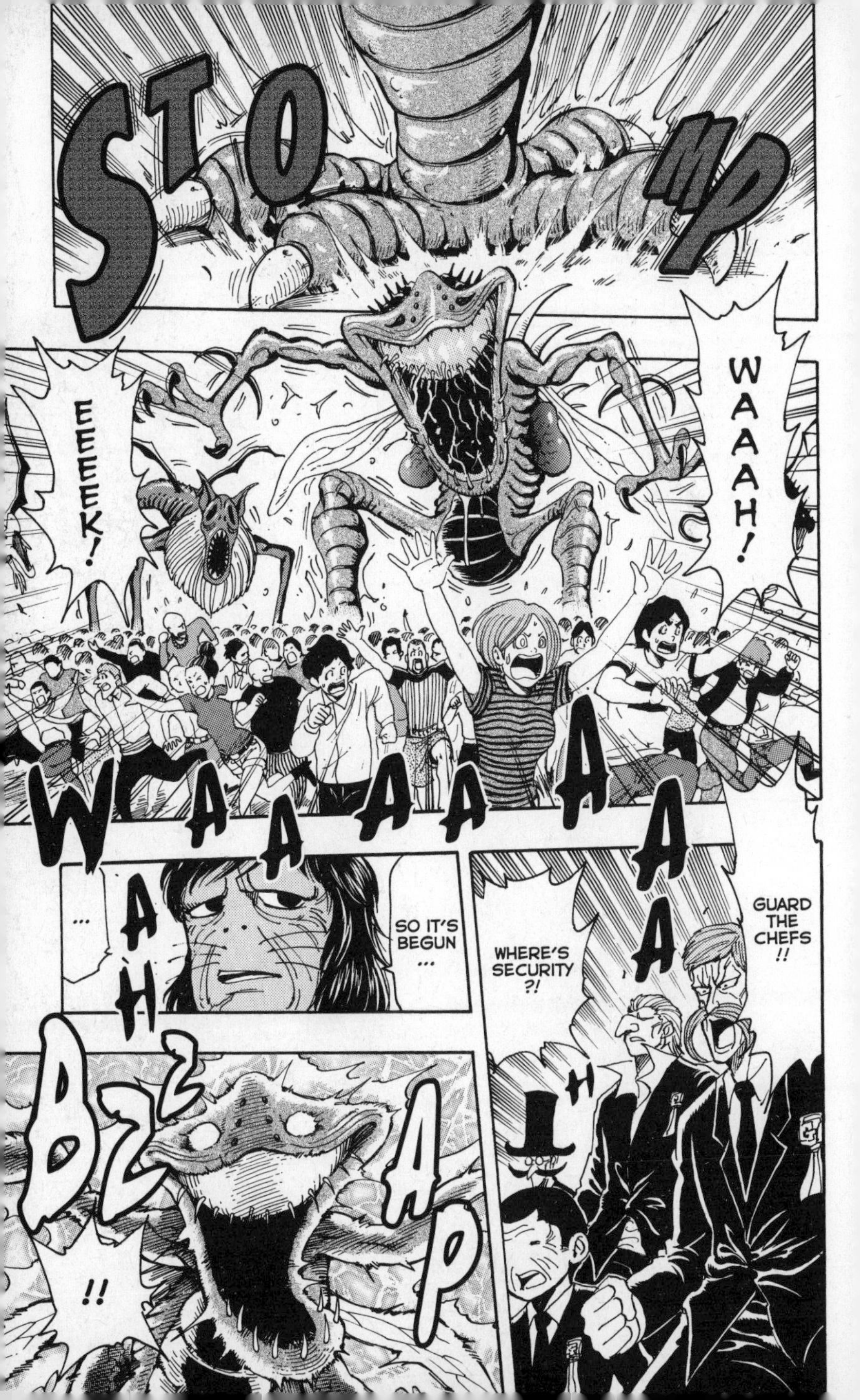
STOMP
WAAAH!
EEEEEK!
WAAAAAAAAAAH
GUARD THE CHEFS!!
WHERE'S SECURITY?!
SO IT'S BEGUN...
...
BZZAP
!!

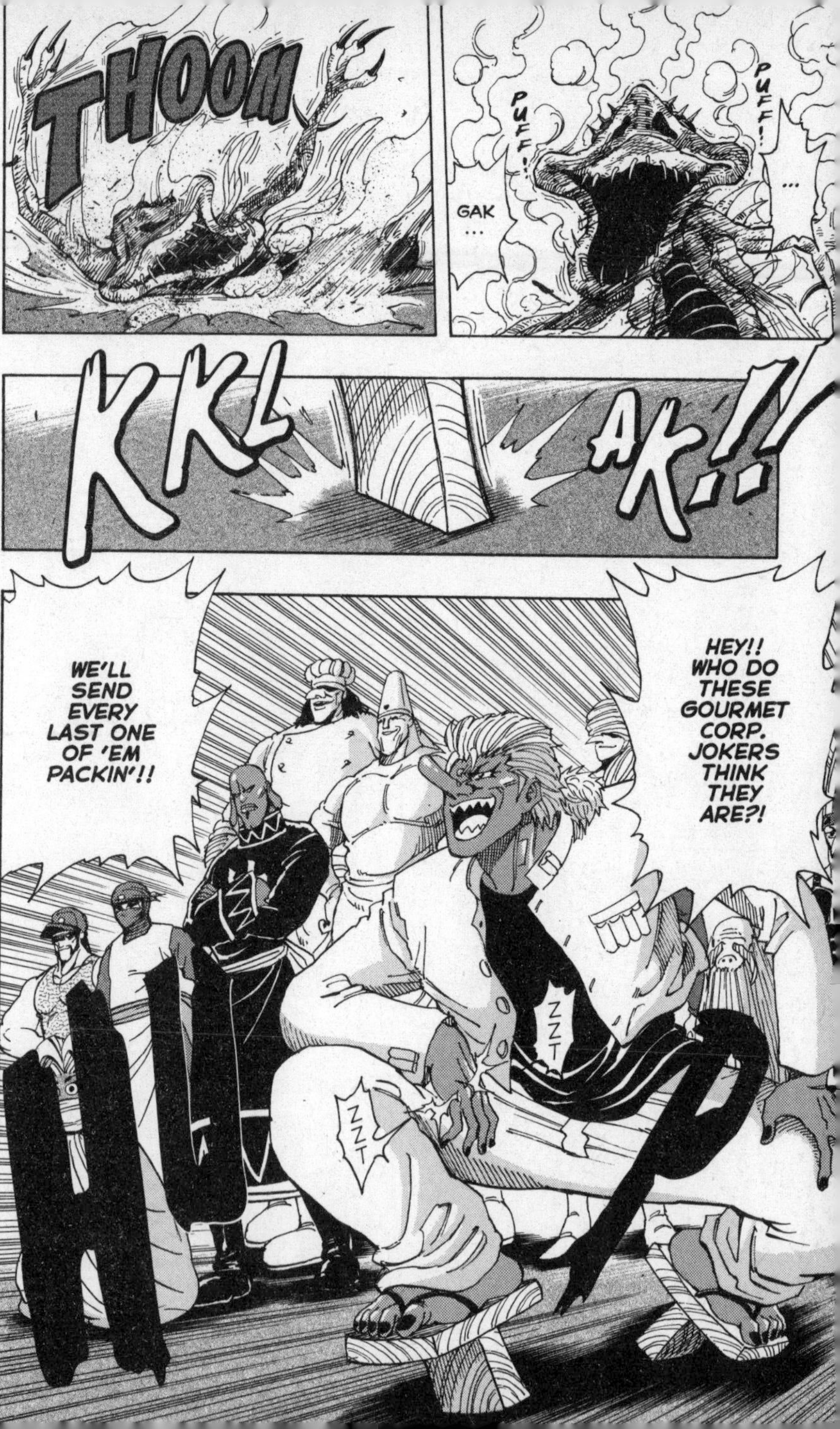
PUFF!!
PUFF...
GAK ...
...
THOOM
KKLAK!!
HEY!! WHO DO THESE GOURMET CORP. JOKERS THINK THEY ARE?!
WE'LL SEND EVERY LAST ONE OF 'EM PACKIN'!!
ZZT
ZZT
HU

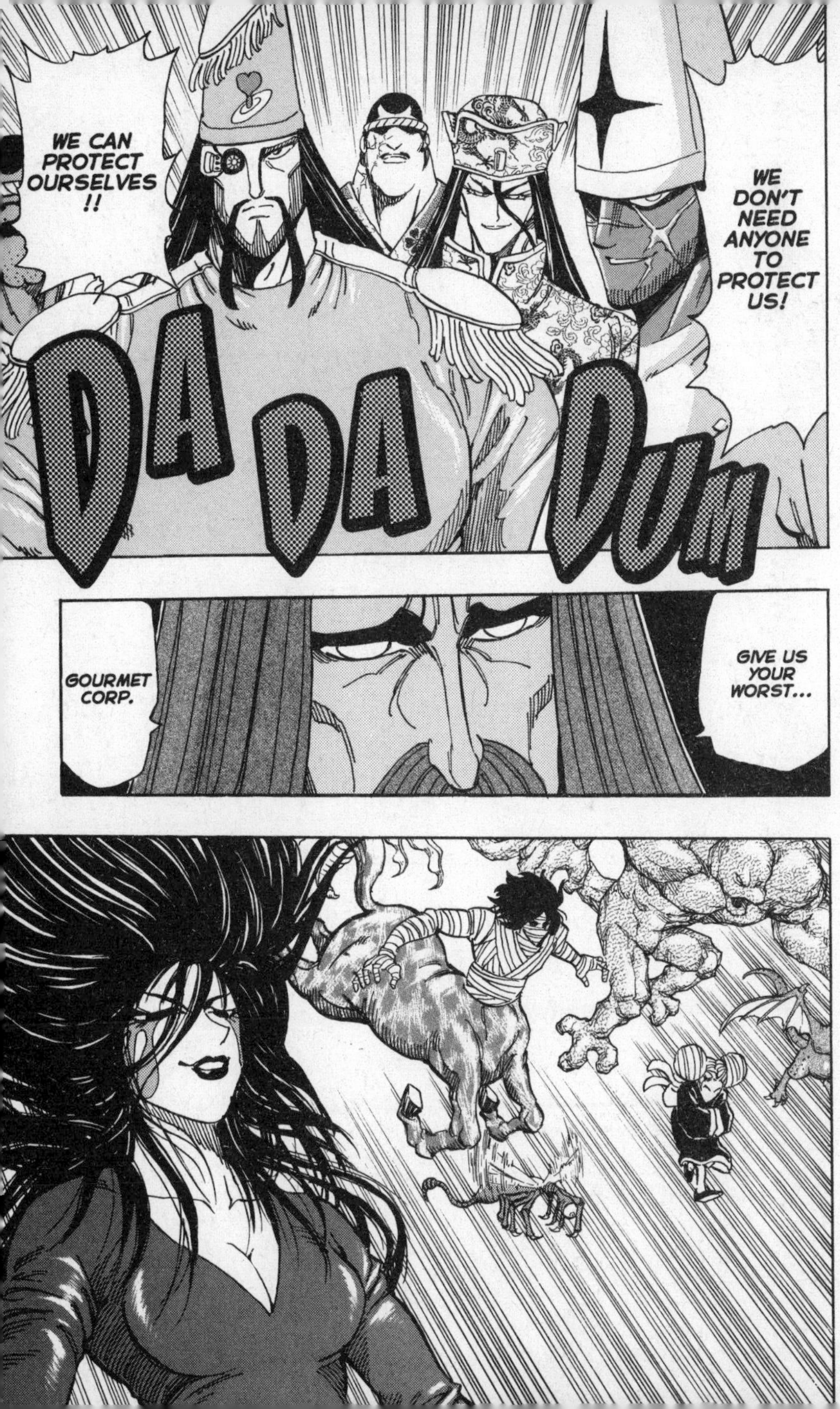
WE DON'T NEED ANYONE TO PROTECT US!
WE CAN PROTECT OURSELVES !!
DA DA DUM
GIVE US YOUR WORST...
GOURMET CORP.

GOURMET CHECKLIST

Vol. 250

GARLIC CRAB
(CRUSTACEAN)

CAPTURE LEVEL: 2

HABITAT: OCEAN

LENGTH: 60 CM

HEIGHT: ---

WEIGHT: 8 KG

PRICE: 150 YEN PER CRAB

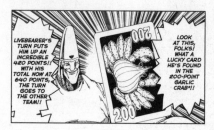

LOOK AT THIS, FOLKS! WHAT A LUCKY CARD HE'S FOUND IN THE 200-POINT GARLIC CRAB*!!
200
200
LIVEBEARER'S TURN PUTS HIM UP AN INCREDIBLE 420 POINTS!! WITH HIS TOTAL NOW AT 640 POINTS, THE TURN GOES TO THE OTHER TEAM!!

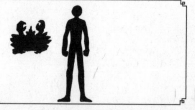

SCALE

THE BODY OF THIS CRAB IS SHAPED LIKE ONE BIG GARLIC BULB! IT TASTES LIKE GARLIC TOO, ADDING THAT SPECIAL SOMETHING TO SOUPS. BUT THE USES OF THIS VERSATILE INGREDIENT GO FAR BEYOND SOUP STOCKS. THE GARLIC CRAB IS CONSIDERED LUCKY IN THE GAME OF GOURMET TASTING THANKS TO ITS RELATIVELY EASY METHOD OF PREPARATION.

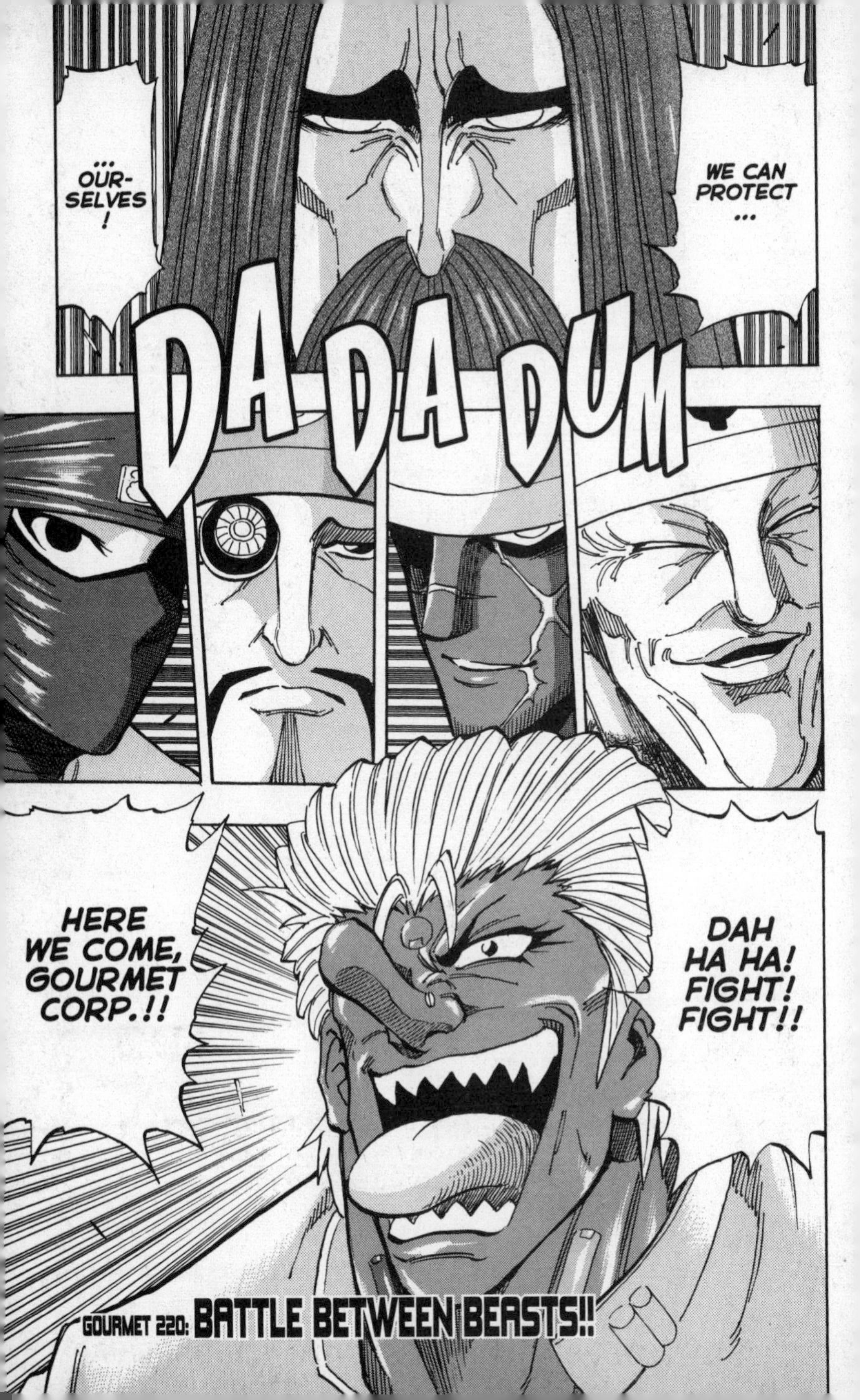
WE CAN PROTECT ...
... OUR-SELVES!
DA DA DUM
DAH HA HA! FIGHT! FIGHT!!
HERE WE COME, GOURMET CORP.!!

GOURMET 220: BATTLE BETWEEN BEASTS!!

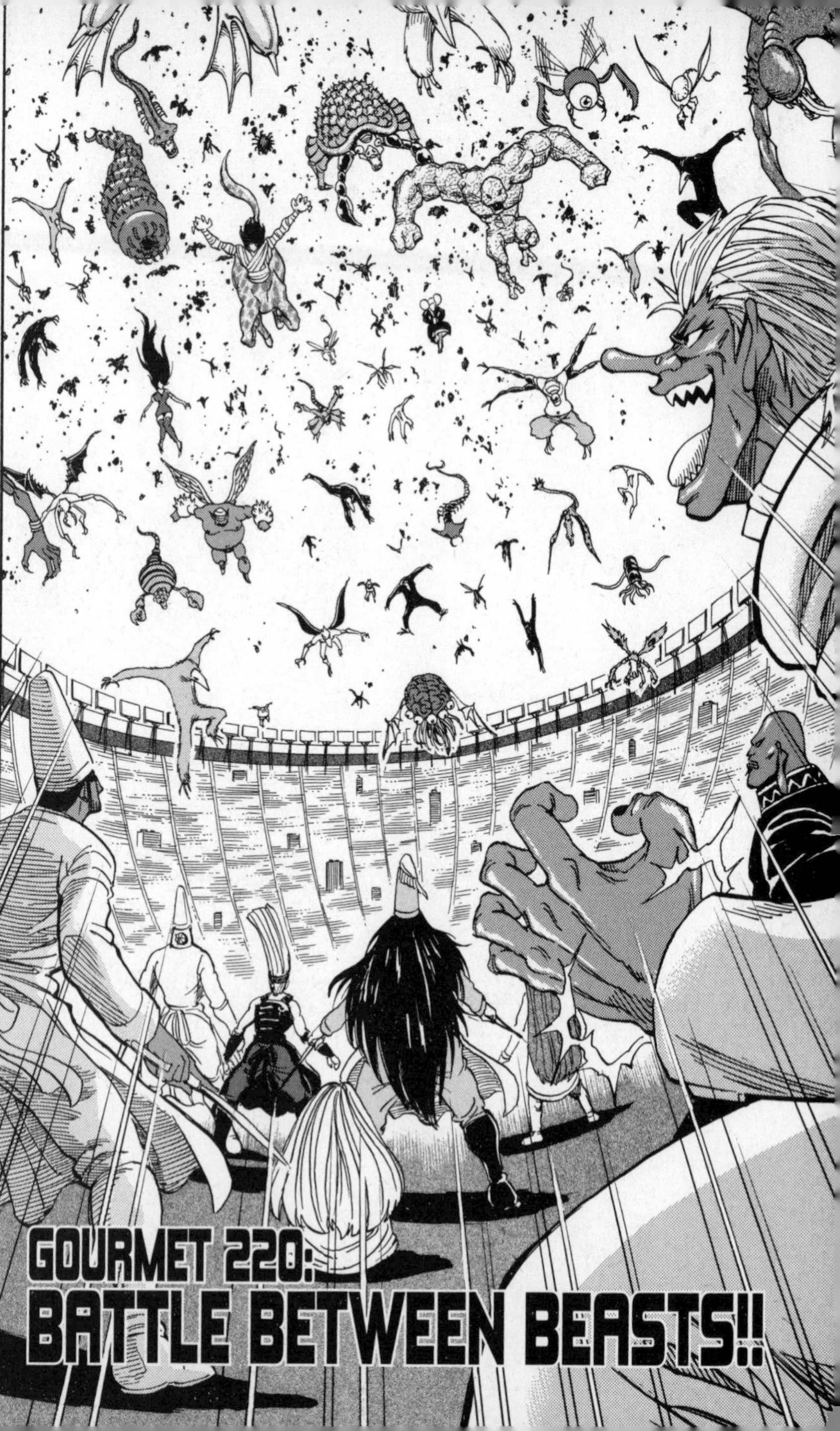
GOURMET 220:
BATTLE BETWEEN BEASTS!!

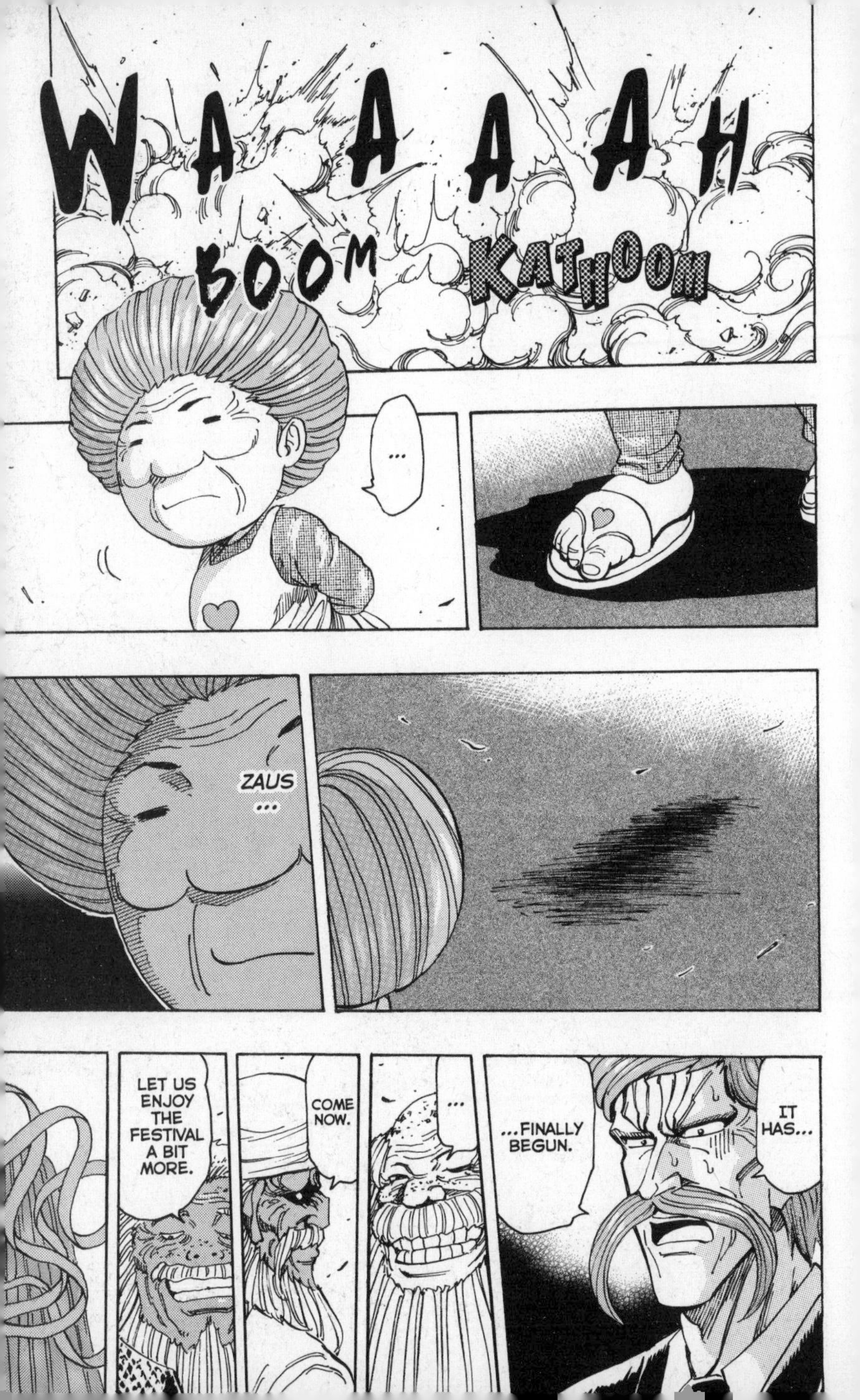
WAAAAAH
KATHOOM
BOOM
...
ZAUS ...
IT HAS...
...FINALLY BEGUN.
...
COME NOW.
LET US ENJOY THE FESTIVAL A BIT MORE.

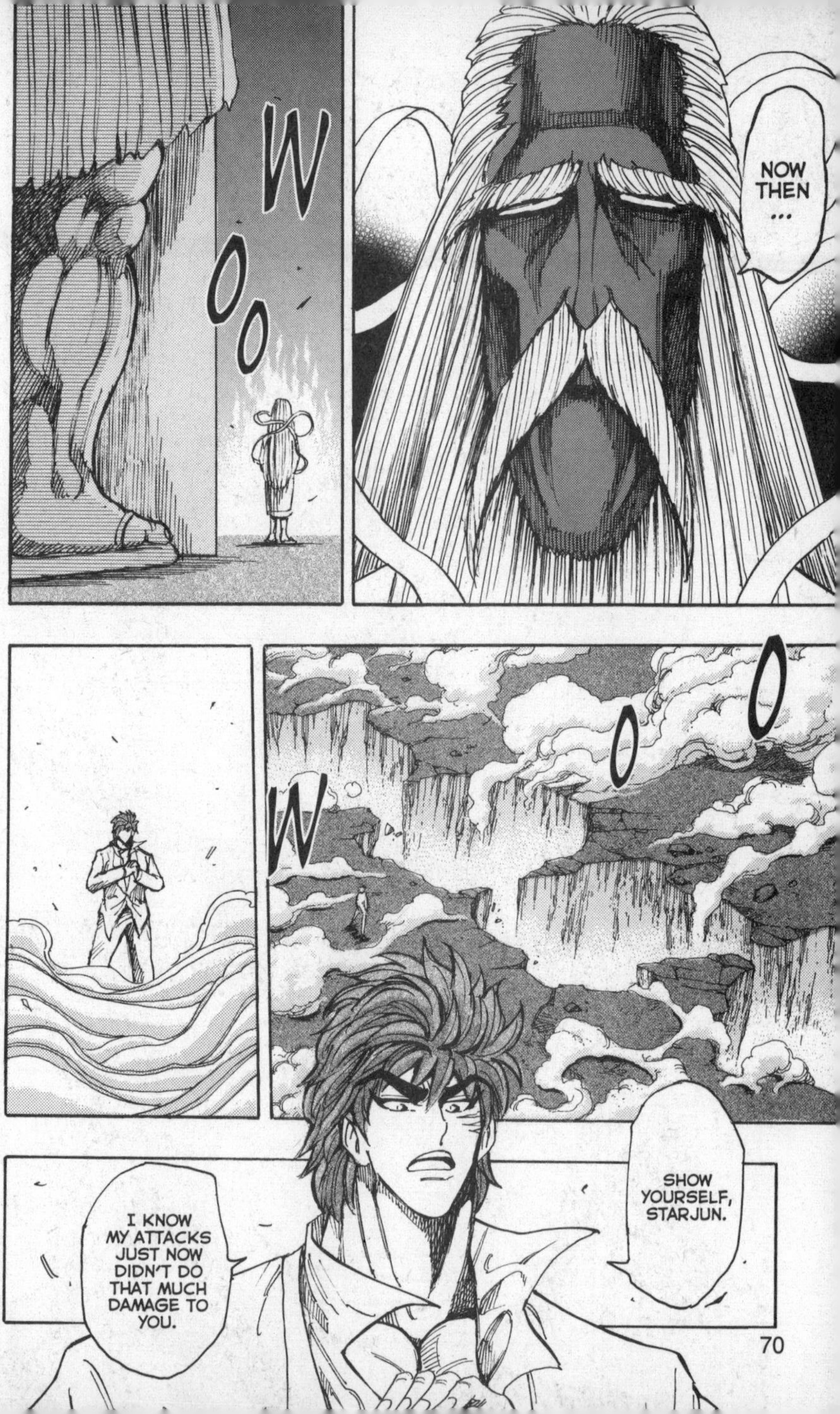

NOW THEN ...
WOO
WOO
SHOW YOURSELF, STARJUN.
I KNOW MY ATTACKS JUST NOW DIDN'T DO THAT MUCH DAMAGE TO YOU.

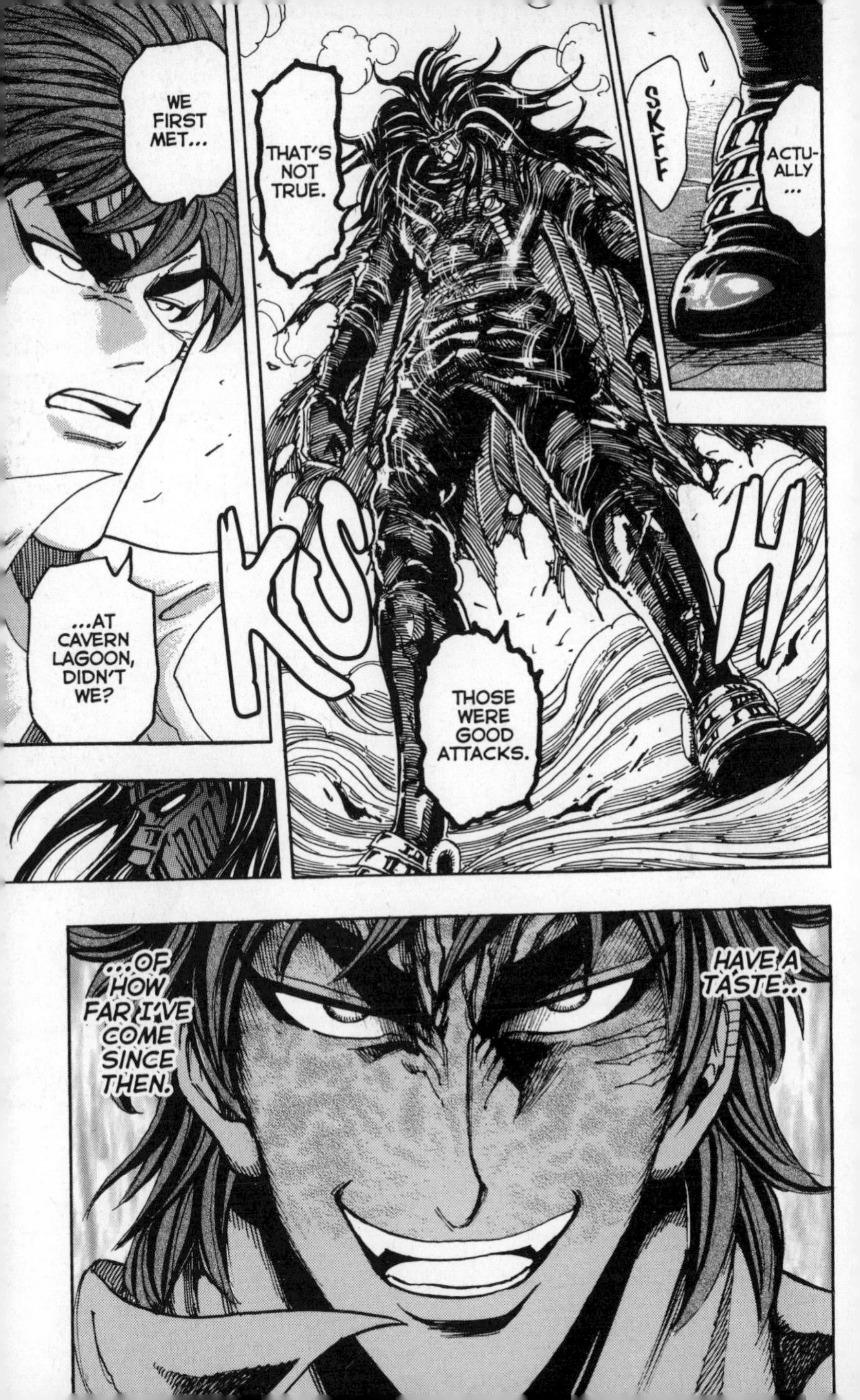
SKEFF
ACTU-ALLY...
THAT'S NOT TRUE.
THOSE WERE GOOD ATTACKS.
WE FIRST MET...
...AT CAVERN LAGOON, DIDN'T WE?
HAVE A TASTE...
...OF HOW FAR I'VE COME SINCE THEN.

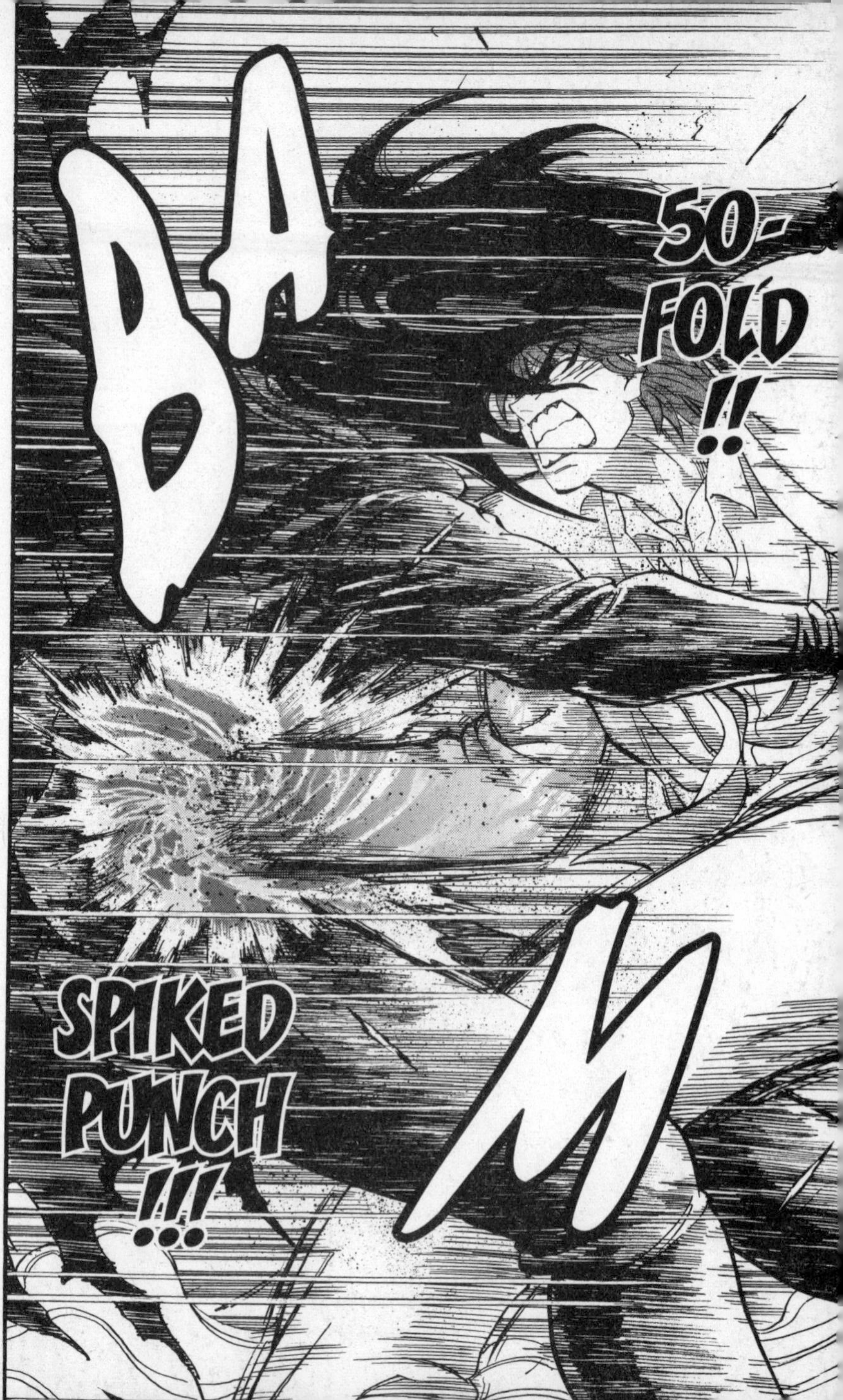
50-FOLD!!
DA
M
SPIKED PUNCH!!!

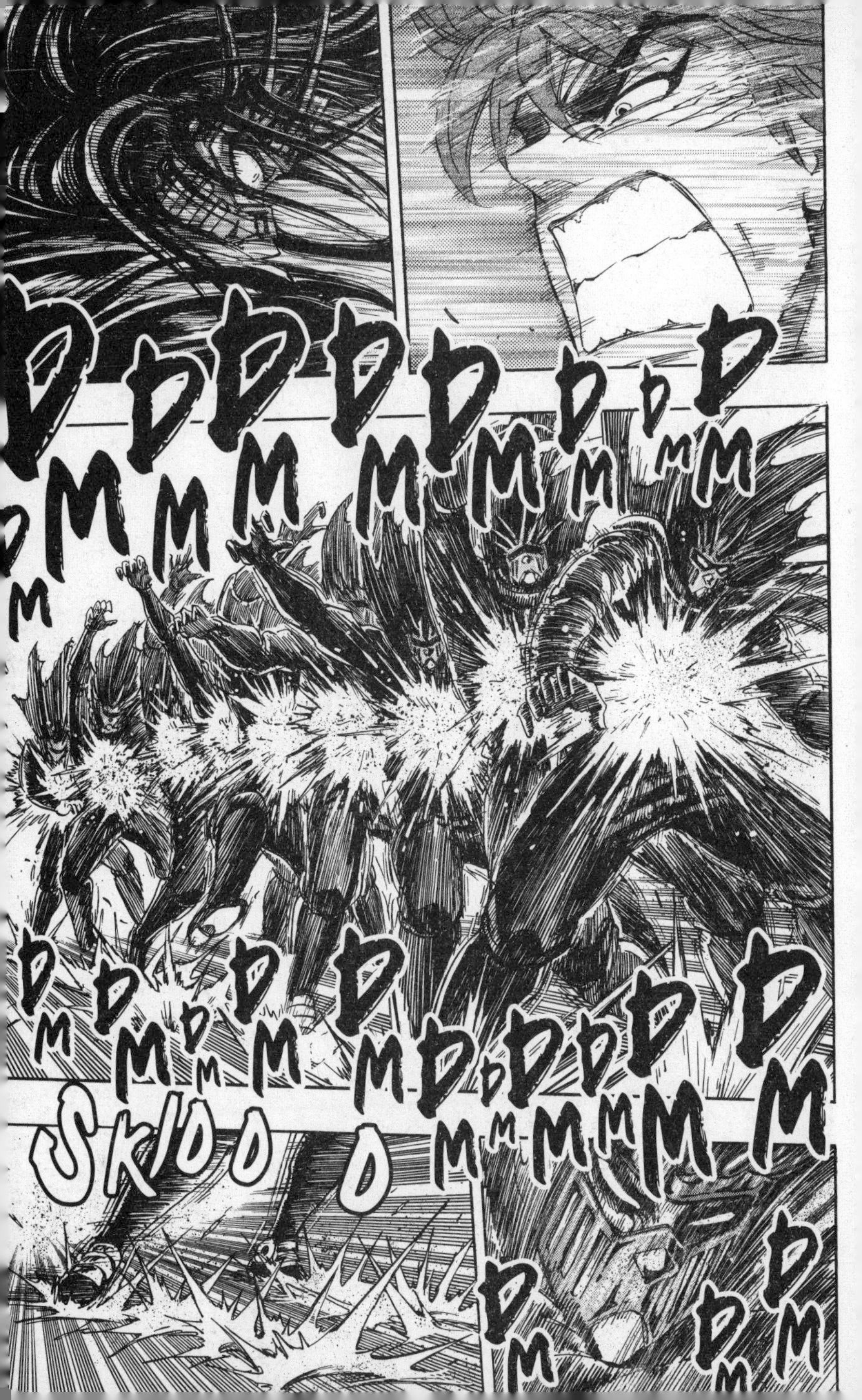
DDDDDDDDDD
DMMMMMMMMMMM
DMDMDMDMMDDDDDDD
MMMMMMM
SKIDOO D
DMDMDM

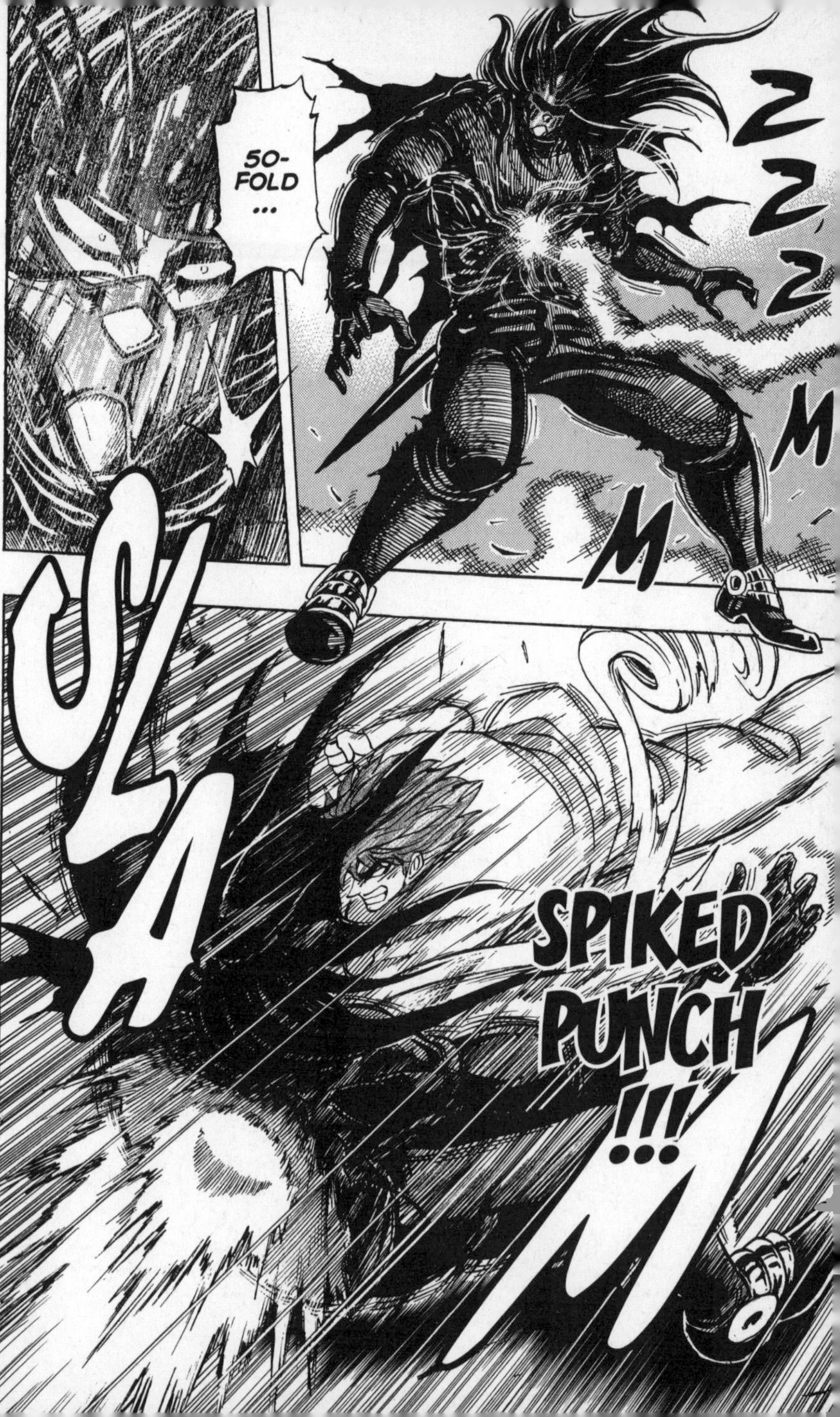
ZZZZMMM
50-FOLD...
SPIKED PUNCH!!!
SLAM

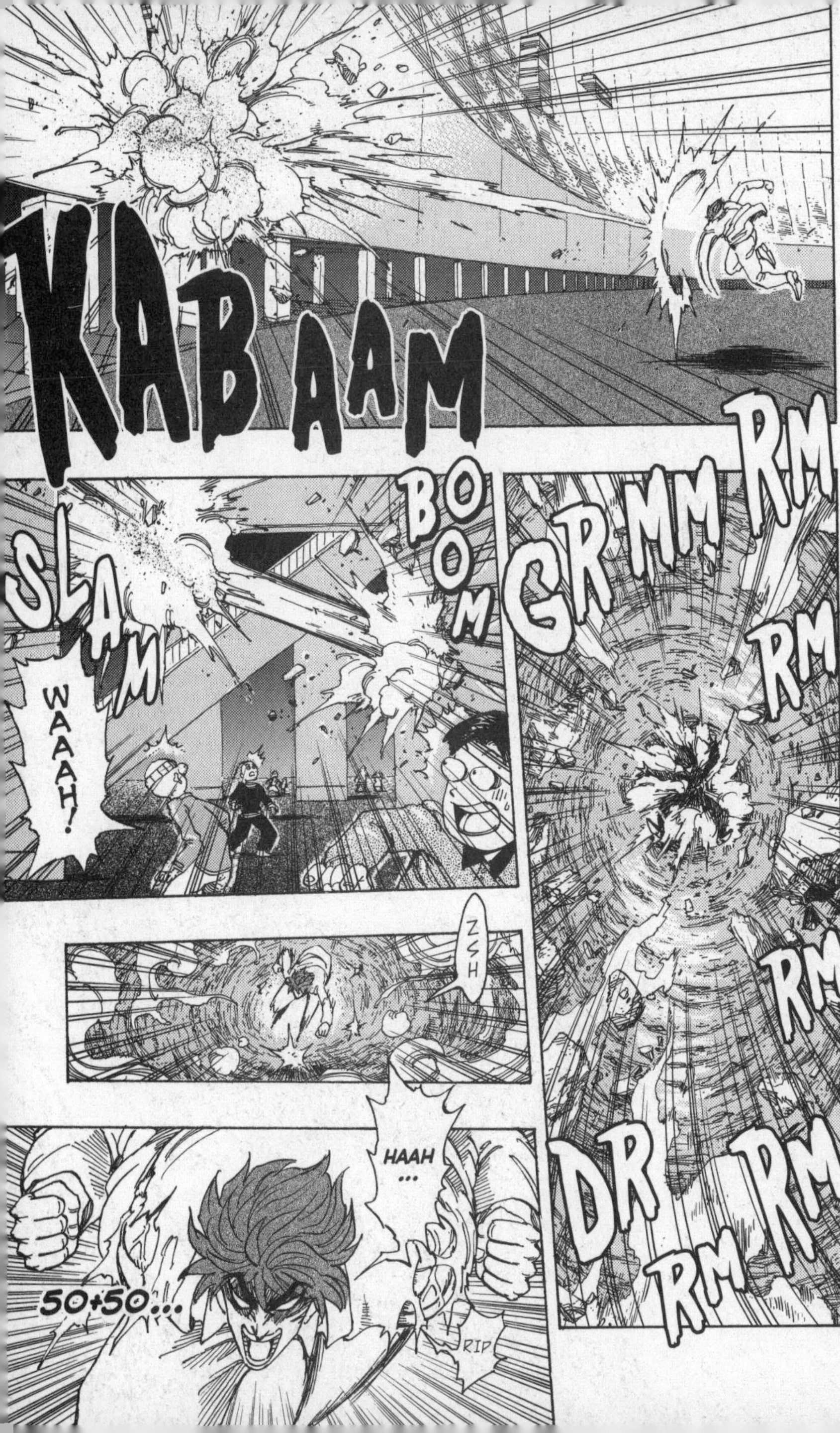
KABAAM
GRMM RM
RM
RM
DR RM RM
BOOM
SLAM
WAAAH!
ZSH
HAAH...
RIP
50+50...

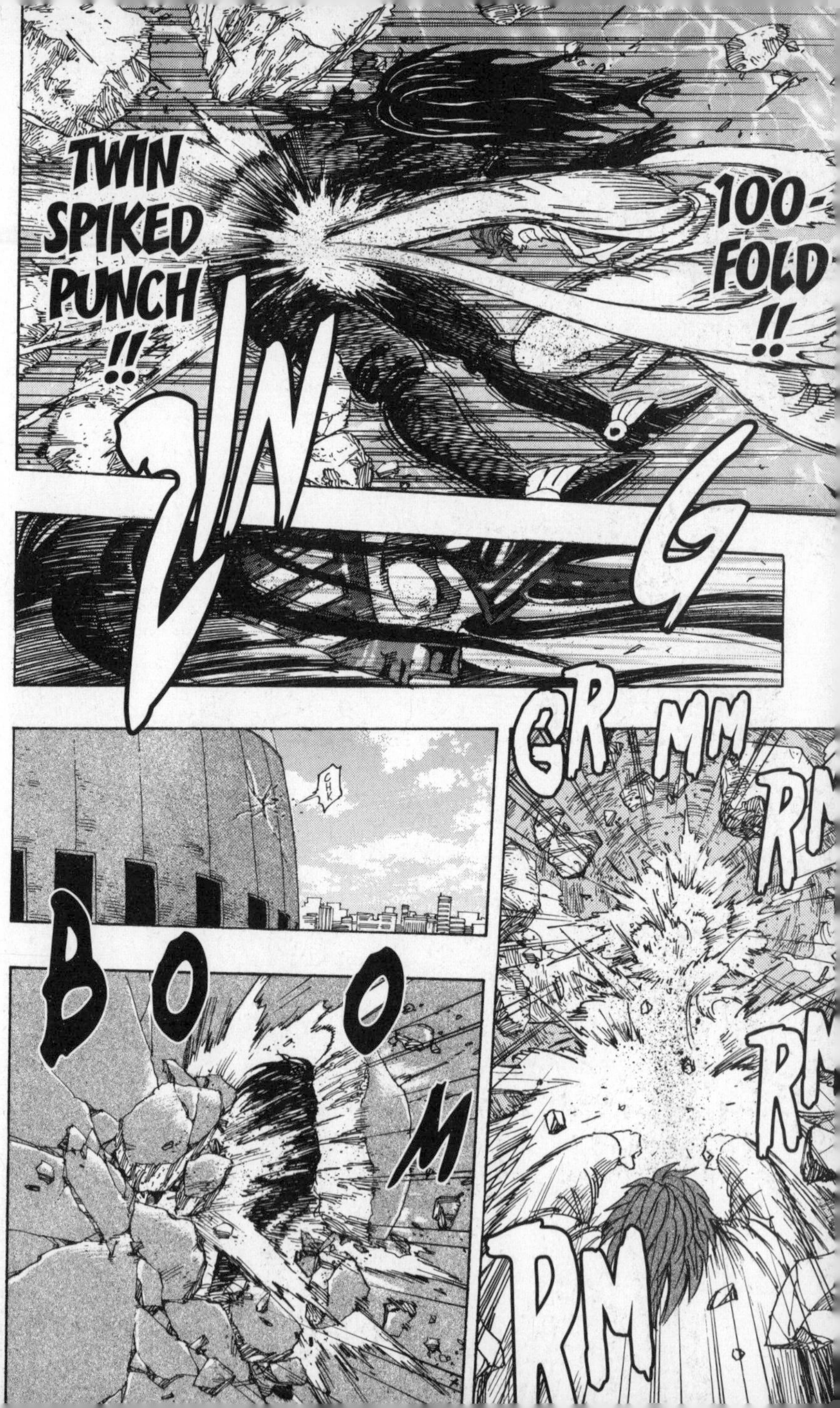
100-FOLD!!
TWIN SPIKED PUNCH!!
GR MM
RM
RM
RM
CHK
BOOM

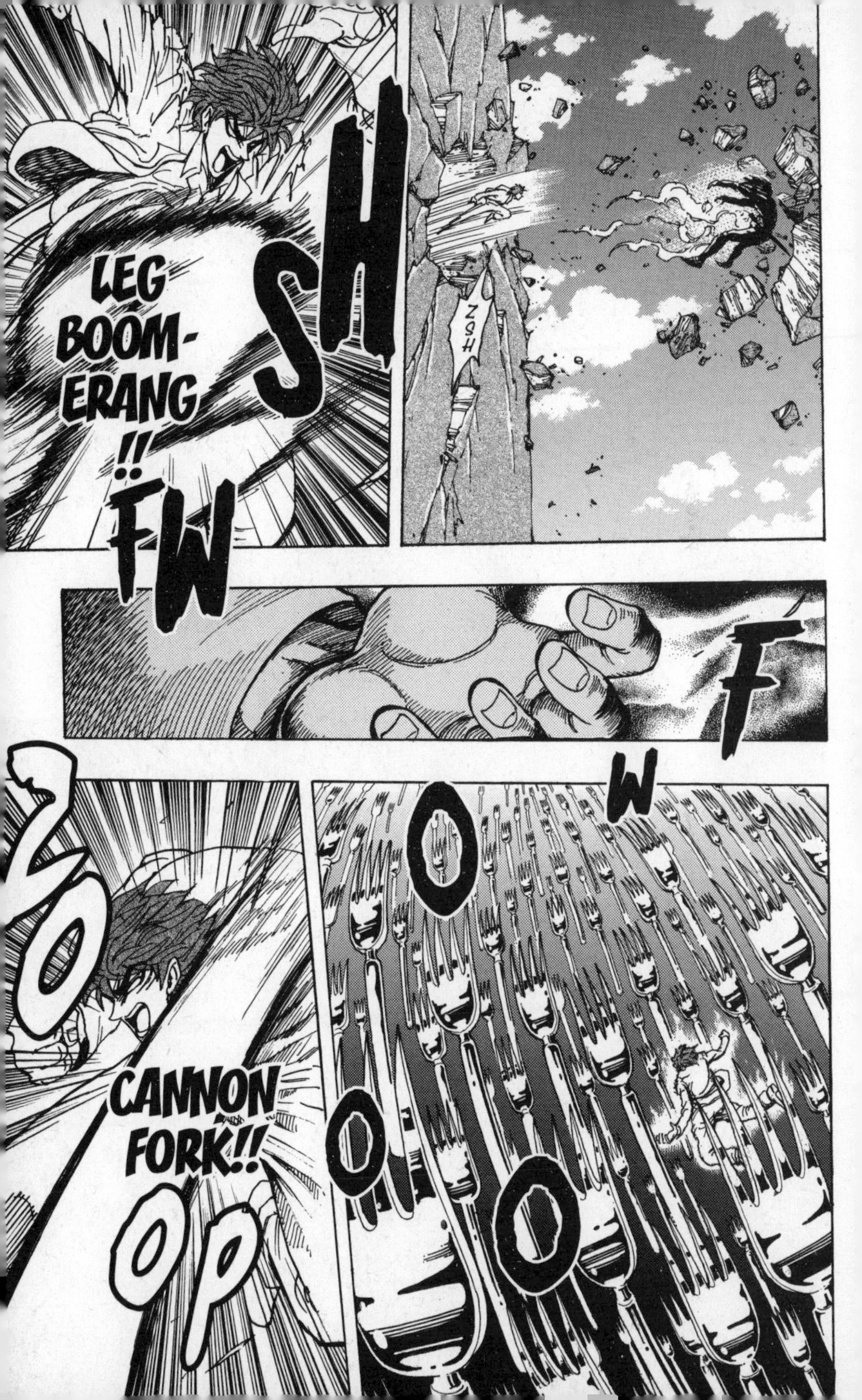

ZSH
LEG BOOM-ERANG!!
SH
FW
F
W
OOOO
CANNON FORK!!
ZO
OP

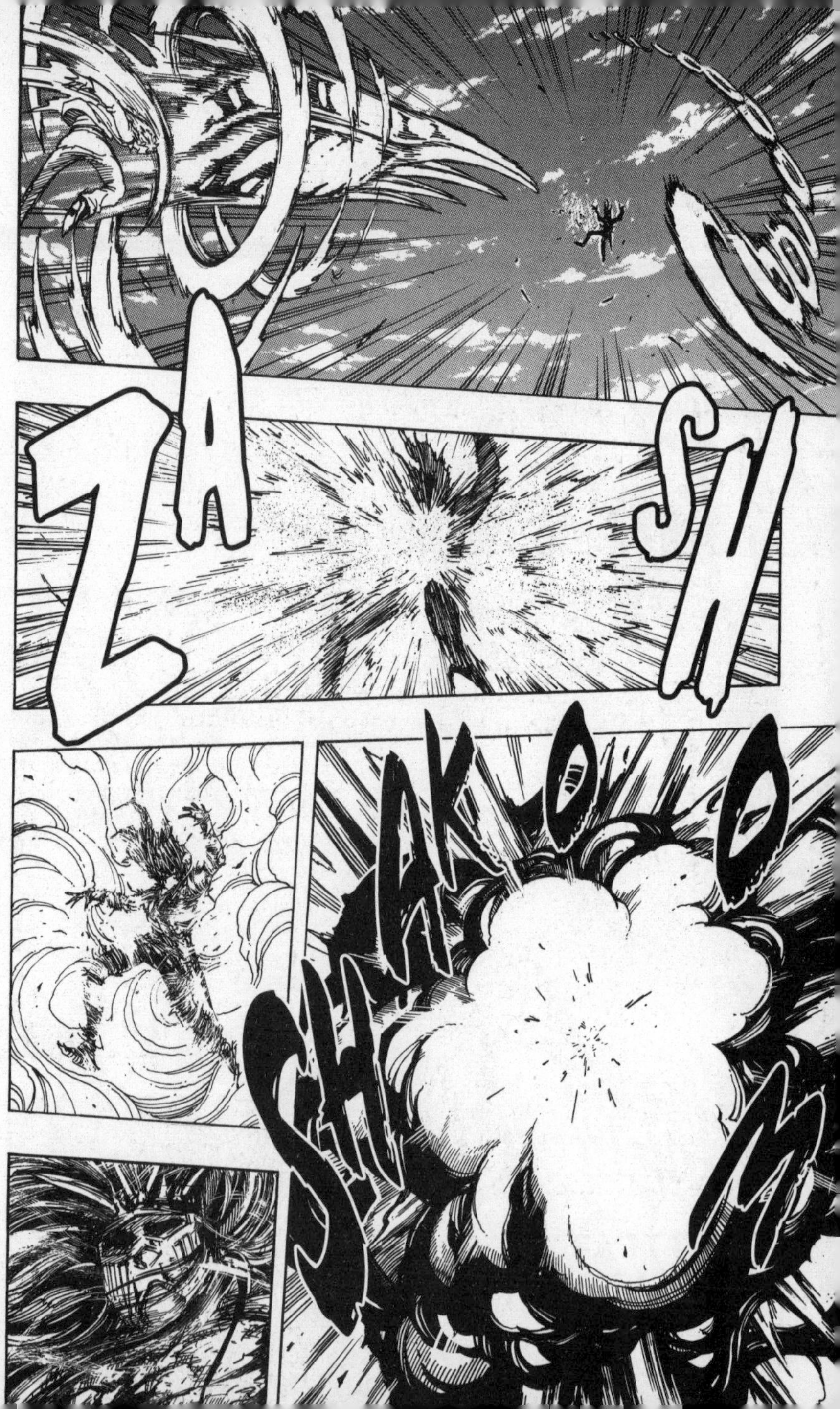
ZASH
CHAKOOM

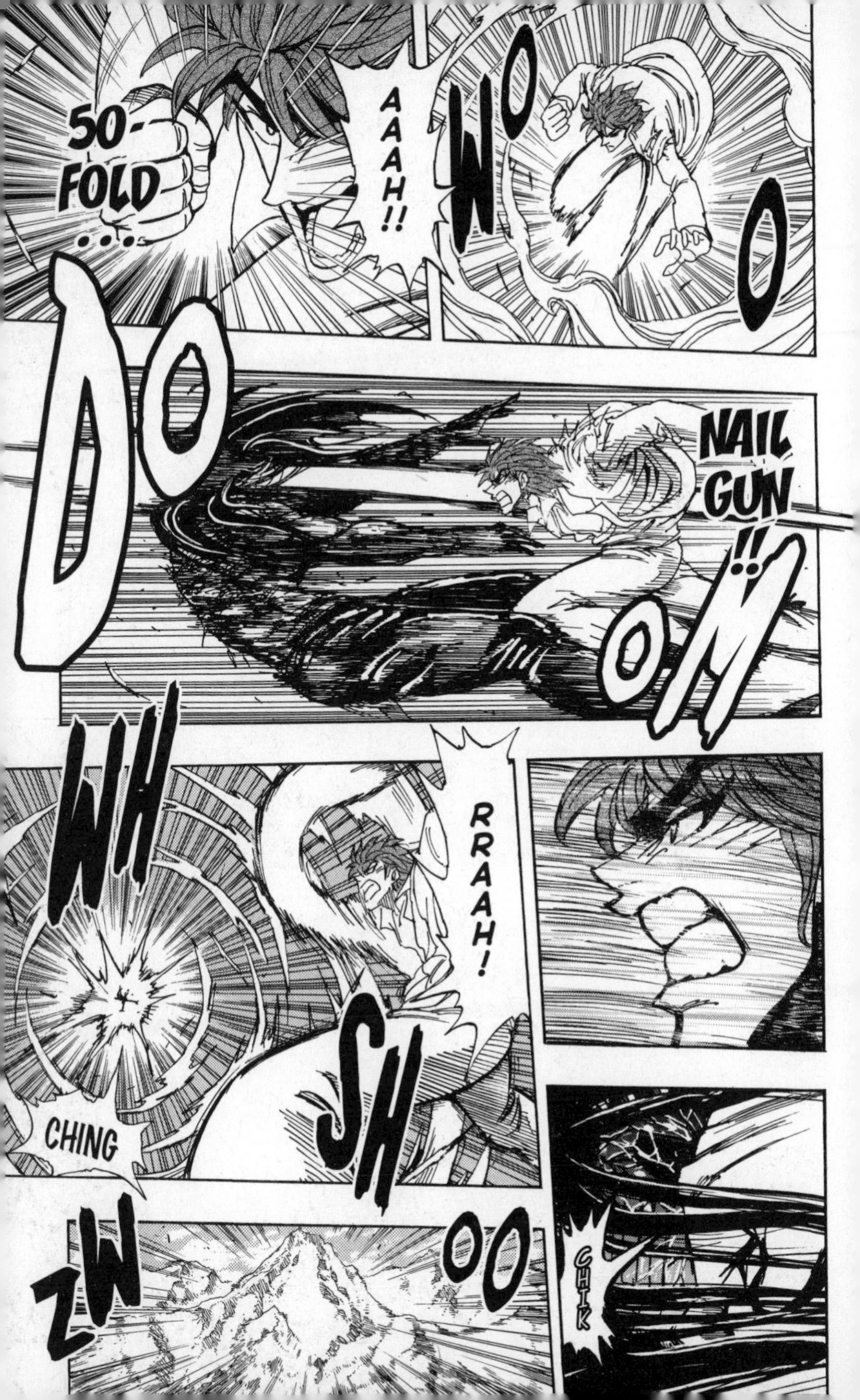
WO
O
AAAAH!!
50-FOLD...
NAIL GUN!!
DO
OM
RRAAAH!
WH
CHING
SH
OO
CHIK
ZW

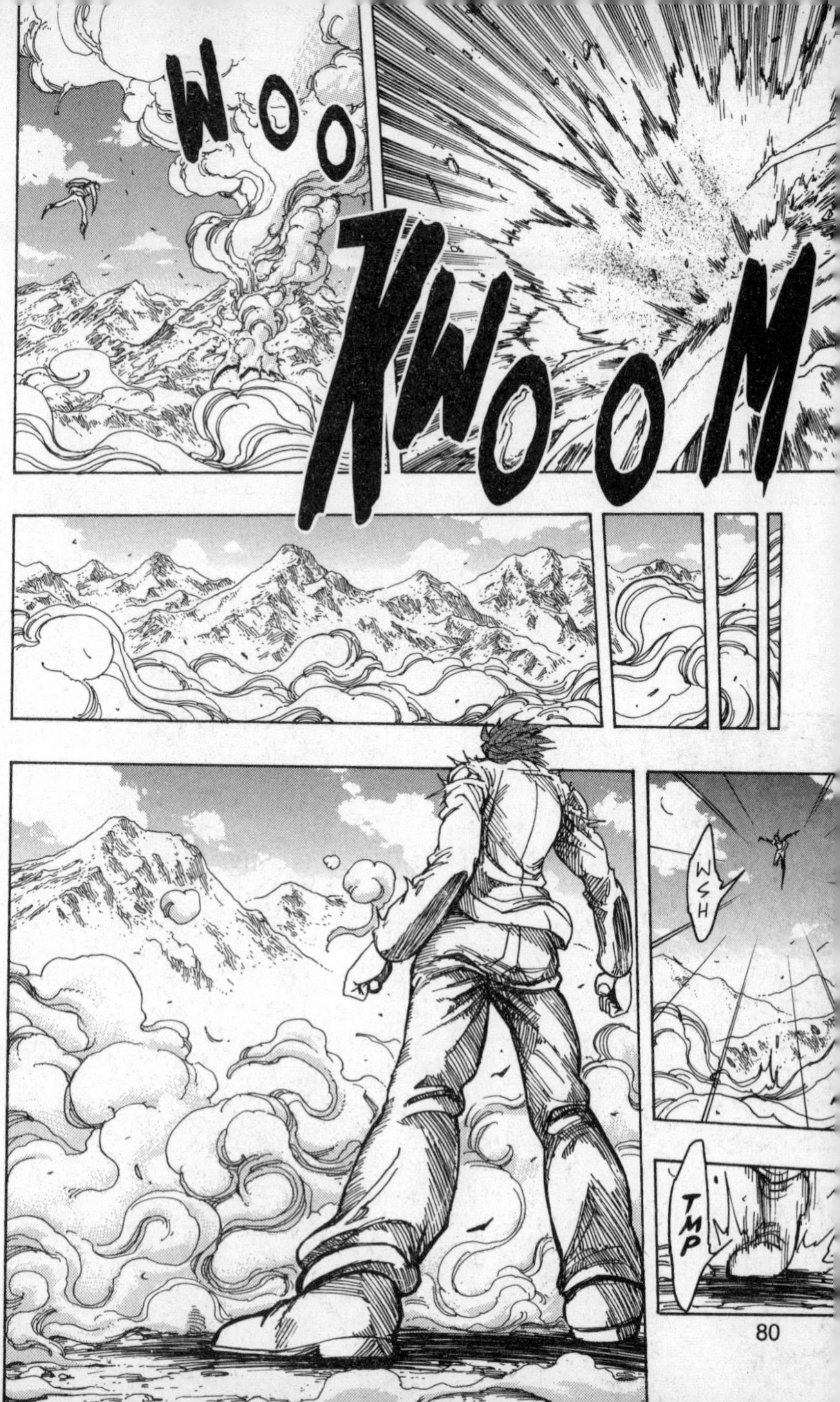
WOOO
KWOOOM
WSH
TMP

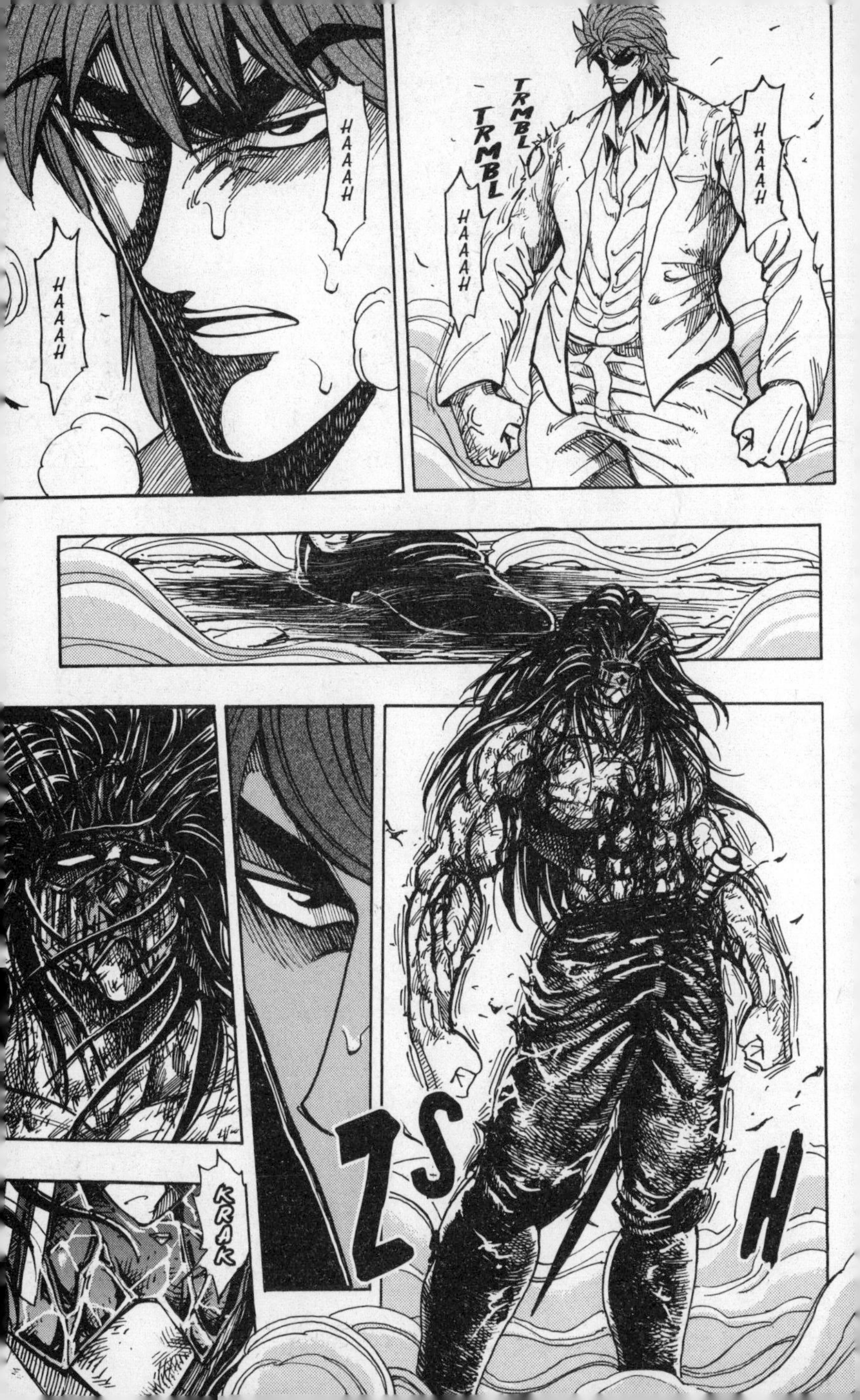
HAAAAH
TRMBL
TRMBL
HAAAAH
HAAAAH
HAAAAH
ZSH
KRAK

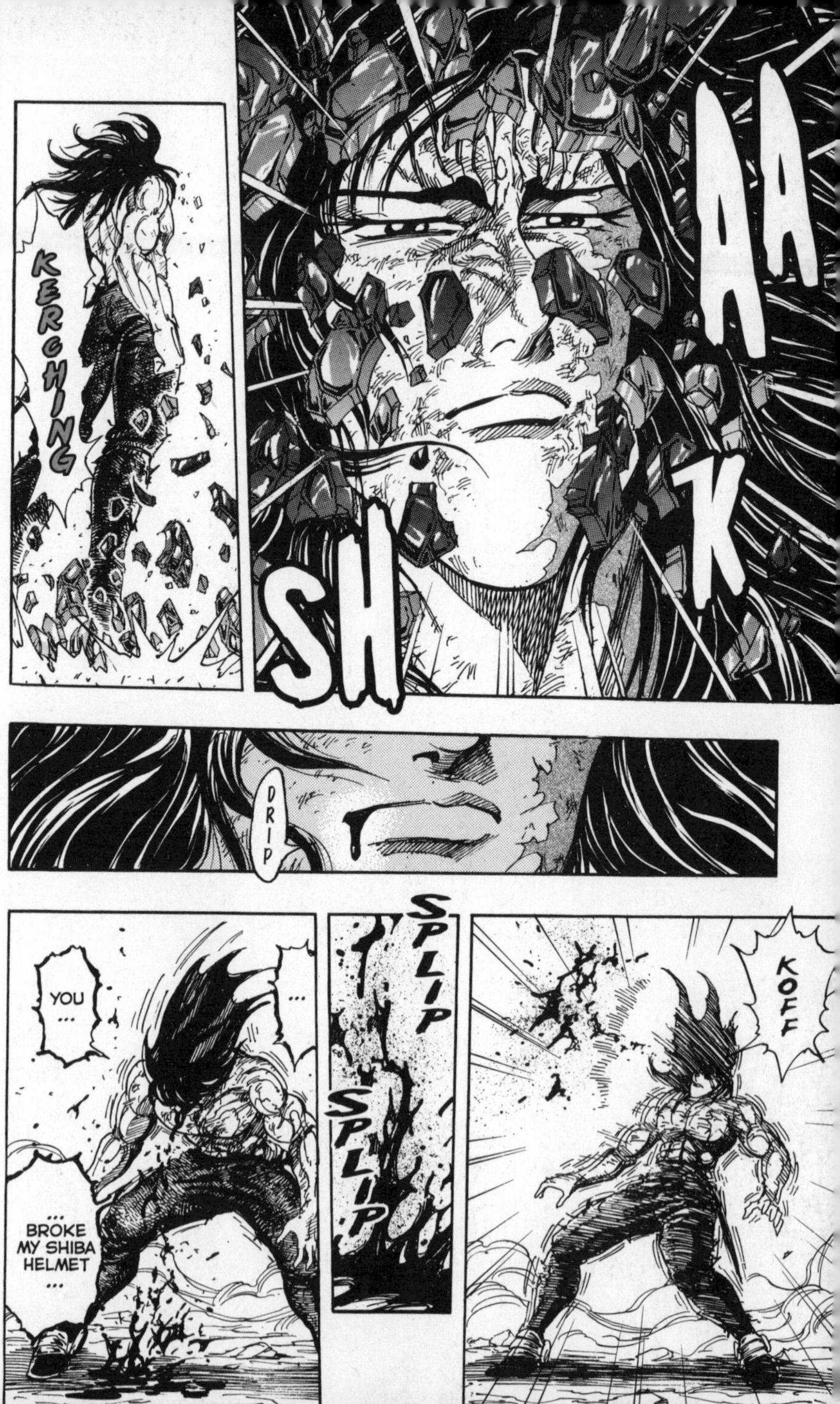

SHAAK
KERCHING
DRIP
KOFF
SPLIP
SPLIP
YOU ...
...
... BROKE MY SHIBA HELMET ...

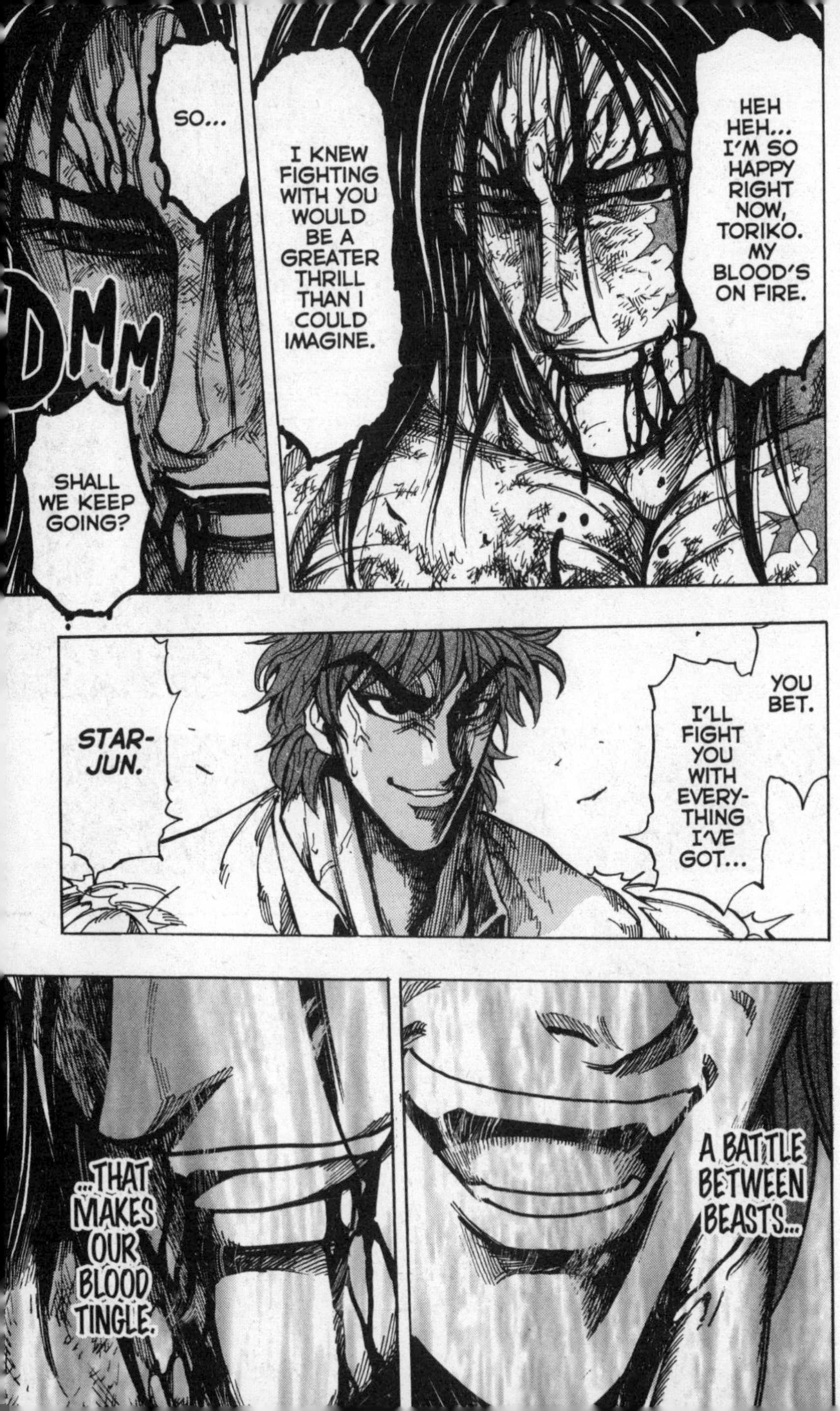
HEH HEH... I'M SO HAPPY RIGHT NOW, TORIKO. MY BLOOD'S ON FIRE.
I KNEW FIGHTING WITH YOU WOULD BE A GREATER THRILL THAN I COULD IMAGINE.
SO...
DMM
SHALL WE KEEP GOING?
YOU BET.
I'LL FIGHT YOU WITH EVERY-THING I'VE GOT...
STAR-JUN.
A BATTLE BETWEEN BEASTS...
...THAT MAKES OUR BLOOD TINGLE.

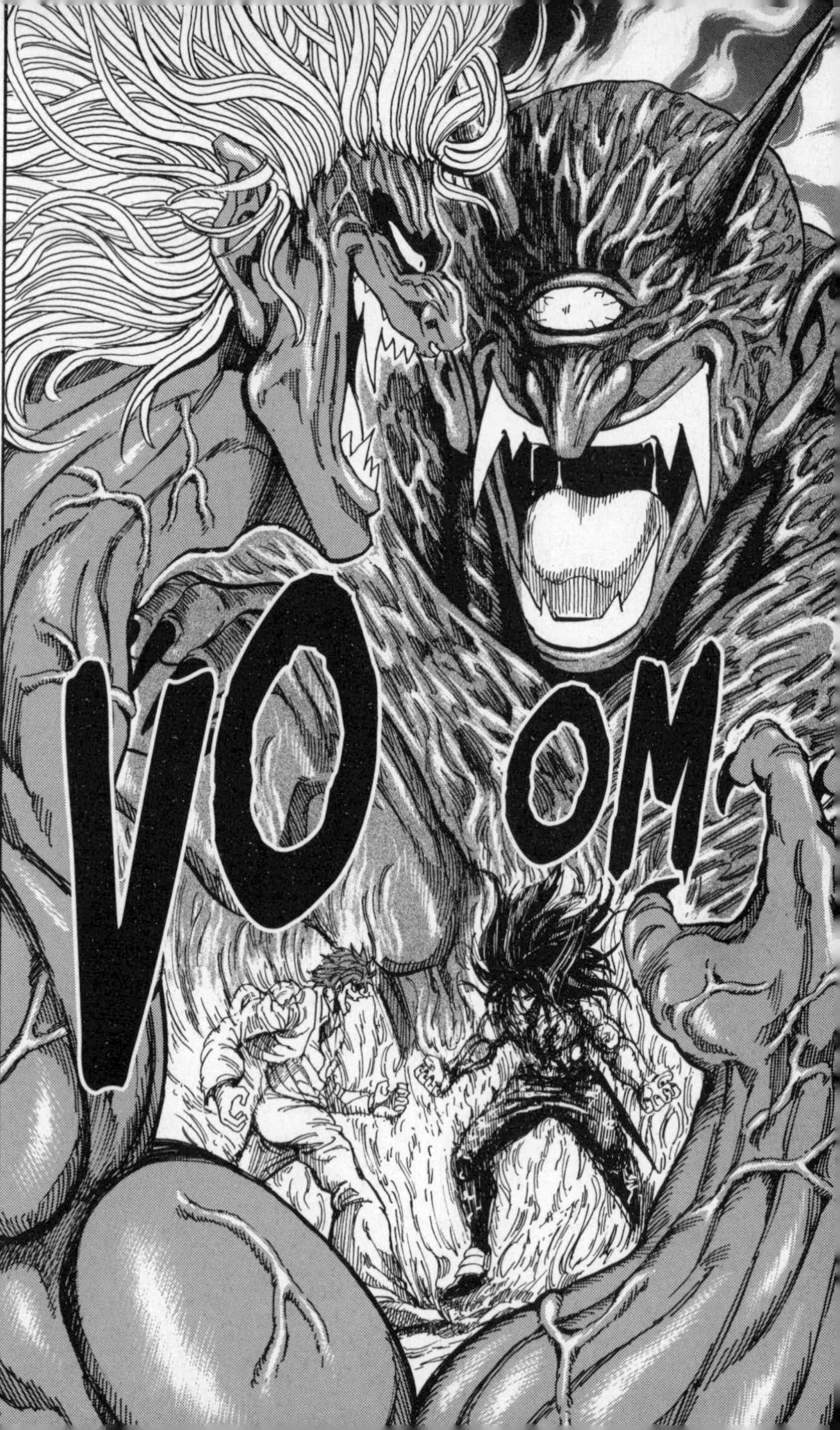
VOOM

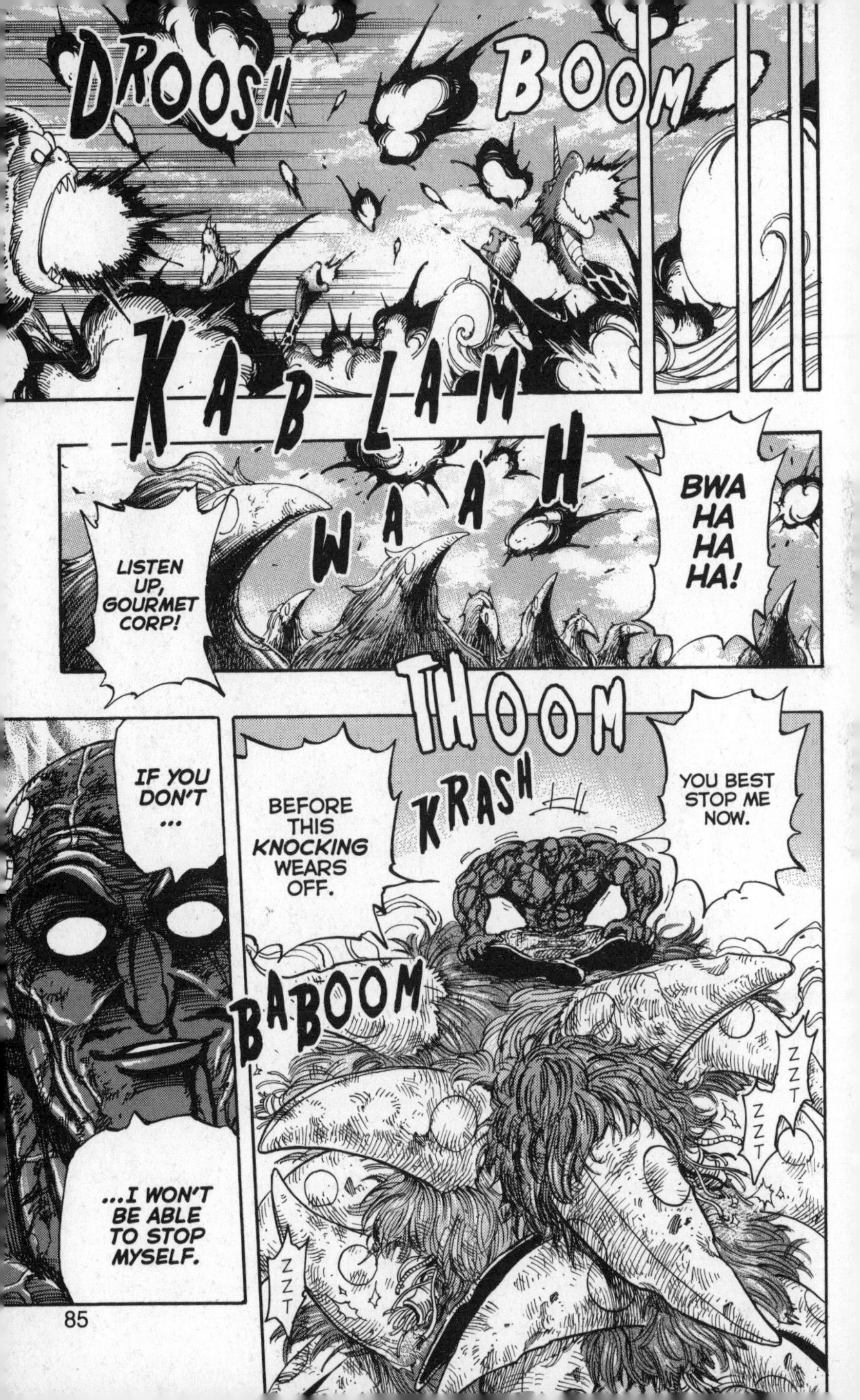
BOOM
DROOSH
KABLAM
BWA HA HA HA!
WAAH
LISTEN UP, GOURMET CORP!
YOU BEST STOP ME NOW.
THOOM
KRASH
BEFORE THIS KNOCKING WEARS OFF.
BABOOM
ZZT
ZZT
ZZT
IF YOU DON'T ...
...I WON'T BE ABLE TO STOP MYSELF.

TORIKO REJECT PAGES CORNER!!

(GOURMET 180)

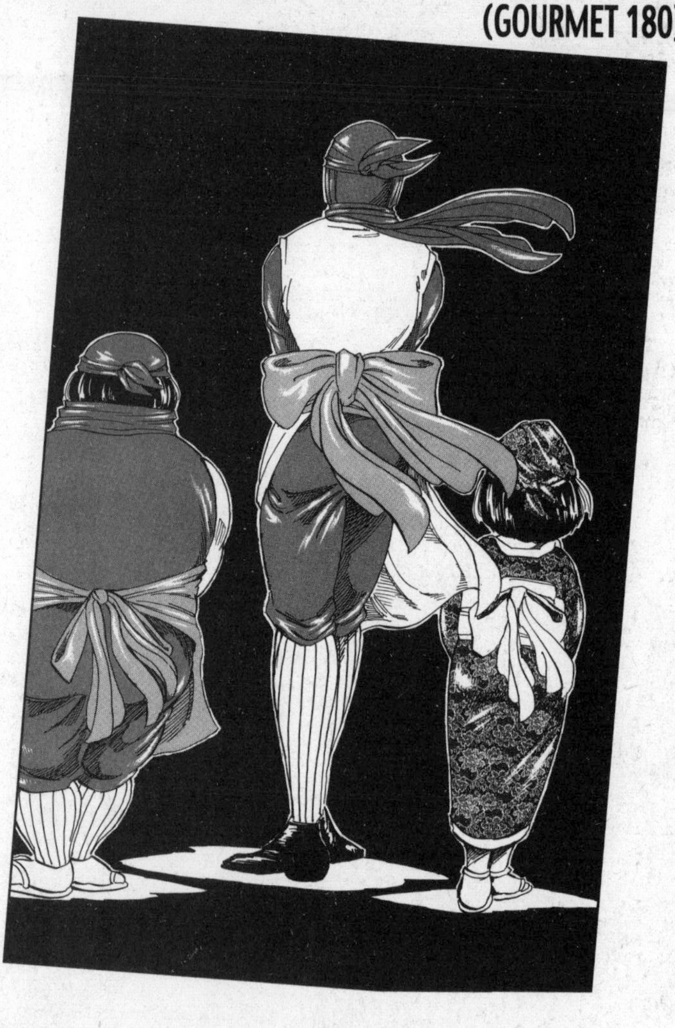

★ All right, here we are again! It's the customary "Reject Pages Corner"! (This is only its second installment, but I'm proclaiming it a custom!) This is the title page of the chapter where Toriko and Komatsu go to "Vanishing Japanese Cuisine." Chiru is in the middle; Chirin is on the left. And on the right...wait, who's that? The truth is, this chapter underwent a massive revision in the pencil stage and almost one entire chapter's worth of storyboards was rejected. So I'm going to showcase a little of it here!

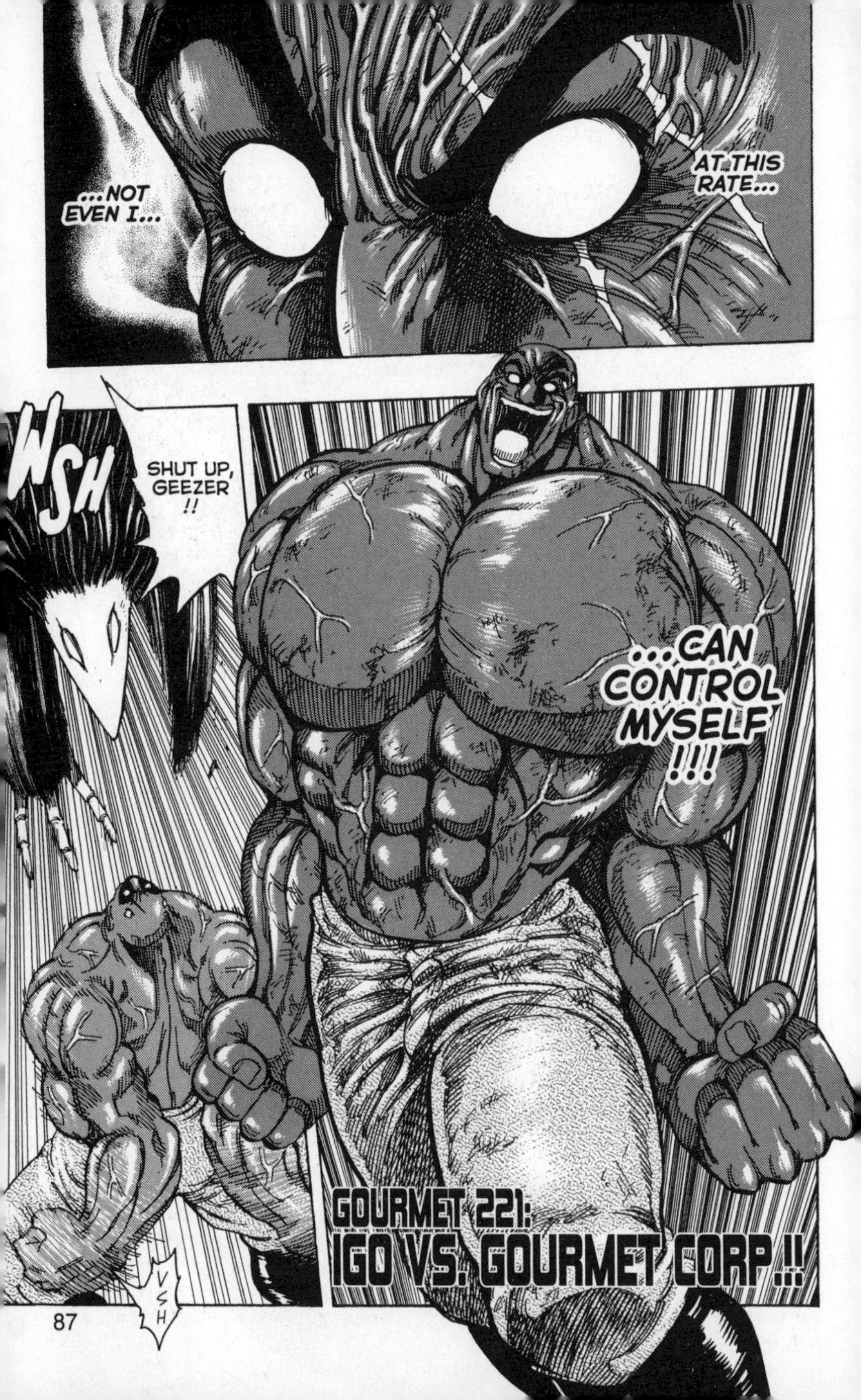
AT THIS RATE...
...NOT EVEN I...
...CAN CONTROL MYSELF!!!
WSH
SHUT UP, GEEZER!!
GOURMET 221:
IGO VS. GOURMET CORP.!!
VSH

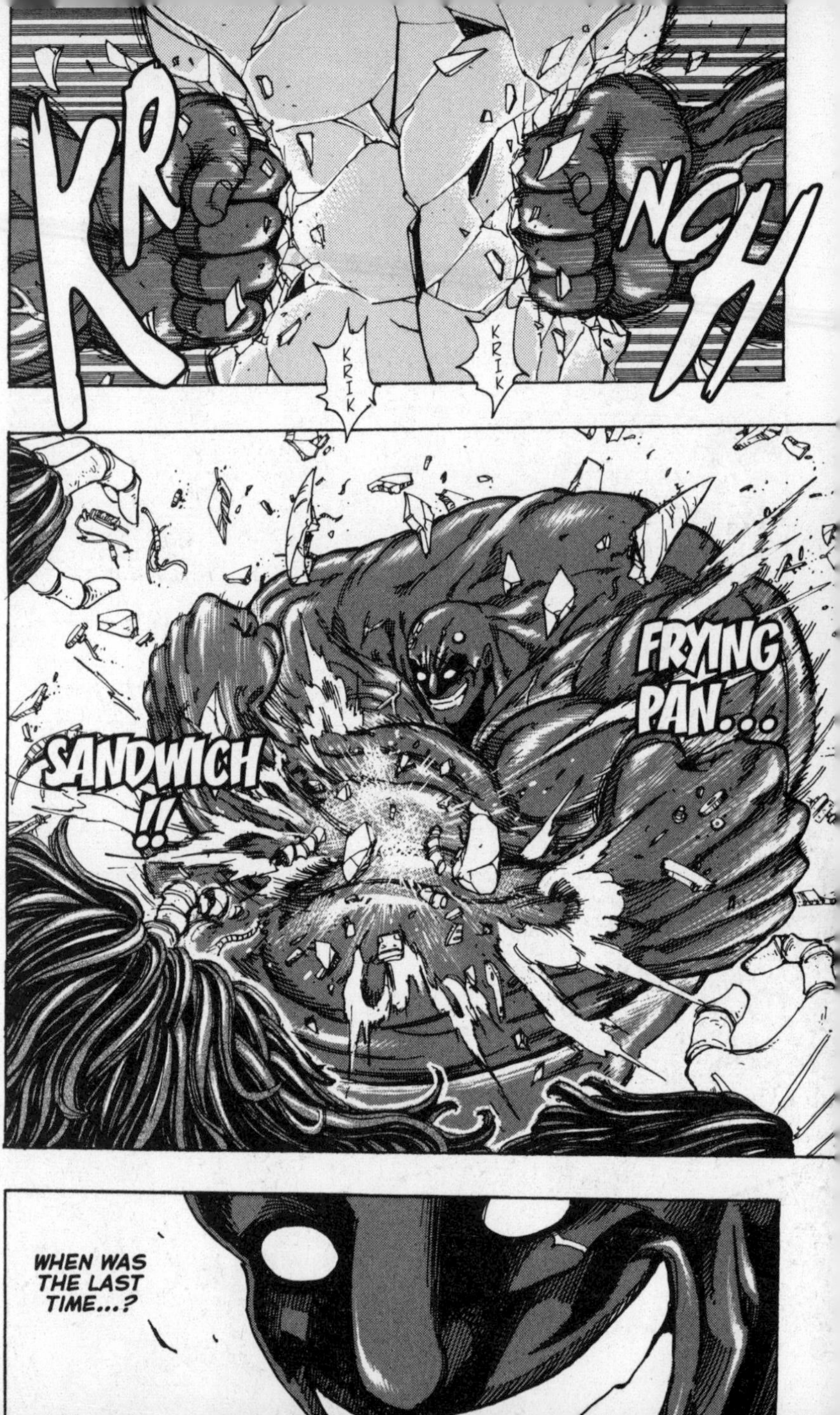
KR NCH
KRIK
KRIK
FRYING PAN...
SANDWICH !!
WHEN WAS THE LAST TIME...?

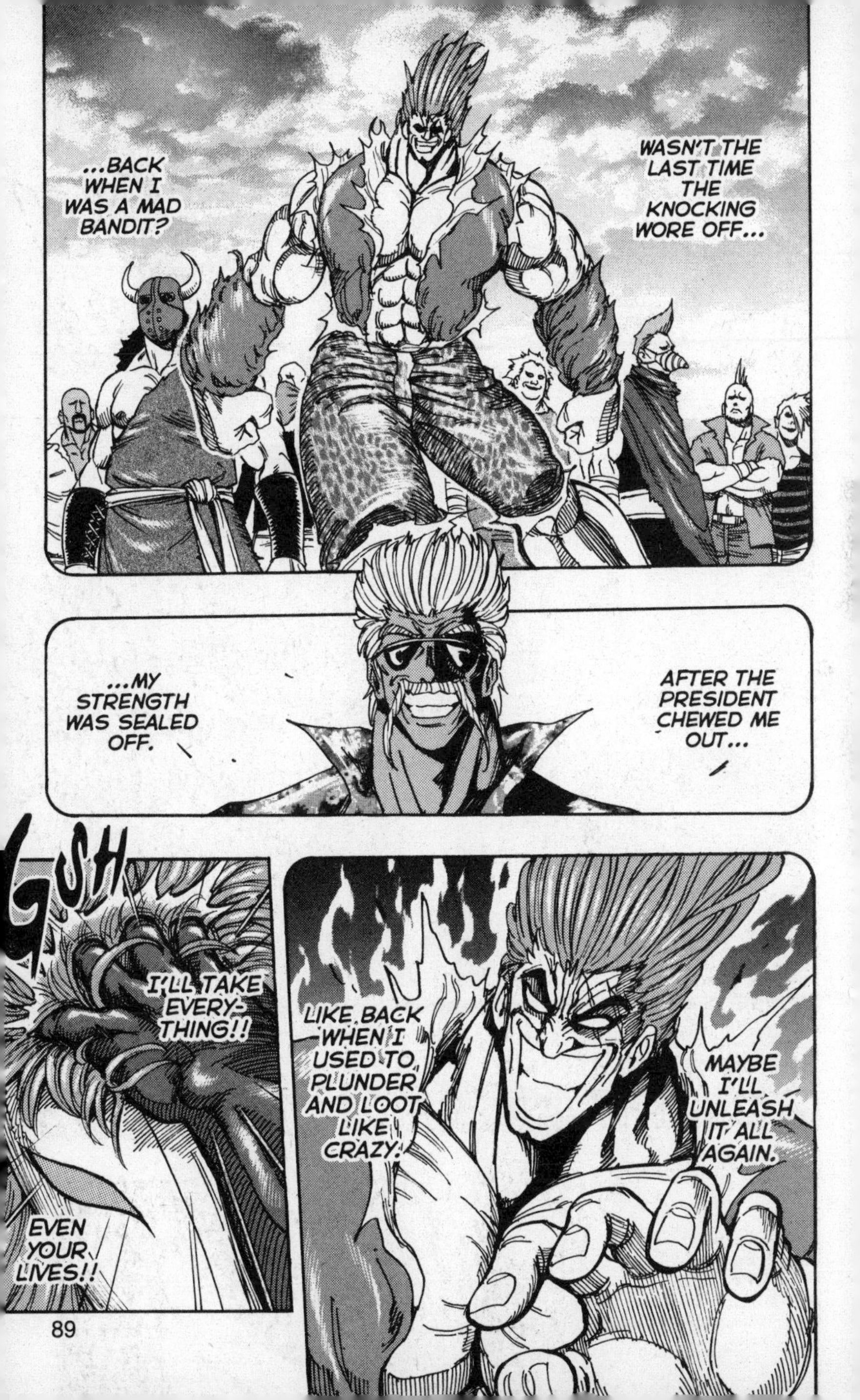

WASN'T THE LAST TIME THE KNOCKING WORE OFF...
...BACK WHEN I WAS A MAD BANDIT?
AFTER THE PRESIDENT CHEWED ME OUT...
...MY STRENGTH WAS SEALED OFF.
MAYBE I'LL UNLEASH IT ALL AGAIN.
LIKE BACK WHEN I USED TO PLUNDER AND LOOT LIKE CRAZY.
GSH
I'LL TAKE EVERY-THING!!
EVEN YOUR LIVES!!

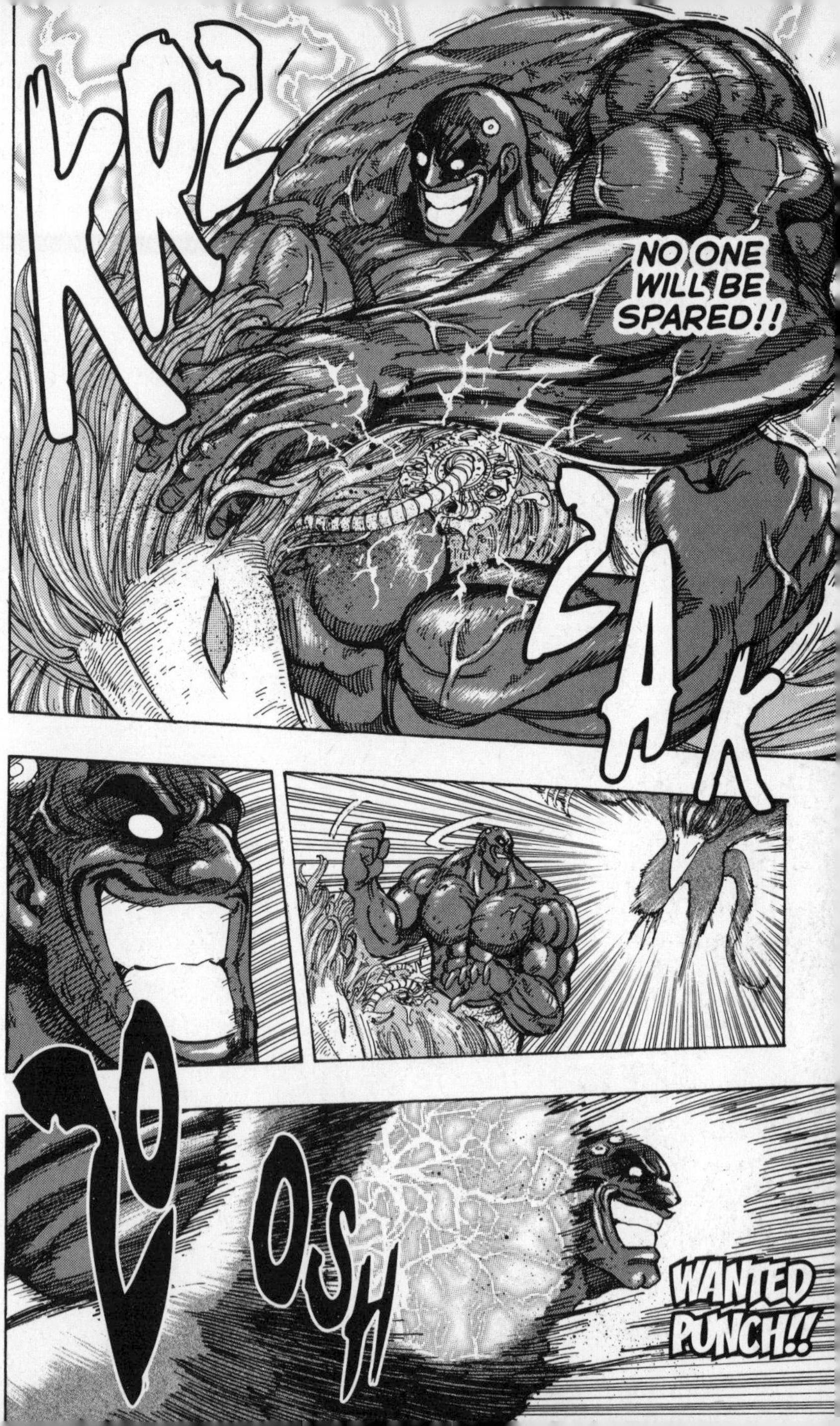
KRZ
NO ONE WILL BE SPARED!!
ZAK
WANTED PUNCH!!
ZOOSH

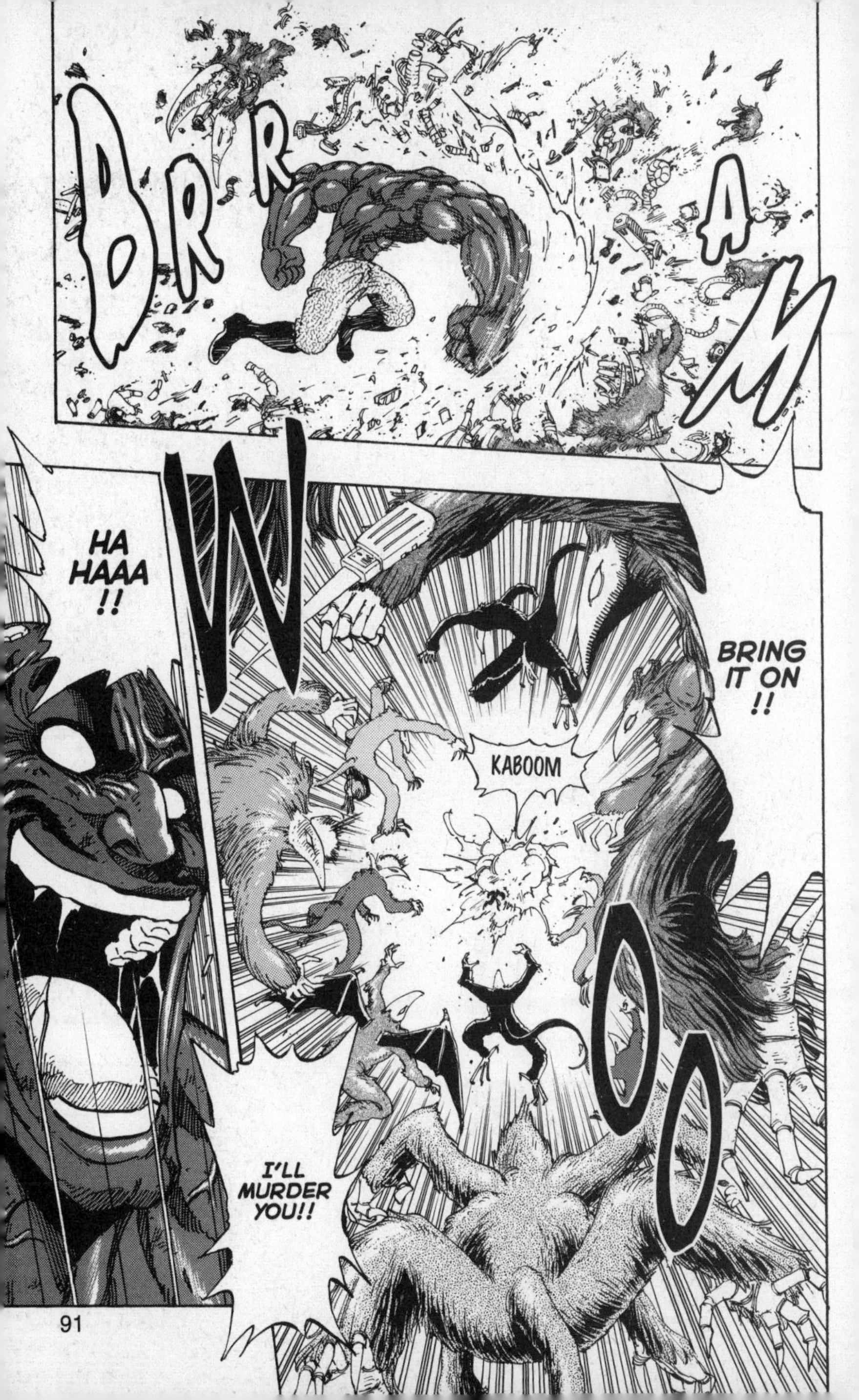
DRRAM
BRING IT ON !!
HA HAAA !!
KABOOM
WOO
I'LL MURDER YOU!!

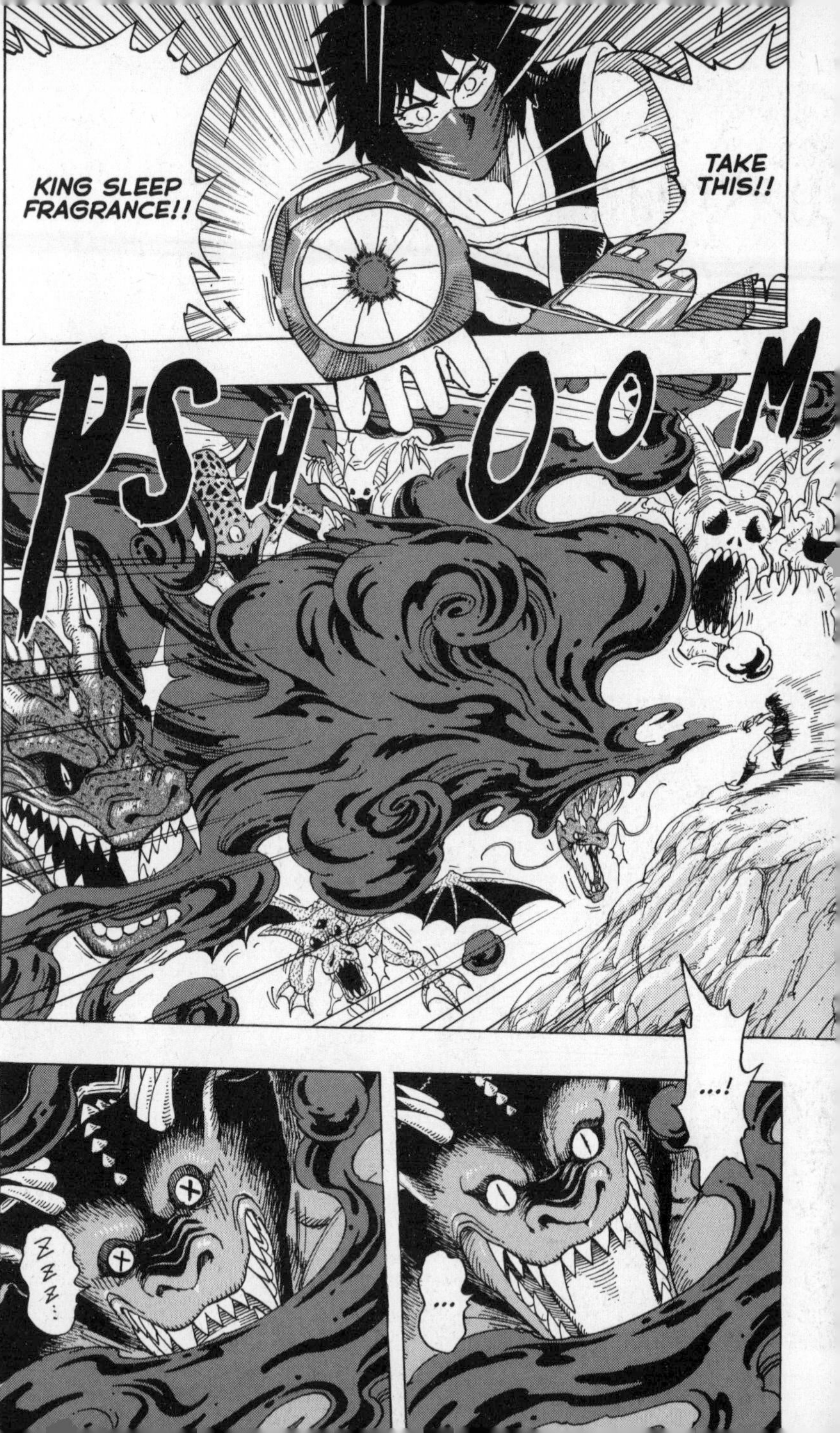
TAKE THIS!!
KING SLEEP FRAGRANCE!!
PSHOOOM
...!
...
ZZZ...

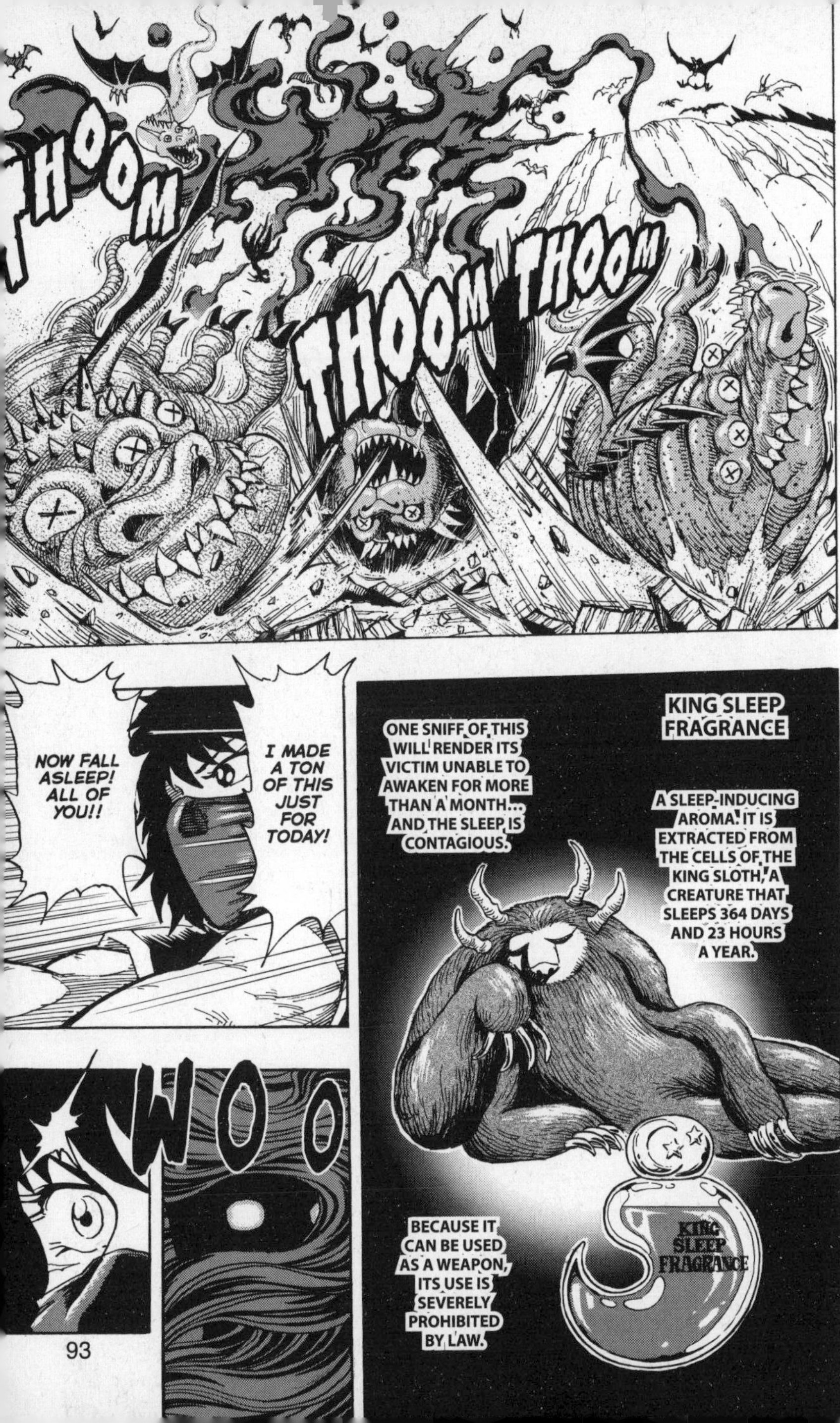
THOOM
THOOM
THOOM
KING SLEEP FRAGRANCE
A SLEEP-INDUCING AROMA. IT IS EXTRACTED FROM THE CELLS OF THE KING SLOTH, A CREATURE THAT SLEEPS 364 DAYS AND 23 HOURS A YEAR.
ONE SNIFF OF THIS WILL RENDER ITS VICTIM UNABLE TO AWAKEN FOR MORE THAN A MONTH... AND THE SLEEP IS CONTAGIOUS.
KING SLEEP FRAGRANCE
BECAUSE IT CAN BE USED AS A WEAPON, ITS USE IS SEVERELY PROHIBITED BY LAW.
I MADE A TON OF THIS JUST FOR TODAY!
NOW FALL ASLEEP! ALL OF YOU!!
WOOO

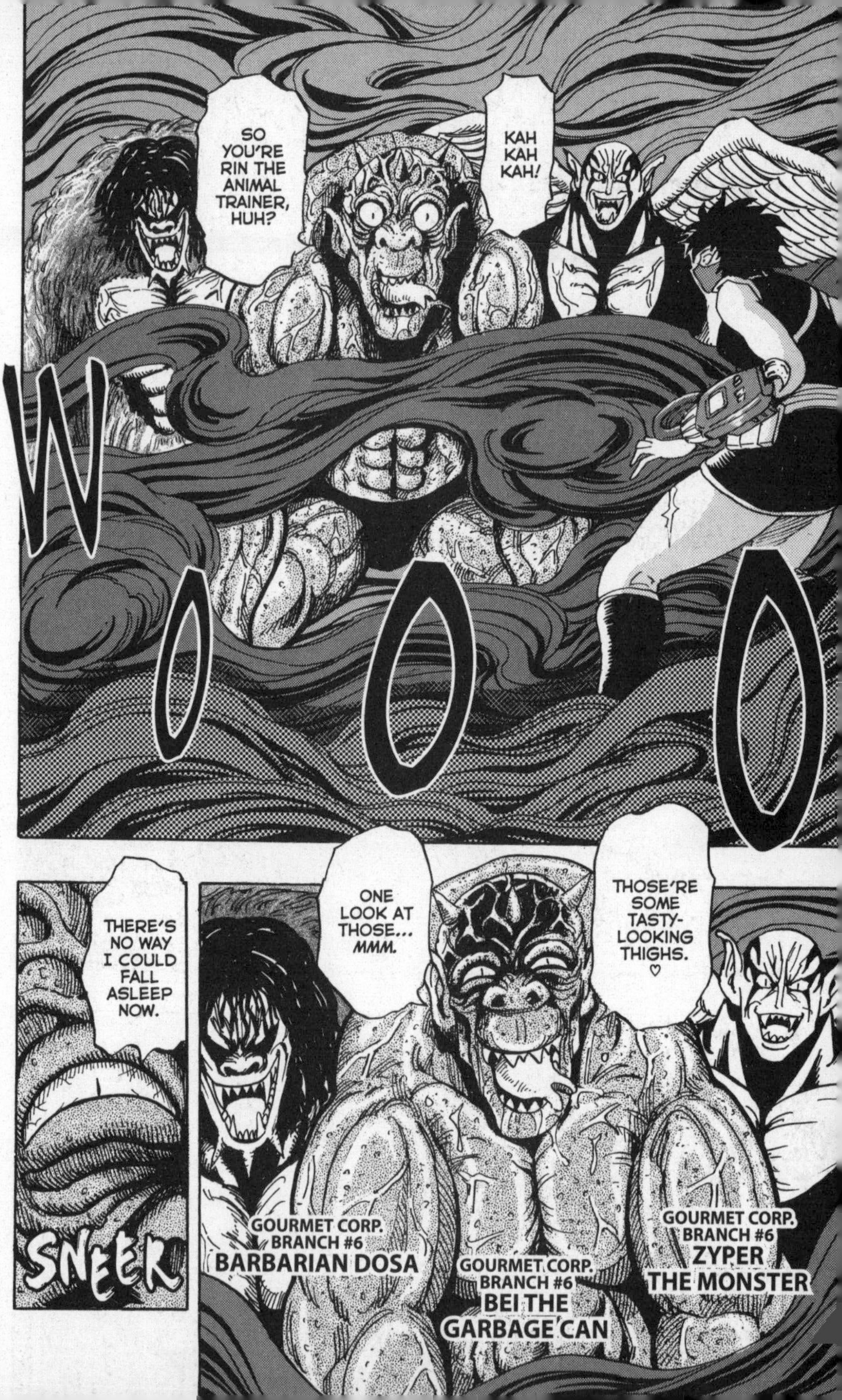
KAH KAH KAH!
SO YOU'RE RIN THE ANIMAL TRAINER, HUH?
WOOOO
THOSE'RE SOME TASTY-LOOKING THIGHS. ♡
ONE LOOK AT THOSE... MMM.
GOURMET CORP. BRANCH #6 ZYPER THE MONSTER
GOURMET CORP. BRANCH #6 BEI THE GARBAGE CAN
GOURMET CORP. BRANCH #6 BARBARIAN DOSA
THERE'S NO WAY I COULD FALL ASLEEP NOW.
SNEER

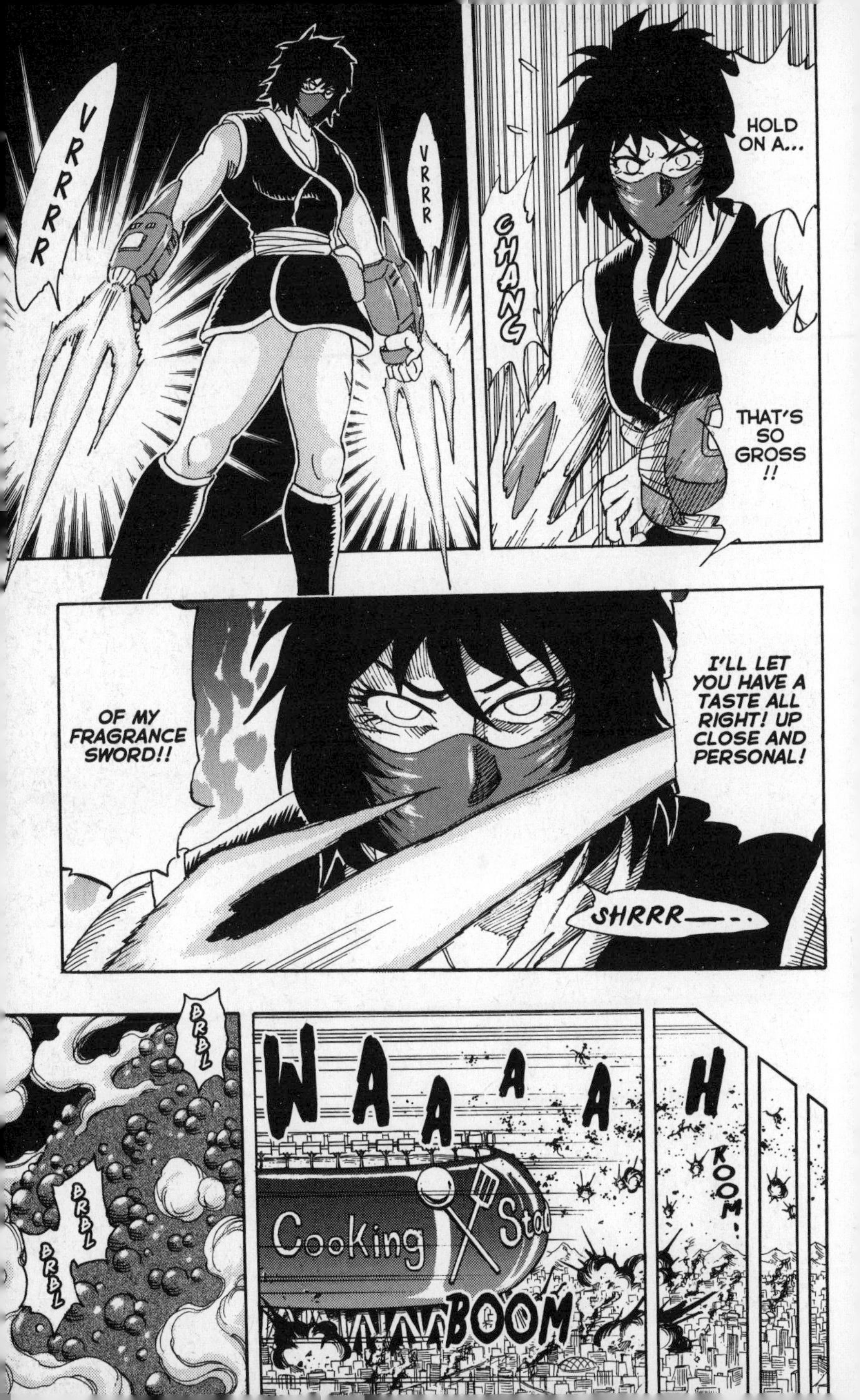
HOLD ON A...
CHANG
THAT'S SO GROSS!!
VRRRRR
VRRR
I'LL LET YOU HAVE A TASTE ALL RIGHT! UP CLOSE AND PERSONAL!
OF MY FRAGRANCE SWORD!!
SHRRR—...
WAAAAH
KOOM
Cooking
BOOM
BRBL
BRBL
BRBL

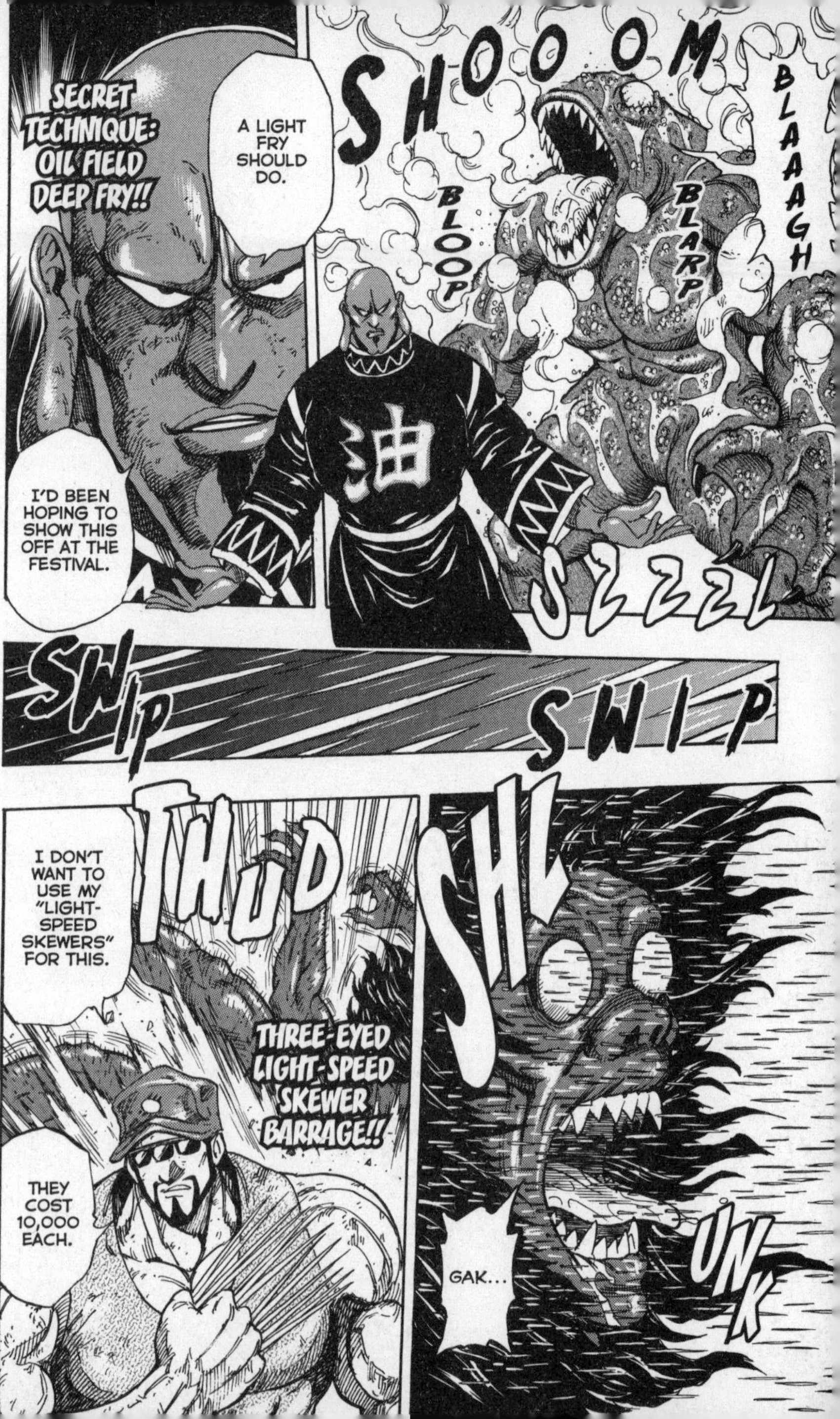
SHOOOM
BLAAAGH
BLARP
BLOOP
SZZZL
A LIGHT FRY SHOULD DO.
SECRET TECHNIQUE: OIL FIELD DEEP FRY!!
I'D BEEN HOPING TO SHOW THIS OFF AT THE FESTIVAL.
SWIP
SWIP
SHL
UNK
GAK...
THUD
I DON'T WANT TO USE MY "LIGHT-SPEED SKEWERS" FOR THIS.
THREE-EYED LIGHT-SPEED SKEWER BARRAGE!!
THEY COST 10,000 EACH.

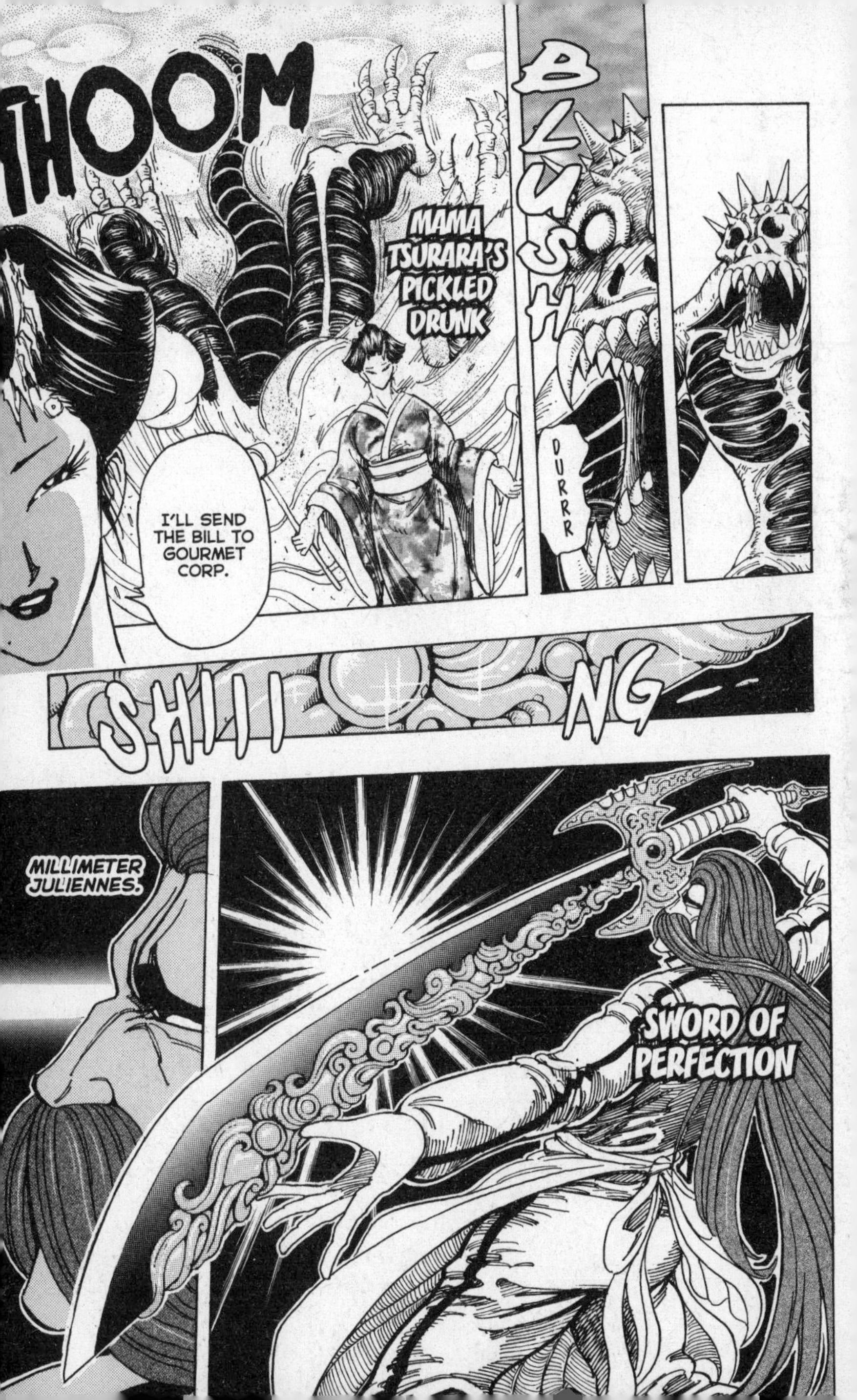
BLUSH
DURRR
THOOM
MAMA TSURARA'S PICKLED DRUNK
I'LL SEND THE BILL TO GOURMET CORP.
SHIII NG
SWORD OF PERFECTION
MILLIMETER JULIENNES.

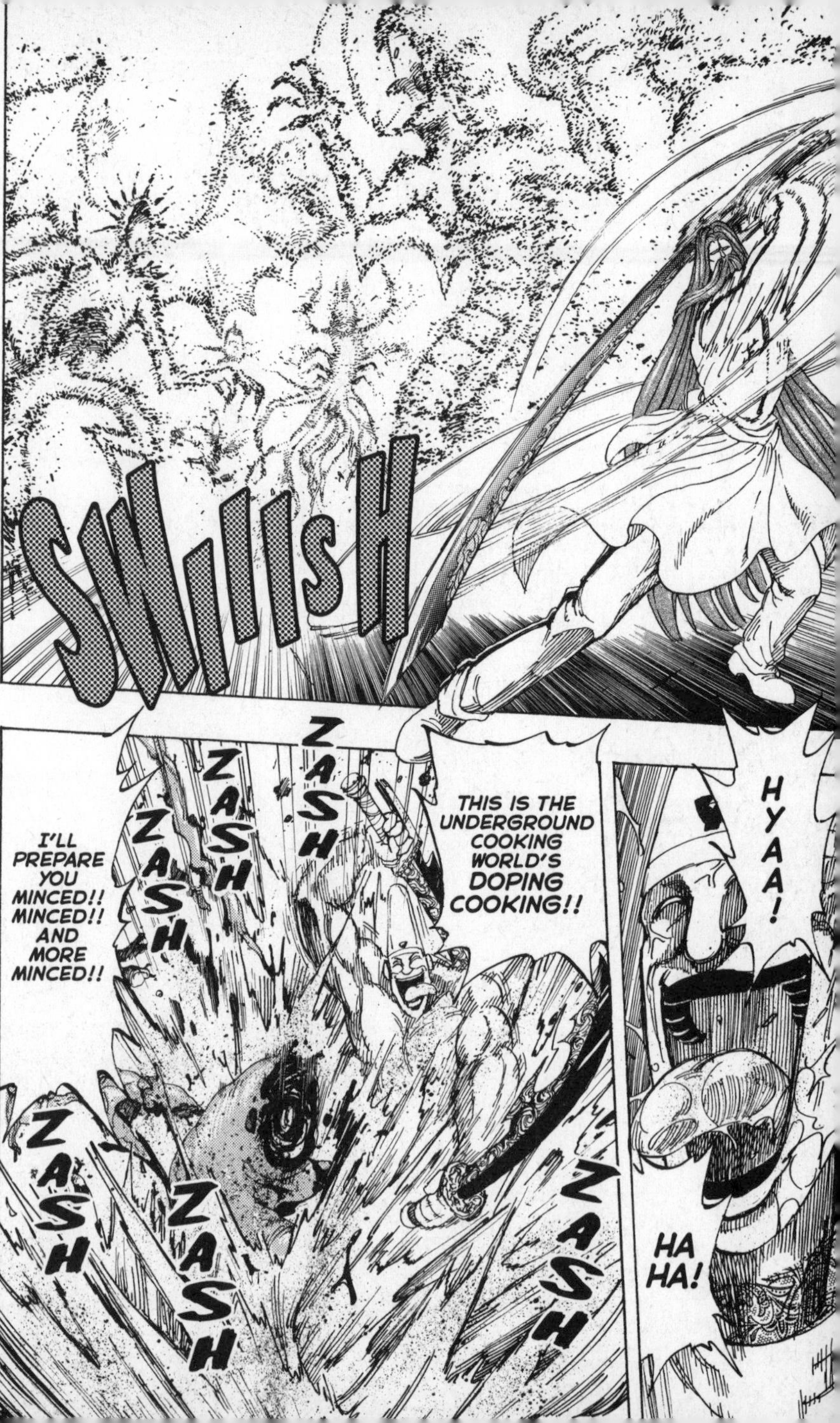
SWIIISH
HYAA!
HA HA!
THIS IS THE UNDERGROUND COOKING WORLD'S DOPING COOKING!!
ZASH
ZASH
ZASH
I'LL PREPARE YOU MINCED!! MINCED!! AND MORE MINCED!!
ZASH
ZASH
ZASH
ZASH

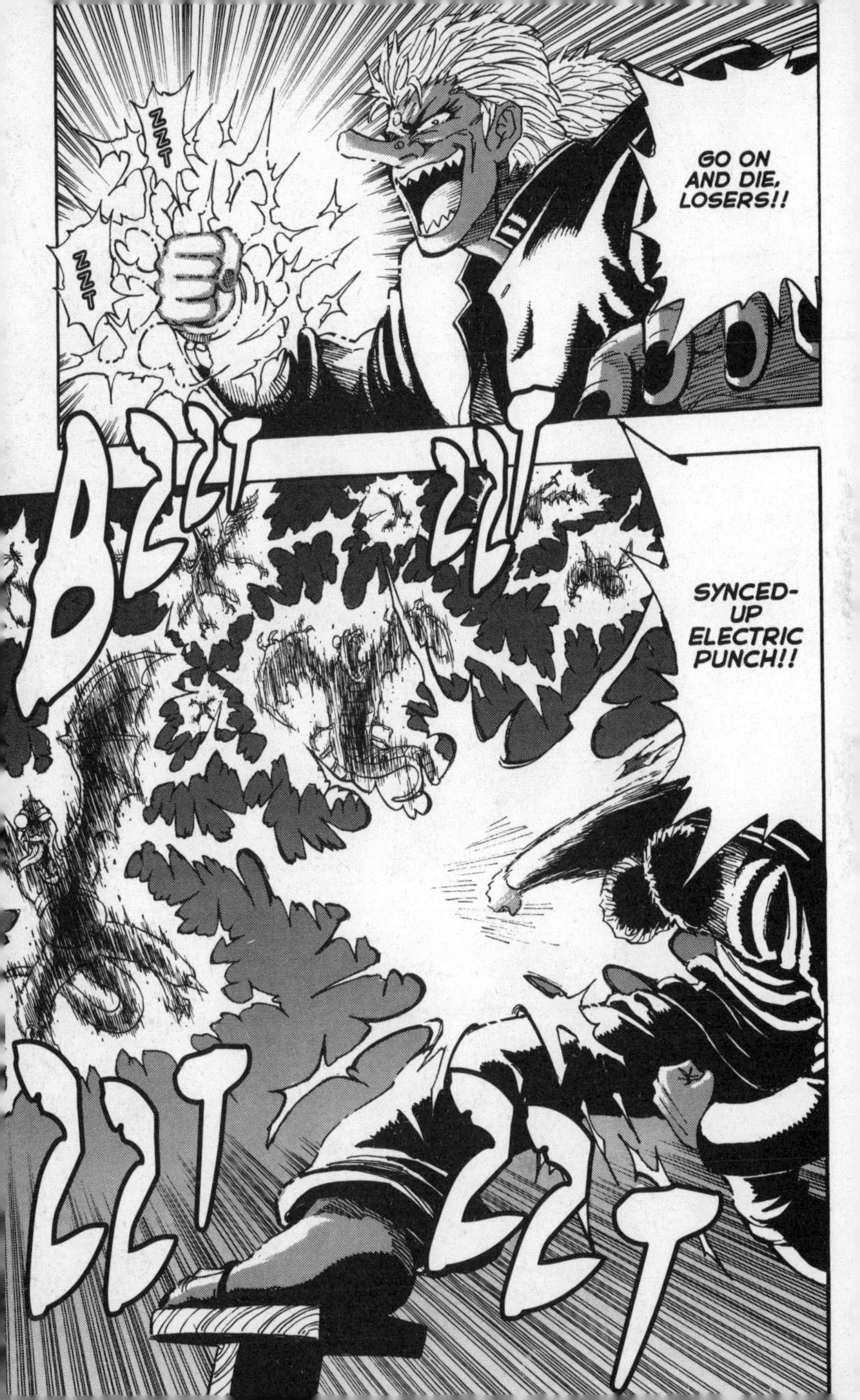
GO ON AND DIE, LOSERS!!
ZZT
ZZT
SYNCED-UP ELECTRIC PUNCH!!

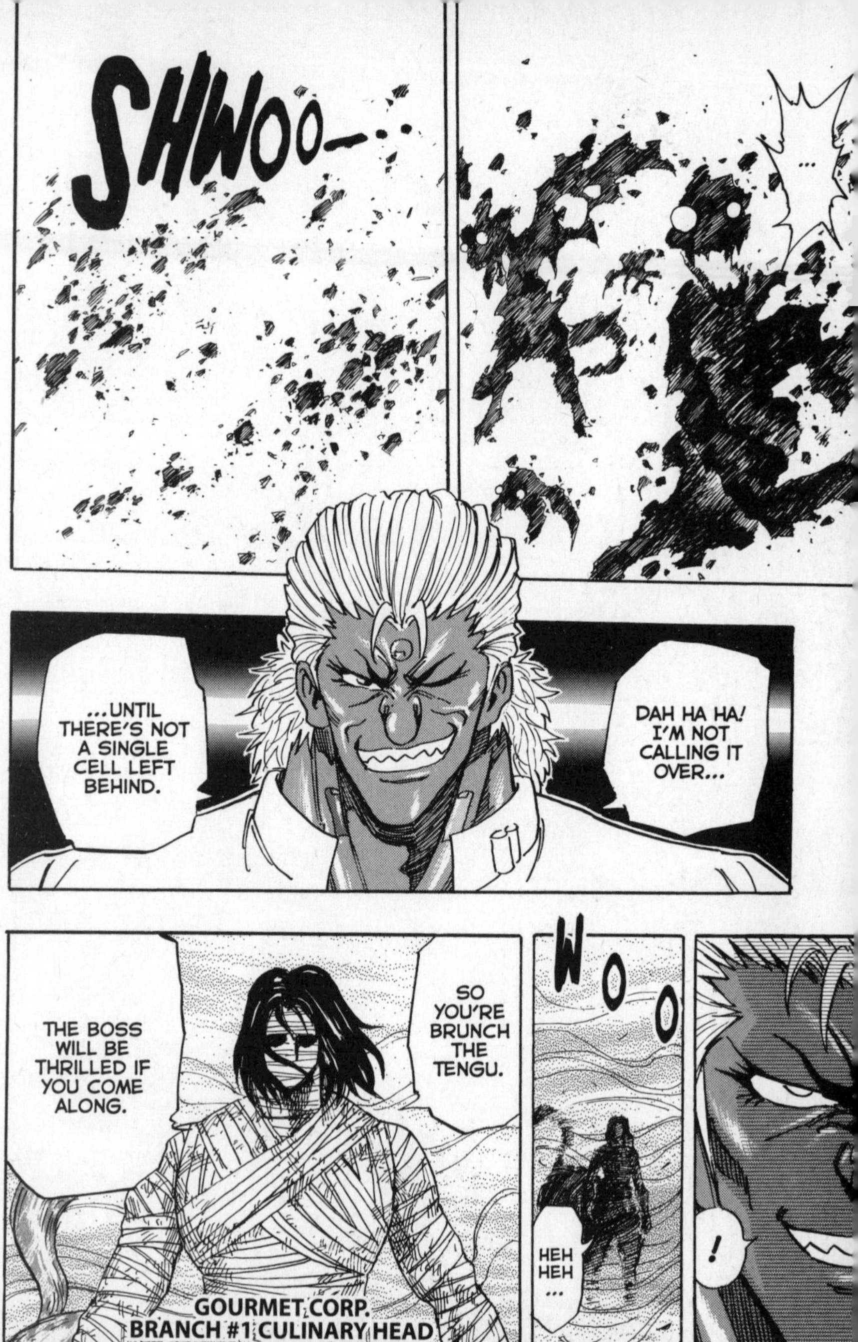
...
SHWOO--
DAH HA HA! I'M NOT CALLING IT OVER...
...UNTIL THERE'S NOT A SINGLE CELL LEFT BEHIND.
!
WOO
HEH HEH ...
SO YOU'RE BRUNCH THE TENGU.
THE BOSS WILL BE THRILLED IF YOU COME ALONG.
GOURMET CORP.
BRANCH #1 CULINARY HEAD
ELG

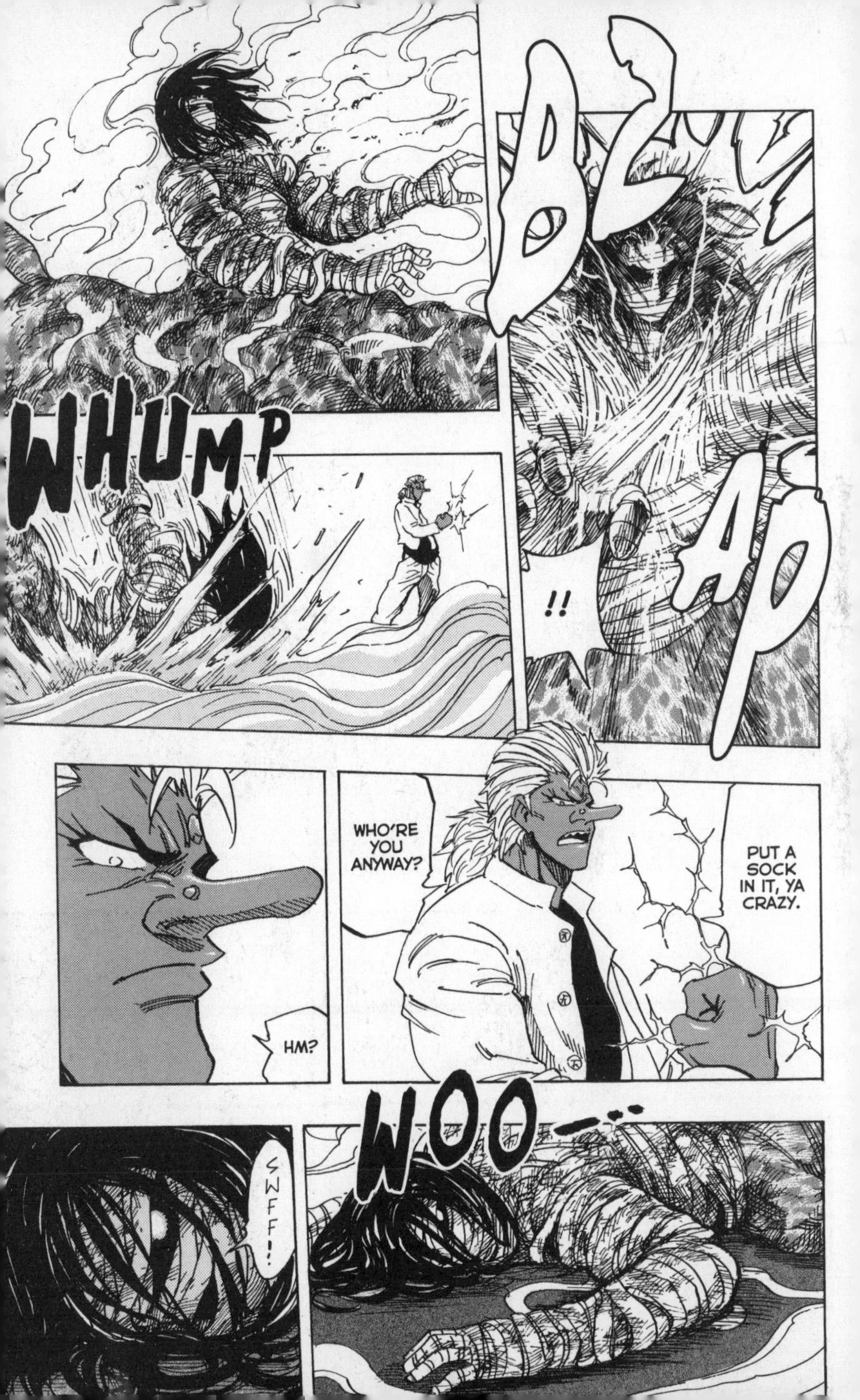
!!
WHUMP
PUT A SOCK IN IT, YA CRAZY.
WHO'RE YOU ANYWAY?
HM?
WOO—..
SWFF!

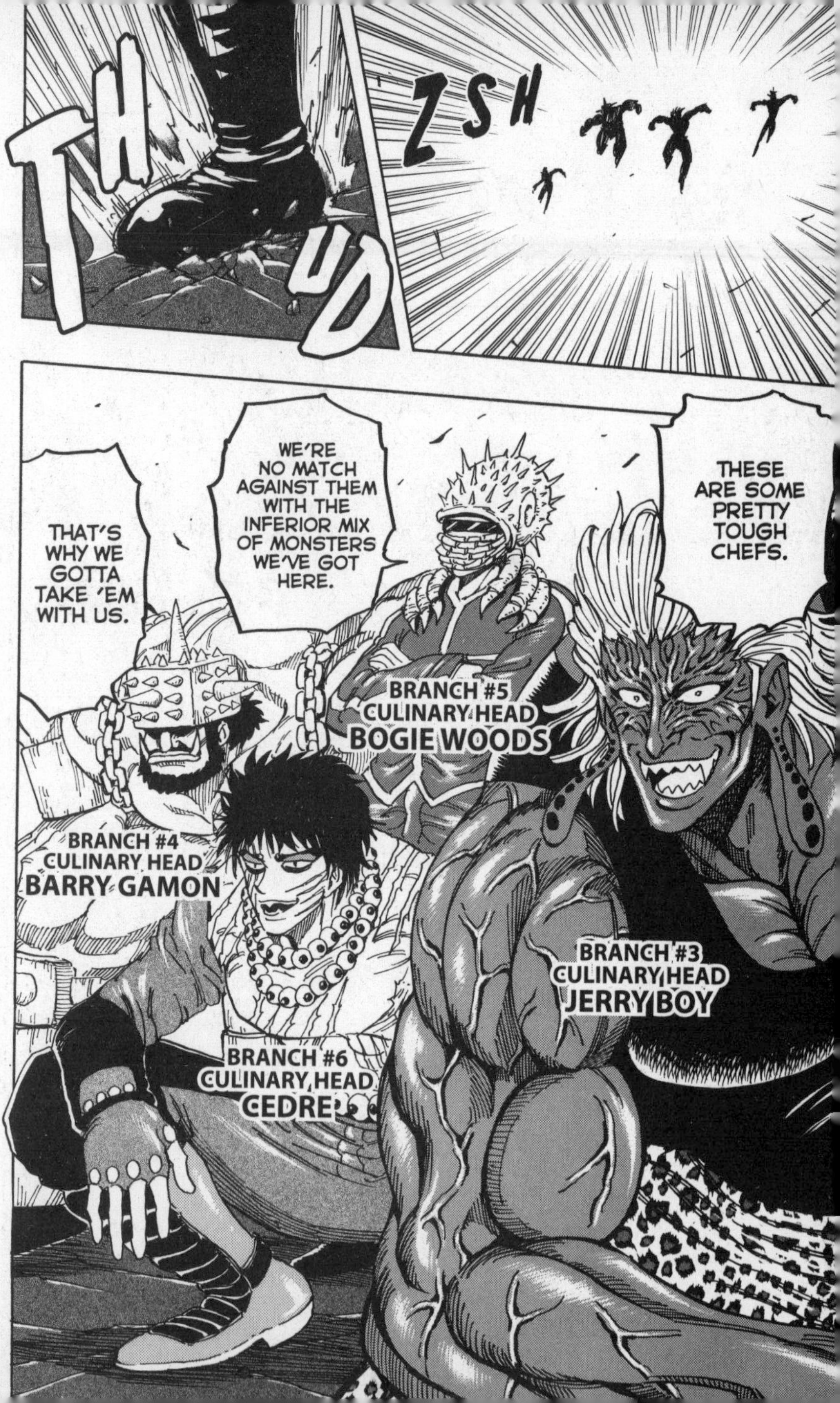
ZSH
THUD
THESE ARE SOME PRETTY TOUGH CHEFS.
WE'RE NO MATCH AGAINST THEM WITH THE INFERIOR MIX OF MONSTERS WE'VE GOT HERE.
THAT'S WHY WE GOTTA TAKE 'EM WITH US.
BRANCH #5 CULINARY HEAD BOGIE WOODS
BRANCH #4 CULINARY HEAD BARRY GAMON
BRANCH #3 CULINARY HEAD JERRY BOY
BRANCH #6 CULINARY HEAD CEDRE

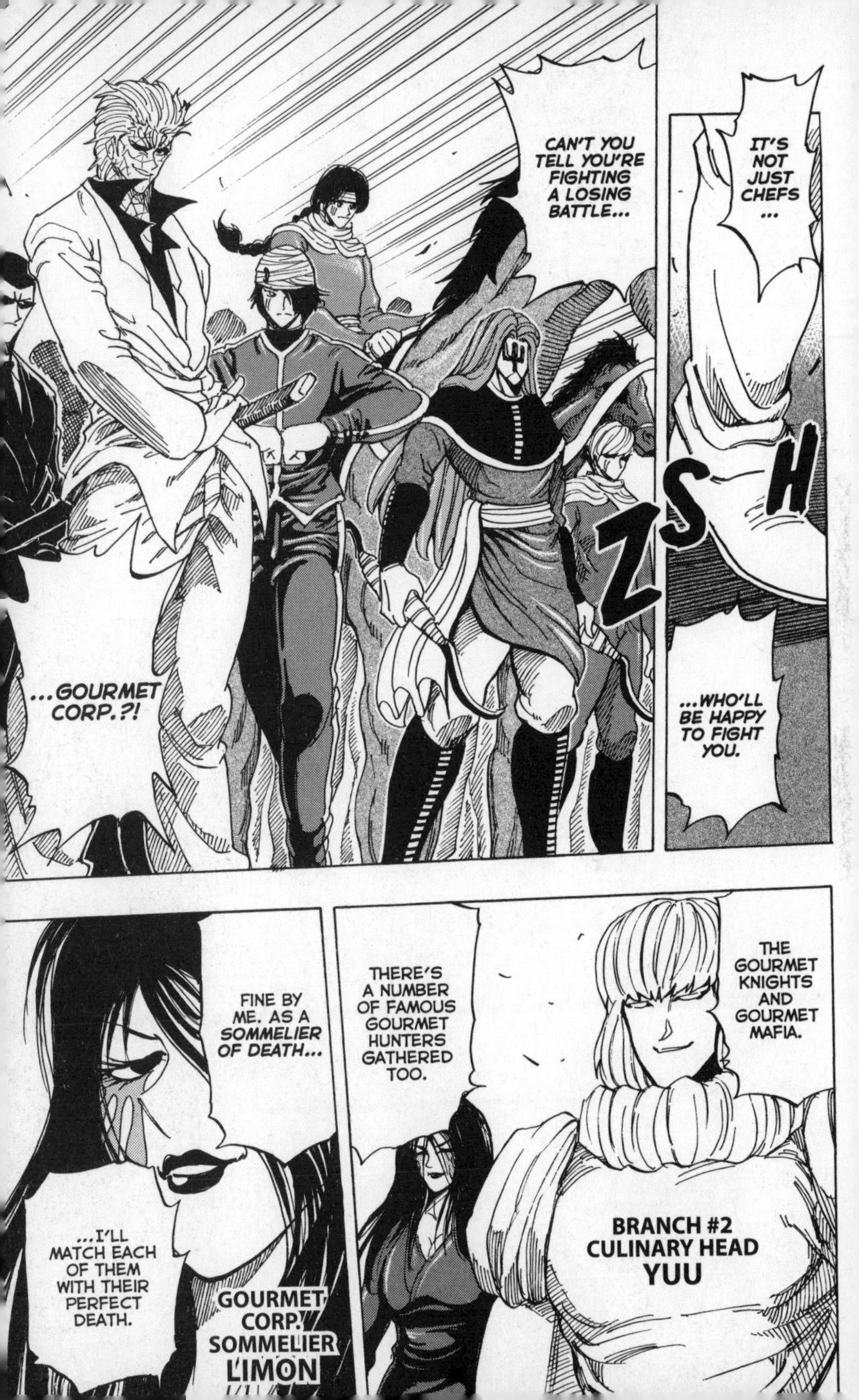
IT'S NOT JUST CHEFS ...
ZSH
...WHO'LL BE HAPPY TO FIGHT YOU.
CAN'T YOU TELL YOU'RE FIGHTING A LOSING BATTLE...
...GOURMET CORP.?!
THE GOURMET KNIGHTS AND GOURMET MAFIA.
THERE'S A NUMBER OF FAMOUS GOURMET HUNTERS GATHERED TOO.
BRANCH #2 CULINARY HEAD YUU
FINE BY ME. AS A SOMMELIER OF DEATH...
...I'LL MATCH EACH OF THEM WITH THEIR PERFECT DEATH.
GOURMET CORP. SOMMELIER LIMON

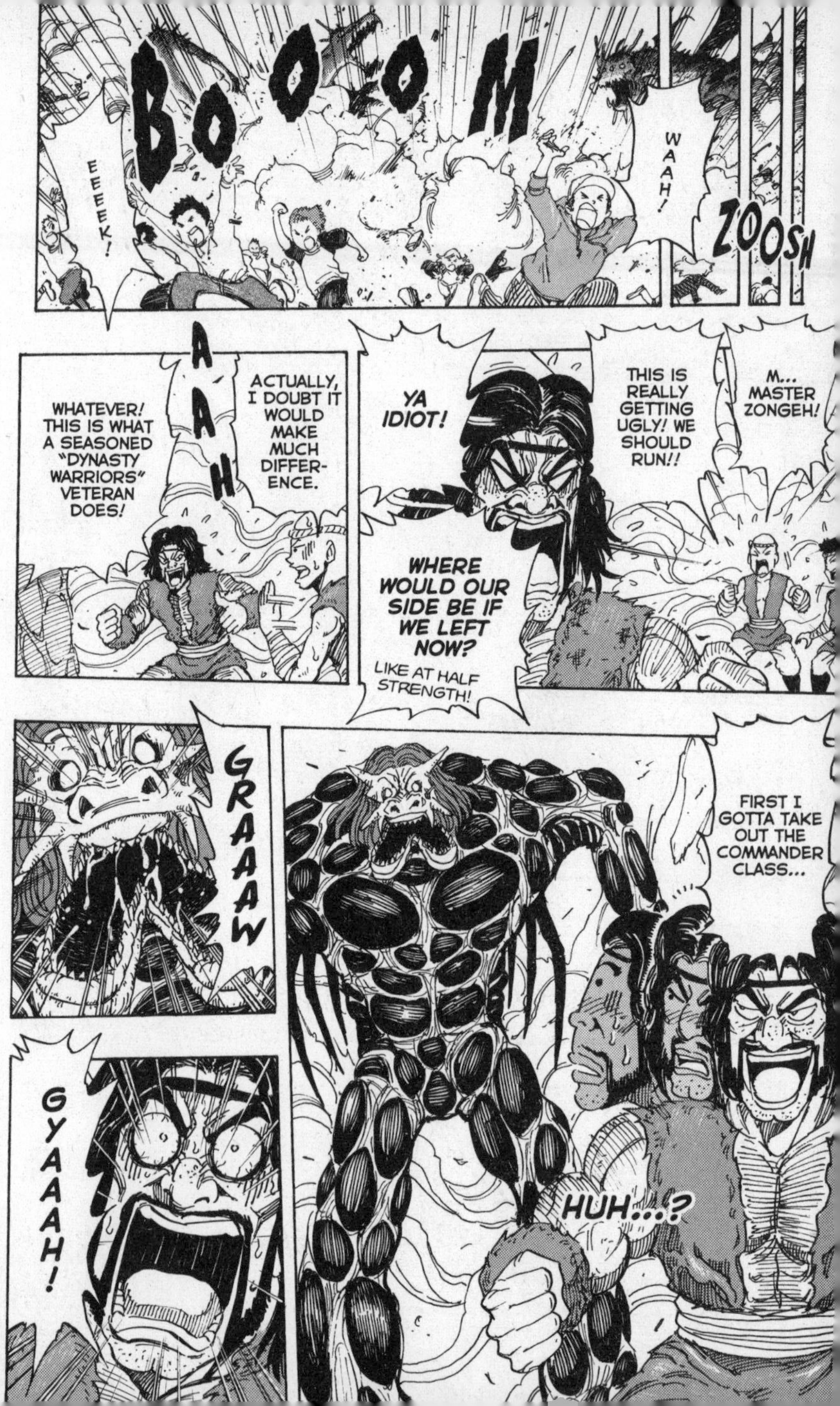
WAAAH!
ZOOSH
BOOOOM
EEEEK!
M... MASTER ZONGEH!
THIS IS REALLY GETTING UGLY! WE SHOULD RUN!!
YA IDIOT!
WHERE WOULD OUR SIDE BE IF WE LEFT NOW?
LIKE AT HALF STRENGTH!
AAAH
ACTUALLY, I DOUBT IT WOULD MAKE MUCH DIFFER-ENCE.
WHATEVER! THIS IS WHAT A SEASONED "DYNASTY WARRIORS" VETERAN DOES!
FIRST I GOTTA TAKE OUT THE COMMANDER CLASS...
HUH...?
GRAAAAW
GYAAAAH!

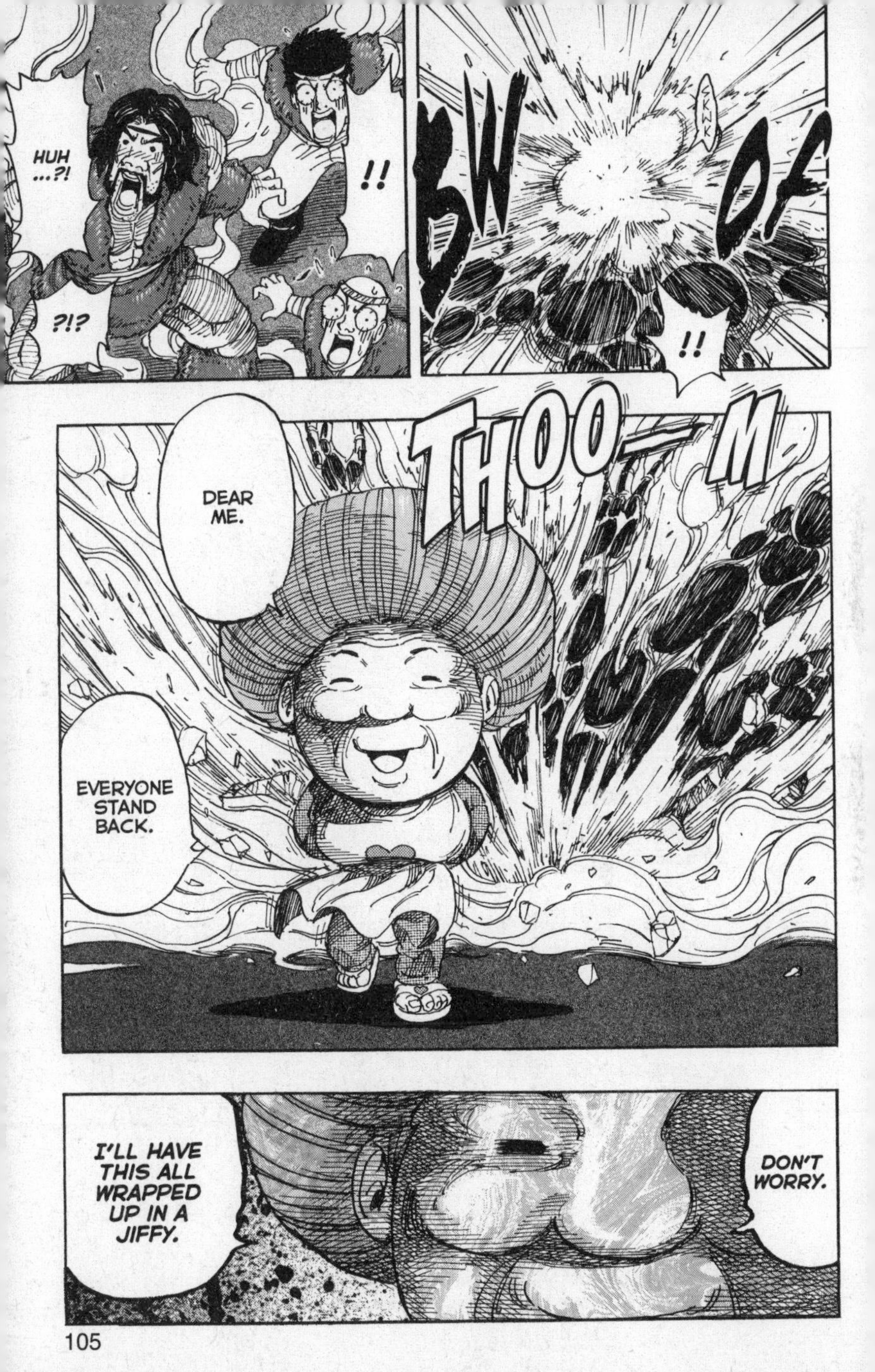
SKWK
BW OF
!!
!!
HUH ...?!
?!?
THOO—M
DEAR ME.
EVERYONE STAND BACK.
DON'T WORRY.
I'LL HAVE THIS ALL WRAPPED UP IN A JIFFY.

TORIKO REJECT PAGES CORNER!!

(GOURMET 180)

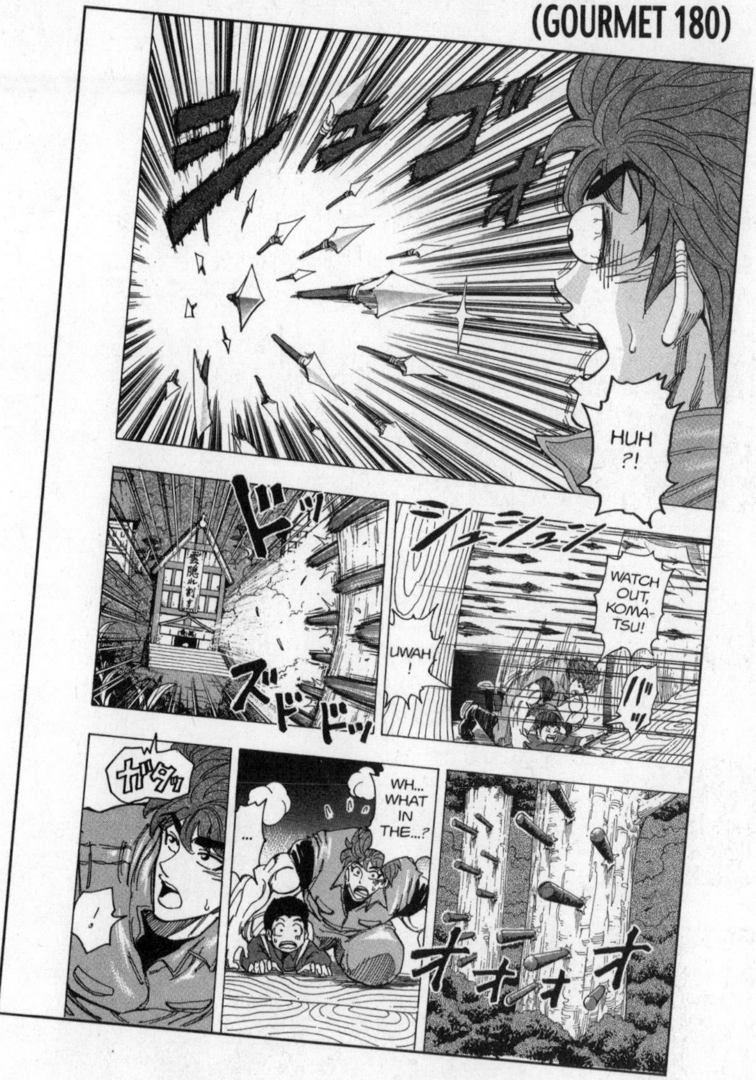
HUH ?!
WATCH OUT, KOMATSU!
UWAH !
WH... WHAT IN THE...?
...
!

★ This is Toriko and Komatsu's first attempt at entering "Vanishing Japanese Cuisine." I made it so they had to face a trap. Scary! This restaurant is scary!!

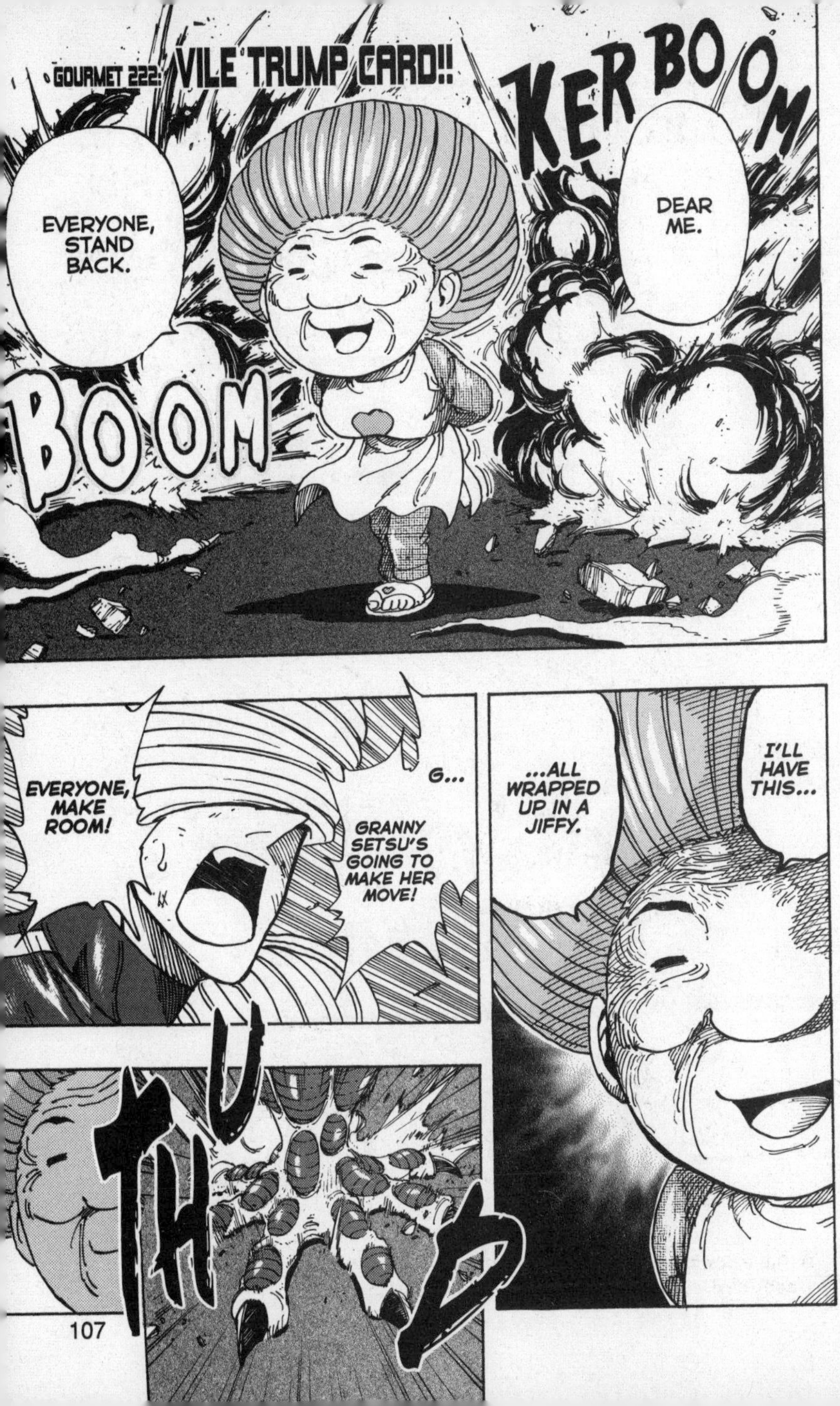
GOURMET 222: VILE TRUMP CARD!!
KERBOOM
DEAR ME.
EVERYONE, STAND BACK.
BOOM
I'LL HAVE THIS...
...ALL WRAPPED UP IN A JIFFY.
G...
GRANNY SETSU'S GOING TO MAKE HER MOVE!
EVERYONE, MAKE ROOM!
THUD

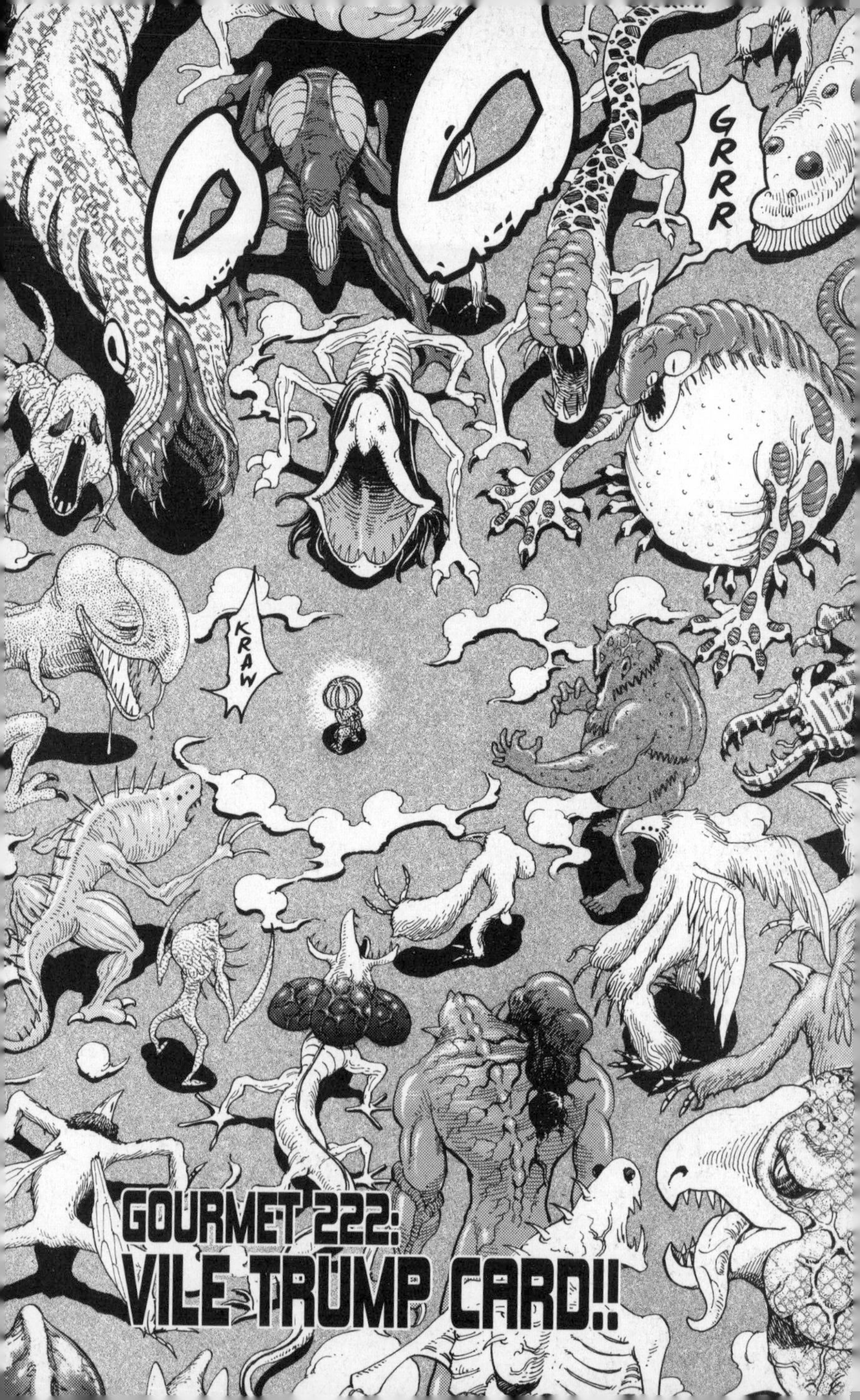
GRRR
KRAW
GOURMET 222:
VILE TRUMP CARD!!

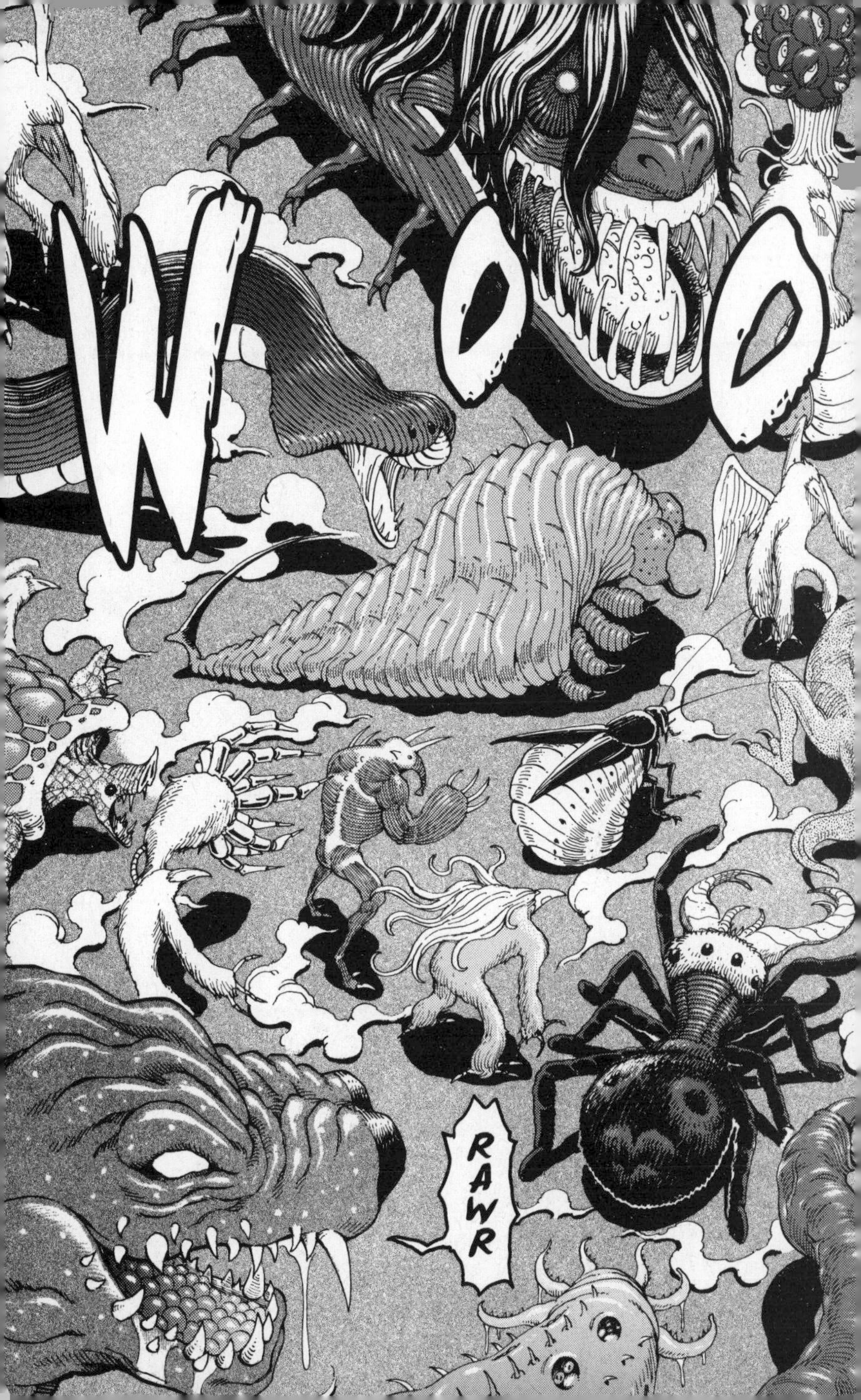
WOOO
RAWR

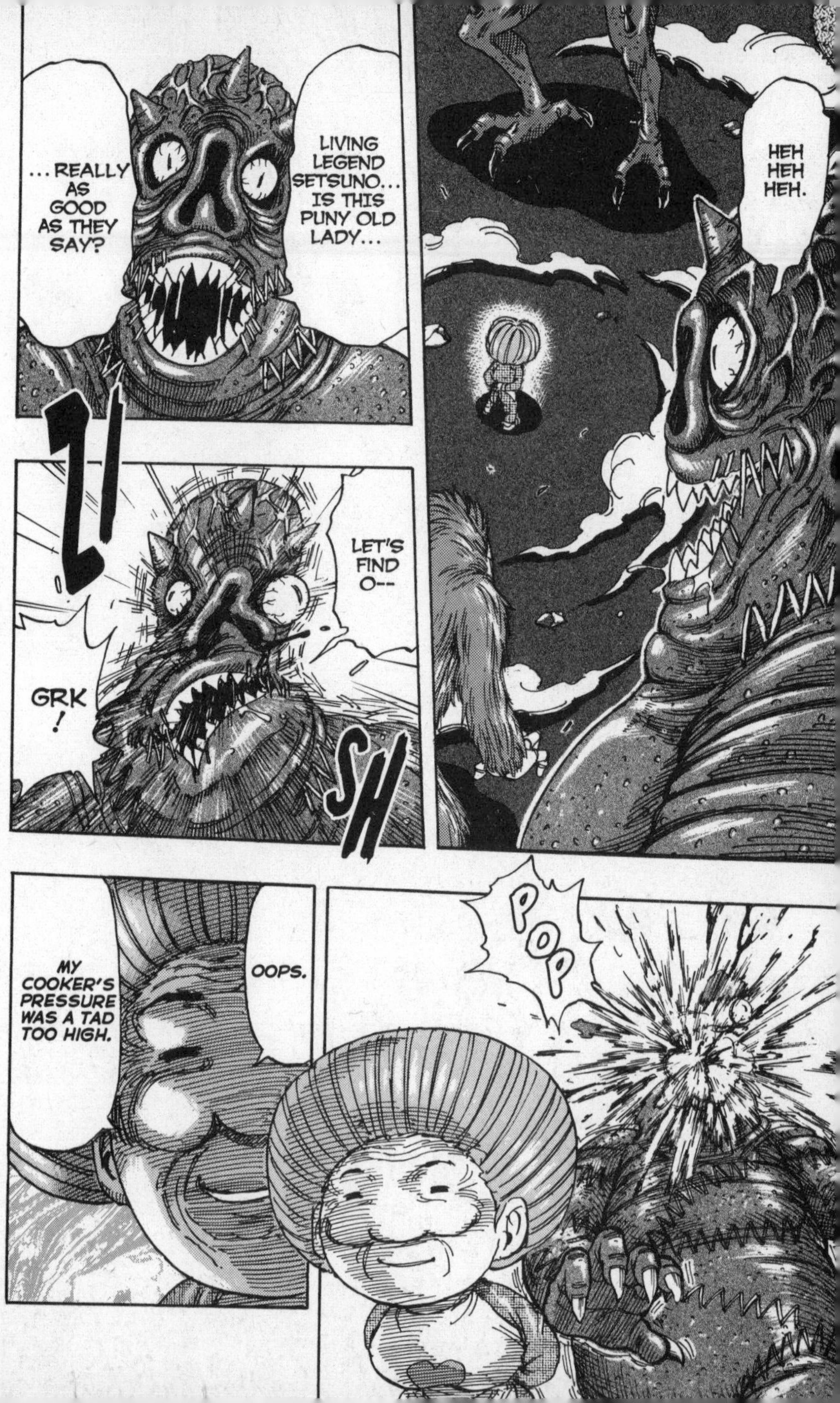
HEH HEH HEH.
LIVING LEGEND SETSUNO... IS THIS PUNY OLD LADY...
...REALLY AS GOOD AS THEY SAY?
LET'S FIND O--
GRK!
SH
POP
OOPS.
MY COOKER'S PRESSURE WAS A TAD TOO HIGH.

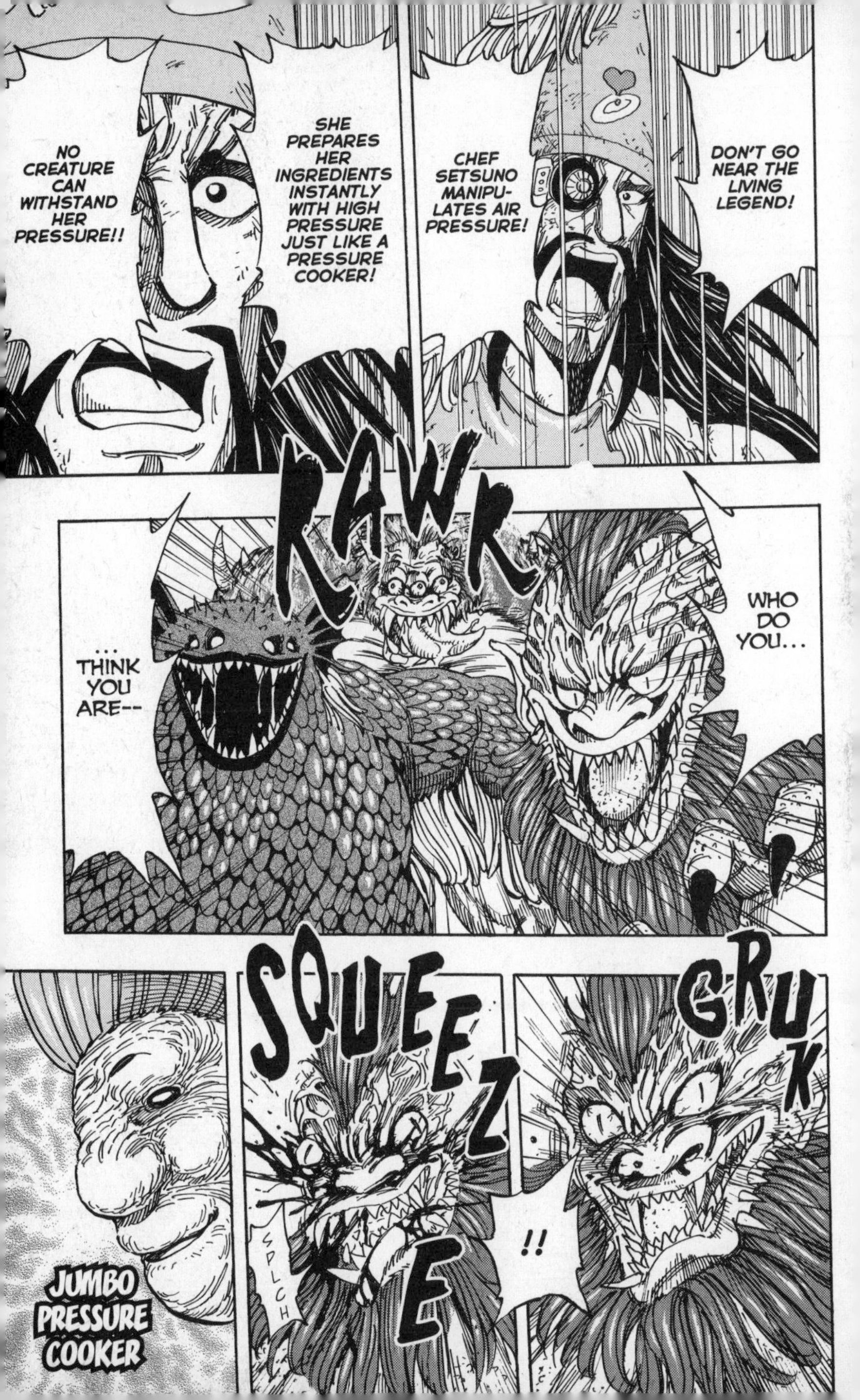
DON'T GO NEAR THE LIVING LEGEND!
CHEF SETSUNO MANIPU-LATES AIR PRESSURE!
SHE PREPARES HER INGREDIENTS INSTANTLY WITH HIGH PRESSURE JUST LIKE A PRESSURE COOKER!
NO CREATURE CAN WITHSTAND HER PRESSURE!!
RAWR
WHO DO YOU...
...THINK YOU ARE--
GRUK
!!
SQUEEZE
SPLCH
JUMBO PRESSURE COOKER

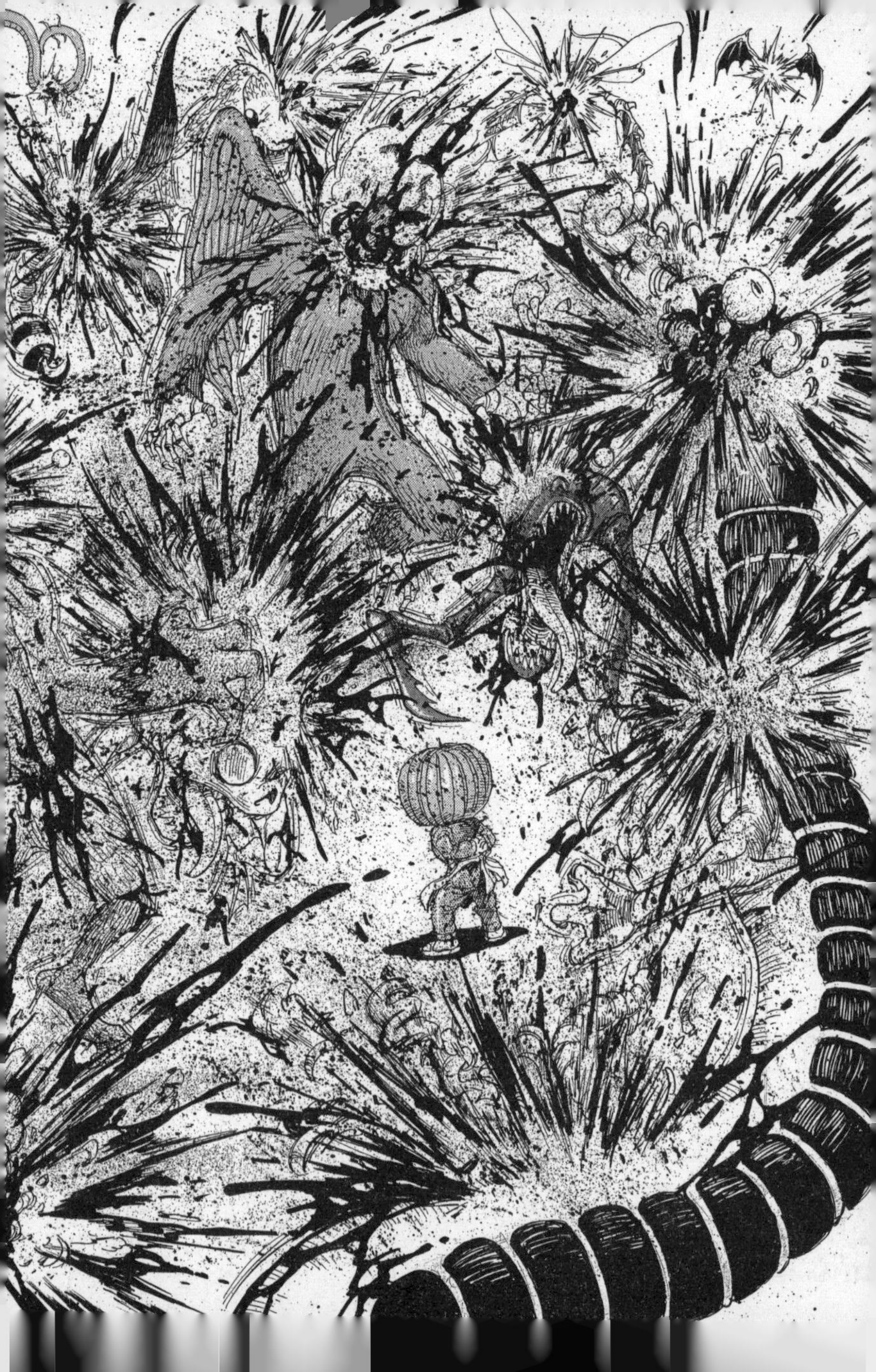

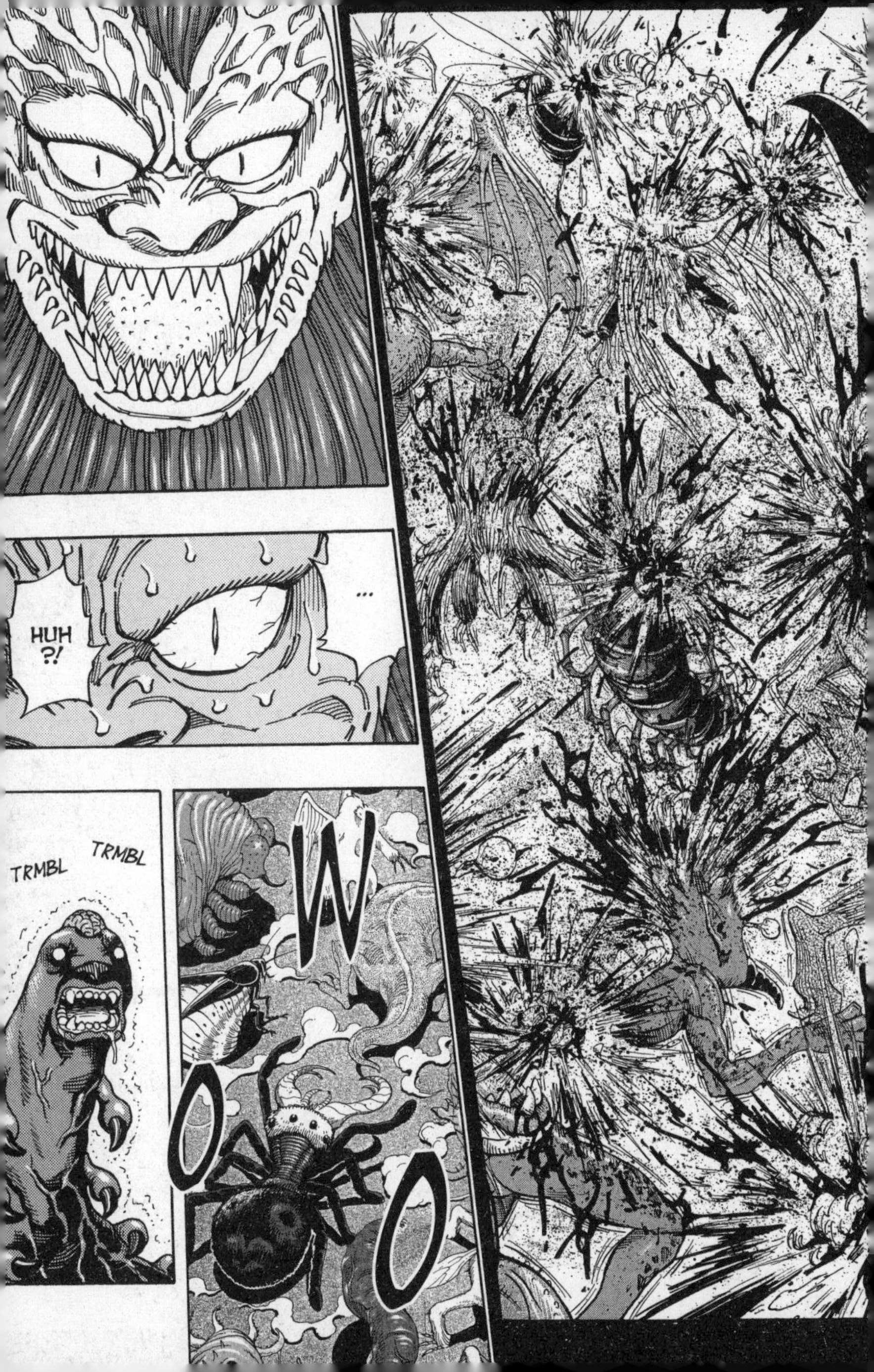
...
HUH ?!
WOOO
TRMBL
TRMBL

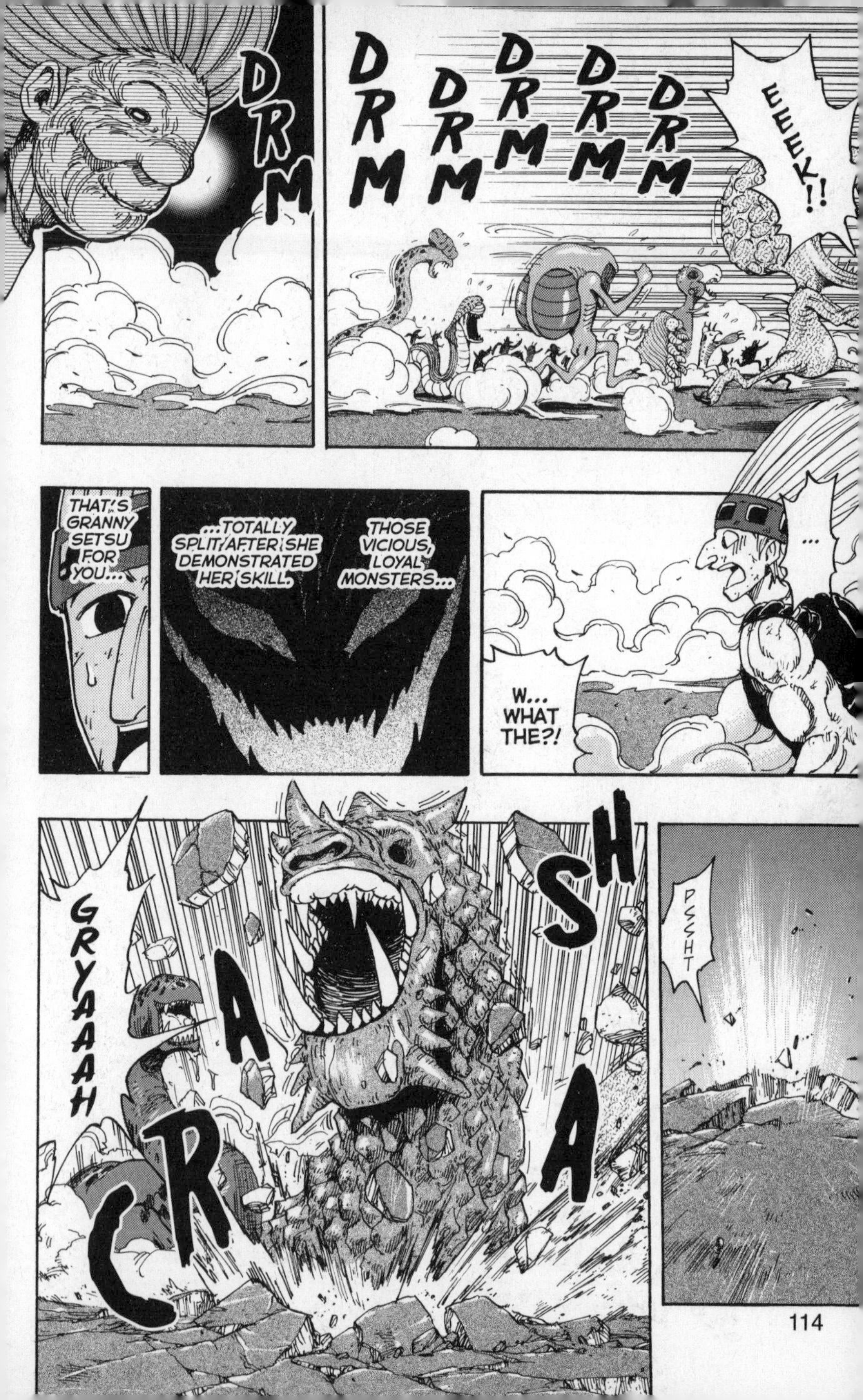
EEEEK!!
DRM DRM DRM DRM DRM
DRM
...
W... WHAT THE?!
THOSE VICIOUS, LOYAL MONSTERS...
...TOTALLY SPLIT AFTER SHE DEMONSTRATED HER SKILL.
THAT'S GRANNY SETSU FOR YOU...
PSSHT
SH
CRAAA
GRYAAAAH

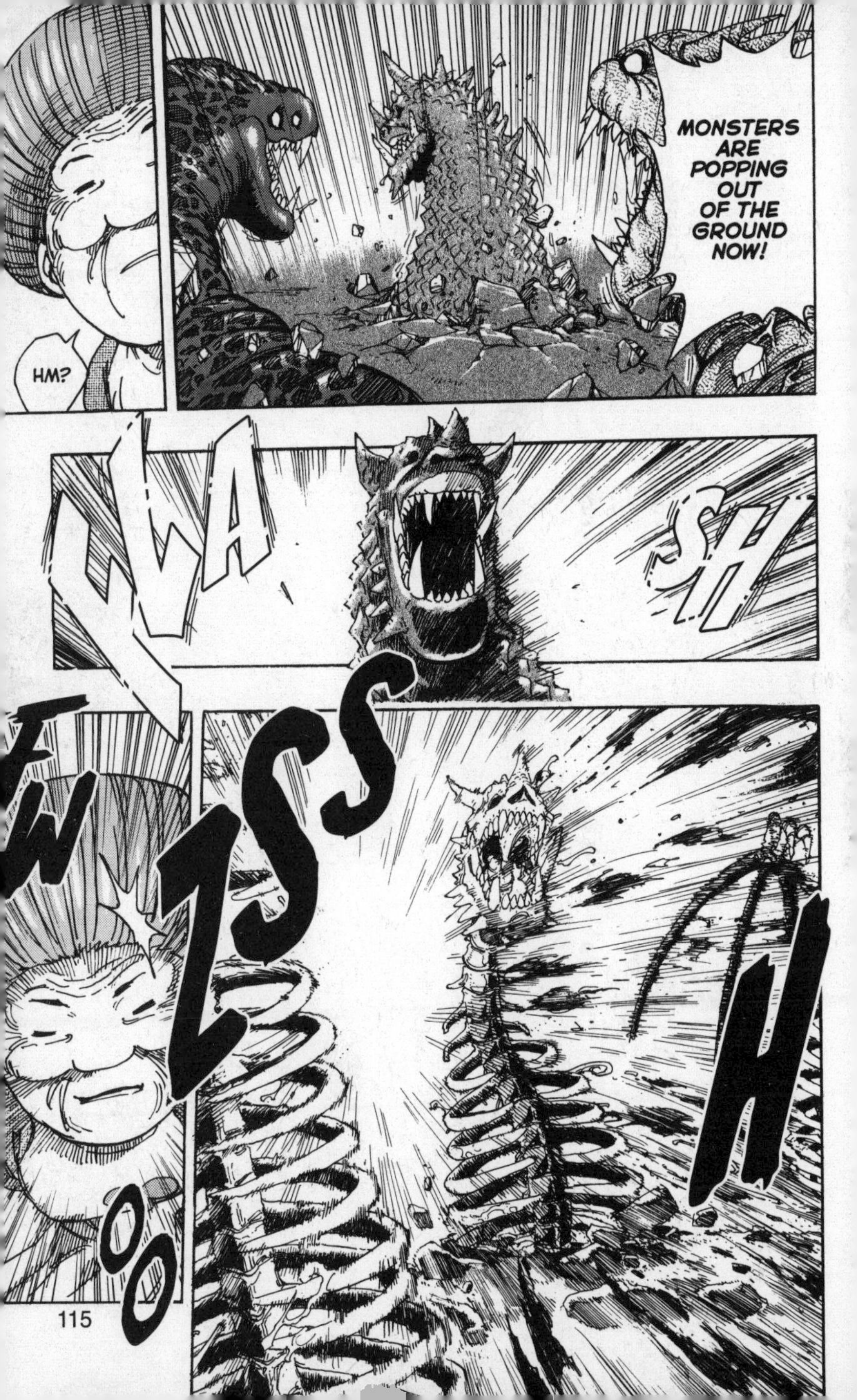
MONSTERS ARE POPPING OUT OF THE GROUND NOW!
HM?
CLASH
ZSSH

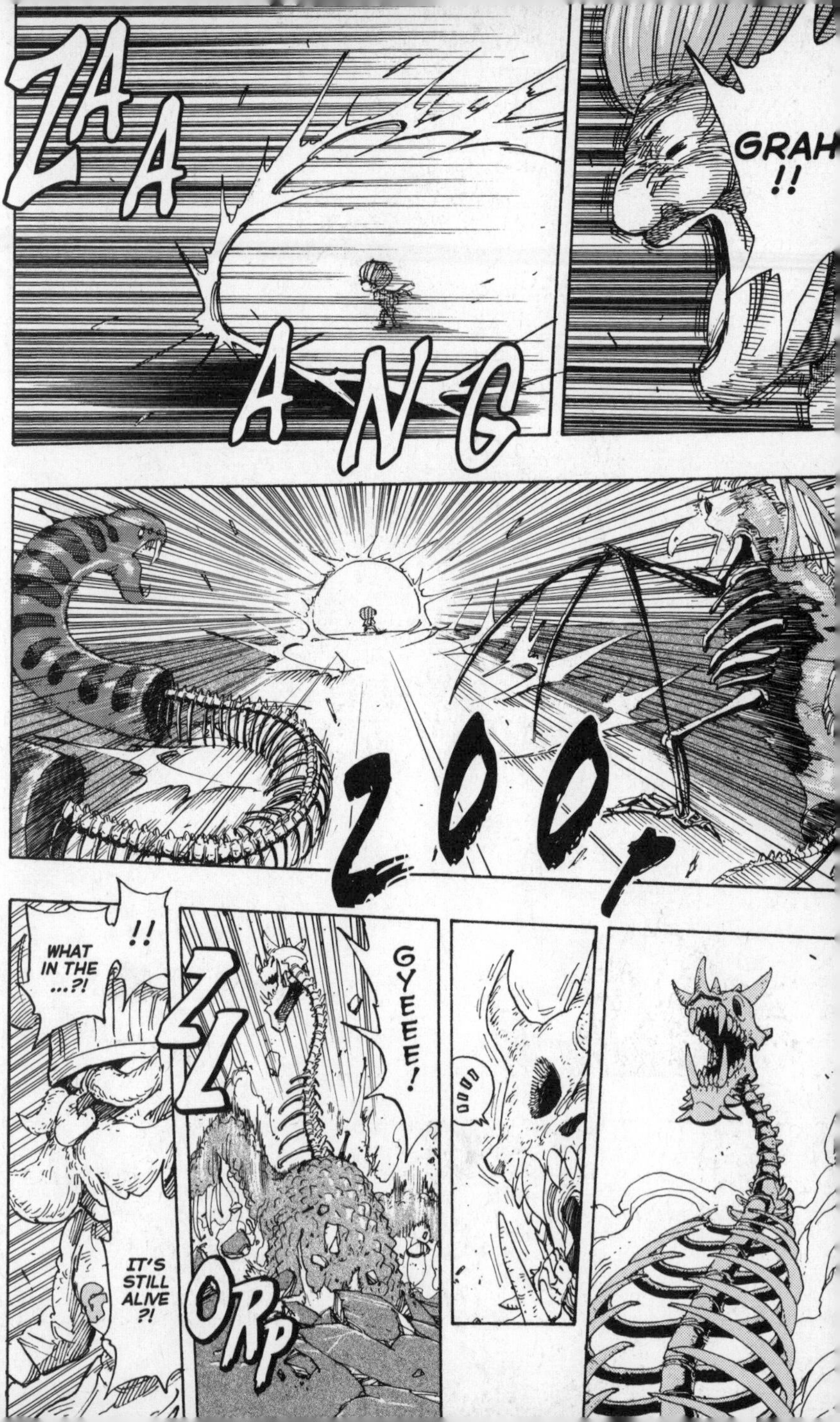
GRAH !!
ZAAANG
GYEEE!
ZZORP
!!
WHAT IN THE ...?!
IT'S STILL ALIVE ?!

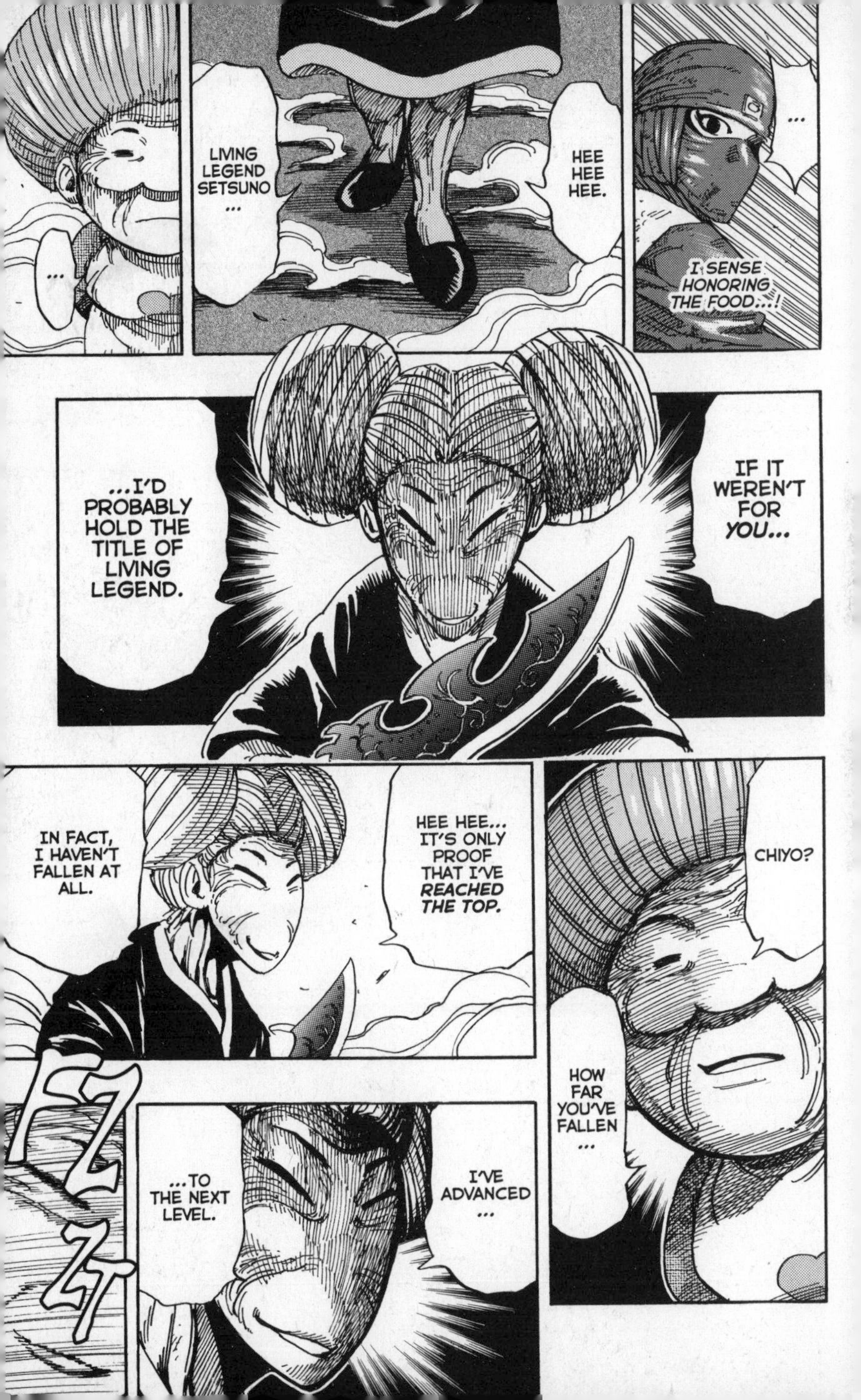
...
I SENSE HONORING THE FOOD...!
HEE HEE HEE.
LIVING LEGEND SETSUNO ...
...
IF IT WEREN'T FOR YOU...
...I'D PROBABLY HOLD THE TITLE OF LIVING LEGEND.
CHIYO?
HOW FAR YOU'VE FALLEN ...
HEE HEE... IT'S ONLY PROOF THAT I'VE REACHED THE TOP.
IN FACT, I HAVEN'T FALLEN AT ALL.
I'VE ADVANCED ...
...TO THE NEXT LEVEL.
FZZZT

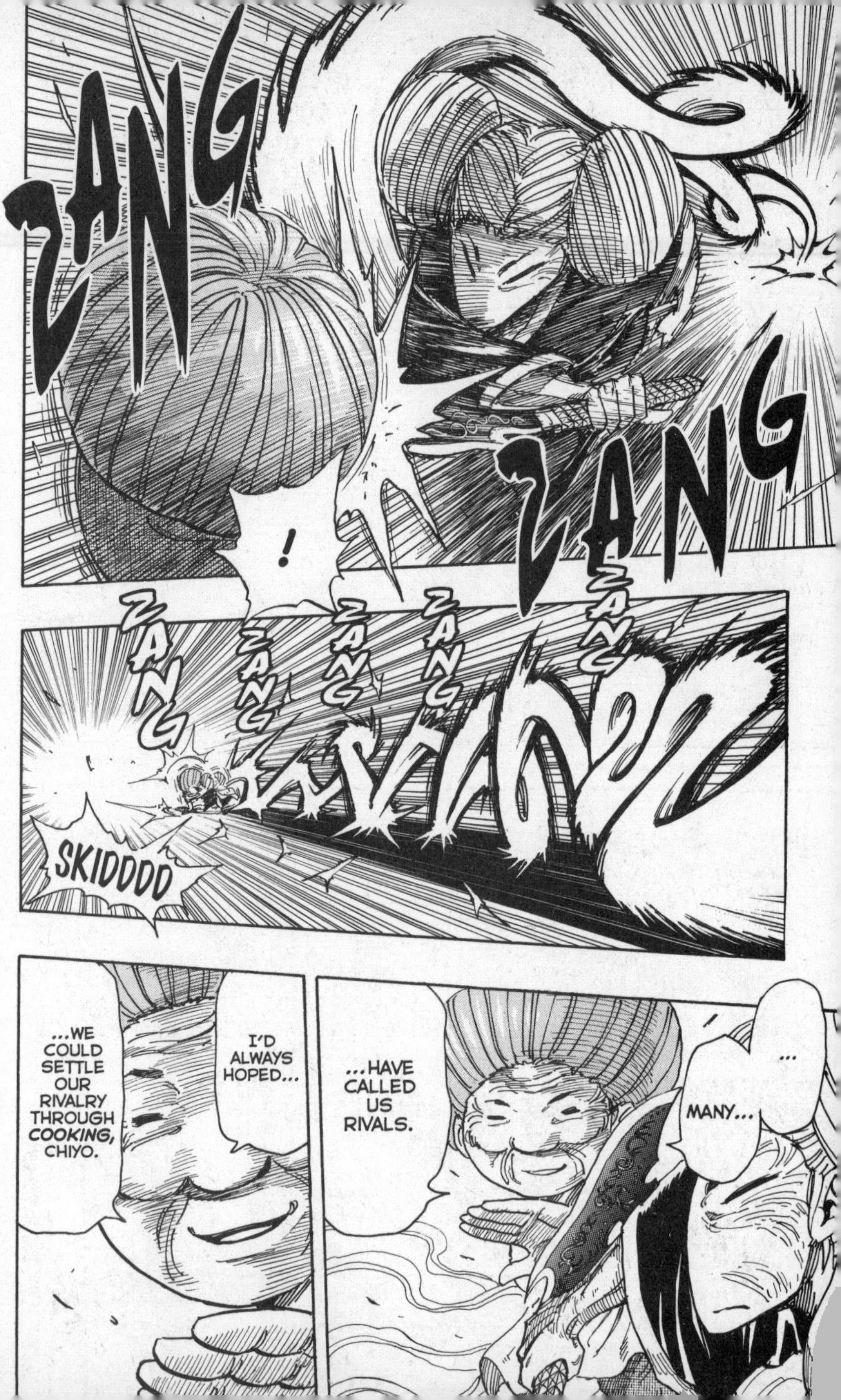
ZANG
ZANG
!
ZANG
ZANG
ZANG
ZANG
ZANG
SKIDDDD
...
MANY...
...HAVE CALLED US RIVALS.
I'D ALWAYS HOPED...
...WE COULD SETTLE OUR RIVALRY THROUGH *COOKING,* CHIYO.

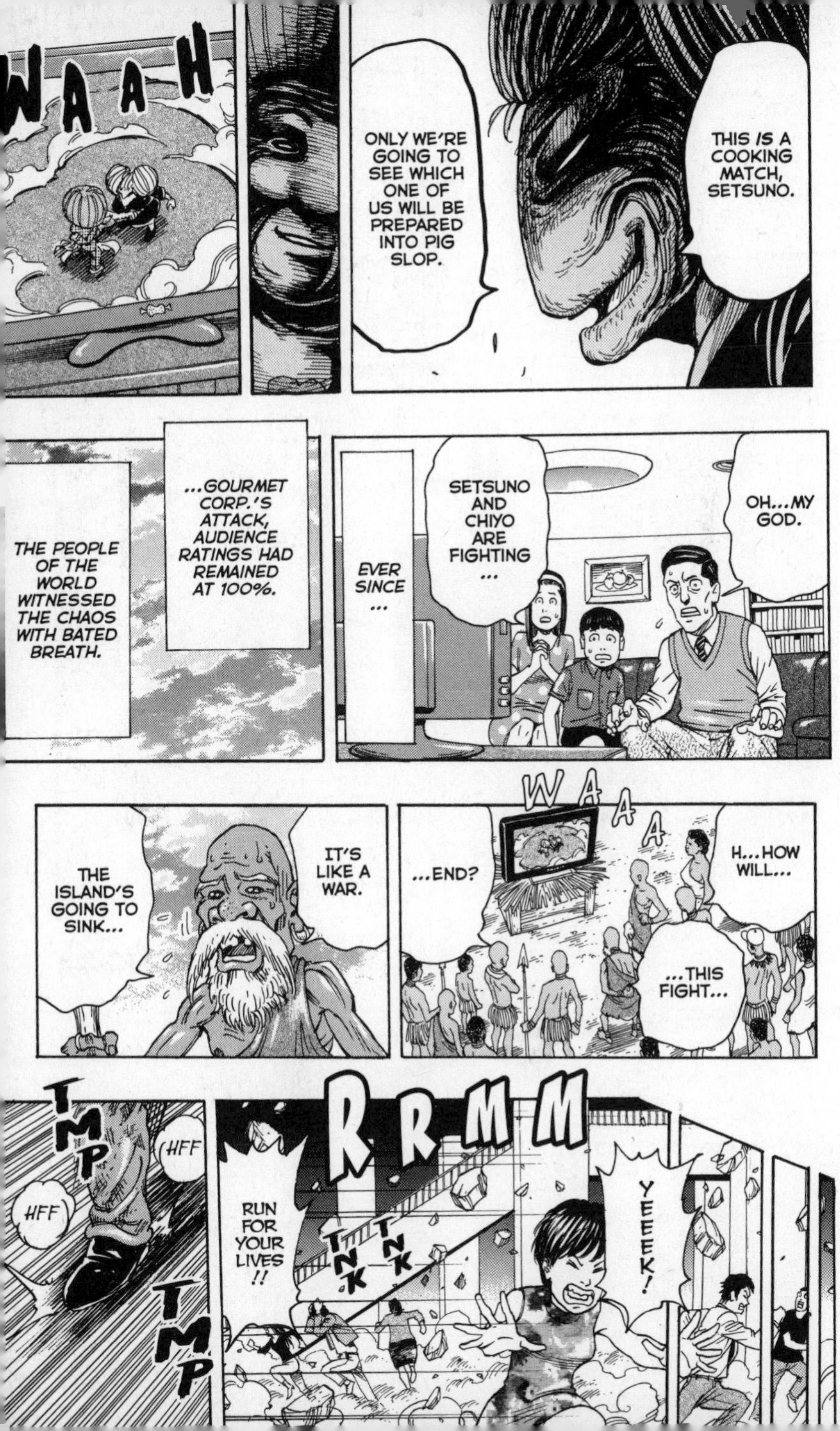
THIS IS A COOKING MATCH, SETSUNO.
ONLY WE'RE GOING TO SEE WHICH ONE OF US WILL BE PREPARED INTO PIG SLOP.
WAAH
OH...MY GOD.
SETSUNO AND CHIYO ARE FIGHTING...
EVER SINCE...
...GOURMET CORP.'S ATTACK, AUDIENCE RATINGS HAD REMAINED AT 100%.
THE PEOPLE OF THE WORLD WITNESSED THE CHAOS WITH BATED BREATH.
WAAA
H...HOW WILL...
...THIS FIGHT...
...END?
IT'S LIKE A WAR.
THE ISLAND'S GOING TO SINK...
RRMM
YEEEK!
TNK
TNK
RUN FOR YOUR LIVES!!
TMP
HFF
HFF
TMP

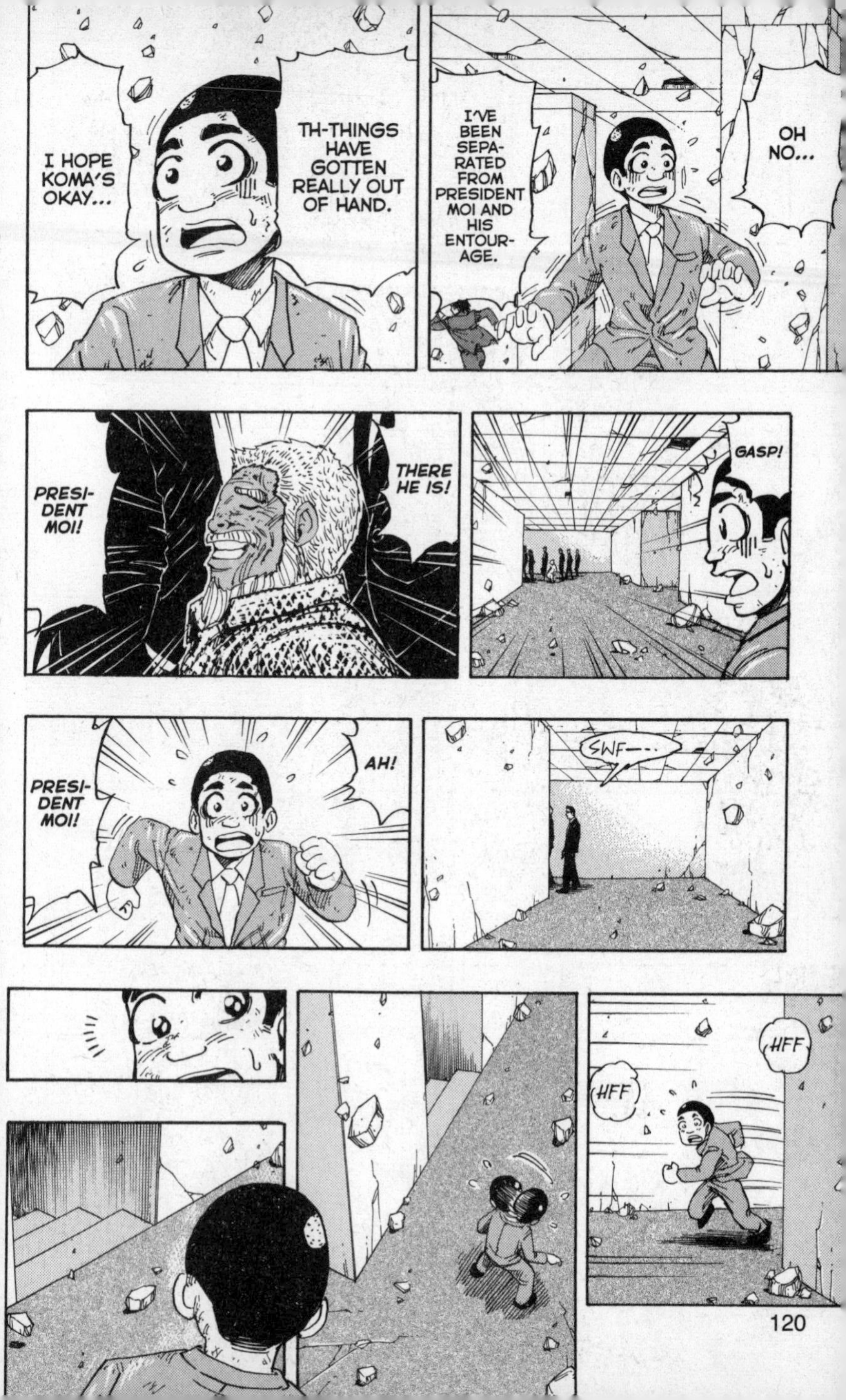
OH NO...
I'VE BEEN SEPARATED FROM PRESIDENT MOI AND HIS ENTOURAGE.
TH-THINGS HAVE GOTTEN REALLY OUT OF HAND.
I HOPE KOMA'S OKAY...
GASP!
THERE HE IS!
PRESIDENT MOI!
SWF—...
AH!
PRESIDENT MOI!
HFF
HFF

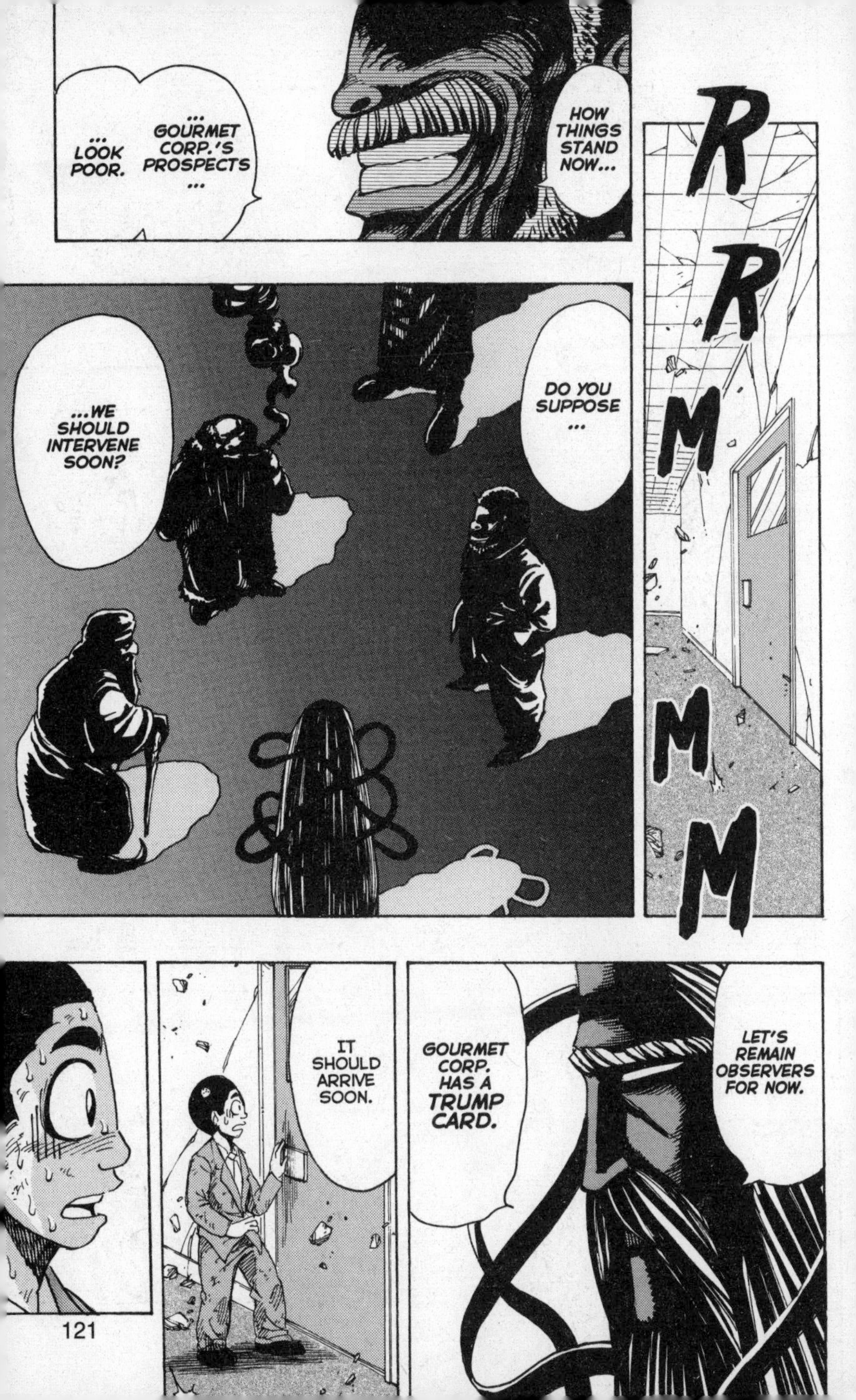
RRMMM
HOW THINGS STAND NOW...
... GOURMET CORP.'S PROSPECTS ...
... LOOK POOR.
DO YOU SUPPOSE ...
...WE SHOULD INTERVENE SOON?
LET'S REMAIN OBSERVERS FOR NOW.
GOURMET CORP. HAS A TRUMP CARD.
IT SHOULD ARRIVE SOON.

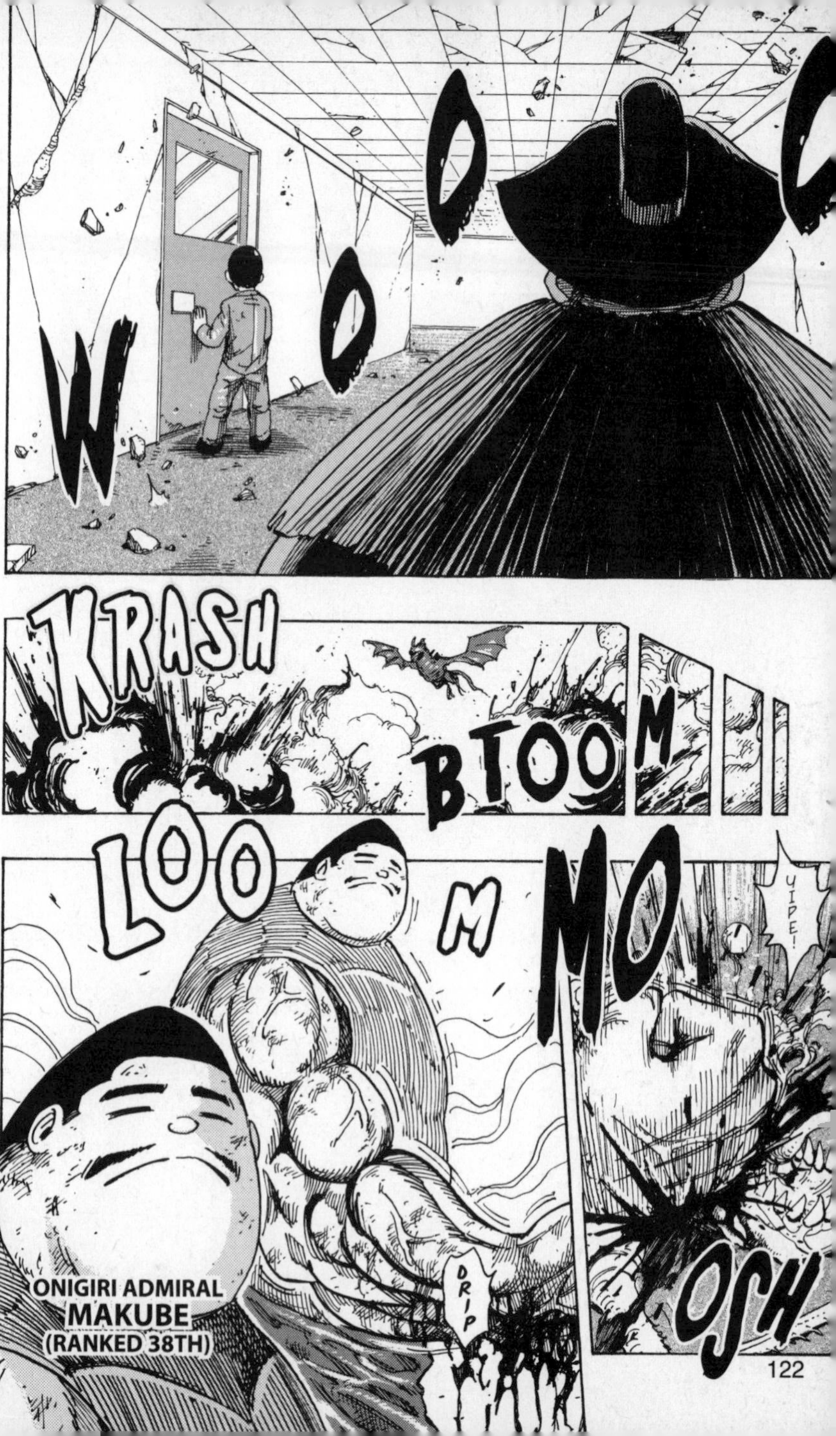
WOOOO
KRASH
BTOOM
YIPE!
MO
OSH
DRIP
LOOM
ONIGIRI ADMIRAL
MAKUBE
(RANKED 38TH)

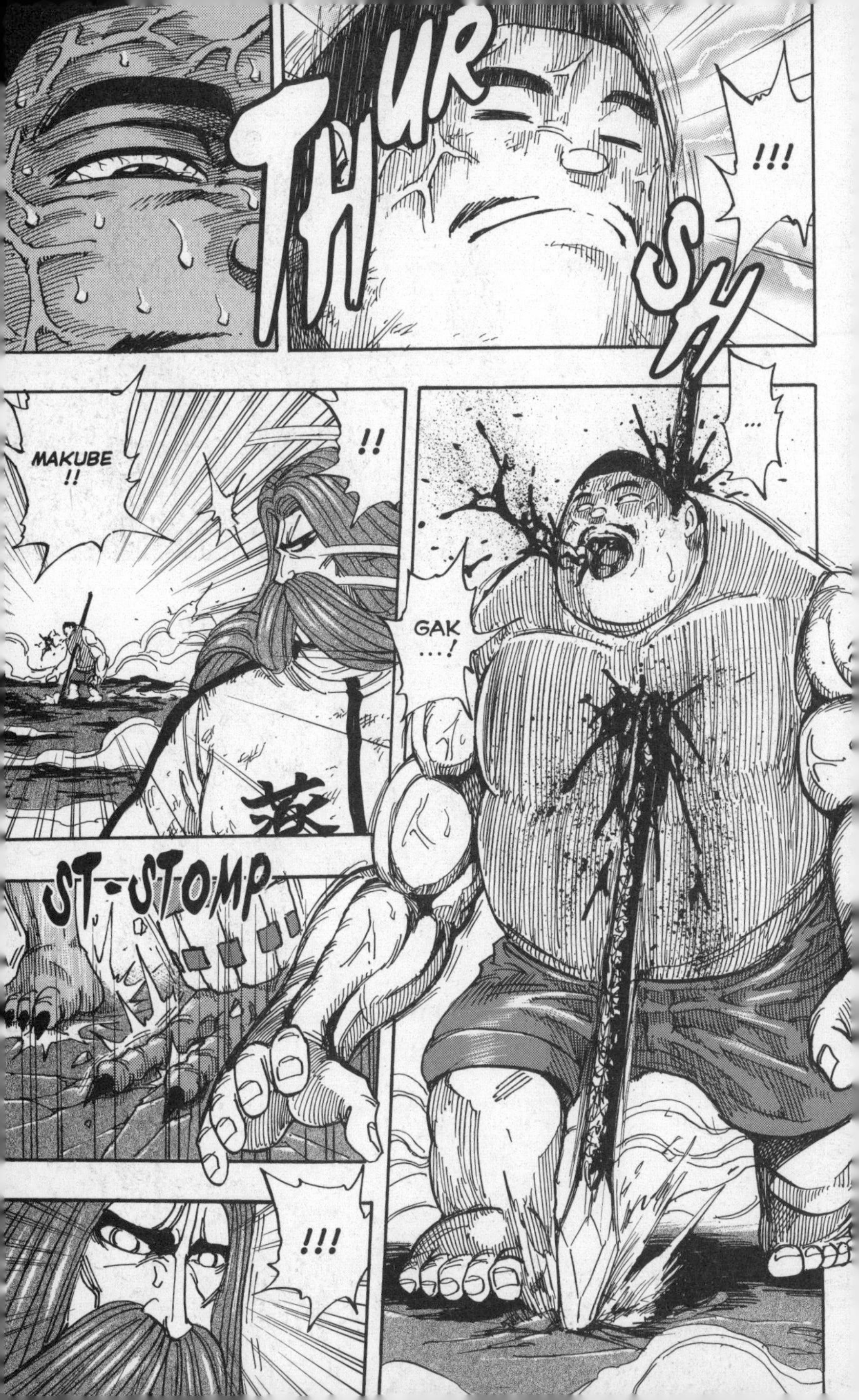
THURSH
!!!
...
GAK ...!
!!
MAKUBE !!
ST-STOMP
!!!

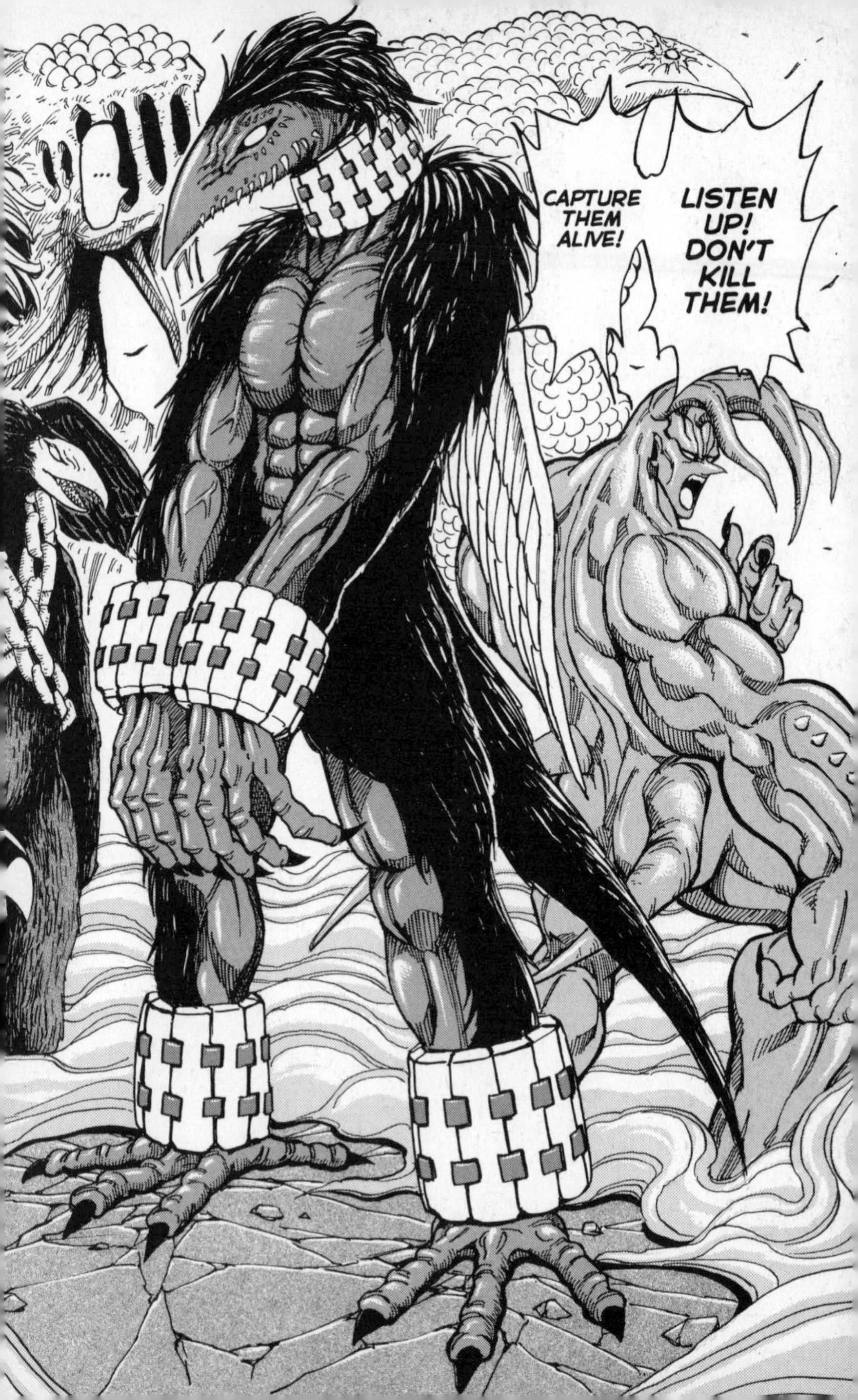
LISTEN UP! DON'T KILL THEM!
CAPTURE THEM ALIVE!
...

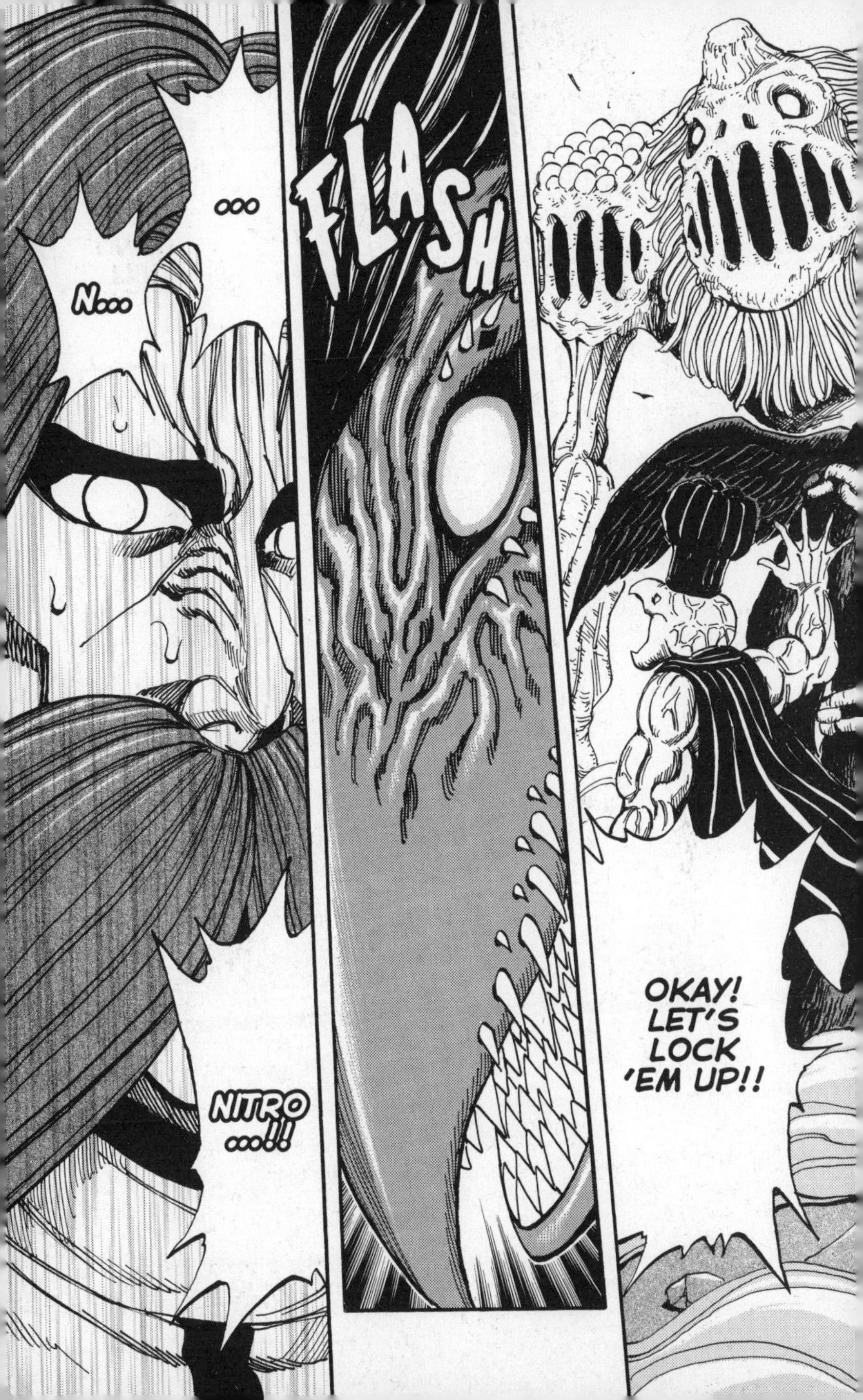

OKAY! LET'S LOCK 'EM UP!!
FLASH
...
N...
NITRO ...!!

TORIKO REJECT PAGES CORNER!!

(GOURMET 180)

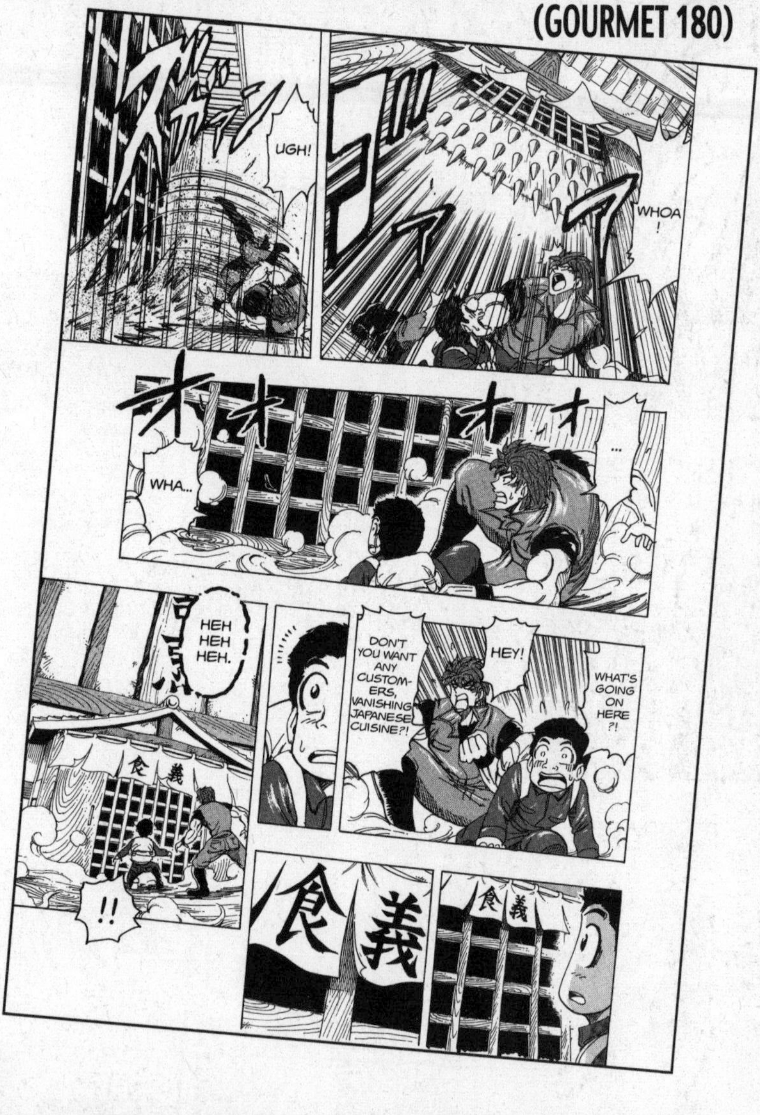
WHOA!
UGH!
...
WHA...
WHAT'S GOING ON HERE?!
HEY!
DON'T YOU WANT ANY CUSTOMERS, VANISHING JAPANESE CUISINE?!
HEH HEH HEH.
!!
食義

★It's one trap after another! Hmmm. I thought that'd be great, but it got rejected. Thing is, even I couldn't tell what was going on (even though I wrote it). I can't believe I wrote something without understanding it!

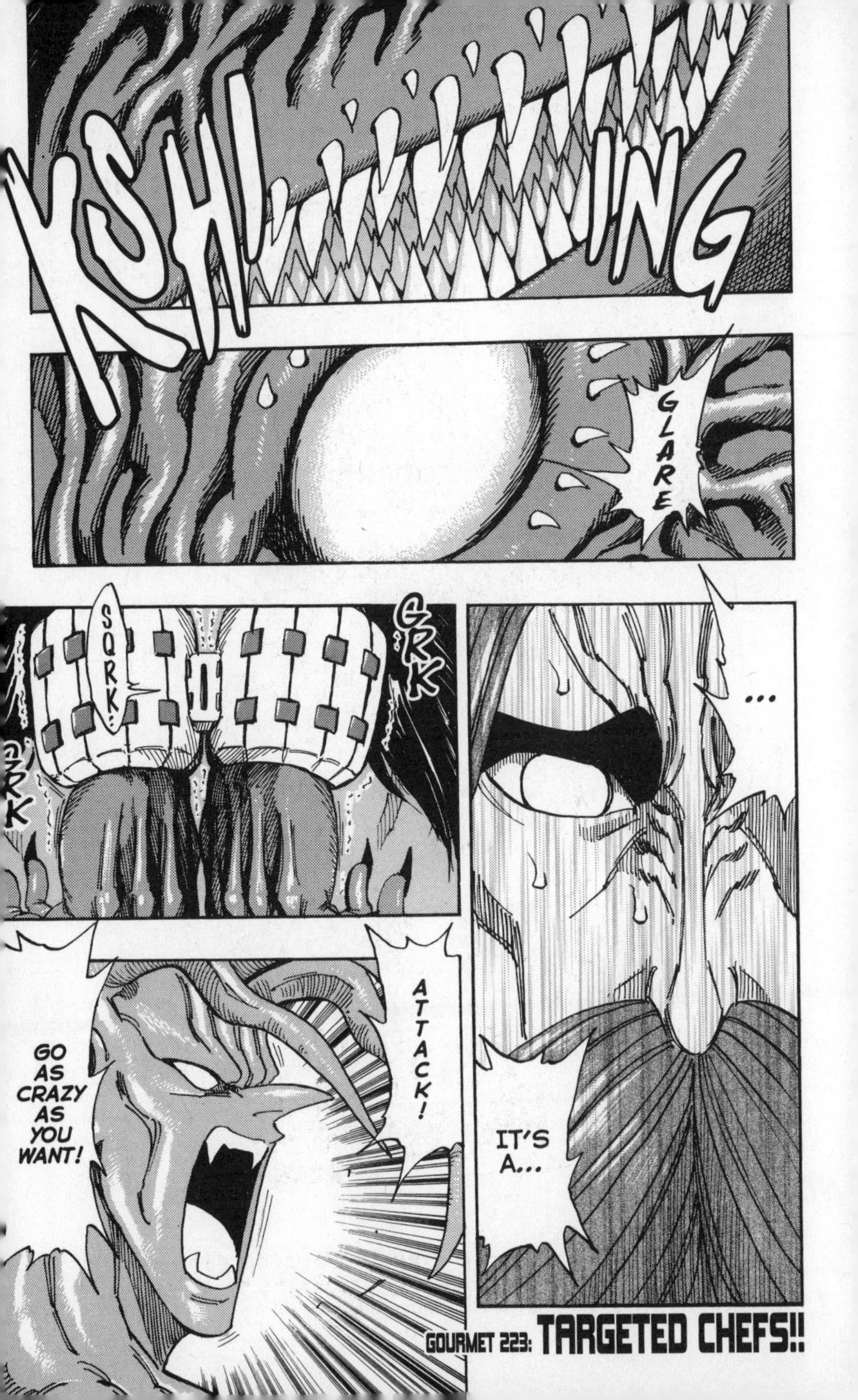
KSHI...ING
GLARE
...
IT'S A...
SQRK
GRK
GRK
ATTACK!
GO AS CRAZY AS YOU WANT!

GOURMET 223: TARGETED CHEFS!!

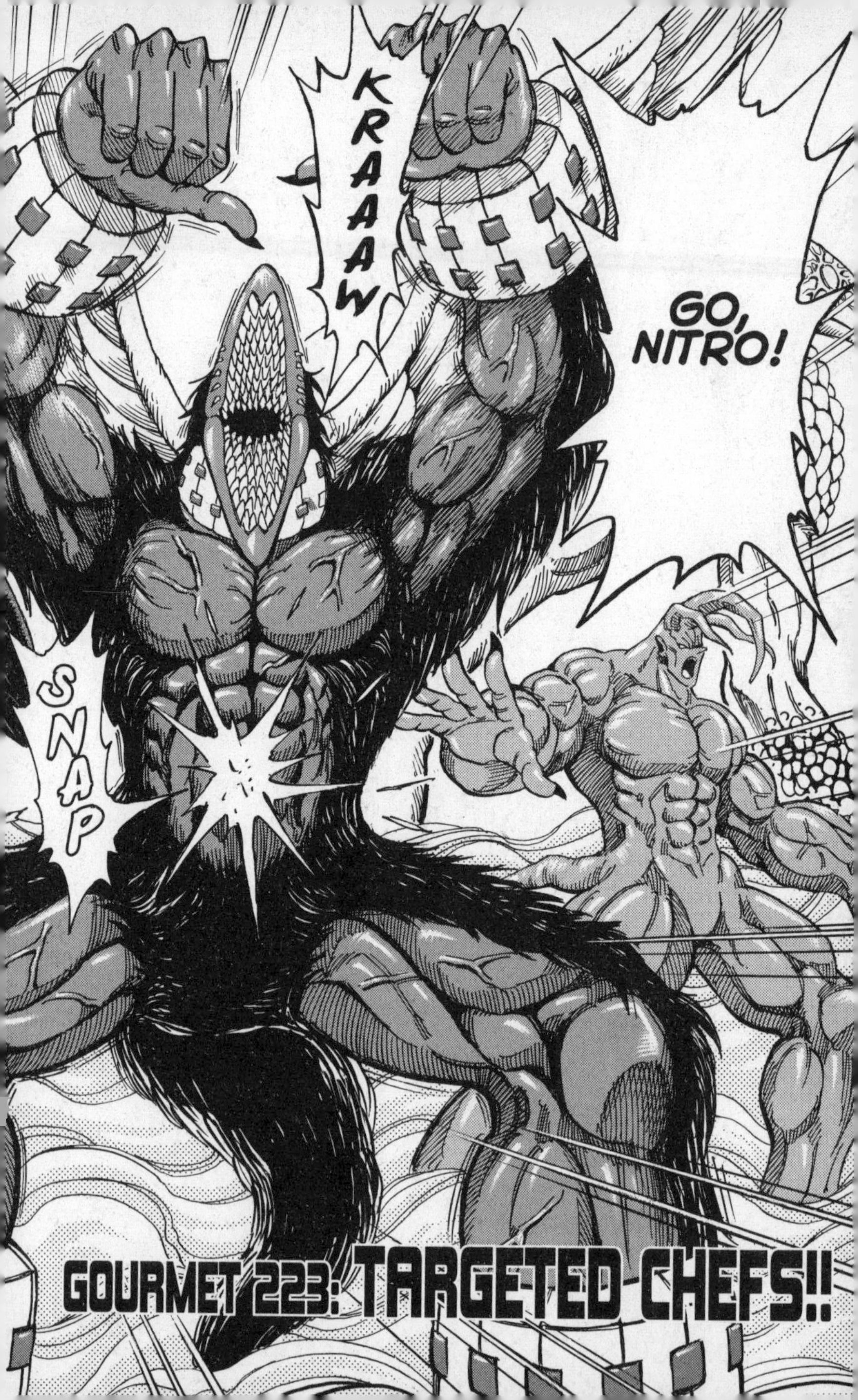
GO, NITRO!
KRAAAAW
SNAP
GOURMET 223: TARGETED CHEFS!!

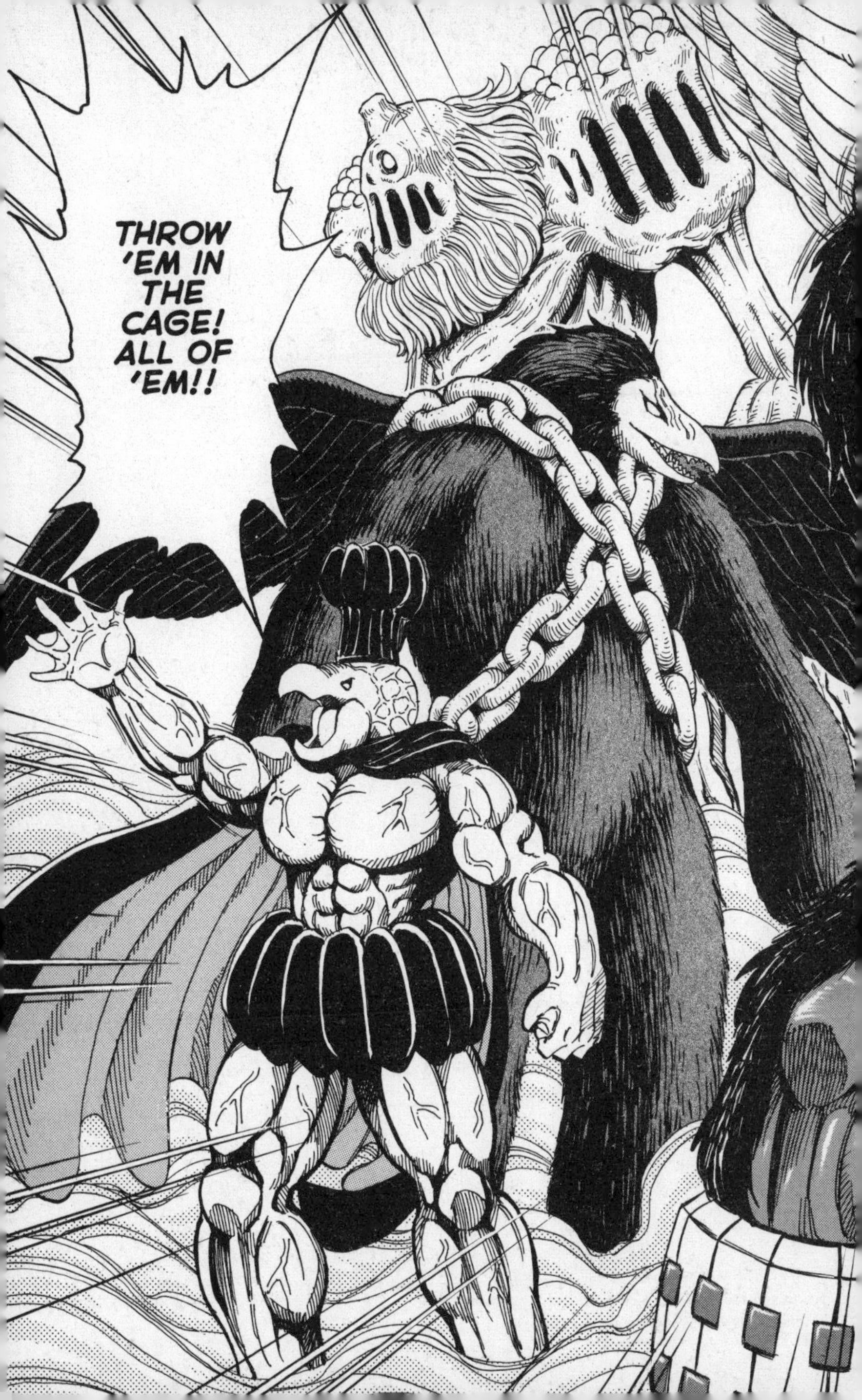
THROW 'EM IN THE CAGE! ALL OF 'EM!!

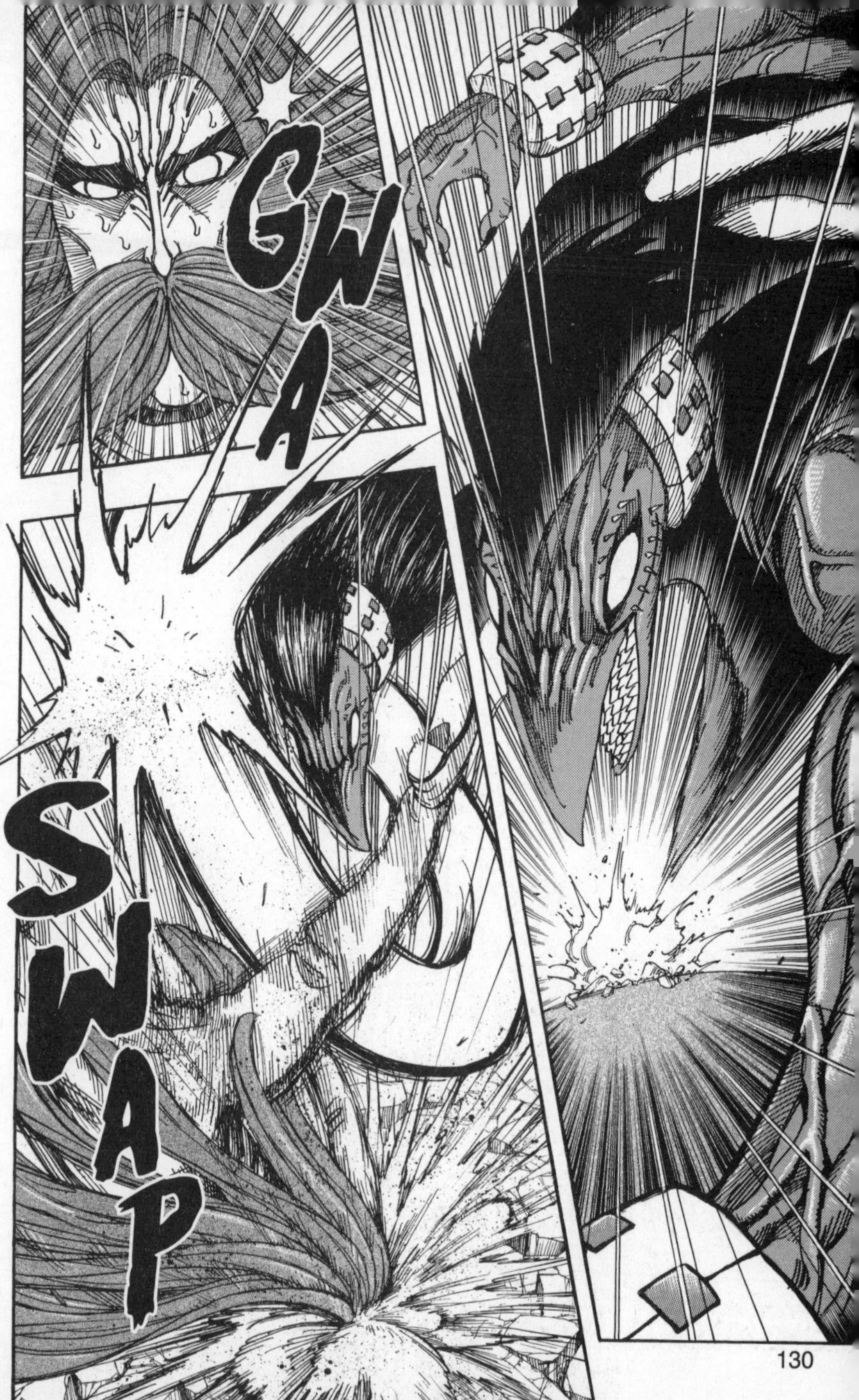
GWA
SWAP

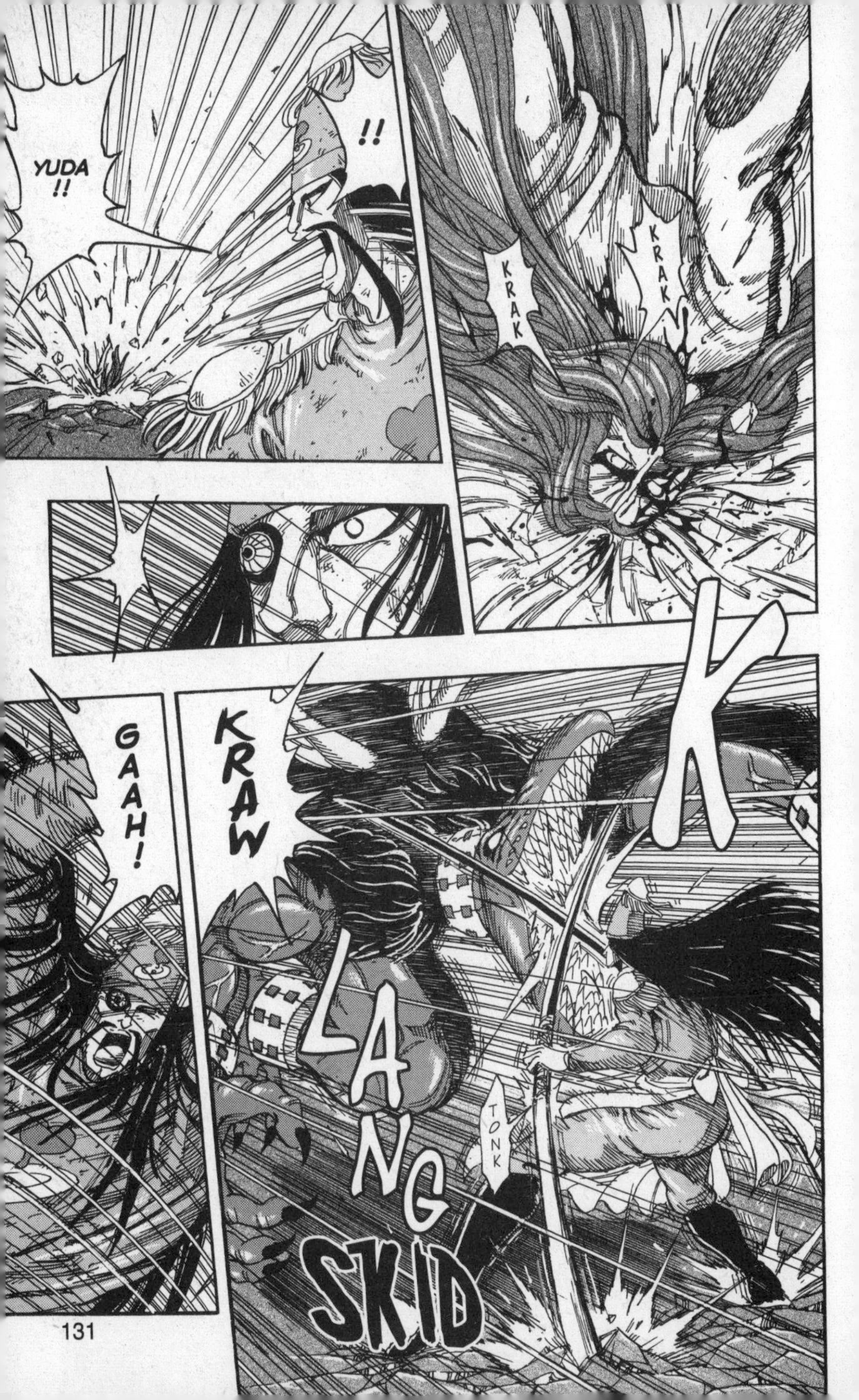
KRAK
KRAK
!!
YUDA !!
K
KRAW
LANG
TONK
SKID
GAAH!

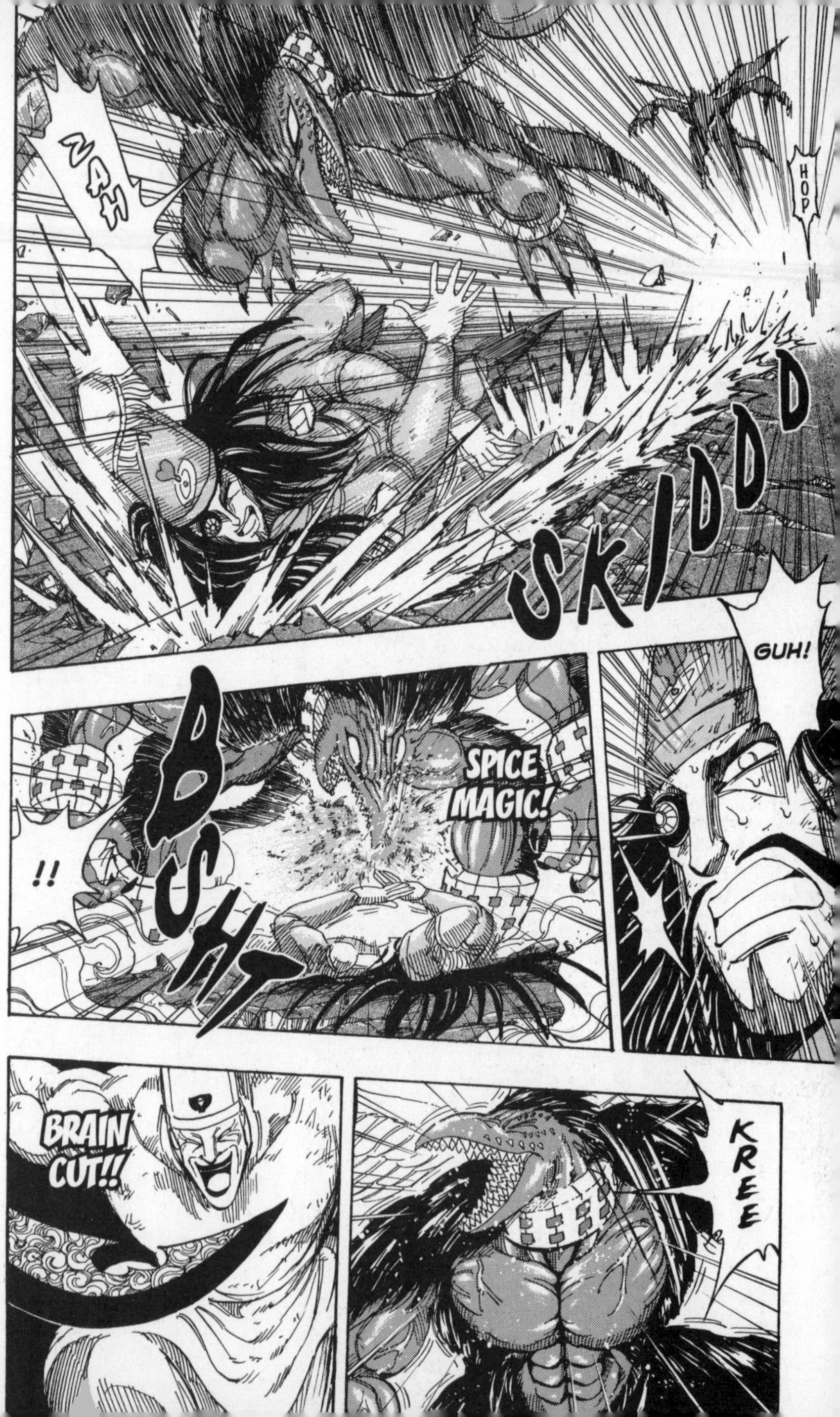
HOP
ZAH
SKIDDD
GUH!
SPICE MAGIC!
BSHT
!!
KREE
BRAIN CUT!!

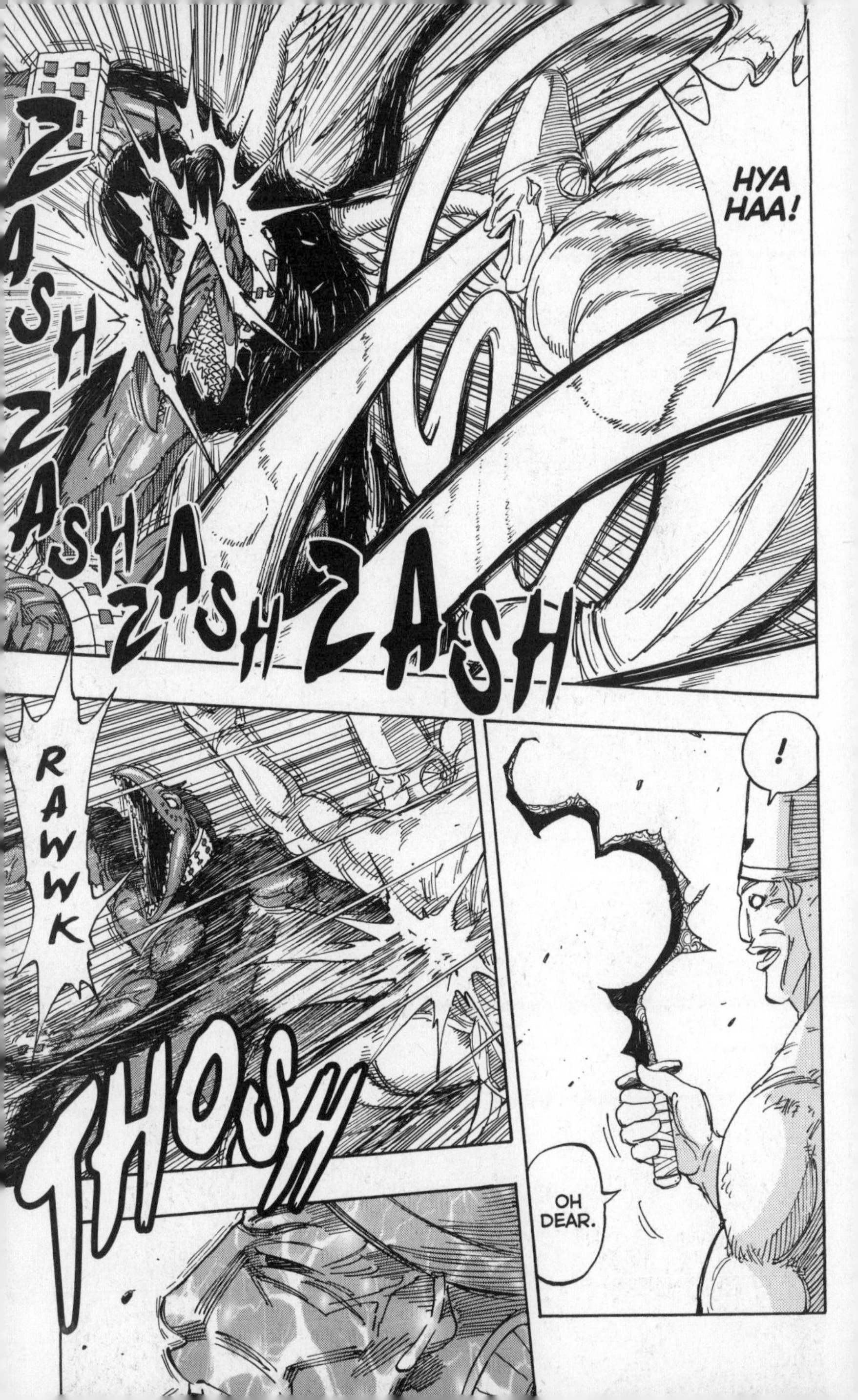
HYA HAA!
ZASH ZASH
ZASH ZASH
!
OH DEAR.
RAWWK
THOSH

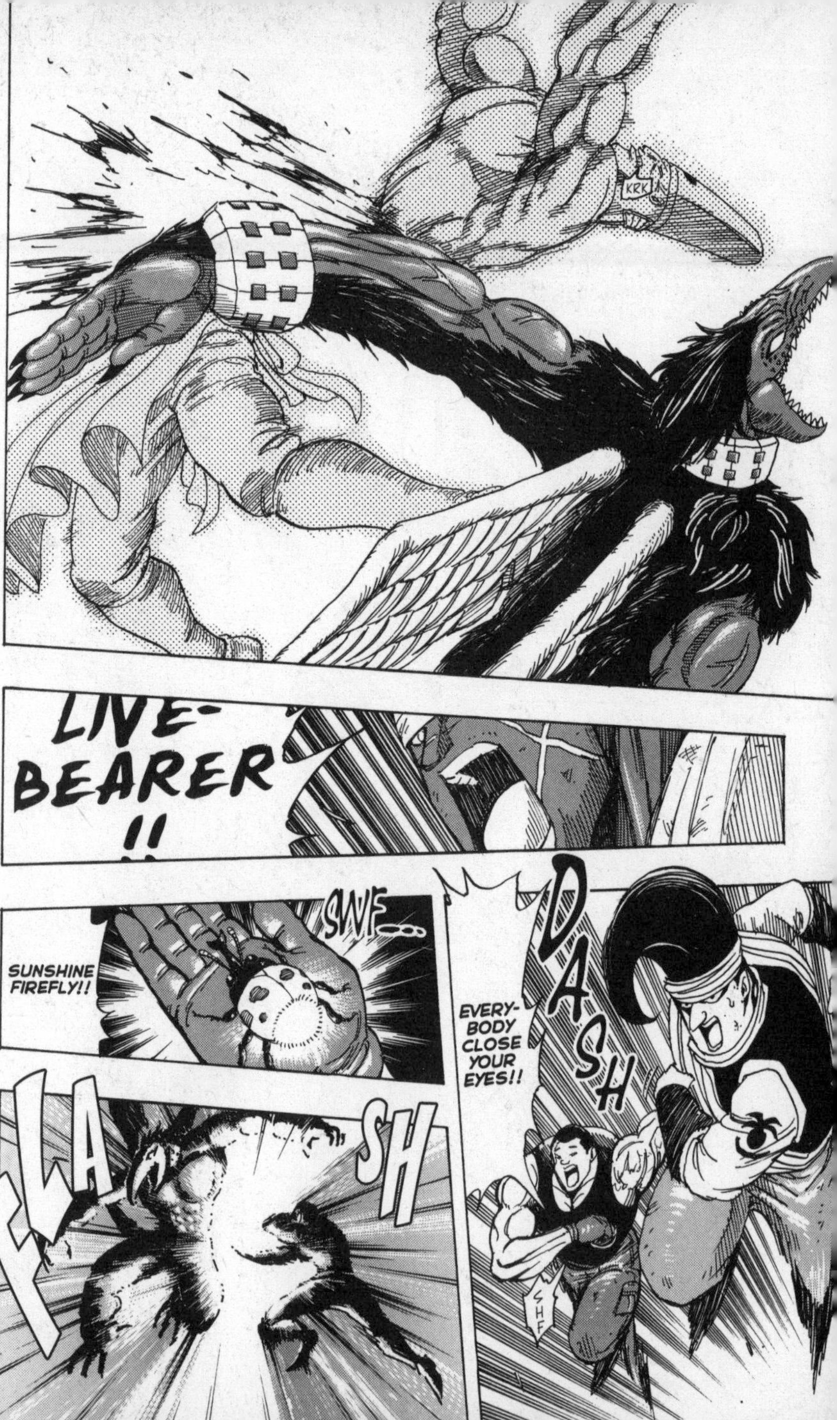
KRK
LIVE-BEARER!!
DASH
EVERY-BODY CLOSE YOUR EYES!!
SHF
SWF...
SUNSHINE FIREFLY!!
FLASH

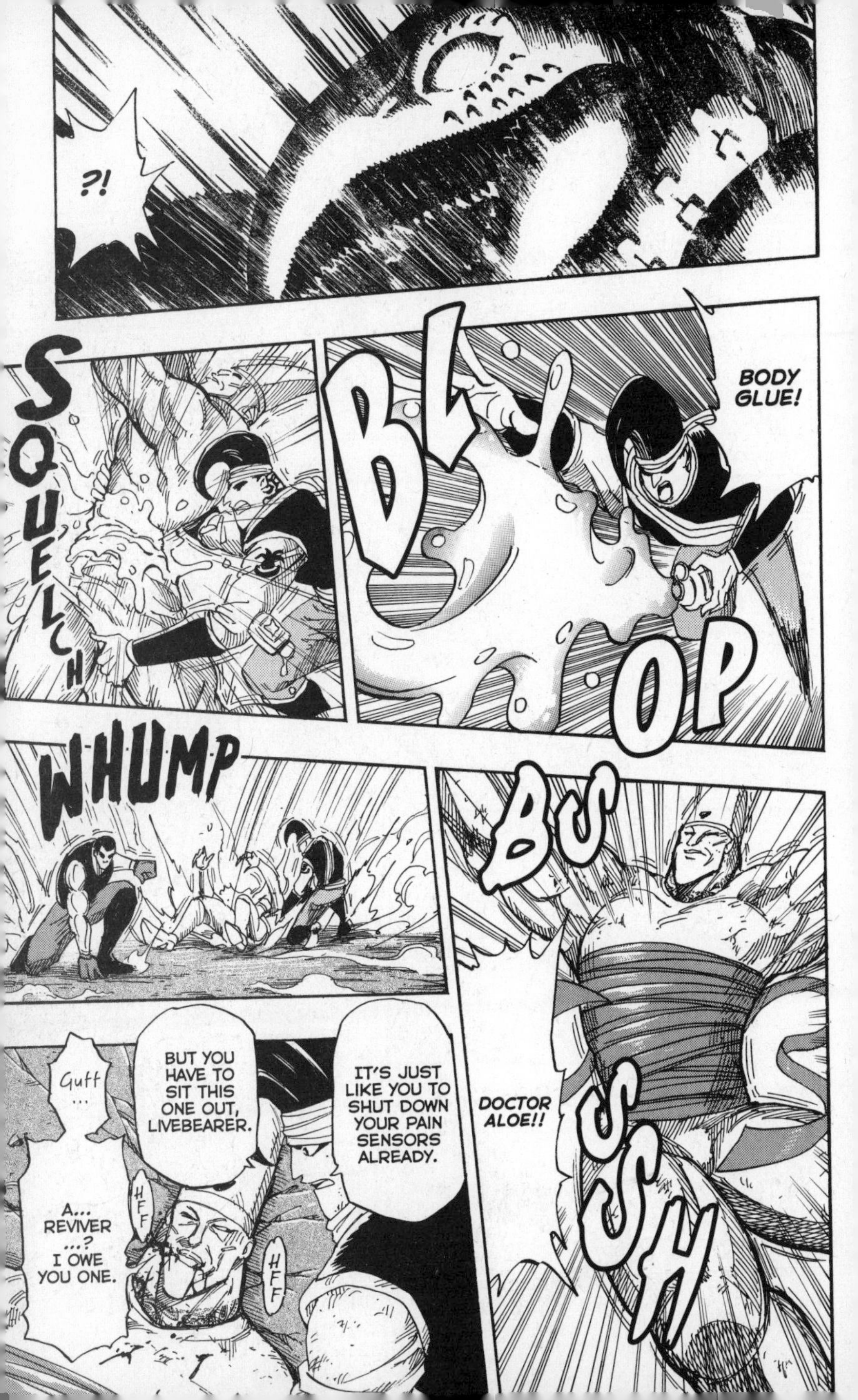
?!
BODY GLUE!
BLOP
SQUELCH
BUSSH
DOCTOR ALOE!!
WHUMP
IT'S JUST LIKE YOU TO SHUT DOWN YOUR PAIN SENSORS ALREADY.
BUT YOU HAVE TO SIT THIS ONE OUT, LIVEBEARER.
Guff ...
HFF
HFF
A... REVIVER ...? I OWE YOU ONE.

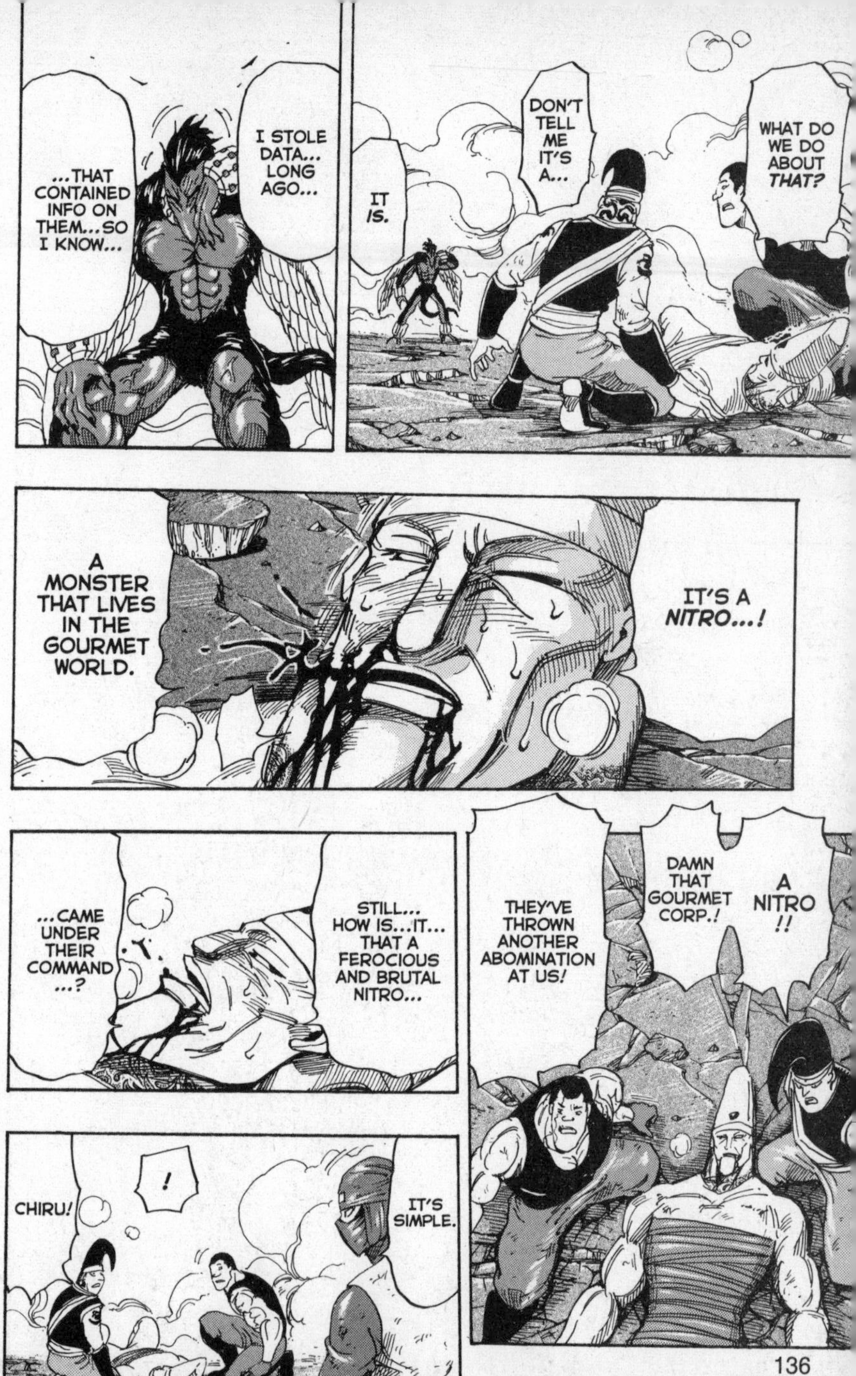
WHAT DO WE DO ABOUT THAT?
DON'T TELL ME IT'S A...
IT IS.
I STOLE DATA... LONG AGO...
...THAT CONTAINED INFO ON THEM...SO I KNOW...
IT'S A NITRO...!
A MONSTER THAT LIVES IN THE GOURMET WORLD.
A NITRO!!
DAMN THAT GOURMET CORP.!
THEY'VE THROWN ANOTHER ABOMINATION AT US!
STILL... HOW IS...IT... THAT A FEROCIOUS AND BRUTAL NITRO...
...CAME UNDER THEIR COMMAND...?
IT'S SIMPLE.
!
CHIRU!

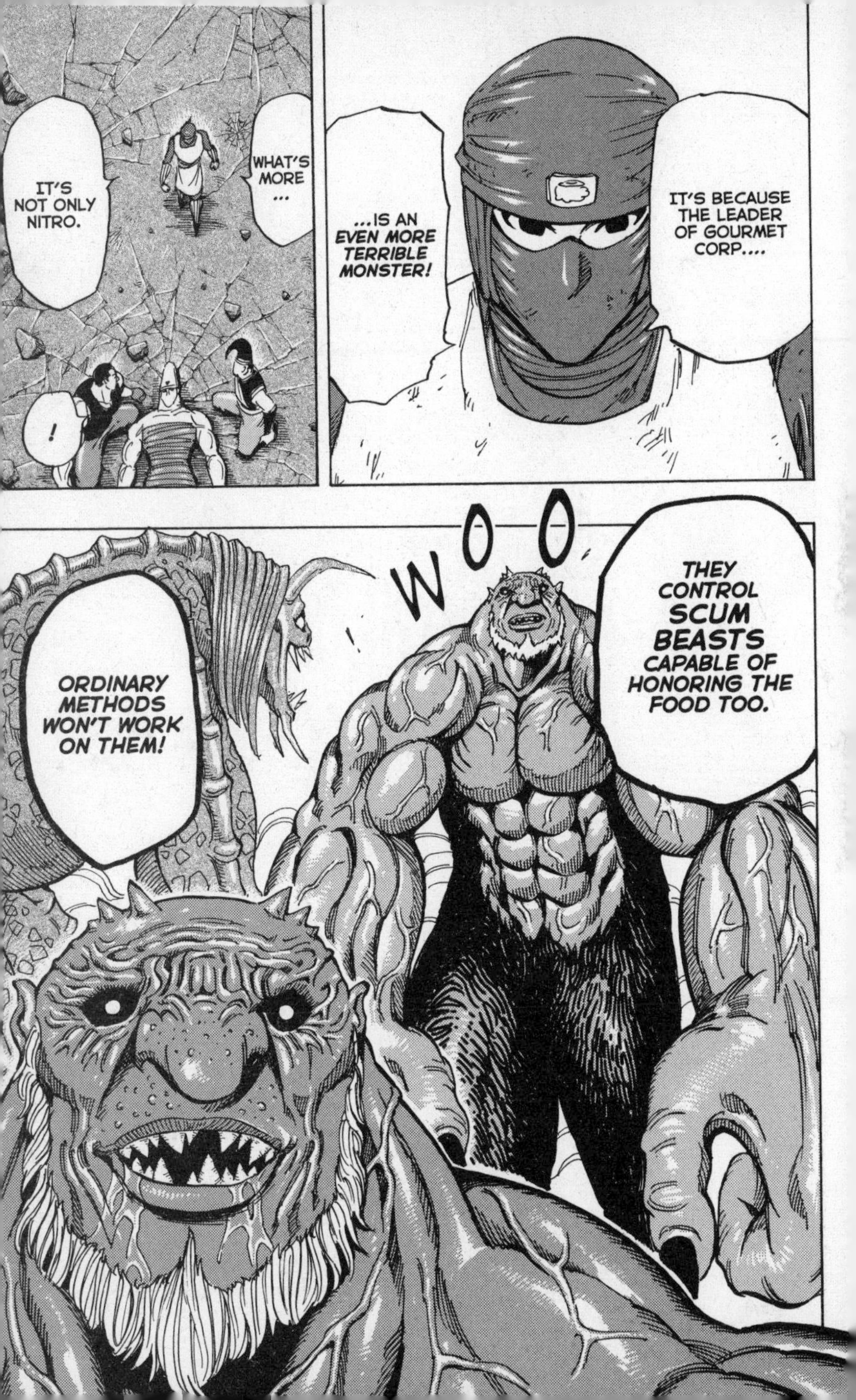
IT'S BECAUSE THE LEADER OF GOURMET CORP....
...IS AN EVEN MORE TERRIBLE MONSTER!
WHAT'S MORE ...
IT'S NOT ONLY NITRO.
!
THEY CONTROL SCUM BEASTS CAPABLE OF HONORING THE FOOD TOO.
WOO
!
ORDINARY METHODS WON'T WORK ON THEM!

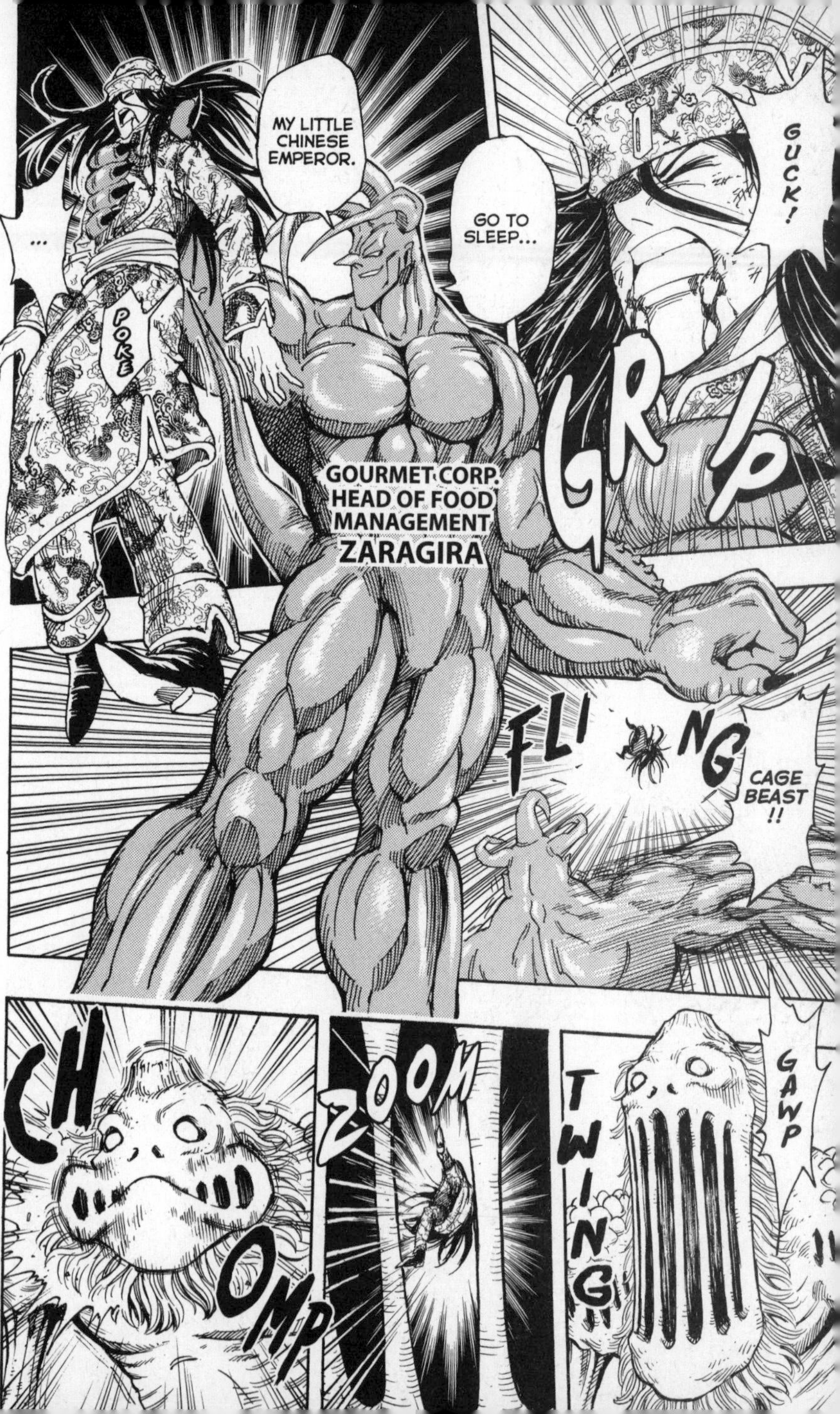

GUCK!
GRIP
GO TO SLEEP...
MY LITTLE CHINESE EMPEROR.
...
POKE
GOURMET CORP. HEAD OF FOOD MANAGEMENT ZARAGIRA
CAGE BEAST !!
FLING
GAWP
!!
TWING
ZOOM
CHOMP

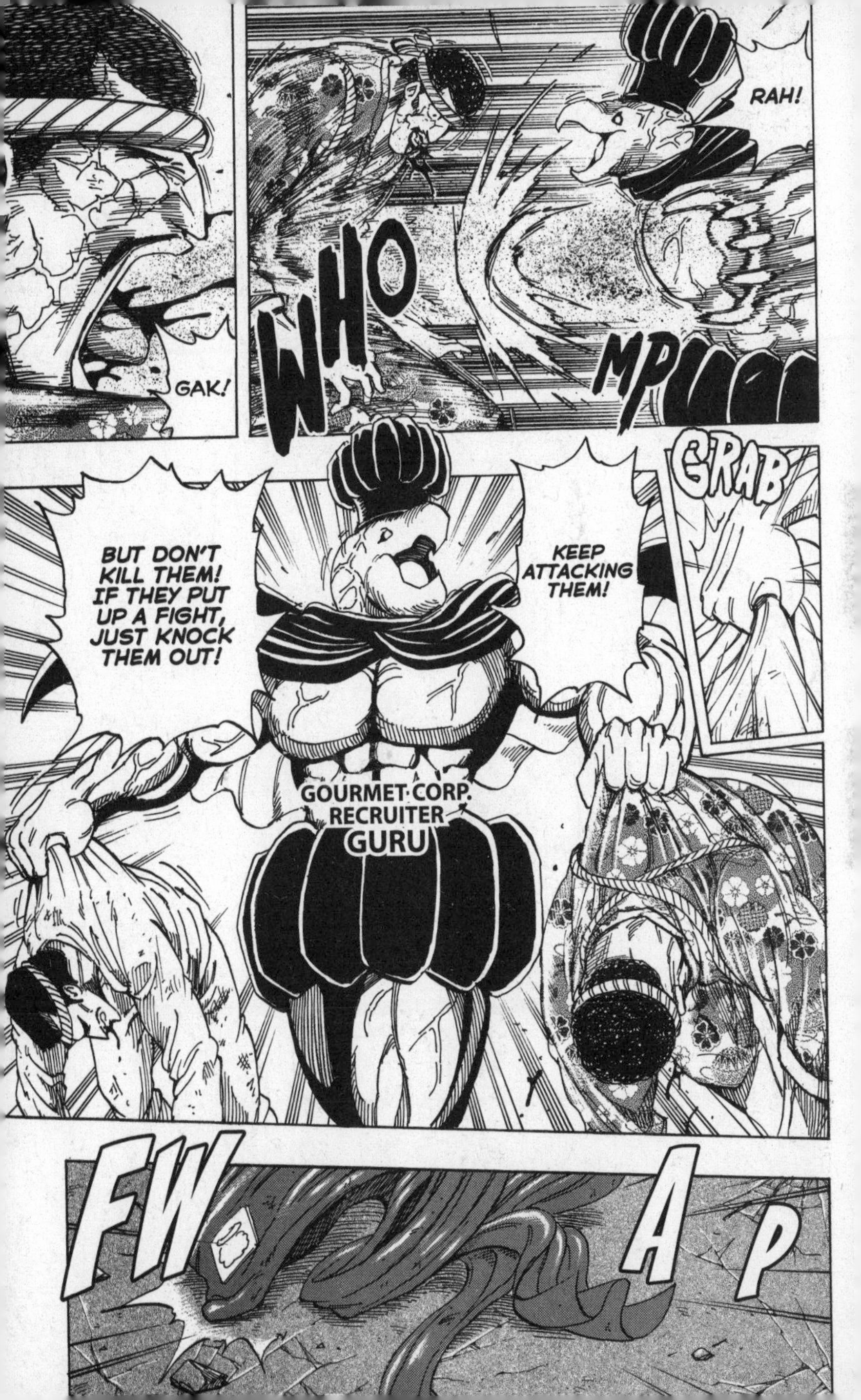
RAH!
WHOMP
GAK!
GRAB
KEEP ATTACKING THEM!
BUT DON'T KILL THEM! IF THEY PUT UP A FIGHT, JUST KNOCK THEM OUT!
GOURMET CORP. RECRUITER GURU
FWAP

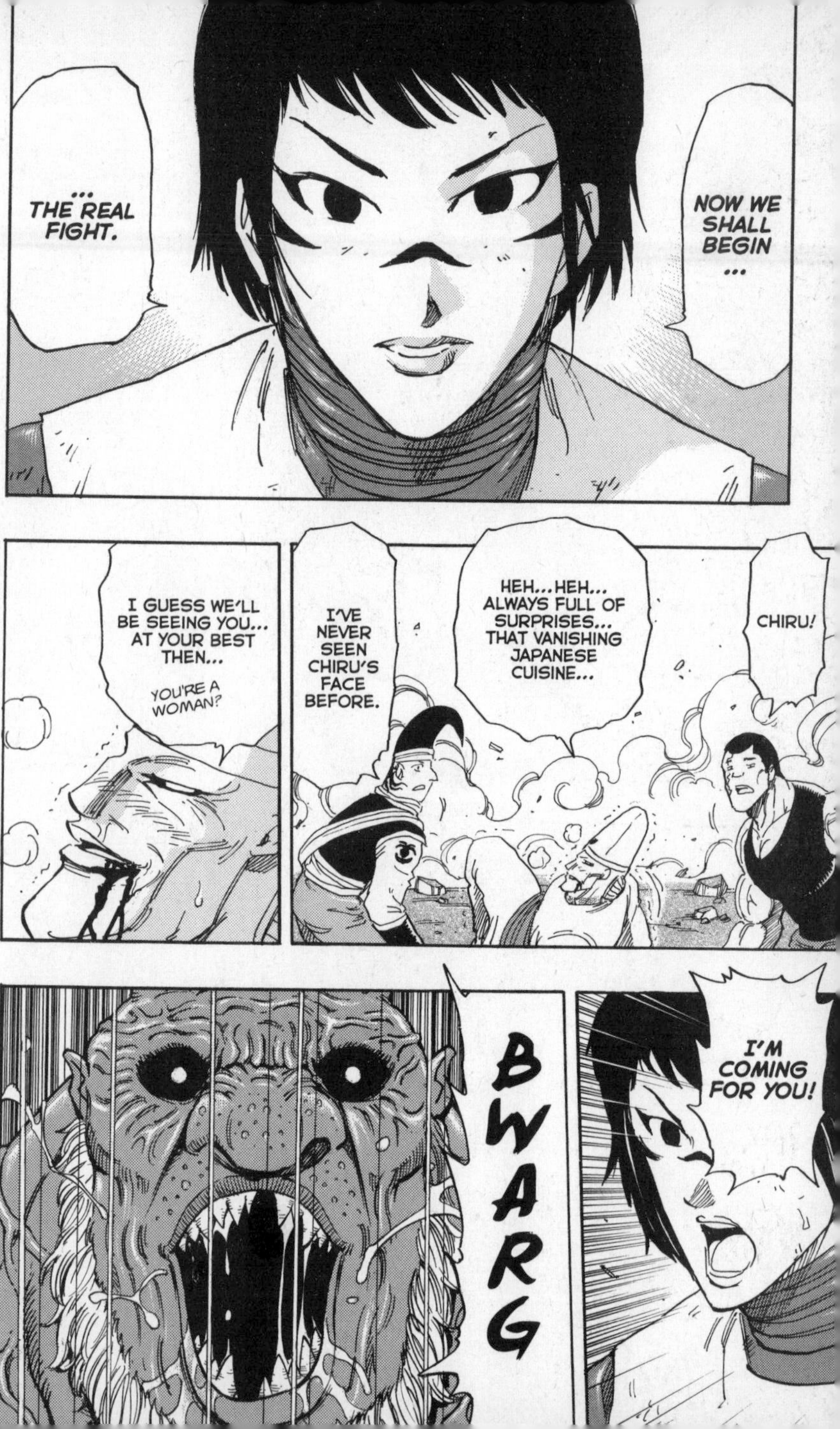
NOW WE SHALL BEGIN ...
... THE REAL FIGHT.
CHIRU!
HEH...HEH... ALWAYS FULL OF SURPRISES... THAT VANISHING JAPANESE CUISINE...
I'VE NEVER SEEN CHIRU'S FACE BEFORE.
I GUESS WE'LL BE SEEING YOU... AT YOUR BEST THEN...
YOU'RE A WOMAN?
I'M COMING FOR YOU!
BWARG

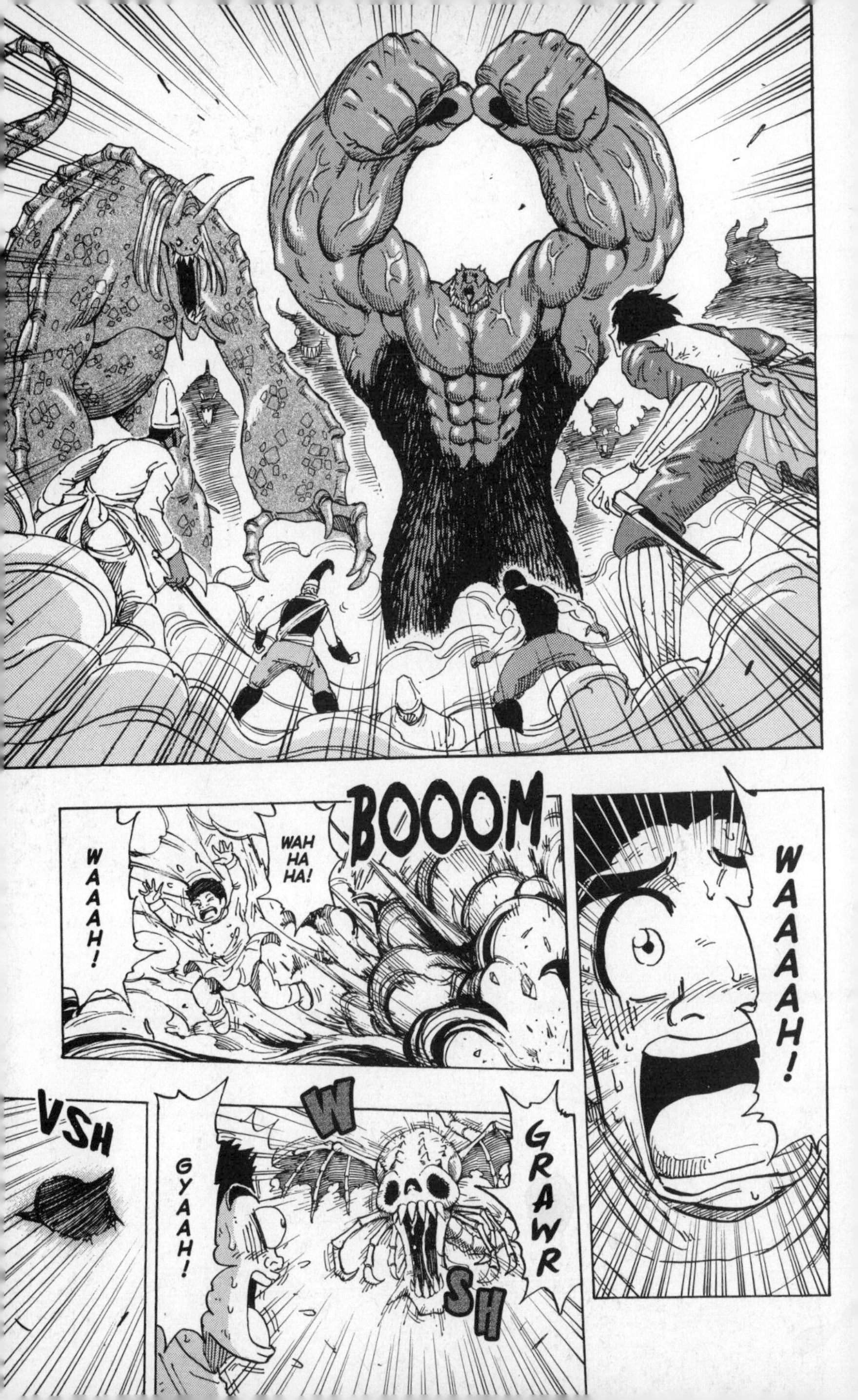
WAAAAAH!
BOOOM
WAH HA HA!
WAAAAH!
GRAWR
W
GYAAH!
SH
VSH

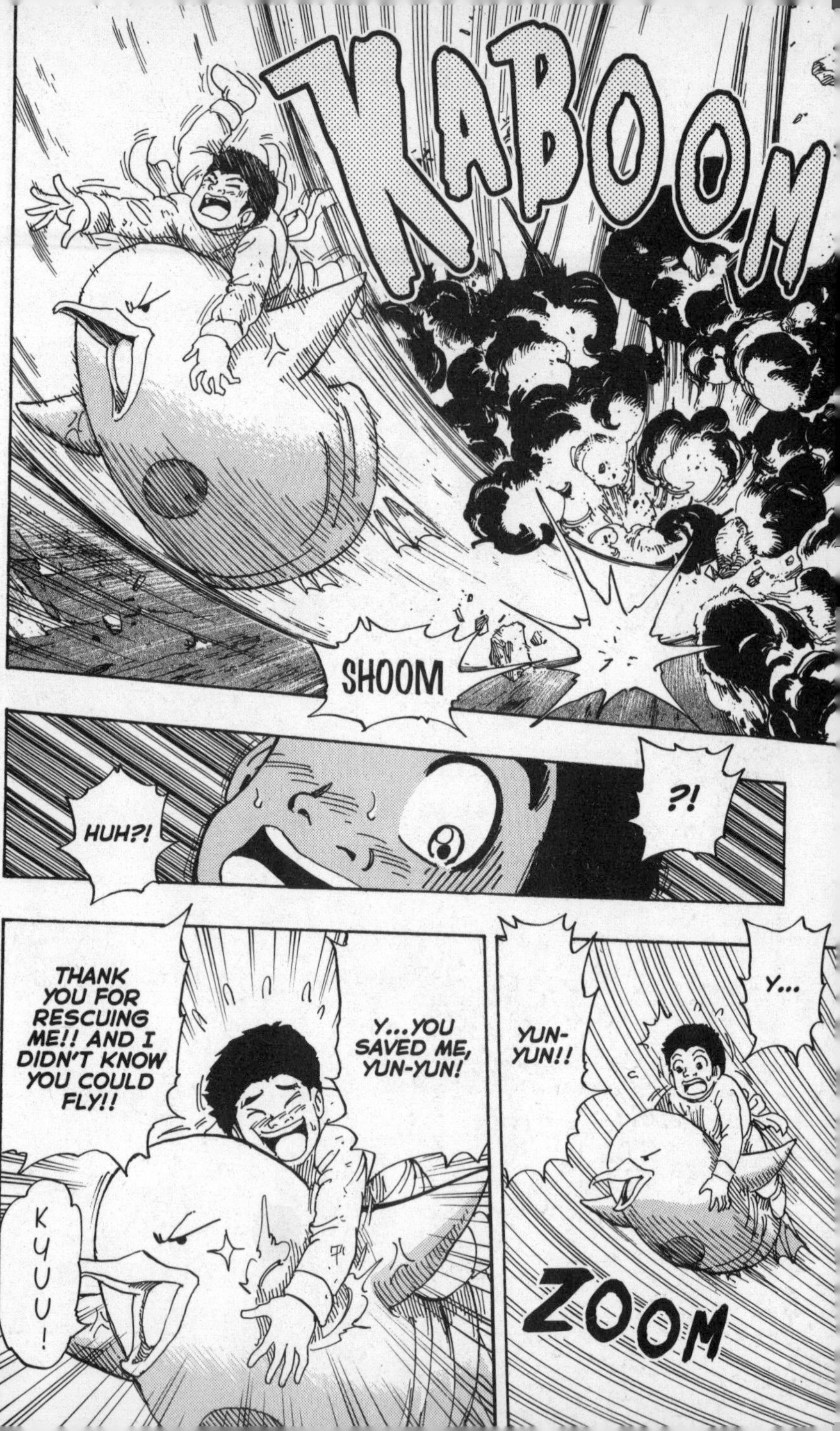
KABOOM
SHOOM
?!
HUH?!
Y...
YUN-YUN!!
ZOOM
Y...YOU SAVED ME, YUN-YUN!
THANK YOU FOR RESCUING ME!! AND I DIDN'T KNOW YOU COULD FLY!!
KYUUU!

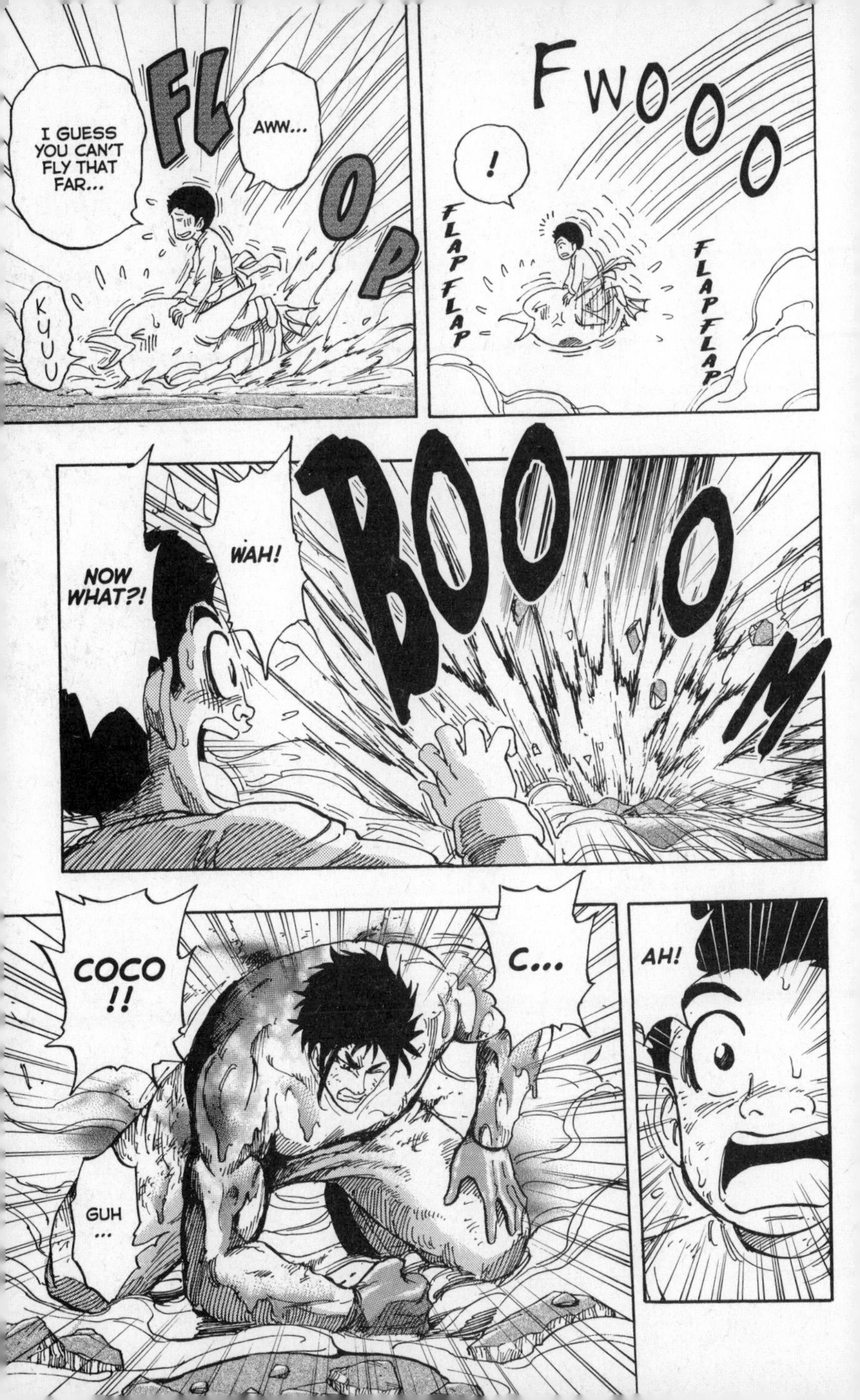
FWOOOO
!
FLAP FLAP
FLAP FLAP
AWW...
FLOOP
I GUESS YOU CAN'T FLY THAT FAR...
KYUU
BOOOM
WAH!
NOW WHAT?!
AH!
C...
COCO!!
GUH...

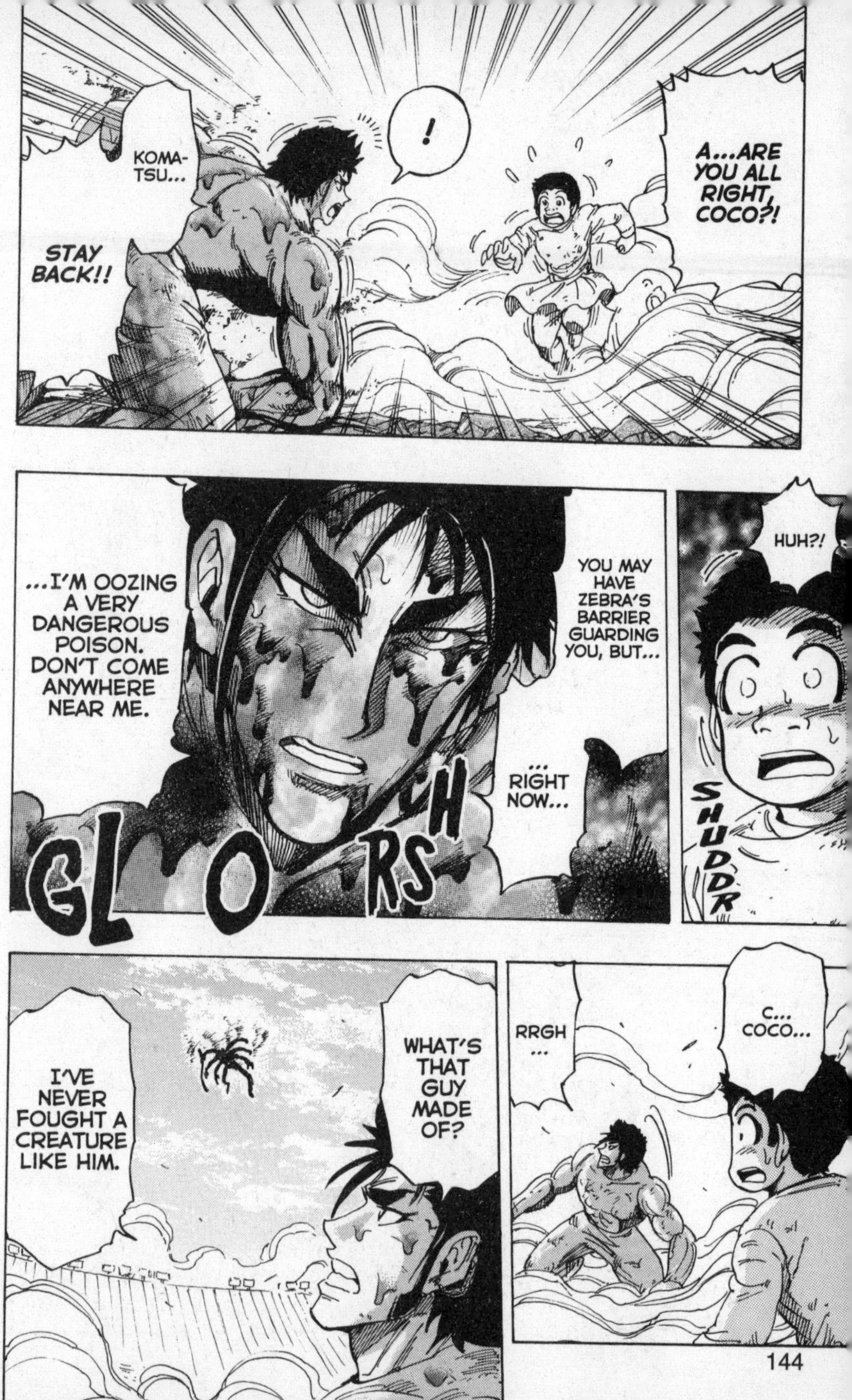

A...ARE YOU ALL RIGHT, COCO?!
!
KOMA-TSU...
STAY BACK!!
HUH?!
SHUDDR
YOU MAY HAVE ZEBRA'S BARRIER GUARDING YOU, BUT...
... RIGHT NOW...
...I'M OOZING A VERY DANGEROUS POISON. DON'T COME ANYWHERE NEAR ME.
GLORSCH
C... COCO...
RRGH ...
WHAT'S THAT GUY MADE OF?
I'VE NEVER FOUGHT A CREATURE LIKE HIM.

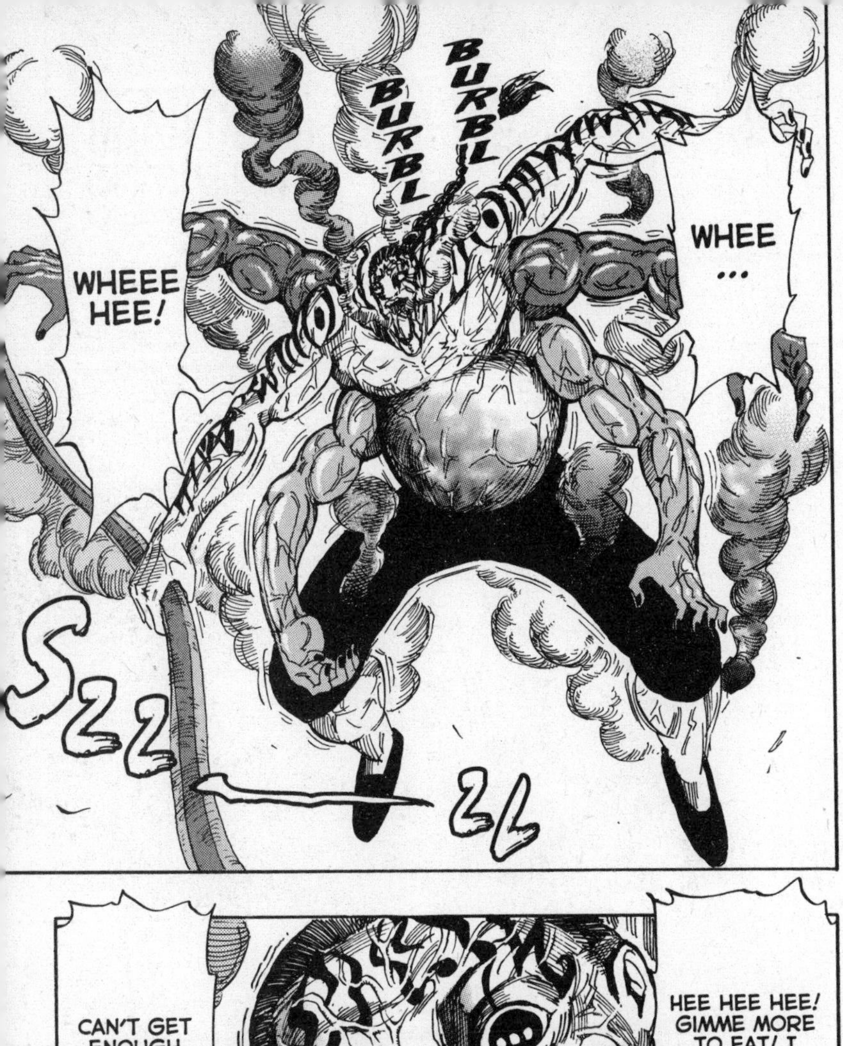
BURBL BURBL
WHEE ...
WHEEE HEE!
SZZZ

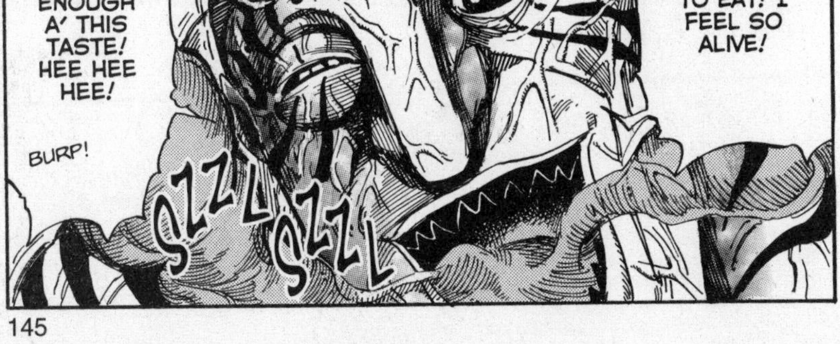
HEE HEE HEE! GIMME MORE TO EAT! I FEEL SO ALIVE!
CAN'T GET ENOUGH A' THIS TASTE! HEE HEE HEE!
BURP!
SZZL SZZL

TORIKO REJECT PAGES CORNER!!

(GOURMET 180)

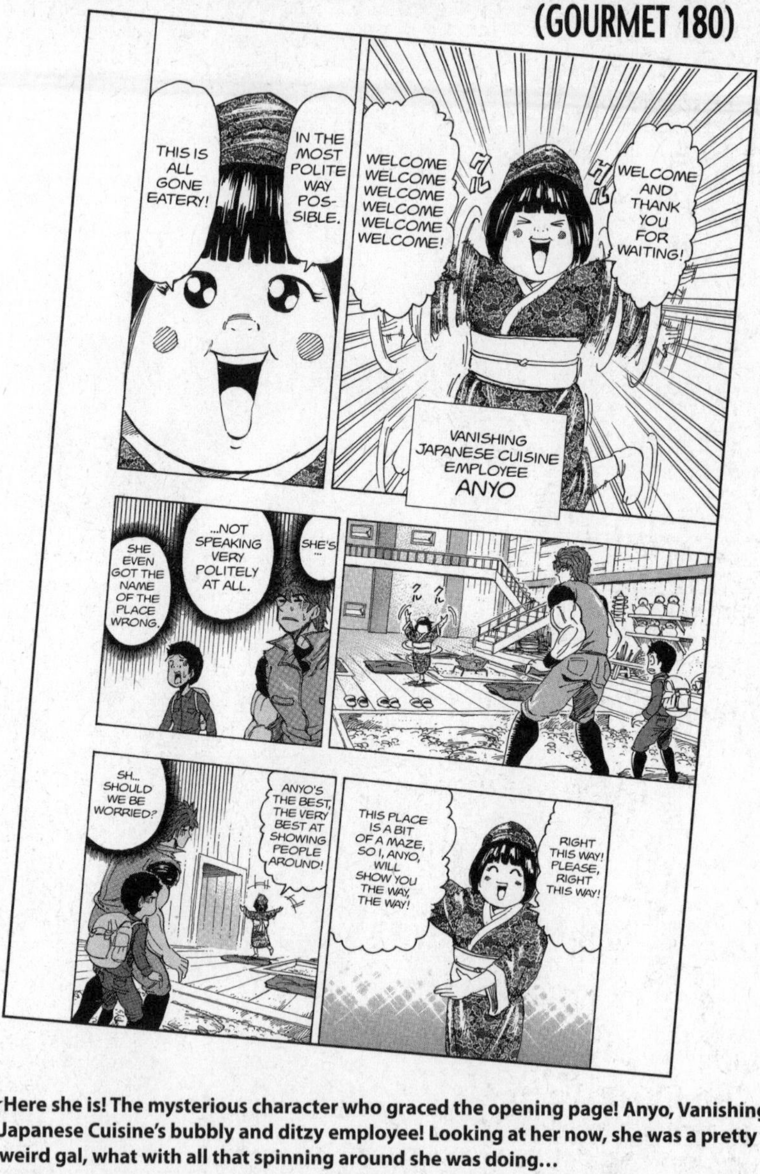
WELCOME AND THANK YOU FOR WAITING!
クル
クル
WELCOME WELCOME WELCOME WELCOME WELCOME WELCOME!
VANISHING JAPANESE CUISINE EMPLOYEE ANYO
IN THE MOST POLITE WAY POS-SIBLE.
THIS IS ALL GONE EATERY!
クル クル
SHE'S...
...NOT SPEAKING VERY POLITELY AT ALL.
SHE EVEN GOT THE NAME OF THE PLACE WRONG.
RIGHT THIS WAY! PLEASE, RIGHT THIS WAY!
THIS PLACE IS A BIT OF A MAZE, SO I, ANYO, WILL SHOW YOU THE WAY, THE WAY!
ANYO'S THE BEST, THE VERY BEST AT SHOWING PEOPLE AROUND!
SH... SHOULD WE BE WORRIED?

★**Here she is! The mysterious character who graced the opening page! Anyo, Vanishing Japanese Cuisine's bubbly and ditzy employee! Looking at her now, she was a pretty weird gal, what with all that spinning around she was doing…**

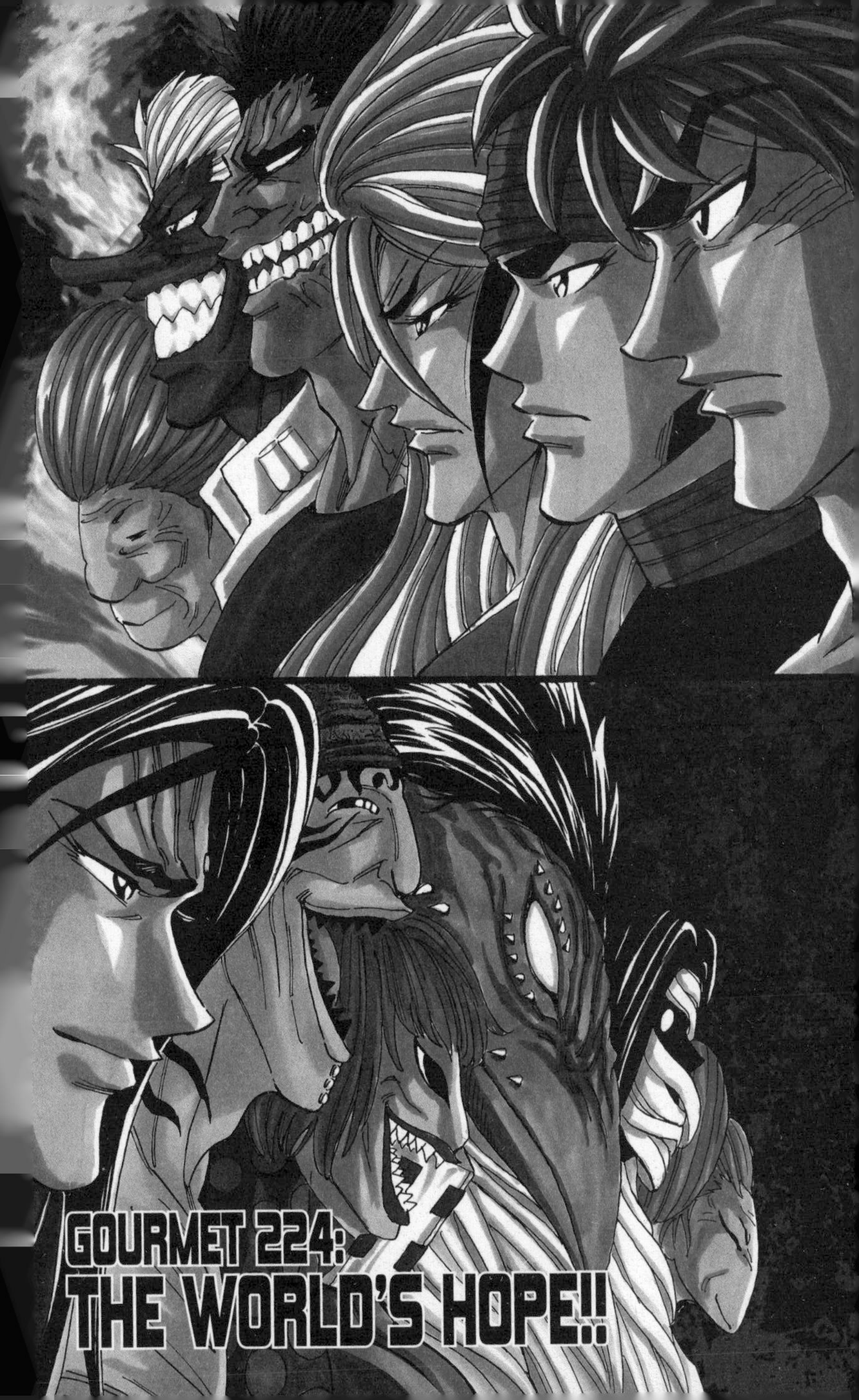
GOURMET 224:
THE WORLD'S HOPE!!

TORIKO REJECT PAGES CORNER!!

(GOURMET 180)

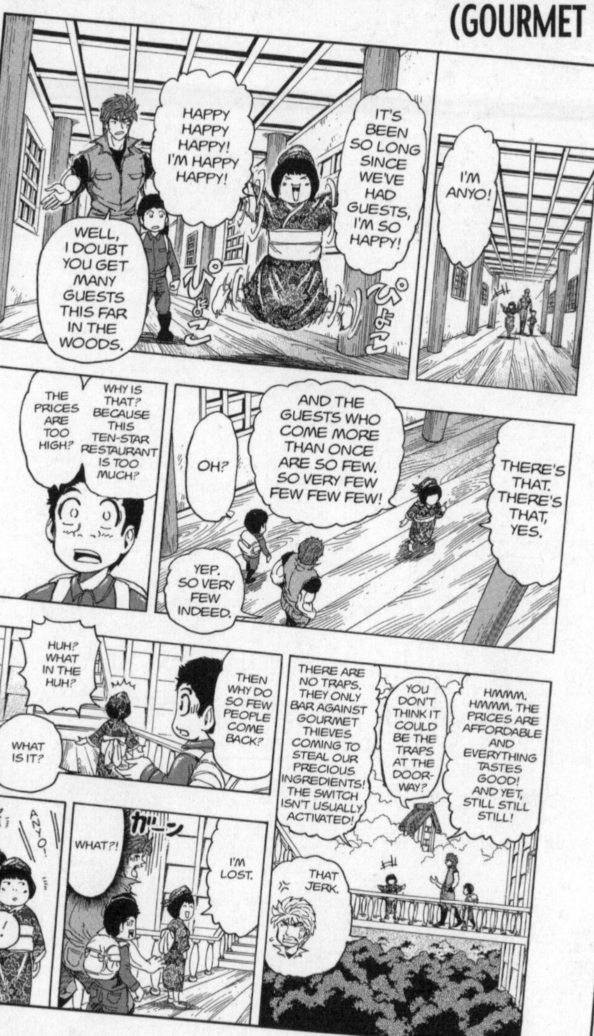
I'M ANYO!
IT'S BEEN SO LONG SINCE WE'VE HAD GUESTS, I'M SO HAPPY!
HAPPY HAPPY HAPPY! I'M HAPPY HAPPY!
WELL, I DOUBT YOU GET MANY GUESTS THIS FAR IN THE WOODS.
THERE'S THAT. THERE'S THAT, YES.
AND THE GUESTS WHO COME MORE THAN ONCE ARE SO FEW. SO VERY FEW FEW FEW FEW!
OH?
YEP. SO VERY FEW INDEED.
WHY IS THAT? BECAUSE THIS TEN-STAR RESTAURANT IS TOO MUCH?
THE PRICES ARE TOO HIGH?
HMMM. HMMM. THE PRICES ARE AFFORDABLE AND EVERYTHING TASTES GOOD! AND YET, STILL STILL STILL!
YOU DON'T THINK IT COULD BE THE TRAPS AT THE DOOR-WAY?
THERE ARE NO TRAPS. THEY ONLY BAR AGAINST GOURMET THIEVES COMING TO STEAL OUR PRECIOUS INGREDIENTS! THE SWITCH ISN'T USUALLY ACTIVATED!
THAT JERK.
THEN WHY DO SO FEW PEOPLE COME BACK?
HUH? WHAT IN THE HUH?
WHAT IS IT?
I'M LOST.
ガーン
WHAT?!
ANYO!

★I can't believe it, I almost completed this page! Having to scrap these pages after having gotten so far wasted an entire week's worth of work. Which means it threw an entire week's schedule out the window. Oh the pain! Since it hurts so much to revisit, this is all I'll showcase of it. Even though I actually have the pages that come after this too. Oh, how it hurts!!

Continued in “Shimabu Speaks” on page 166

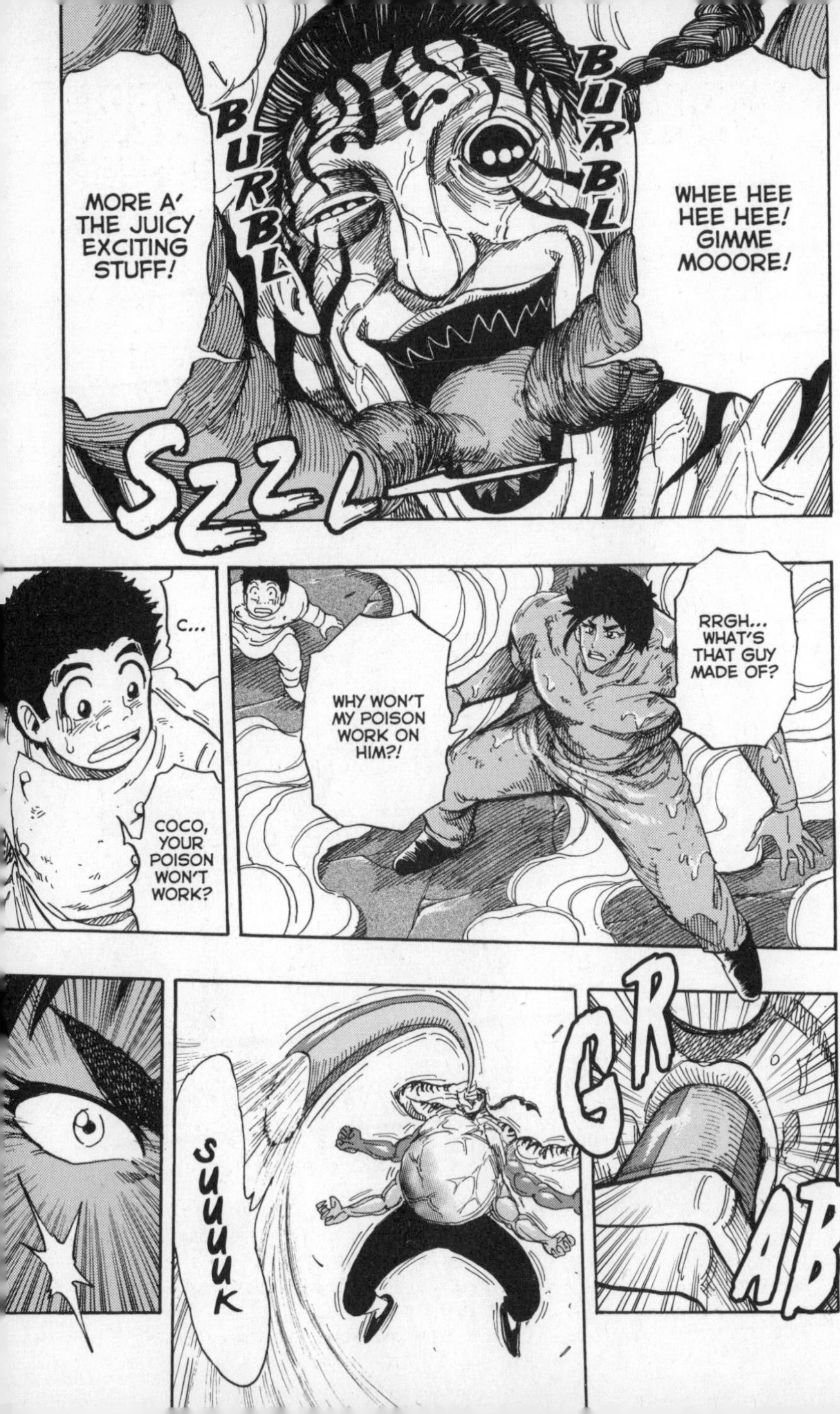
BURBL
BURBL
WHEE HEE HEE HEE! GIMME MOOORE!
MORE A' THE JUICY EXCITING STUFF!
SZZL
RRGH... WHAT'S THAT GUY MADE OF?
WHY WON'T MY POISON WORK ON HIM?!
C...
COCO, YOUR POISON WON'T WORK?
CRAB
SUUUUK

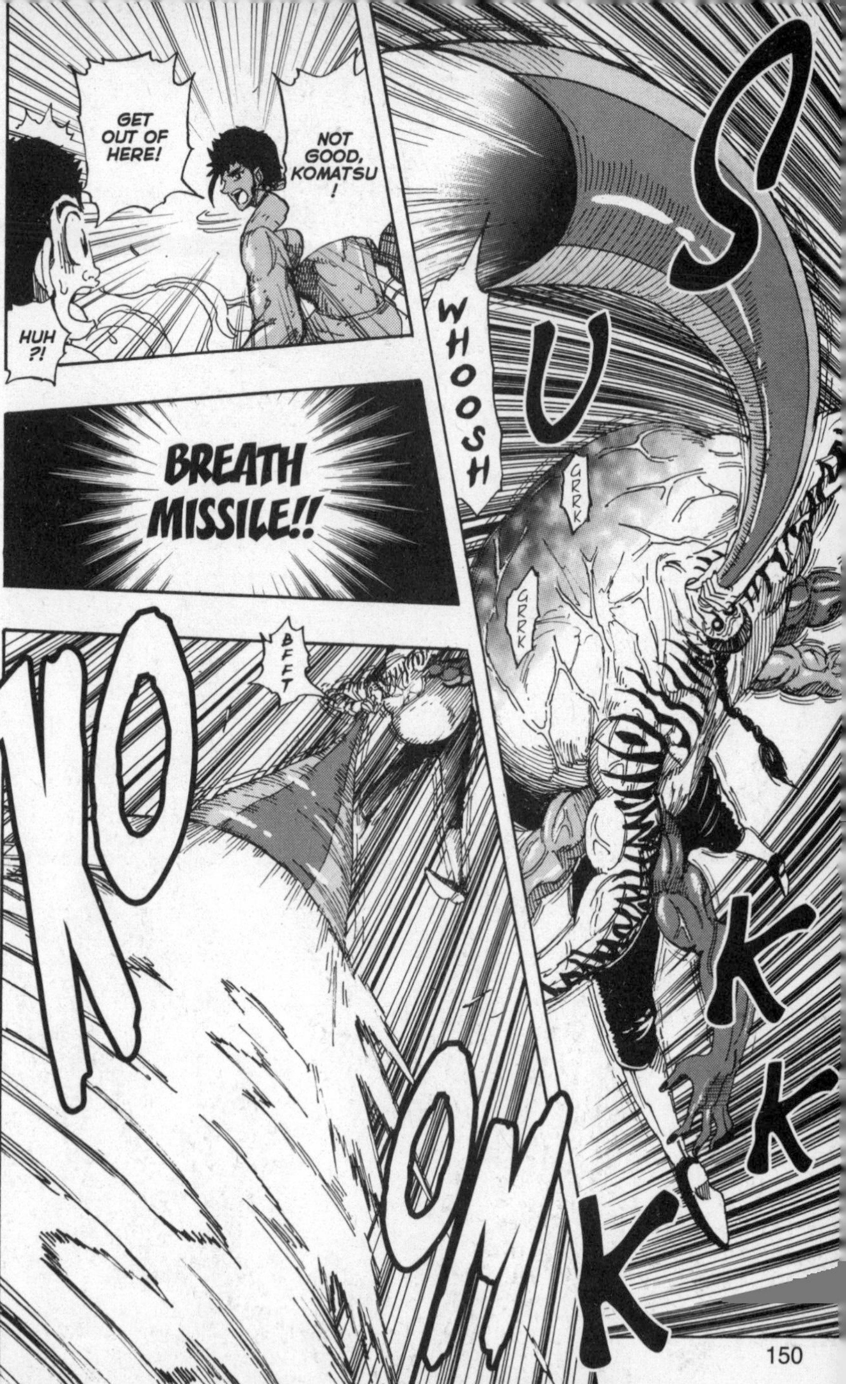
WHOOSH
GRRK
GRRK
NOT GOOD, KOMATSU!
GET OUT OF HERE!
HUH?!
BREATH MISSILE!!
BFFT

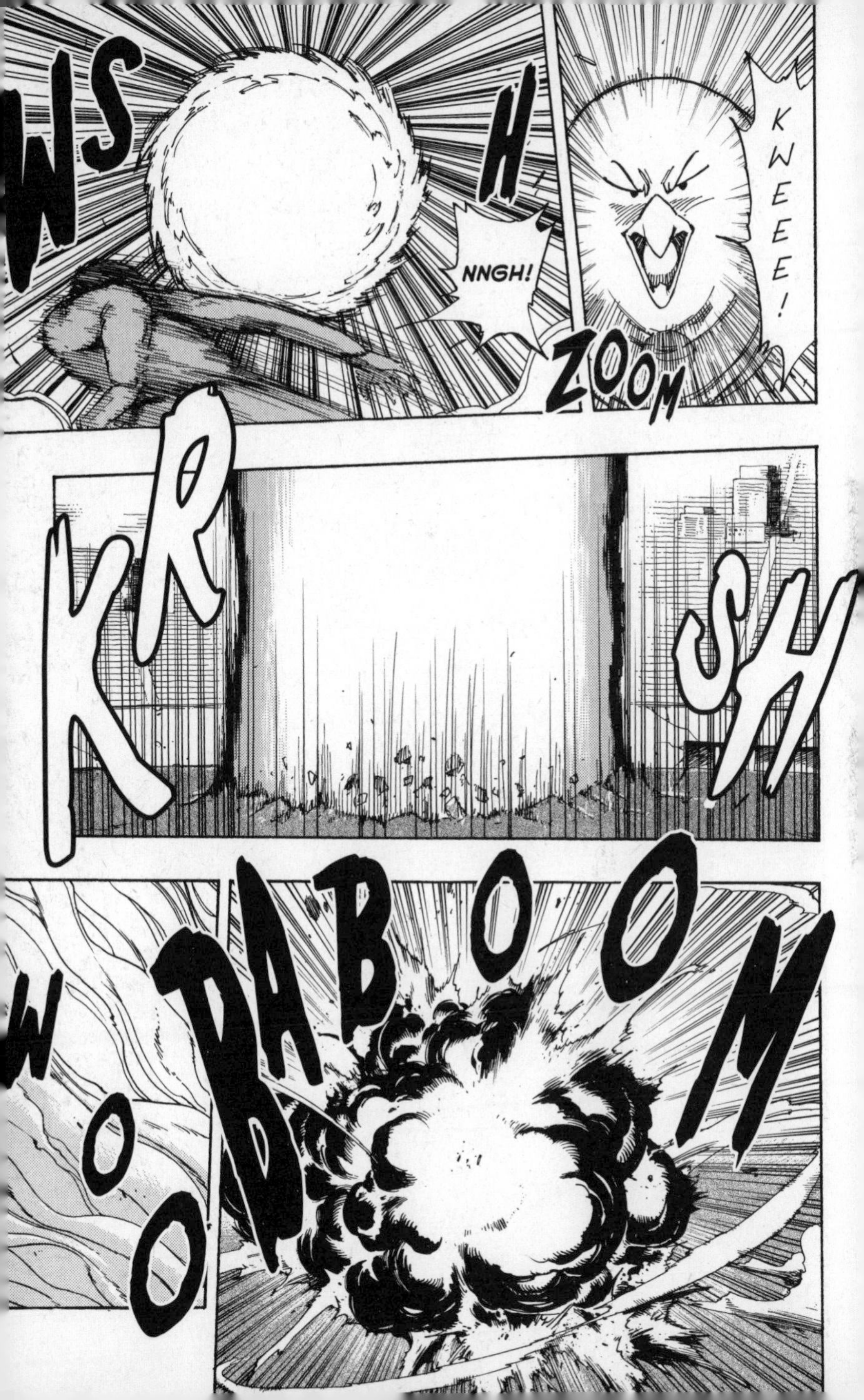
KWEEE!
ZOOM
WSH
NNGH!
KRSH
DABOOM
WOO

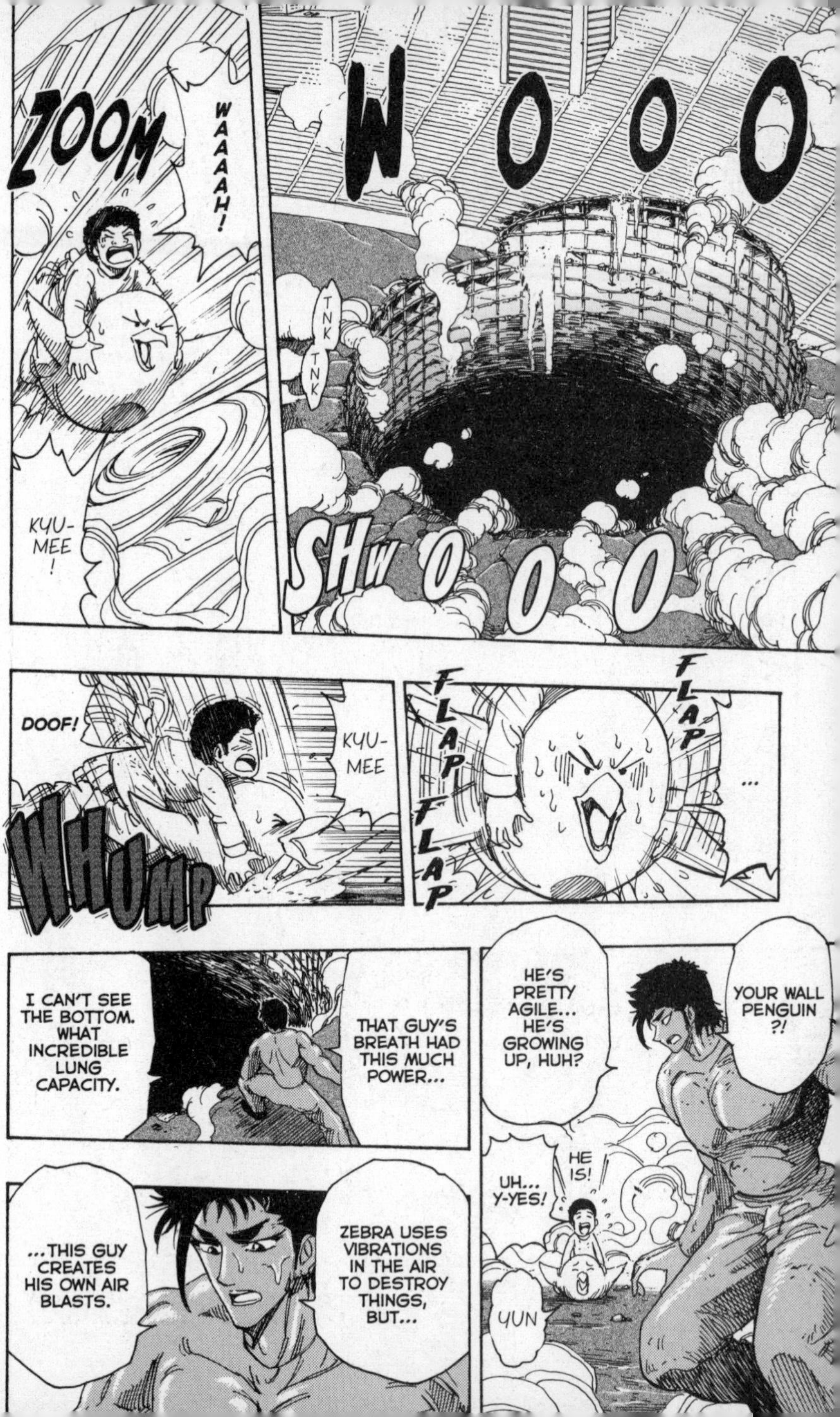
WOOOO
TNK TNK
SHWOOOO
ZOOM
WAAAAAH!
KYU-MEE!
FLAP FLAP
FLAP FLAP
...
DOOF!
KYU-MEE
WHUMP
YOUR WALL PENGUIN?!
HE'S PRETTY AGILE... HE'S GROWING UP, HUH?
HE IS!
UH... Y-YES!
YUN
THAT GUY'S BREATH HAD THIS MUCH POWER...
I CAN'T SEE THE BOTTOM. WHAT INCREDIBLE LUNG CAPACITY.
ZEBRA USES VIBRATIONS IN THE AIR TO DESTROY THINGS, BUT...
...THIS GUY CREATES HIS OWN AIR BLASTS.

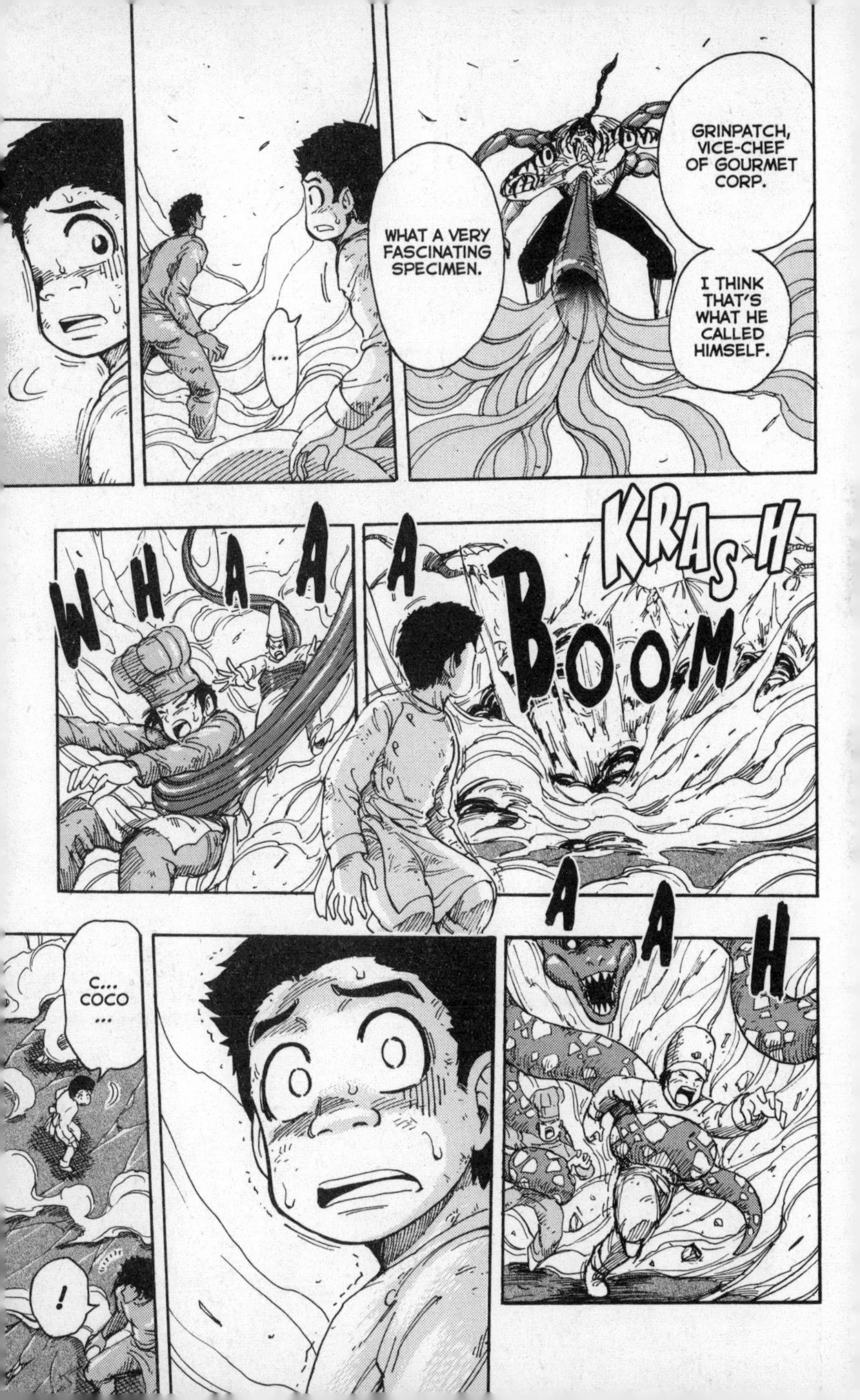

GRINPATCH, VICE-CHEF OF GOURMET CORP.
I THINK THAT'S WHAT HE CALLED HIMSELF.
WHAT A VERY FASCINATING SPECIMEN.
...
KRASH
BOOM
WHAAAAAH
C... COCO ...
!

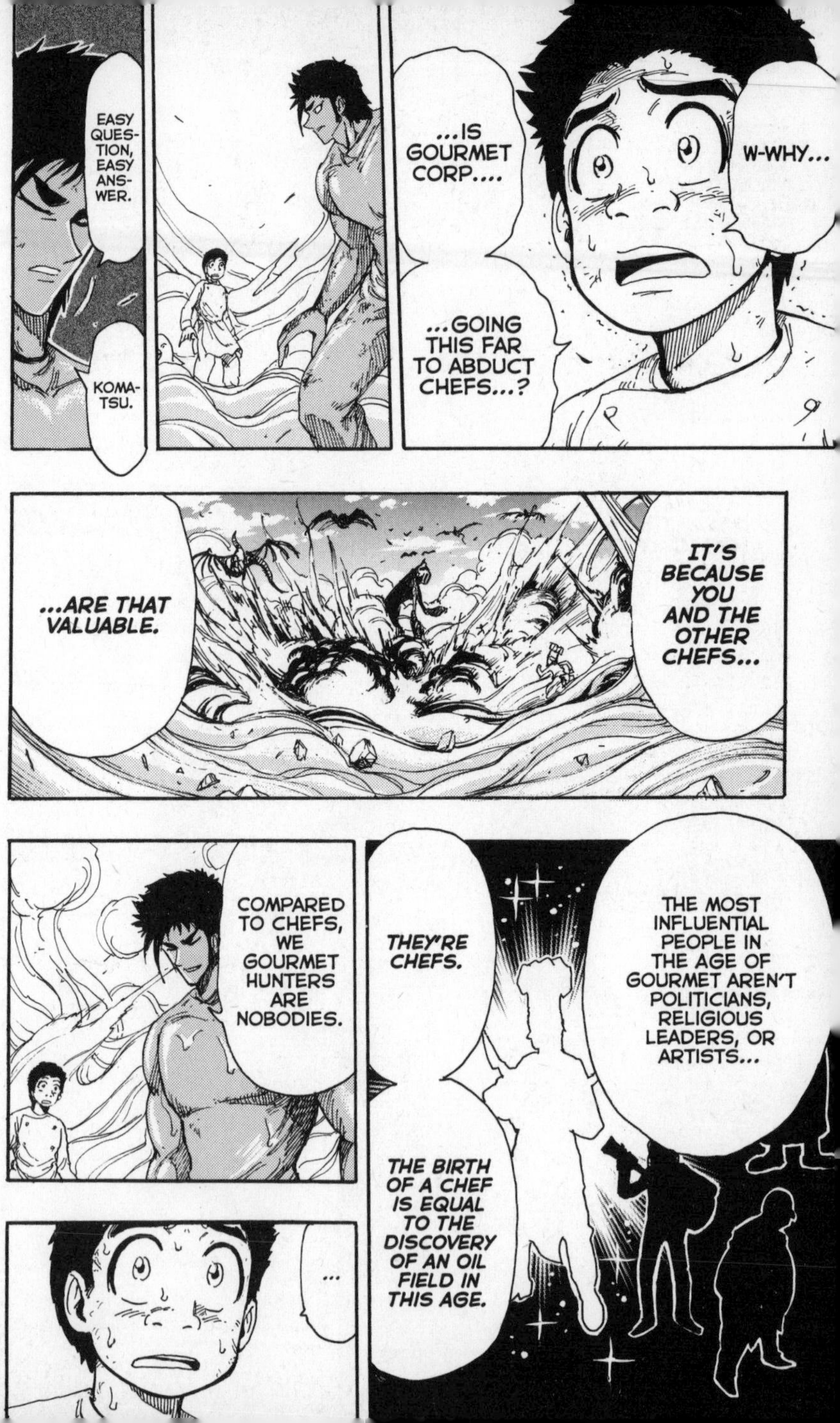
W-WHY...
...IS GOURMET CORP....
...GOING THIS FAR TO ABDUCT CHEFS...?
EASY QUESTION, EASY ANSWER.
KOMATSU.
IT'S BECAUSE YOU AND THE OTHER CHEFS...
...ARE THAT VALUABLE.
THE MOST INFLUENTIAL PEOPLE IN THE AGE OF GOURMET AREN'T POLITICIANS, RELIGIOUS LEADERS, OR ARTISTS...
THEY'RE CHEFS.
THE BIRTH OF A CHEF IS EQUAL TO THE DISCOVERY OF AN OIL FIELD IN THIS AGE.
COMPARED TO CHEFS, WE GOURMET HUNTERS ARE NOBODIES.
...

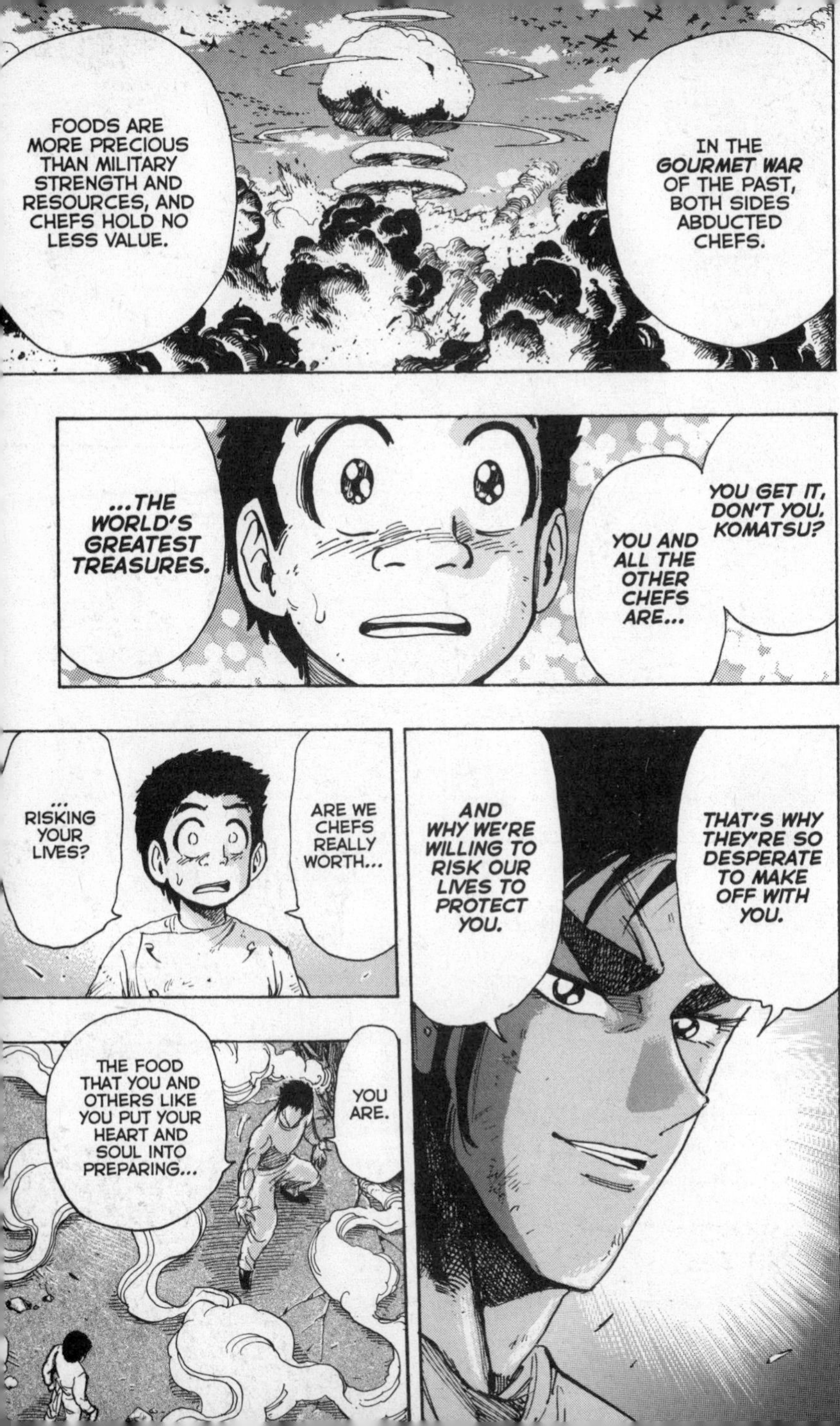
IN THE *GOURMET WAR* OF THE PAST, BOTH SIDES ABDUCTED CHEFS.
FOODS ARE MORE PRECIOUS THAN MILITARY STRENGTH AND RESOURCES, AND CHEFS HOLD NO LESS VALUE.
YOU GET IT, DON'T YOU, KOMATSU?
YOU AND ALL THE OTHER CHEFS ARE...
...THE WORLD'S GREATEST TREASURES.
THAT'S WHY THEY'RE SO DESPERATE TO MAKE OFF WITH YOU.
AND WHY WE'RE WILLING TO RISK OUR LIVES TO PROTECT YOU.
ARE WE CHEFS REALLY WORTH...
...RISKING YOUR LIVES?
YOU ARE.
THE FOOD THAT YOU AND OTHERS LIKE YOU PUT YOUR HEART AND SOUL INTO PREPARING...

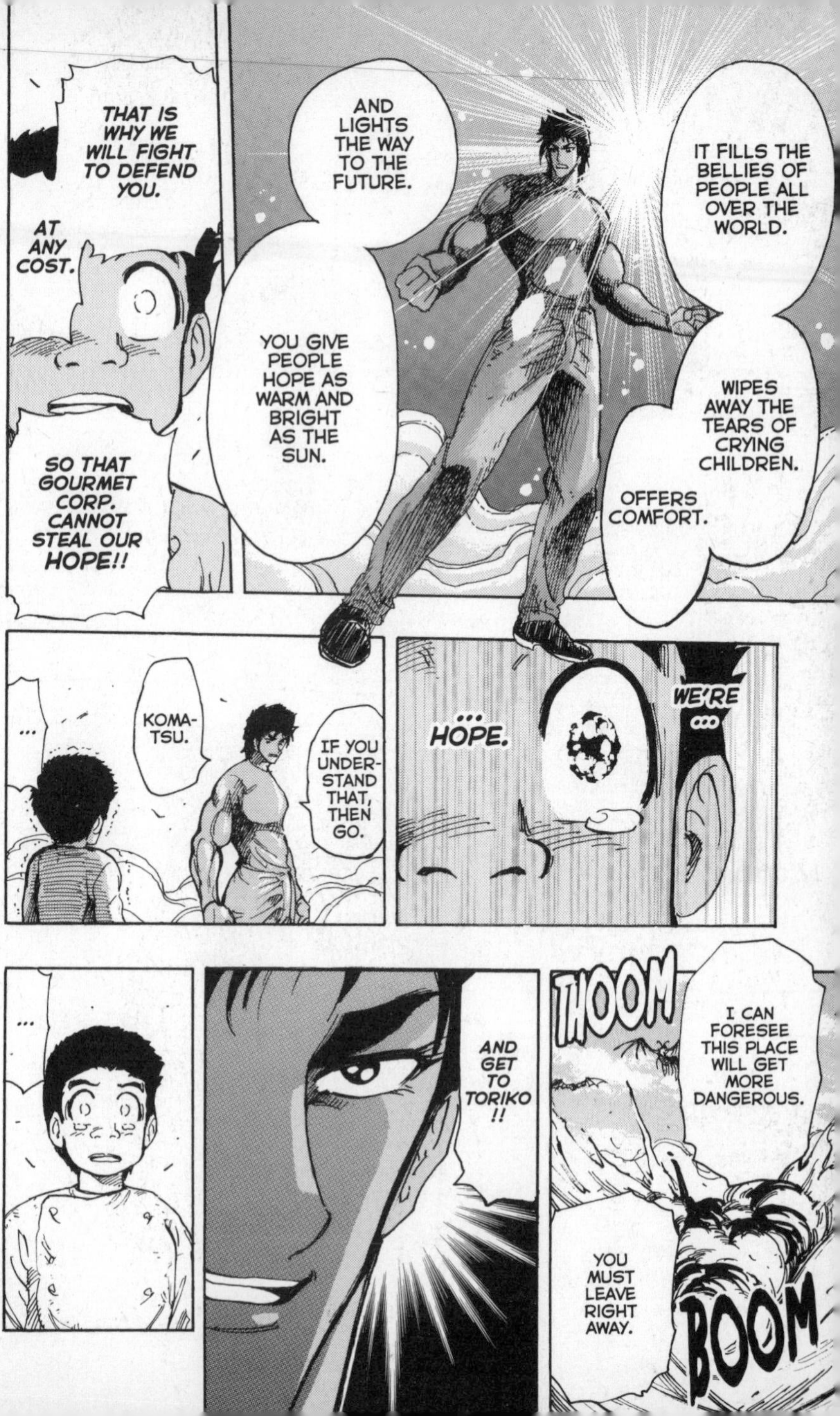
IT FILLS THE BELLIES OF PEOPLE ALL OVER THE WORLD.
WIPES AWAY THE TEARS OF CRYING CHILDREN.
OFFERS COMFORT.
AND LIGHTS THE WAY TO THE FUTURE.
YOU GIVE PEOPLE HOPE AS WARM AND BRIGHT AS THE SUN.
THAT IS WHY WE WILL FIGHT TO DEFEND YOU.
AT ANY COST.
SO THAT GOURMET CORP. CANNOT STEAL OUR HOPE!!
WE'RE ...
... HOPE.
KOMA-TSU.
IF YOU UNDER-STAND THAT, THEN GO.
...
THOOM
I CAN FORESEE THIS PLACE WILL GET MORE DANGEROUS.
YOU MUST LEAVE RIGHT AWAY.
BOOM
AND GET TO TORIKO!!
...

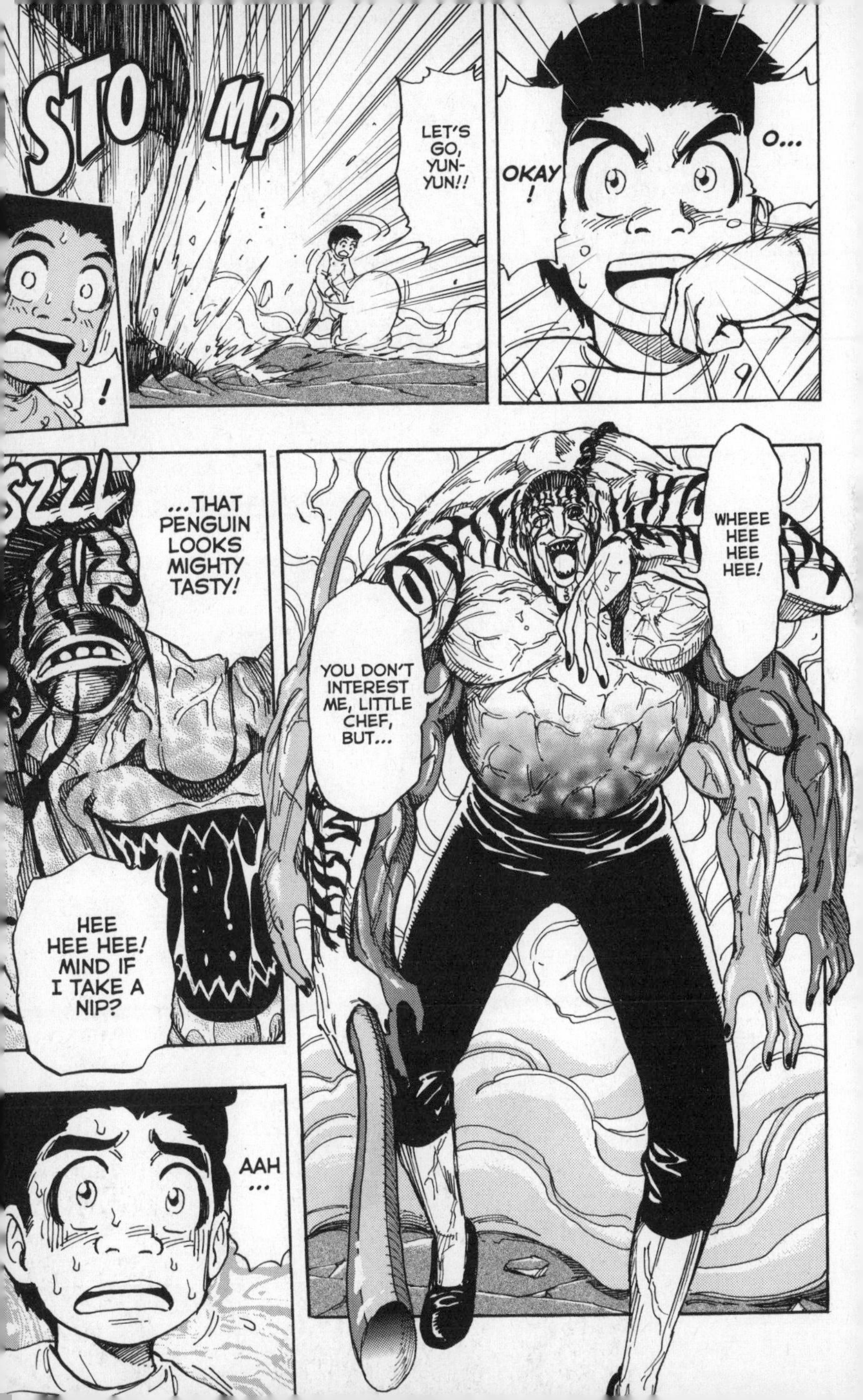
O... OKAY!
LET'S GO, YUN-YUN!!
STOMP
!
WHEEE HEE HEE HEE!
YOU DON'T INTEREST ME, LITTLE CHEF, BUT...
SZZL
...THAT PENGUIN LOOKS MIGHTY TASTY!
HEE HEE HEE! MIND IF I TAKE A NIP?
AAH ...

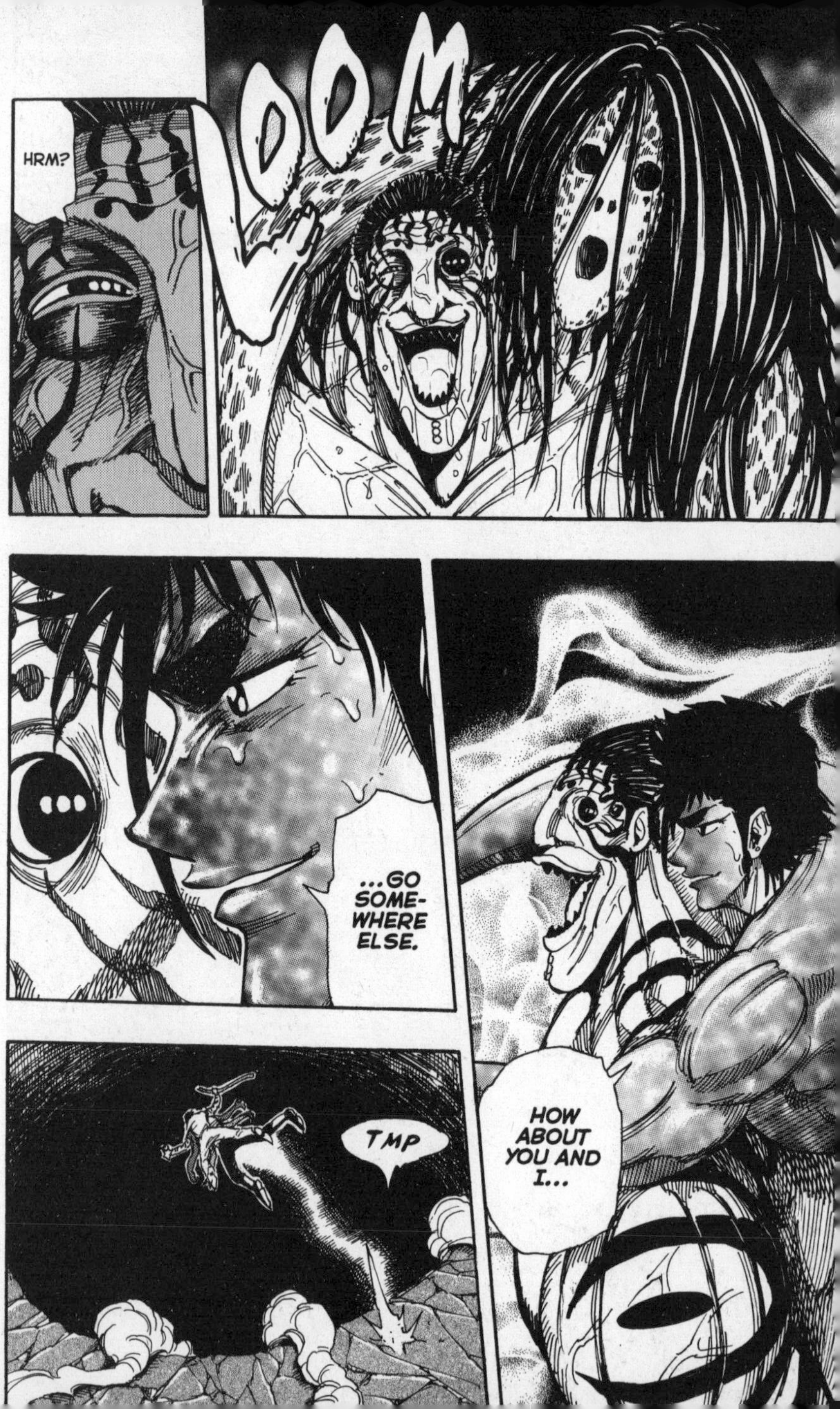
LOOM
HRM?
HOW ABOUT YOU AND I...
...GO SOMEWHERE ELSE.
TMP

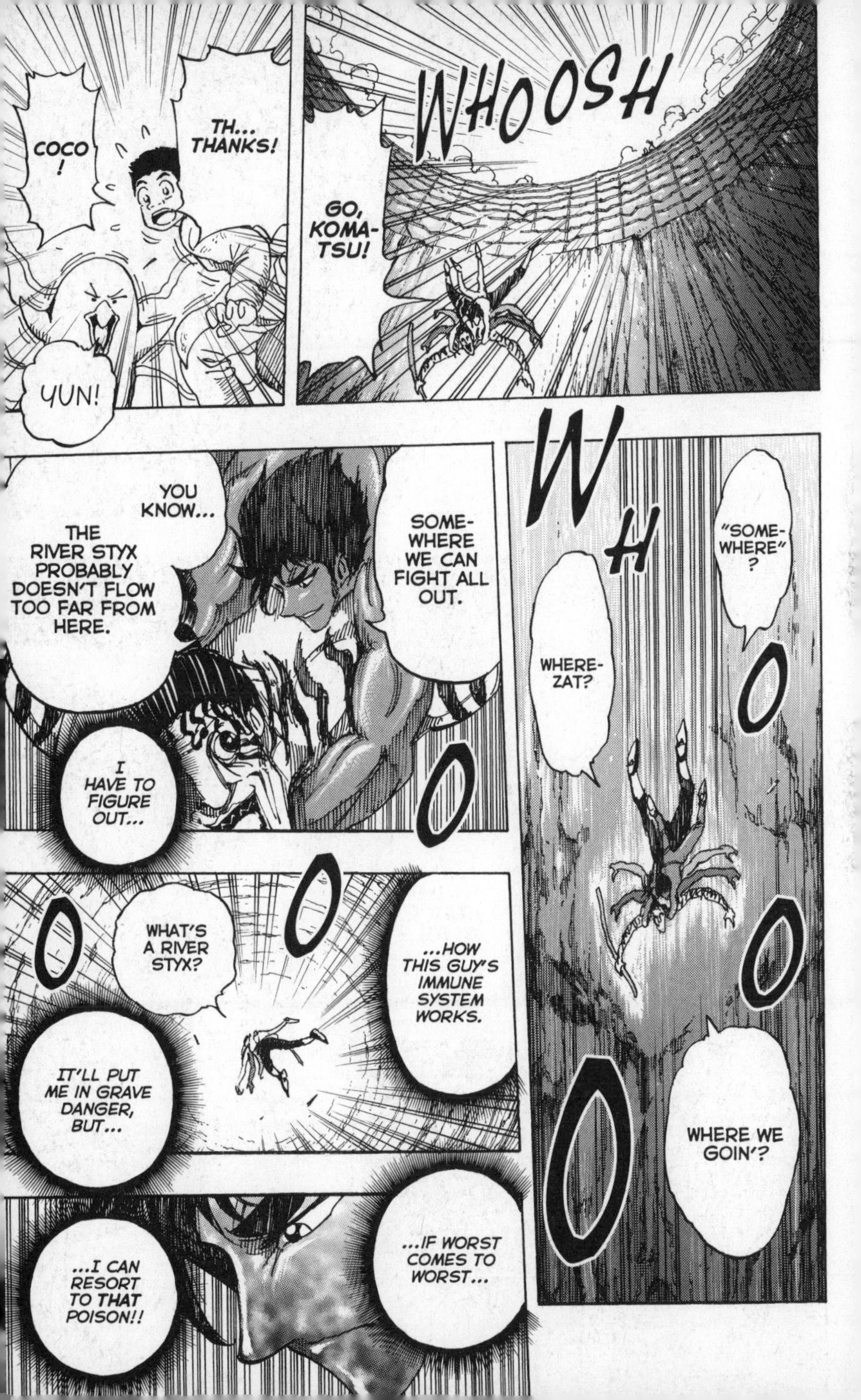
WHOOSH
GO, KOMA-TSU!
TH... THANKS!
COCO!
YUN!
WHOOOOO
"SOME-WHERE"?
WHERE-ZAT?
WHERE WE GOIN'?
SOME-WHERE WE CAN FIGHT ALL OUT.
YOU KNOW... THE RIVER STYX PROBABLY DOESN'T FLOW TOO FAR FROM HERE.
I HAVE TO FIGURE OUT...
...HOW THIS GUY'S IMMUNE SYSTEM WORKS.
WHAT'S A RIVER STYX?
IT'LL PUT ME IN GRAVE DANGER, BUT...
...IF WORST COMES TO WORST...
...I CAN RESORT TO THAT POISON!!

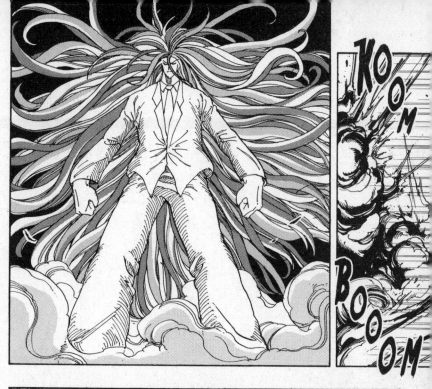

KOOM

BOOOM

WHAT'S MAKING ALL THAT RACKET?

HEY, HEY.

BZZZ

I DO, DON'T I?

DO I HAVE TO LOOK?

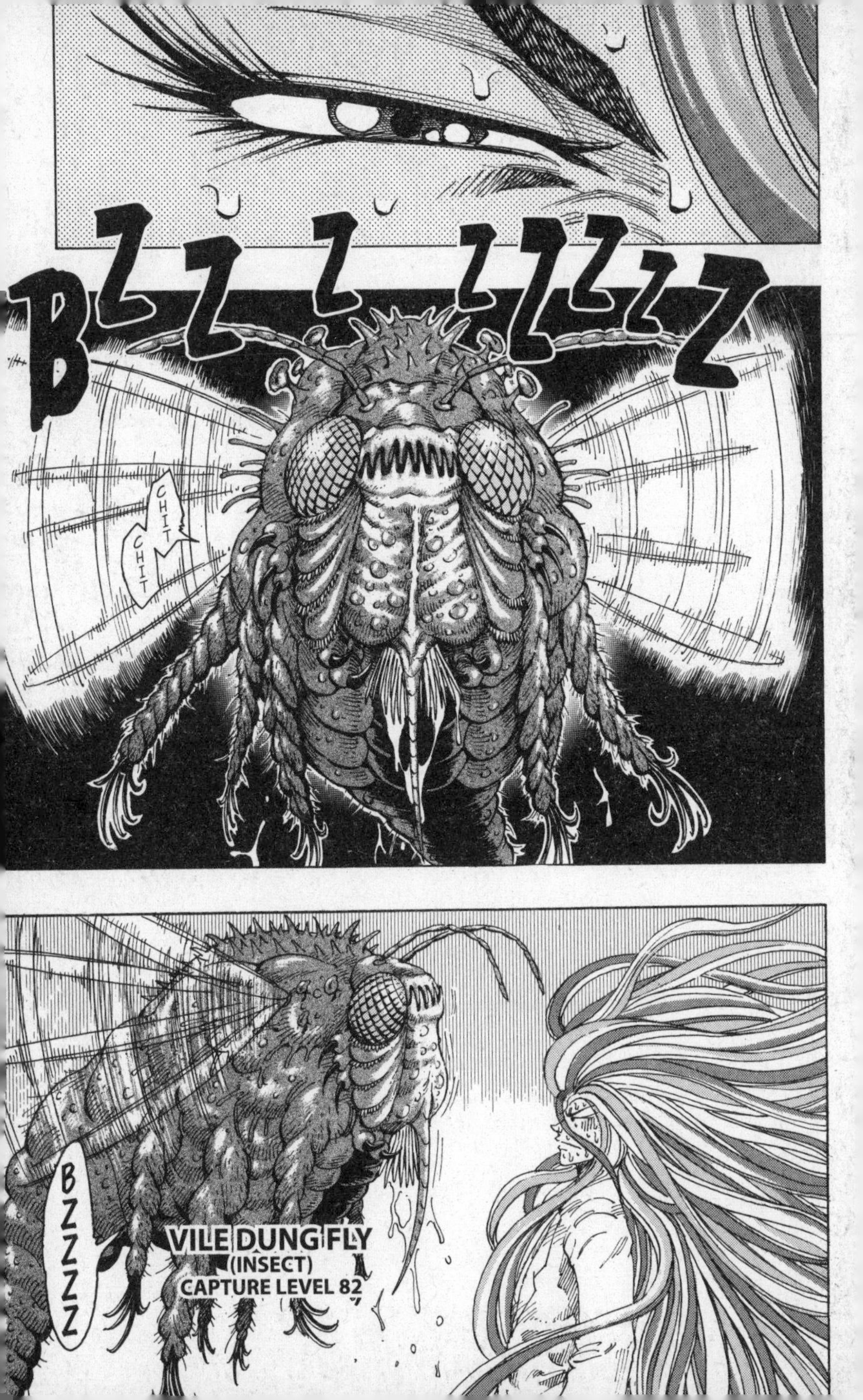
BZZ Z ZZZZZ
CHIT CHIT
BZZZZ
VILE DUNG FLY
(INSECT)
CAPTURE LEVEL 82

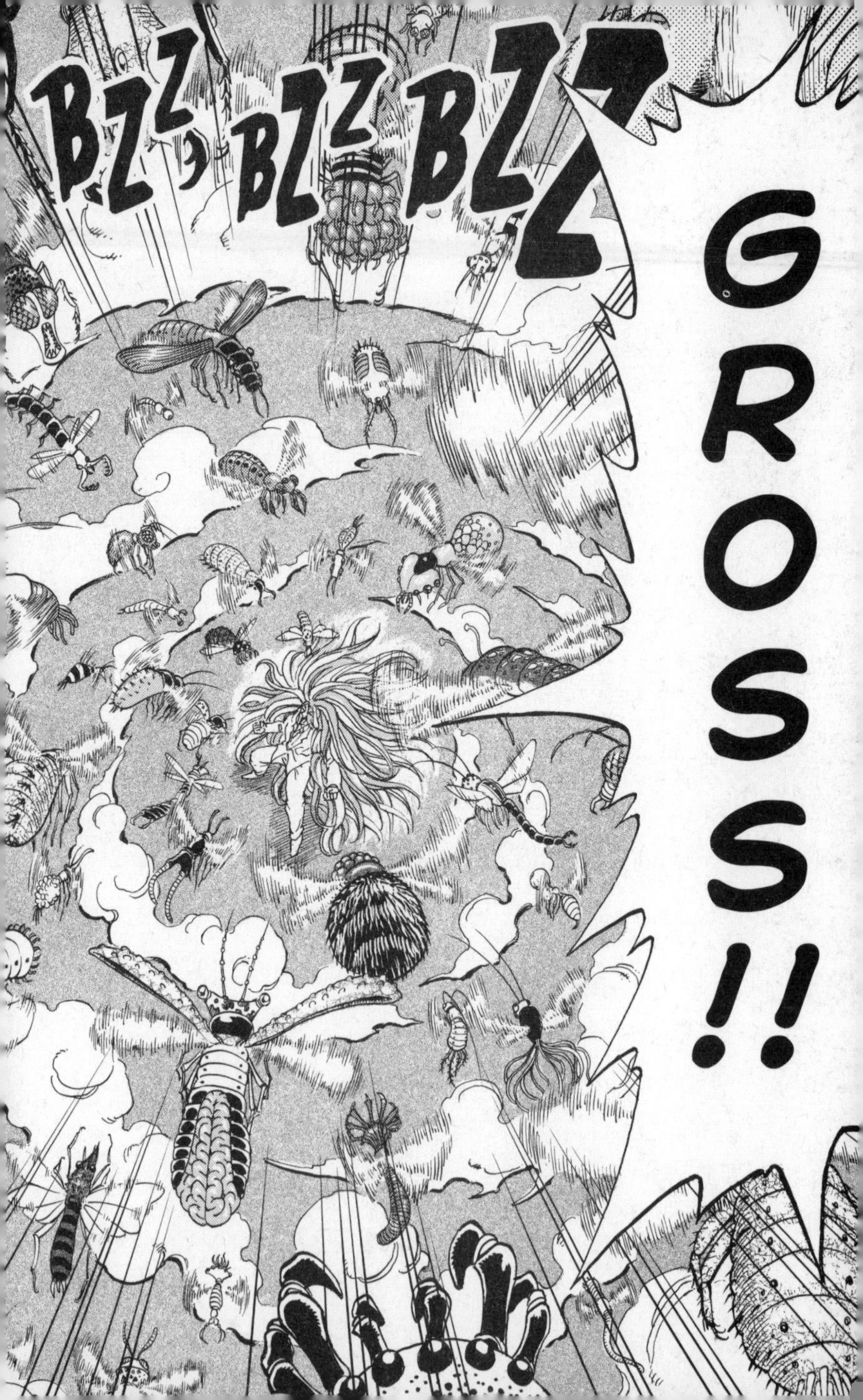
GROSS!!
BZZ, BZZ BZZ

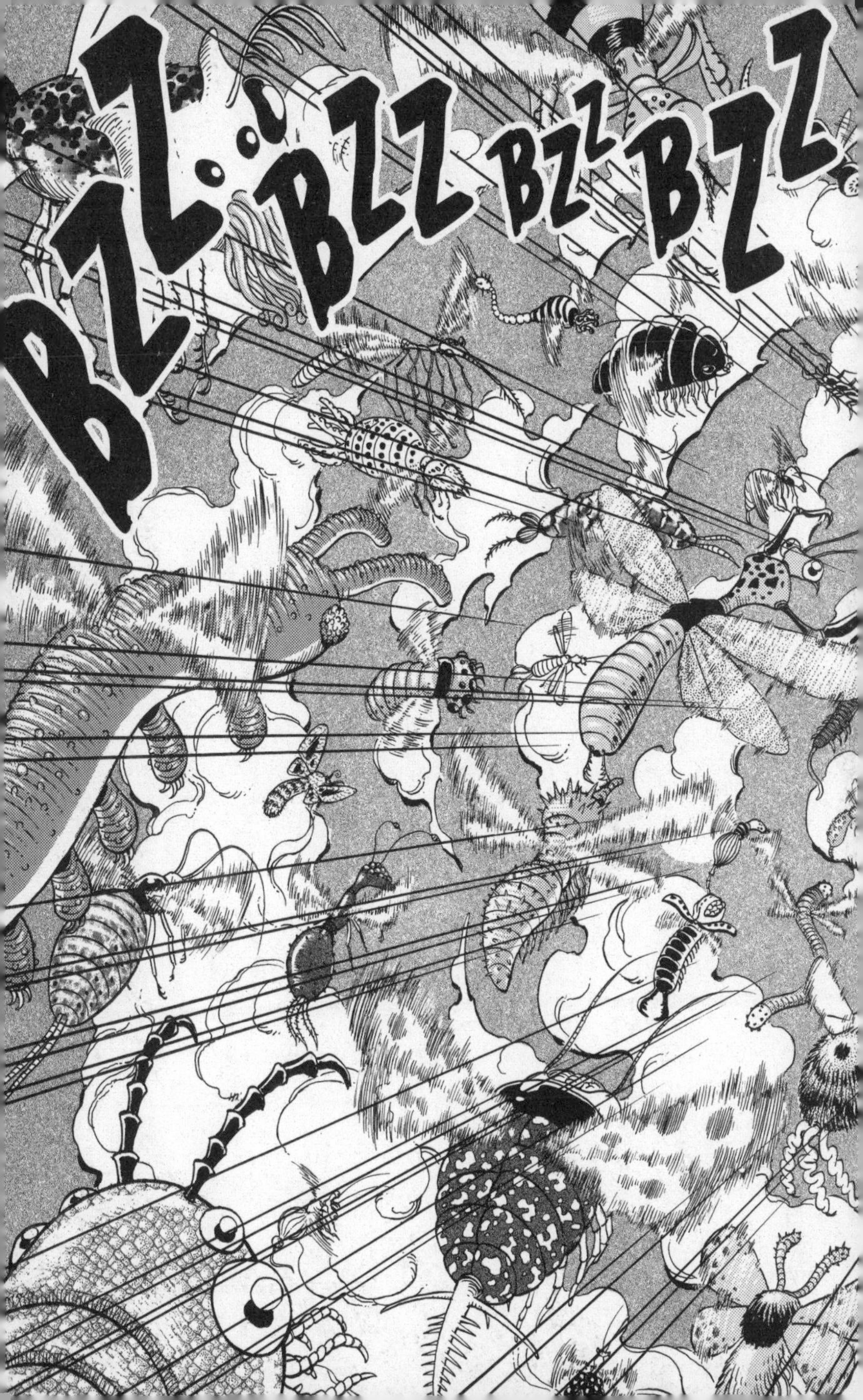
BZZ... BZZ BZZ BZZ

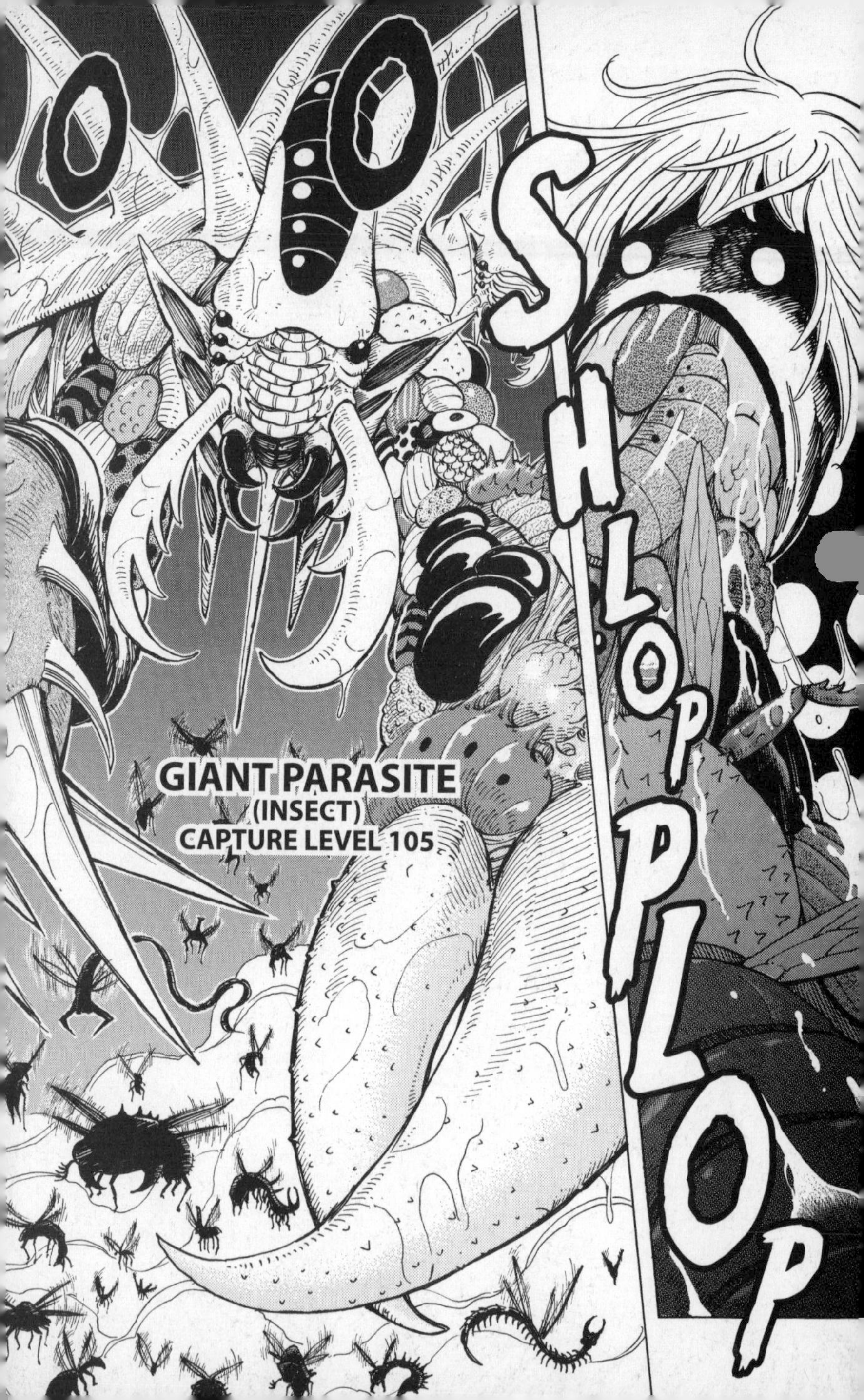
SHLOP
SHLOP
GIANT PARASITE
(INSECT)
CAPTURE LEVEL 105
SPLOP

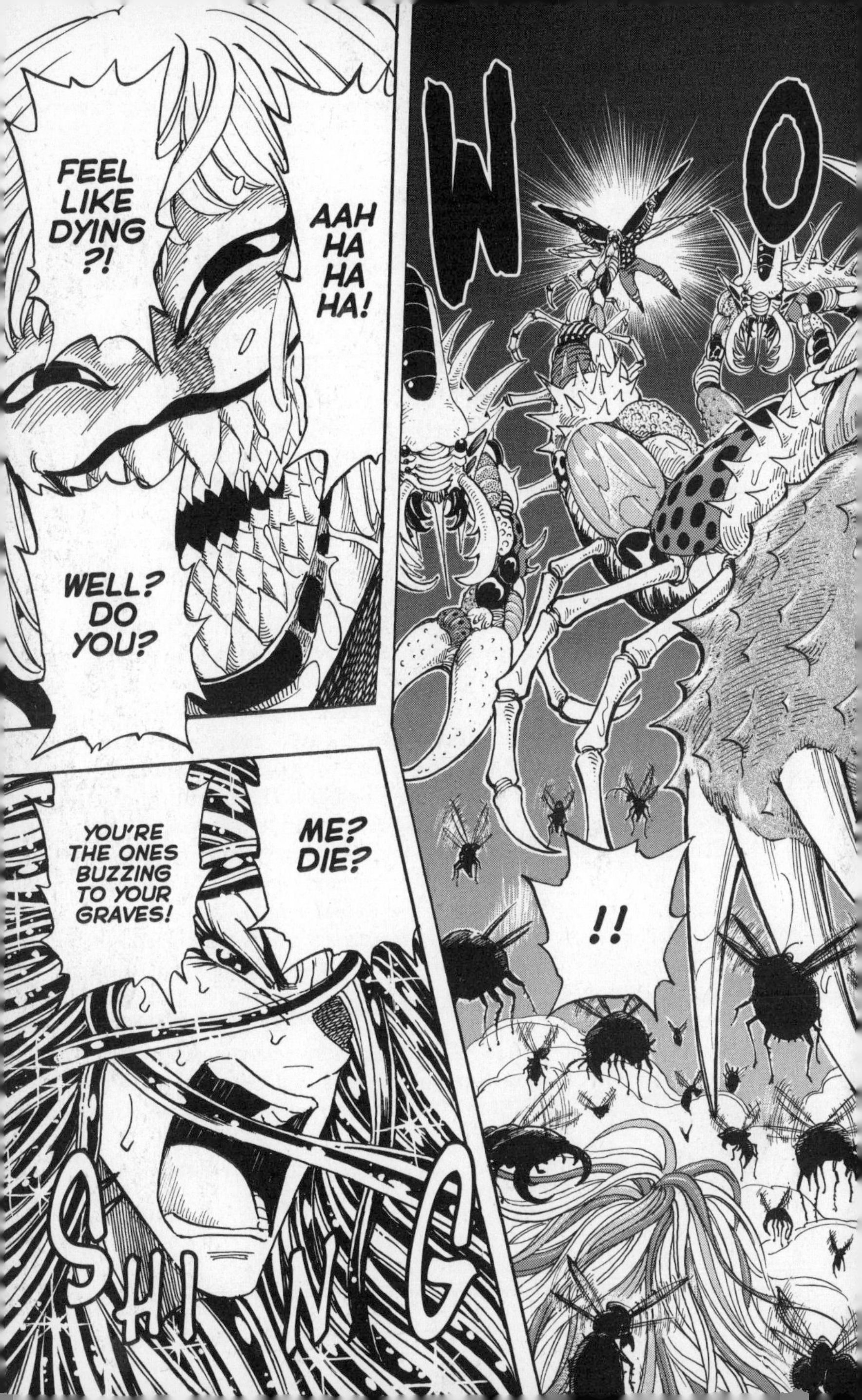
W O
!!
AAH HA HA HA!
FEEL LIKE DYING ?!
WELL? DO YOU?
ME? DIE?
YOU'RE THE ONES BUZZING TO YOUR GRAVES!
SHING

SHIMABU SPEAKS

All right! How did everyone enjoy this volume's install-ment of the Reject Pages Corner? Those were all quite the rejects, huh? It feels good to just scrap something without a moment's hesitation! Yep! It's like getting the gold medal in wasting time! (What's that supposed to mean?!) And on that note, let's take a little trip down memory lane.

Master Chin shows up at the end of Gourmet 180, but origi-nally I had planned on having "Vanishing Japanese Cuisine" span two or three chapters. Like having Komatsu learn some cooking from Chiru and stuff. So Master Chin never actually showed up in any of these reject storyboards. As you saw, that plot was going to develop leisurely, which is very much not my style. But that realization didn't come to me until after I'd written everything, so I reluctantly had to draw the entire chapter over again. I wish I had thought of that sooner! And didn't you think it had something go-ing for it? Namely, that great character Anyo! Oh, well... No use crying over spilled milk. I'm going to handle it grace-fully, have no regrets over the rejections in my life and let it rest in peace. That's how the Reject Pages Corner came to be! There are sure to be many, many more rejects, so I'll showcase them someday! La la la~! (What's all this confidence about rejection?) This is Shimabu, signing off and thinking, as I do every year, how I look forward to the ineffective mist that does little to clear away the occasional heat wave. See you again soon! Oh wait, there's more "Speaks" to be had!

Continued on page 186

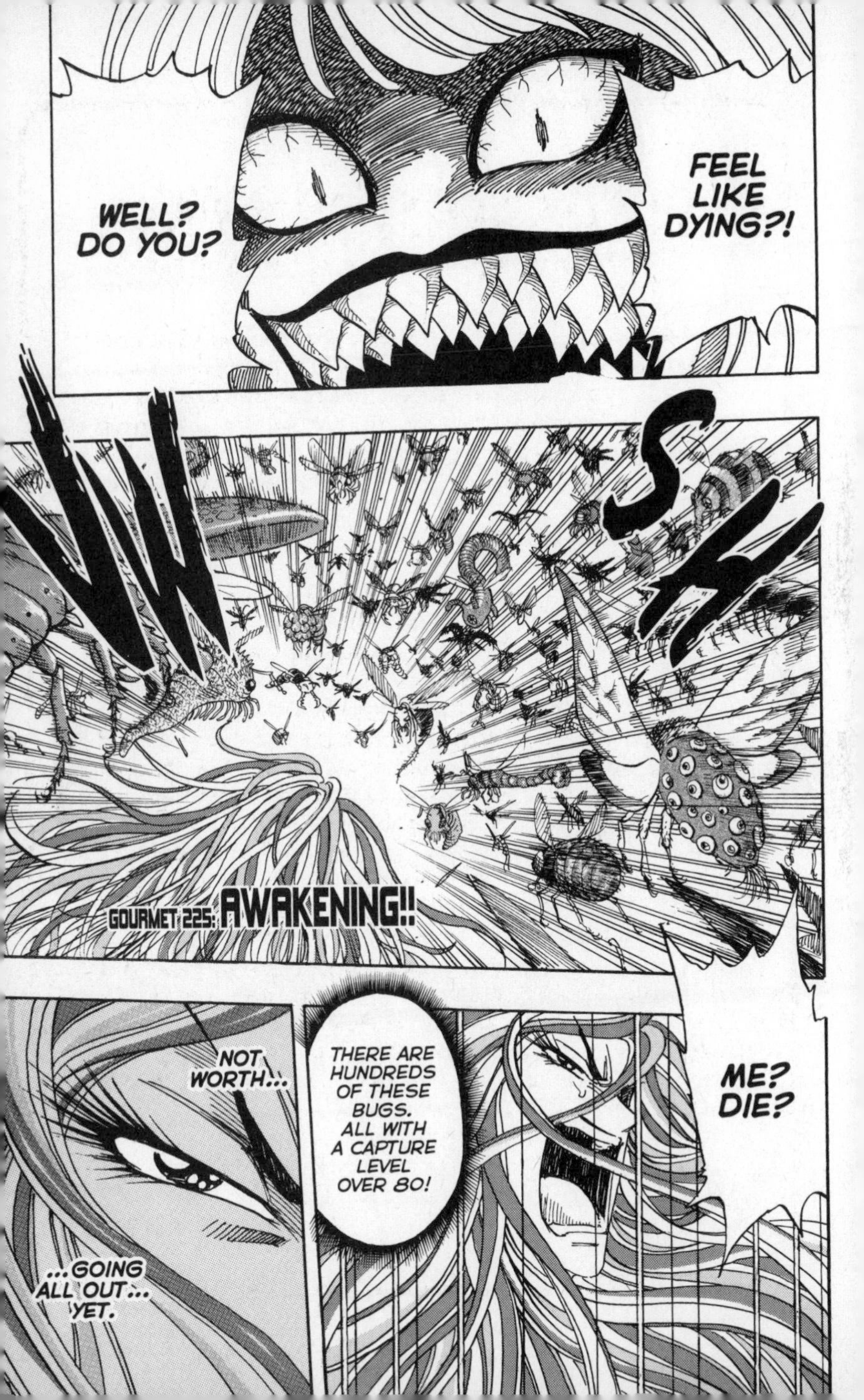
FEEL LIKE DYING?!
WELL? DO YOU?
SH
WW
GOURMET 225: AWAKENING!!
ME? DIE?
THERE ARE HUNDREDS OF THESE BUGS. ALL WITH A CAPTURE LEVEL OVER 80!
NOT WORTH...
...GOING ALL OUT... YET.

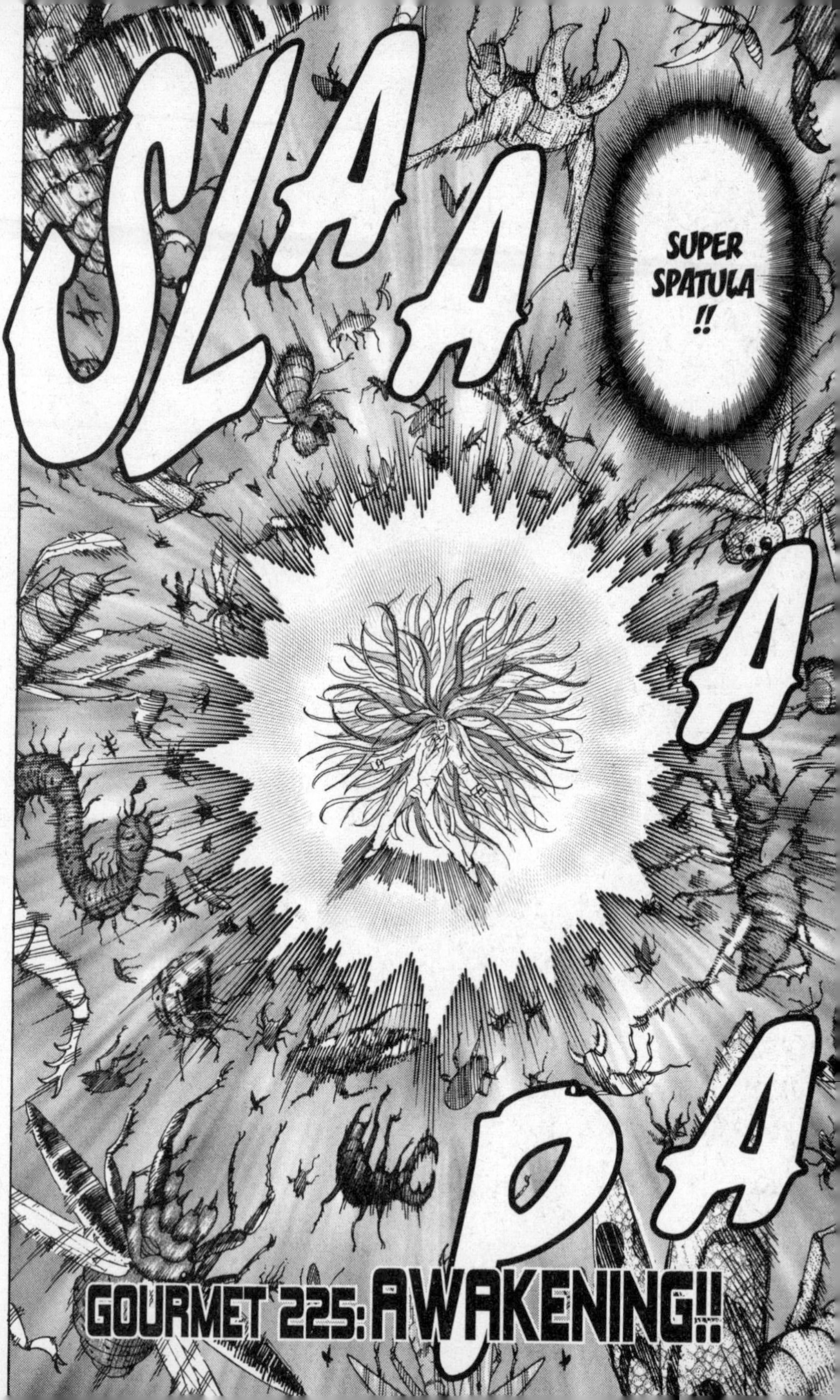
SUPER SPATULA !!
SLAAAA
PA
GOURMET 225: AWAKENING!!

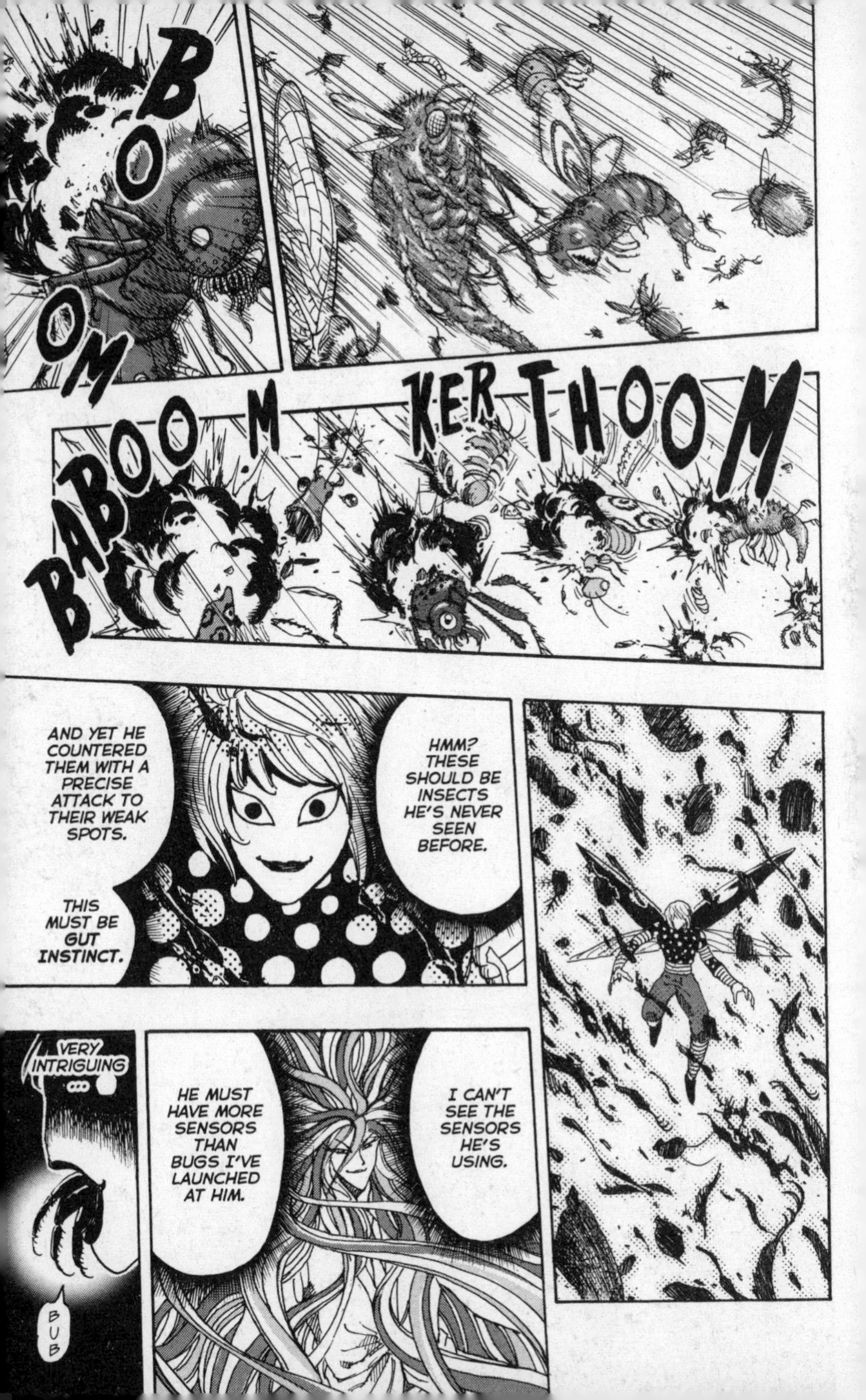
BOOM
KERTHOOM
BABOOM
HMM? THESE SHOULD BE INSECTS HE'S NEVER SEEN BEFORE.
AND YET HE COUNTERED THEM WITH A PRECISE ATTACK TO THEIR WEAK SPOTS.
THIS MUST BE GUT INSTINCT.
I CAN'T SEE THE SENSORS HE'S USING.
HE MUST HAVE MORE SENSORS THAN BUGS I'VE LAUNCHED AT HIM.
VERY INTRIGUING...
BUB

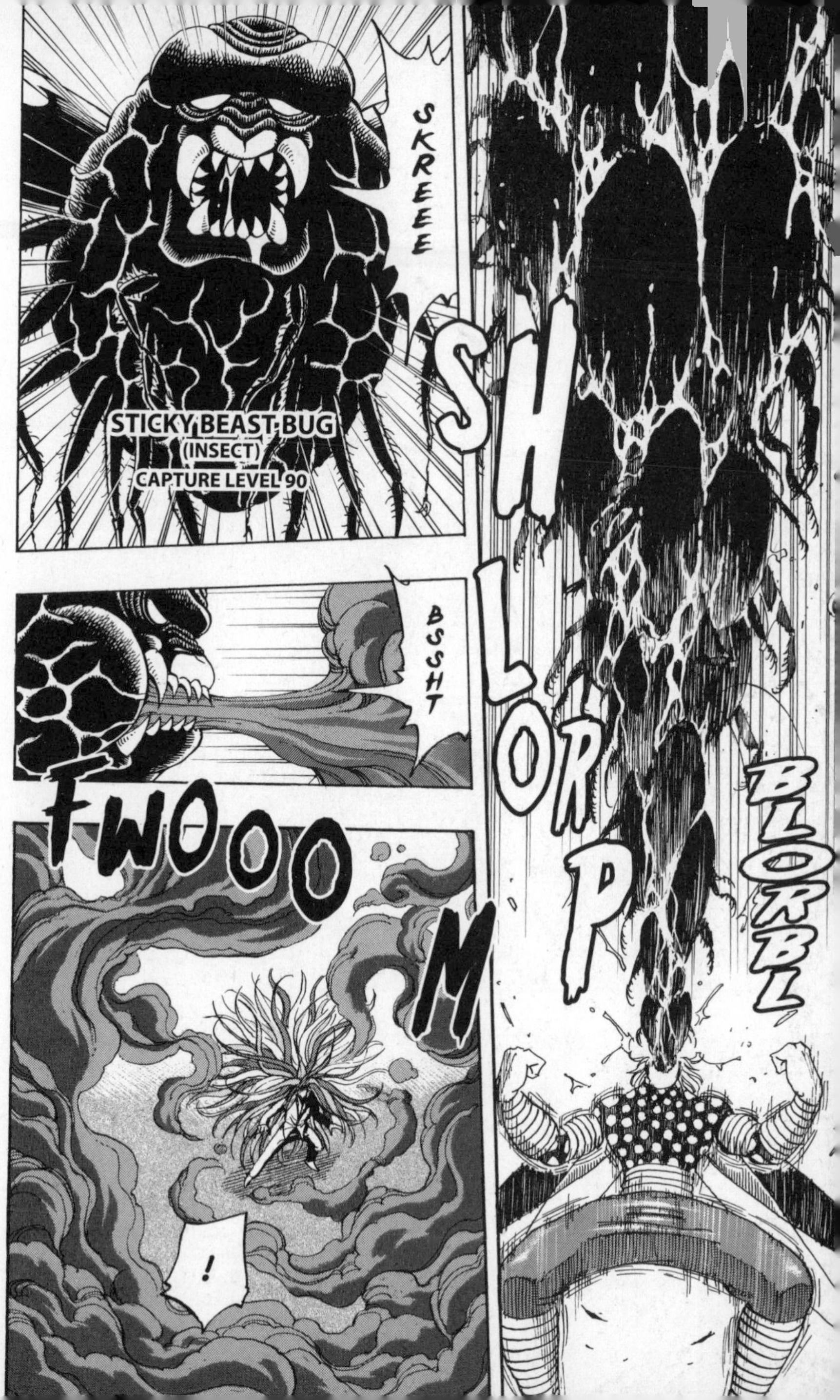
SHLORP
BLORBL
SKREEE
STICKY BEAST BUG
(INSECT)
CAPTURE LEVEL 90
BSSHT
TWOOOM
!

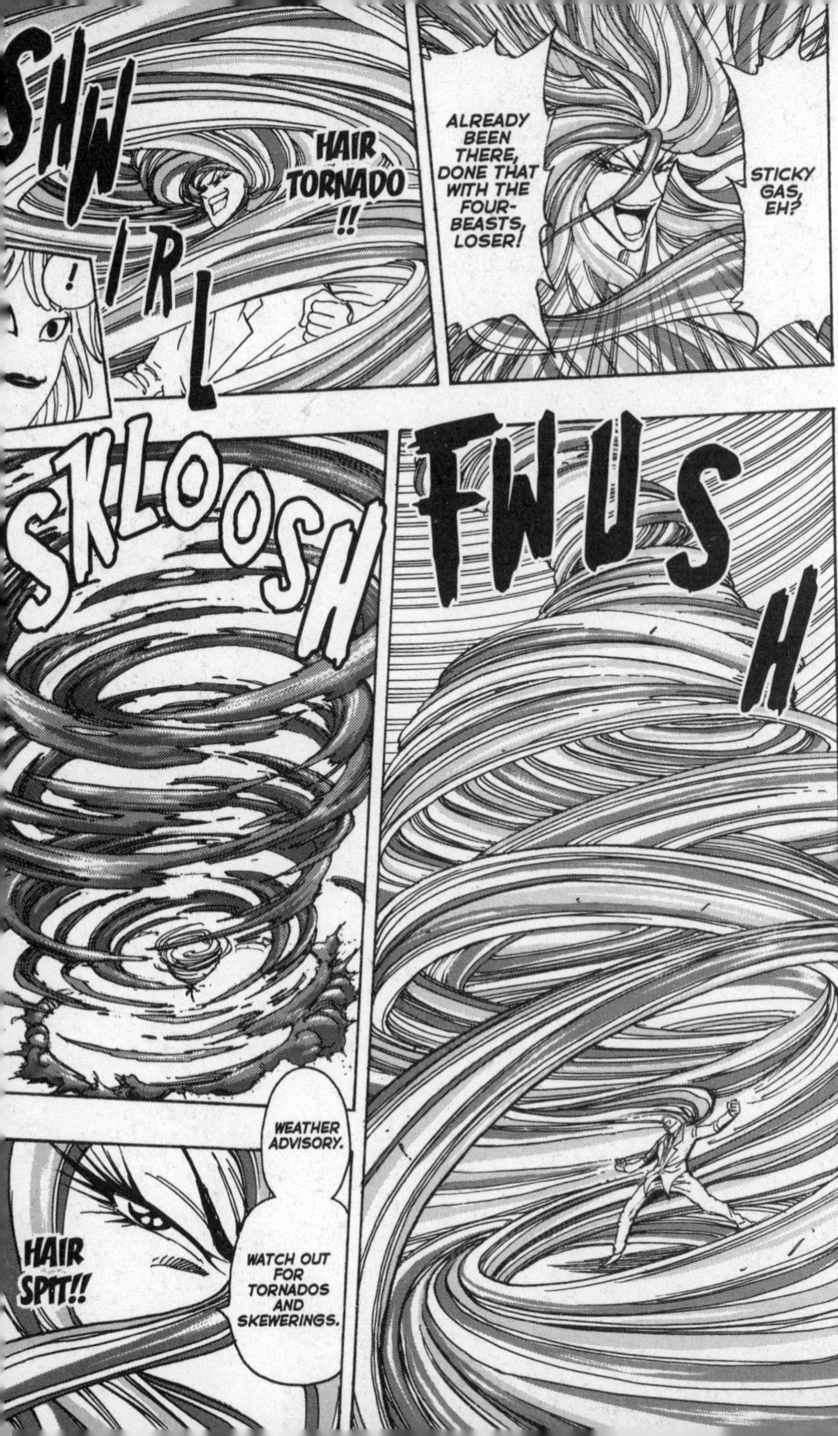
STICKY GAS, EH?
ALREADY BEEN THERE, DONE THAT WITH THE FOUR-BEASTS, LOSER!
HAIR TORNADO!!
SHWIRL
!
FWUSH
SKLOOSH
WEATHER ADVISORY.
WATCH OUT FOR TORNADOS AND SKEWERINGS.
HAIR SPIT!!

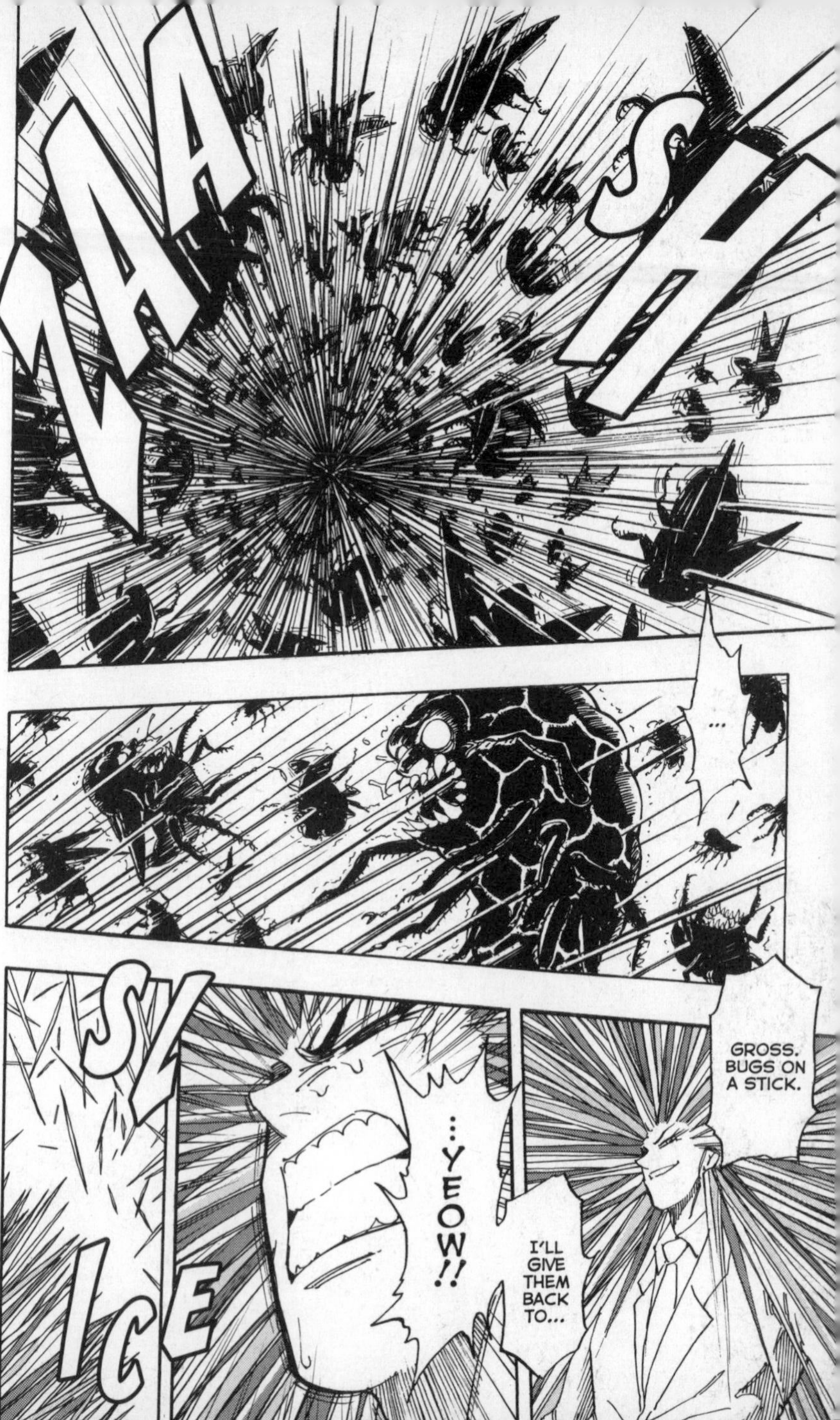
ZAASH
...
GROSS. BUGS ON A STICK.
I'LL GIVE THEM BACK TO...
...YEOW!!
SY
ICE

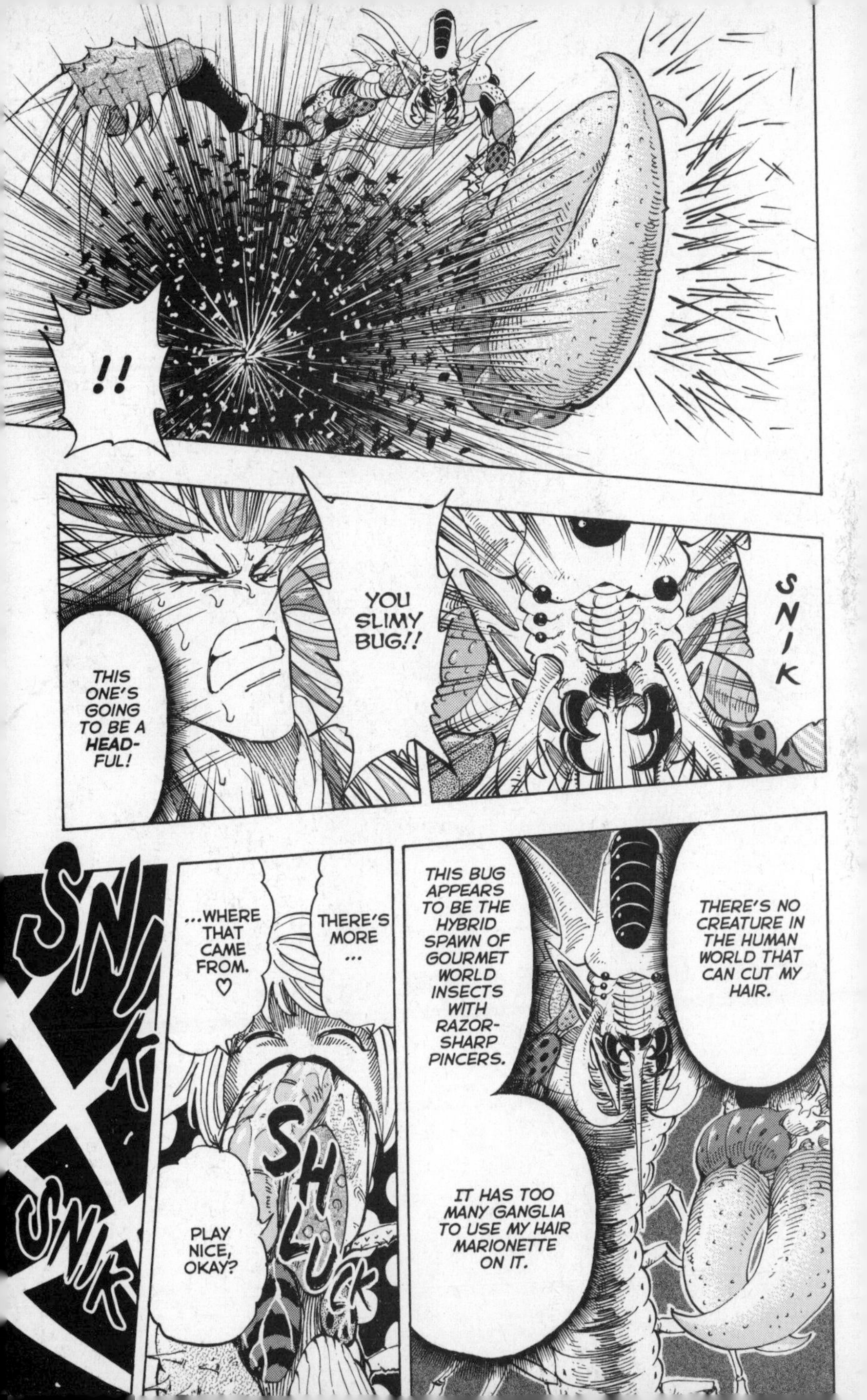
!!
SNIK SNIK
YOU SLIMY BUG!!
THIS ONE'S GOING TO BE A HEAD-FUL!
THERE'S NO CREATURE IN THE HUMAN WORLD THAT CAN CUT MY HAIR.
THIS BUG APPEARS TO BE THE HYBRID SPAWN OF GOURMET WORLD INSECTS WITH RAZOR-SHARP PINCERS.
IT HAS TOO MANY GANGLIA TO USE MY HAIR MARIONETTE ON IT.
THERE'S MORE ...
...WHERE THAT CAME FROM. ♡
SHLUCK
PLAY NICE, OKAY?
SNIK SNIK SNIK

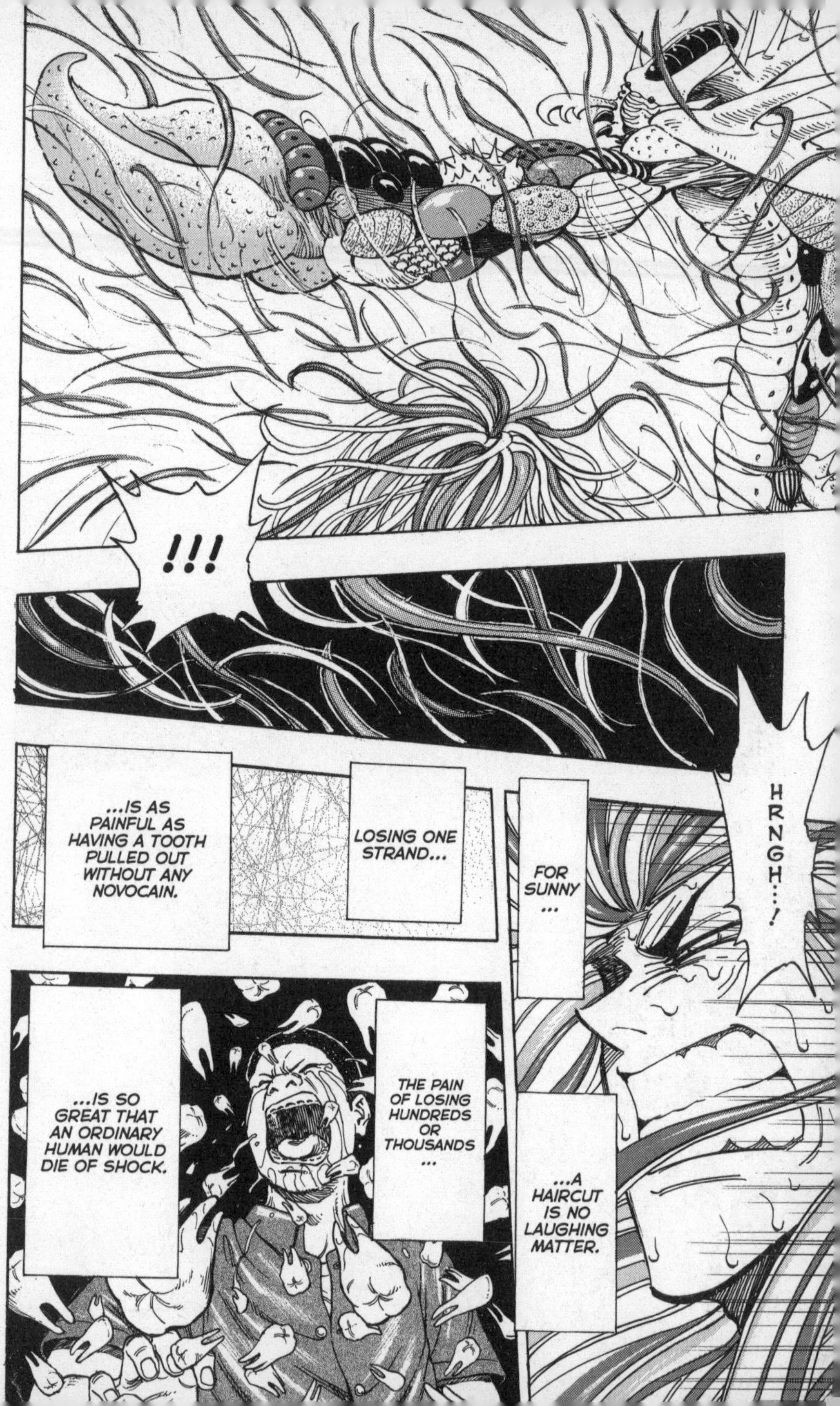
!!!
HRNGH...!
FOR SUNNY...
...A HAIRCUT IS NO LAUGHING MATTER.
LOSING ONE STRAND...
...IS AS PAINFUL AS HAVING A TOOTH PULLED OUT WITHOUT ANY NOVOCAIN.
THE PAIN OF LOSING HUNDREDS OR THOUSANDS...
...IS SO GREAT THAT AN ORDINARY HUMAN WOULD DIE OF SHOCK.

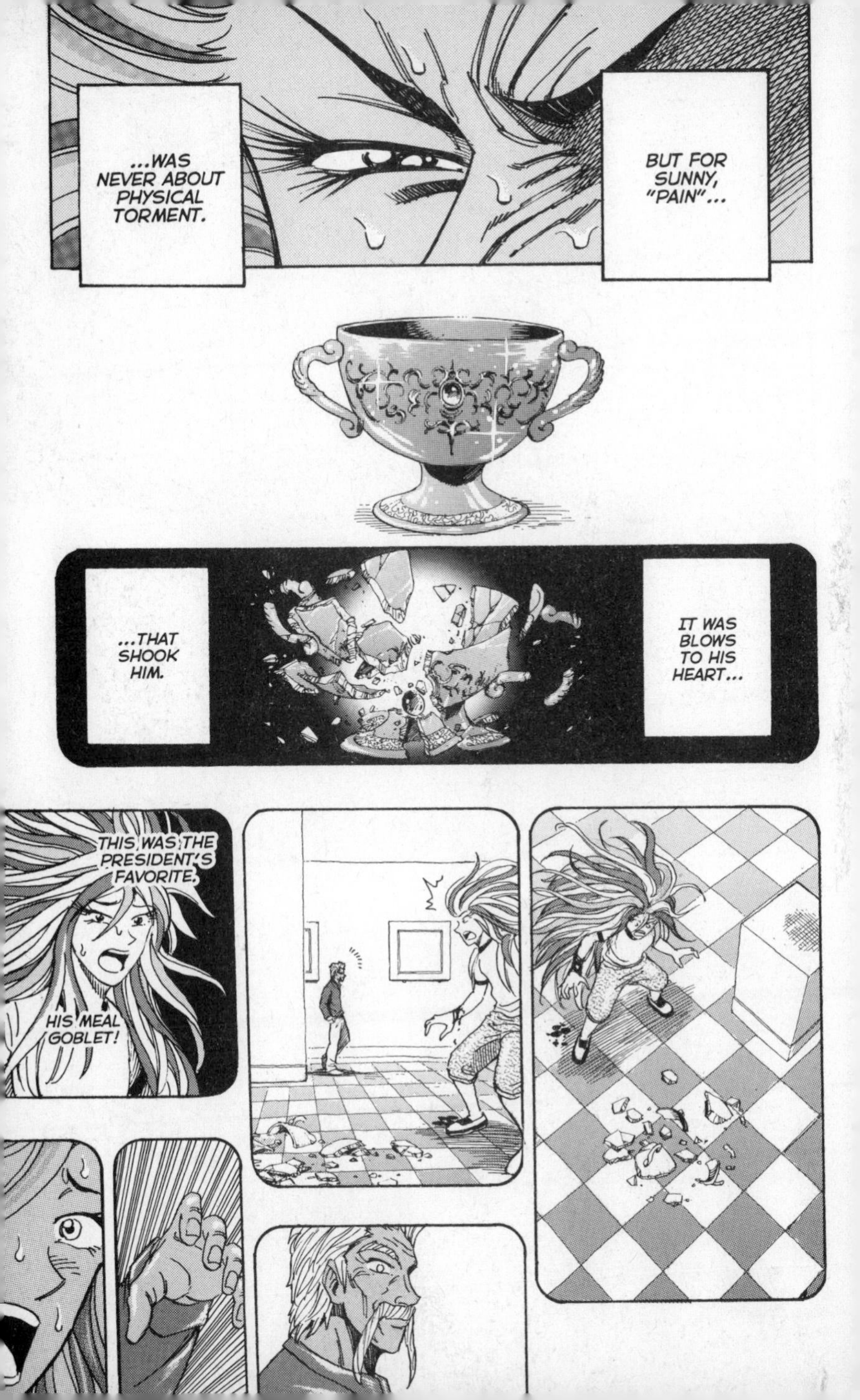
BUT FOR SUNNY, "PAIN"...
...WAS NEVER ABOUT PHYSICAL TORMENT.
IT WAS BLOWS TO HIS HEART...
...THAT SHOOK HIM.
THIS WAS THE PRESIDENT'S FAVORITE.
HIS MEAL GOBLET!

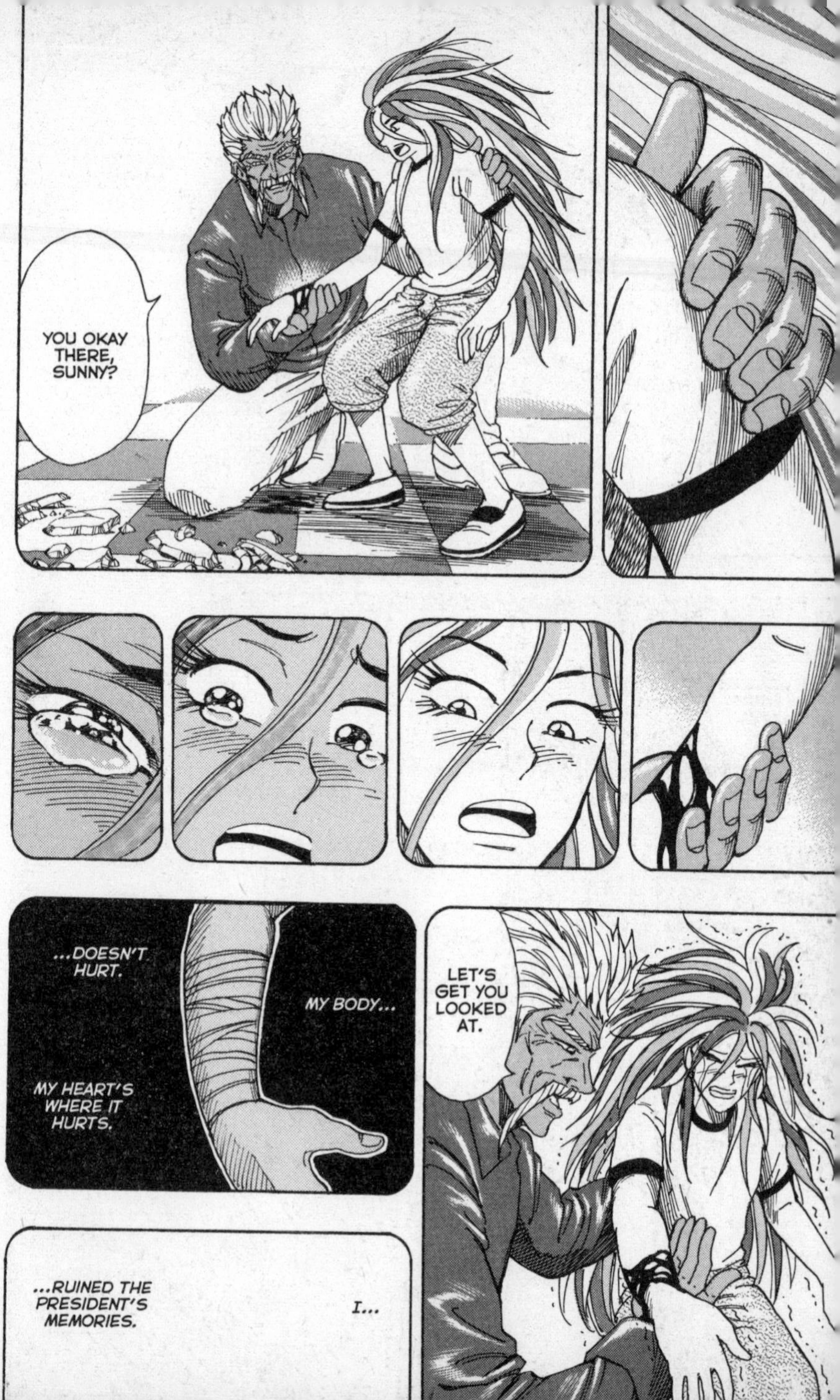
YOU OKAY THERE, SUNNY?
LET'S GET YOU LOOKED AT.
MY BODY...
...DOESN'T HURT.
MY HEART'S WHERE IT HURTS.
I...
...RUINED THE PRESIDENT'S MEMORIES.

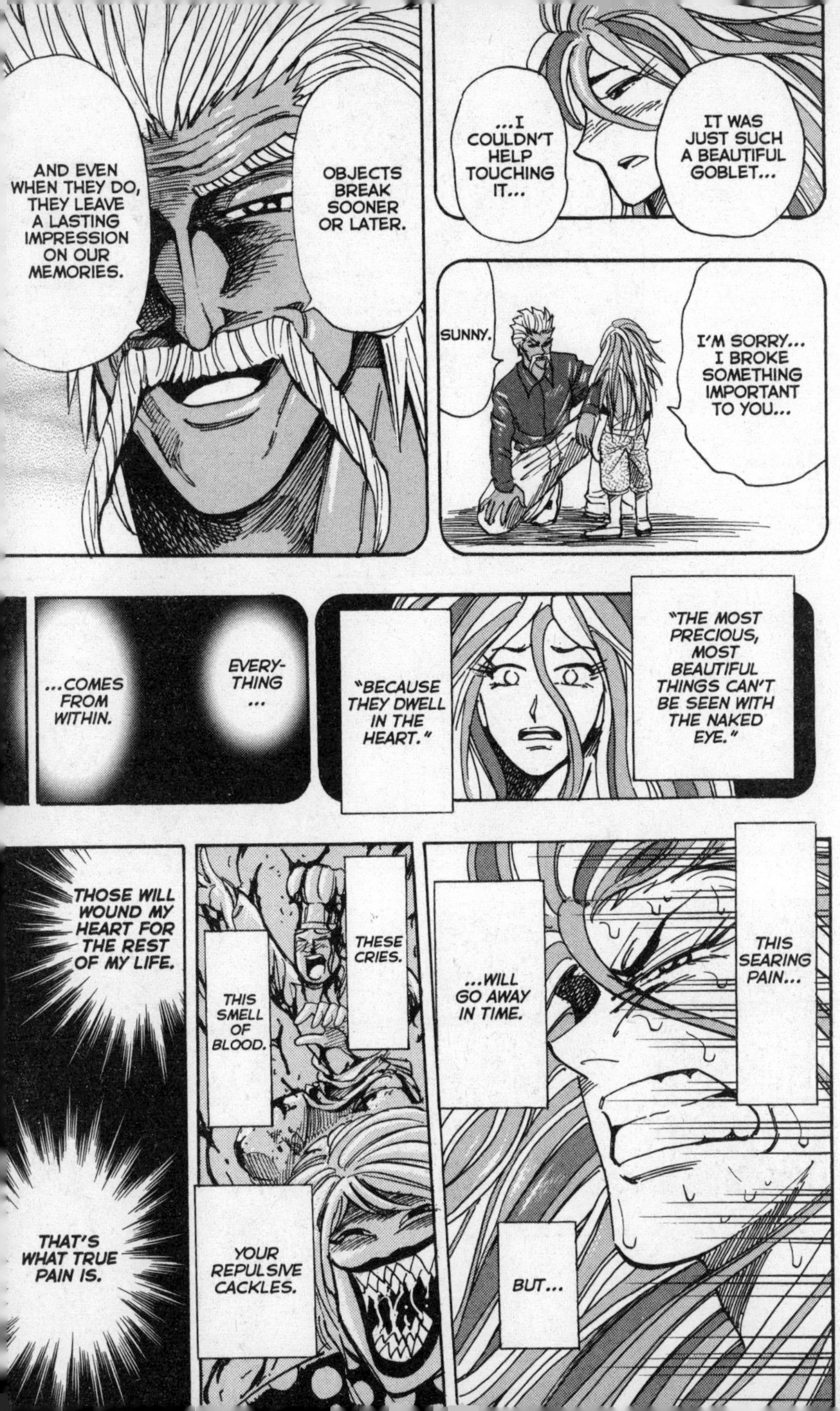
IT WAS JUST SUCH A BEAUTIFUL GOBLET...
...I COULDN'T HELP TOUCHING IT...
I'M SORRY... I BROKE SOMETHING IMPORTANT TO YOU...
SUNNY.
OBJECTS BREAK SOONER OR LATER.
AND EVEN WHEN THEY DO, THEY LEAVE A LASTING IMPRESSION ON OUR MEMORIES.
"THE MOST PRECIOUS, MOST BEAUTIFUL THINGS CAN'T BE SEEN WITH THE NAKED EYE."
"BECAUSE THEY DWELL IN THE HEART."
EVERY-THING...
...COMES FROM WITHIN.
THIS SEARING PAIN...
...WILL GO AWAY IN TIME.
BUT...
THESE CRIES.
THIS SMELL OF BLOOD.
YOUR REPULSIVE CACKLES.
THOSE WILL WOUND MY HEART FOR THE REST OF MY LIFE.
THAT'S WHAT TRUE PAIN IS.

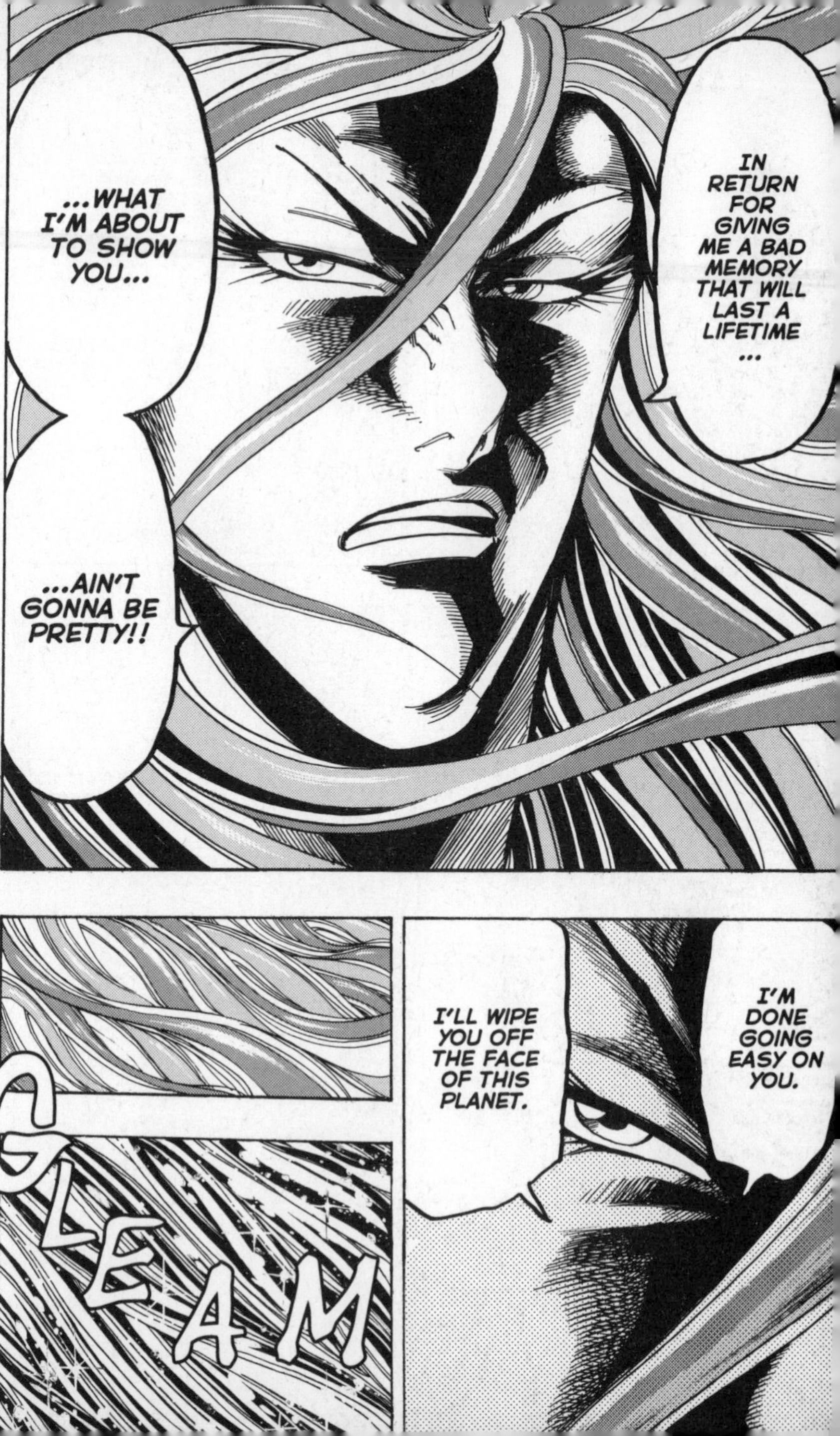
IN RETURN FOR GIVING ME A BAD MEMORY THAT WILL LAST A LIFETIME...
...WHAT I'M ABOUT TO SHOW YOU...
...AIN'T GONNA BE PRETTY!!
I'M DONE GOING EASY ON YOU.
I'LL WIPE YOU OFF THE FACE OF THIS PLANET.
GLEAM

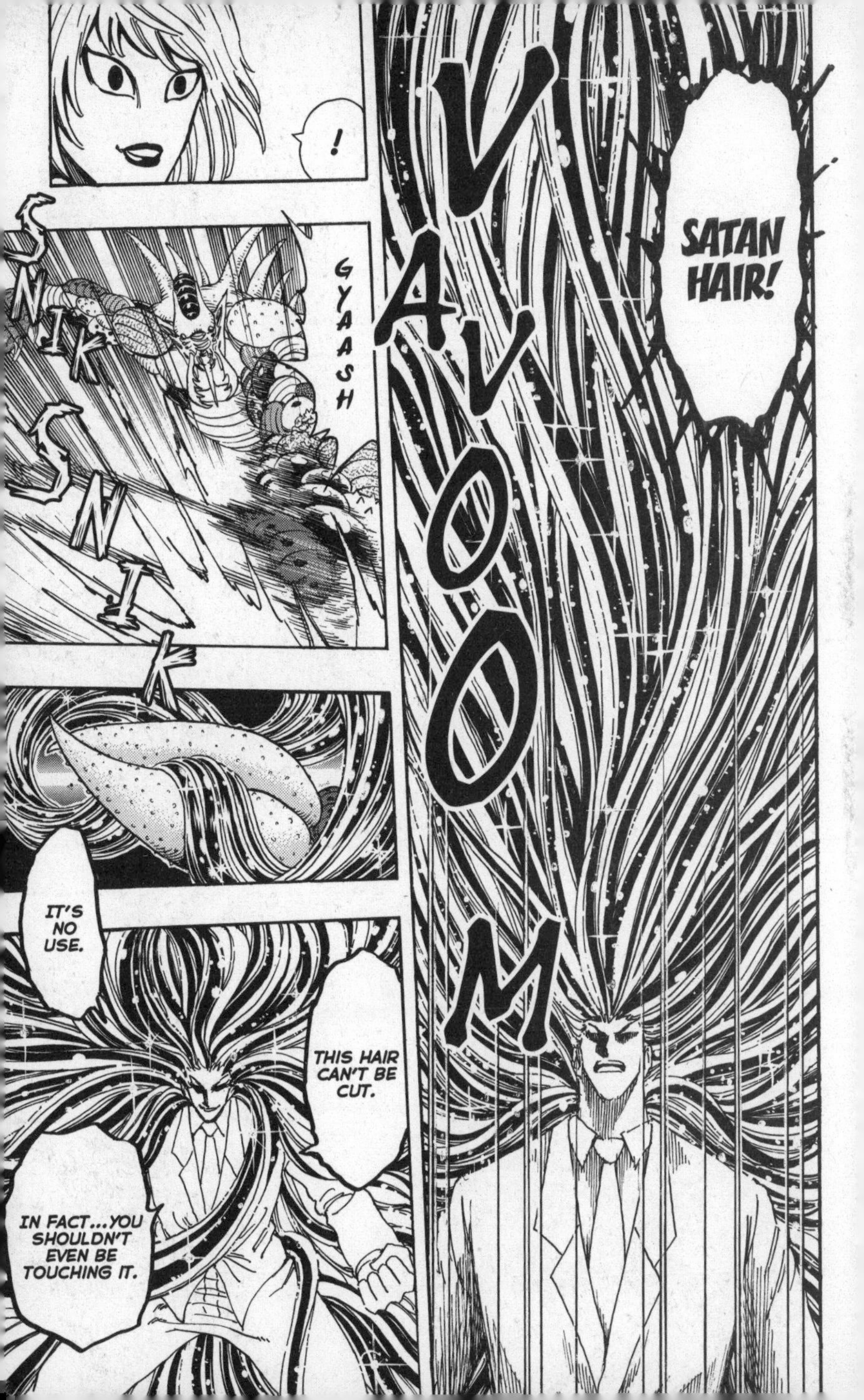
SATAN HAIR!
VAVOOM
!
GYAASH
SNIK
SNIK
IT'S NO USE.
THIS HAIR CAN'T BE CUT.
IN FACT...YOU SHOULDN'T EVEN BE TOUCHING IT.

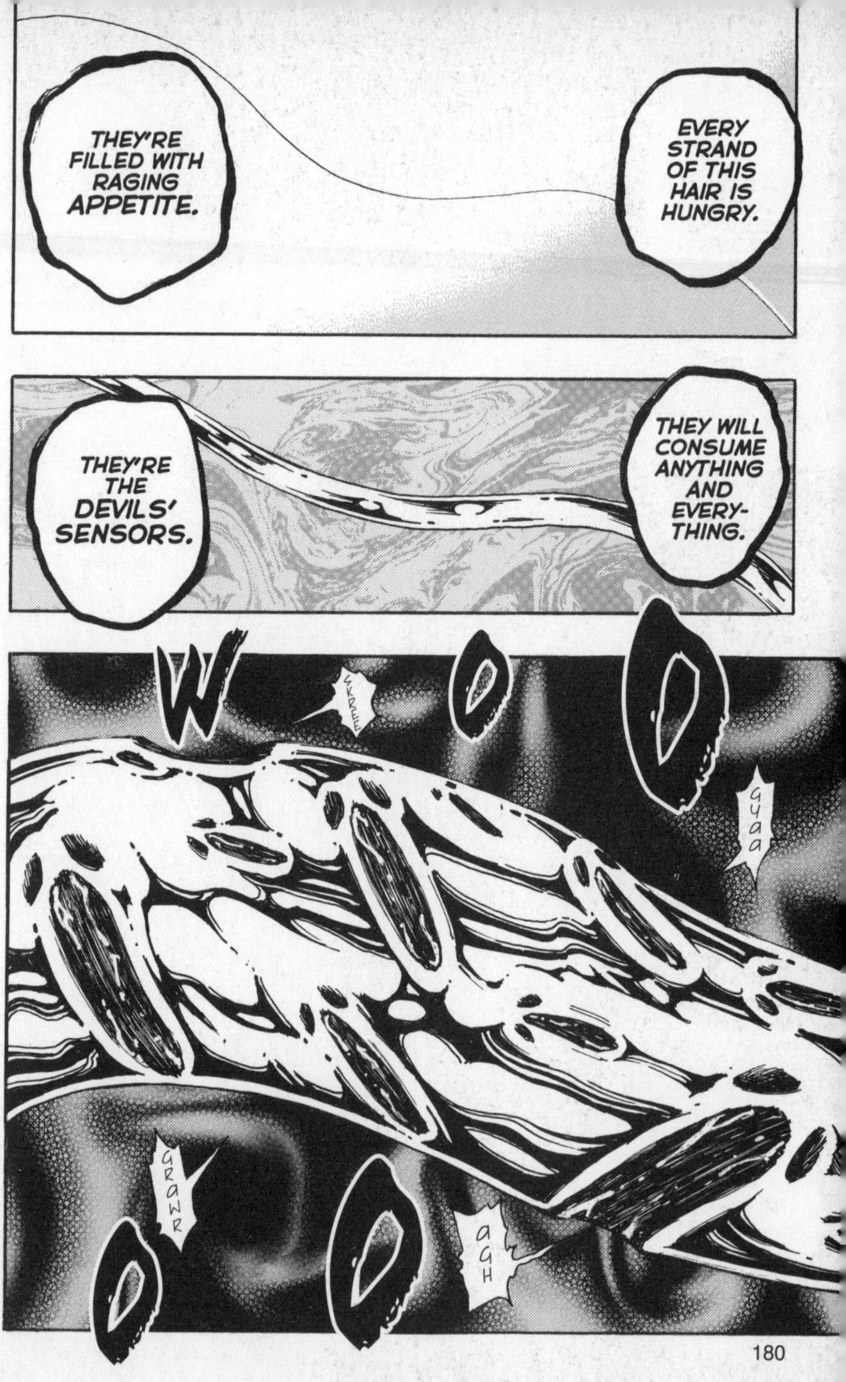
EVERY STRAND OF THIS HAIR IS HUNGRY.
THEY'RE FILLED WITH RAGING APPETITE.
THEY WILL CONSUME ANYTHING AND EVERYTHING.
THEY'RE THE DEVILS' SENSORS.
GYAA
SKREE
W
GRAWR
AGH

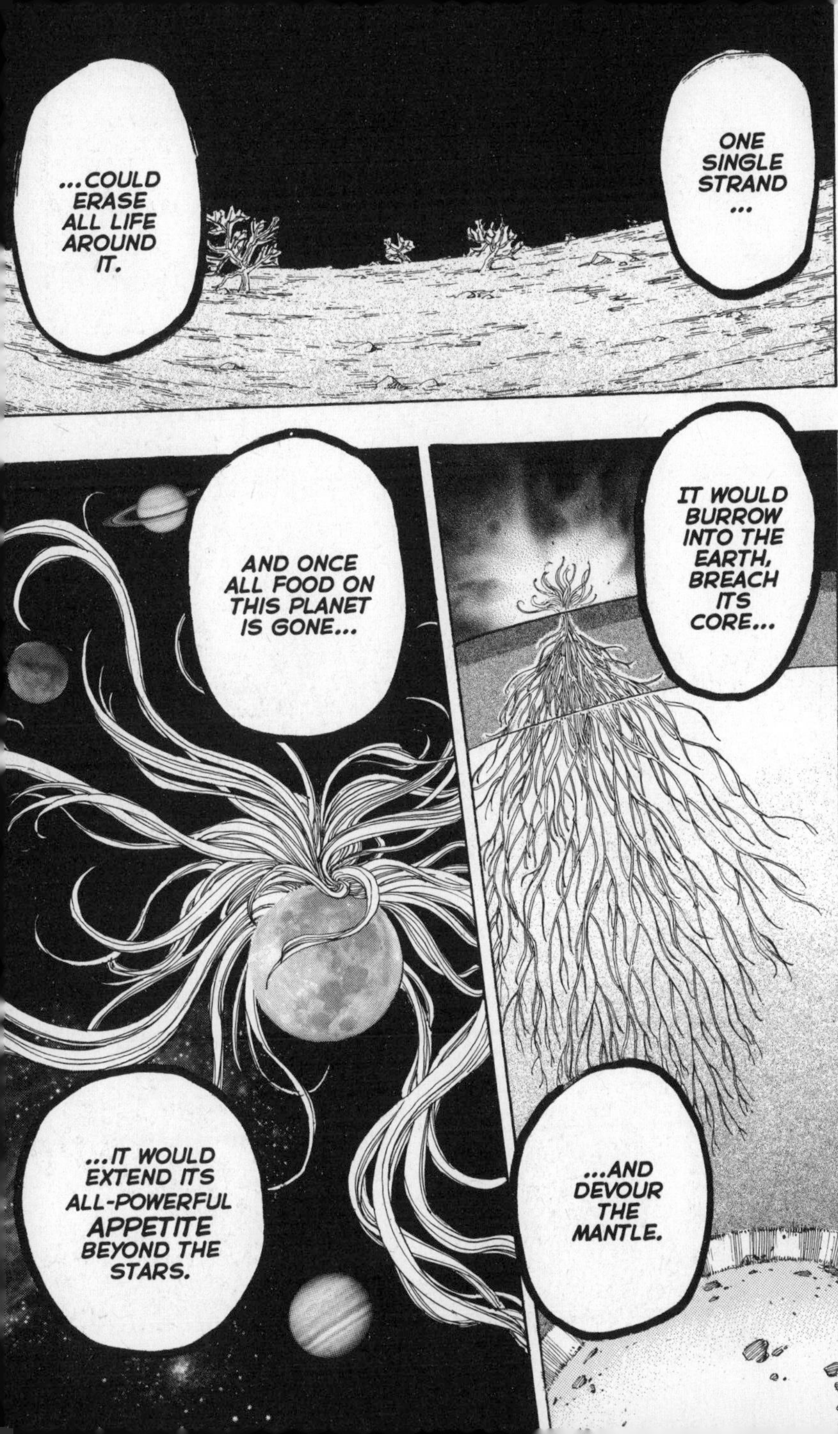
ONE SINGLE STRAND...
...COULD ERASE ALL LIFE AROUND IT.
IT WOULD BURROW INTO THE EARTH, BREACH ITS CORE...
...AND DEVOUR THE MANTLE.
AND ONCE ALL FOOD ON THIS PLANET IS GONE...
...IT WOULD EXTEND ITS ALL-POWERFUL APPETITE BEYOND THE STARS.

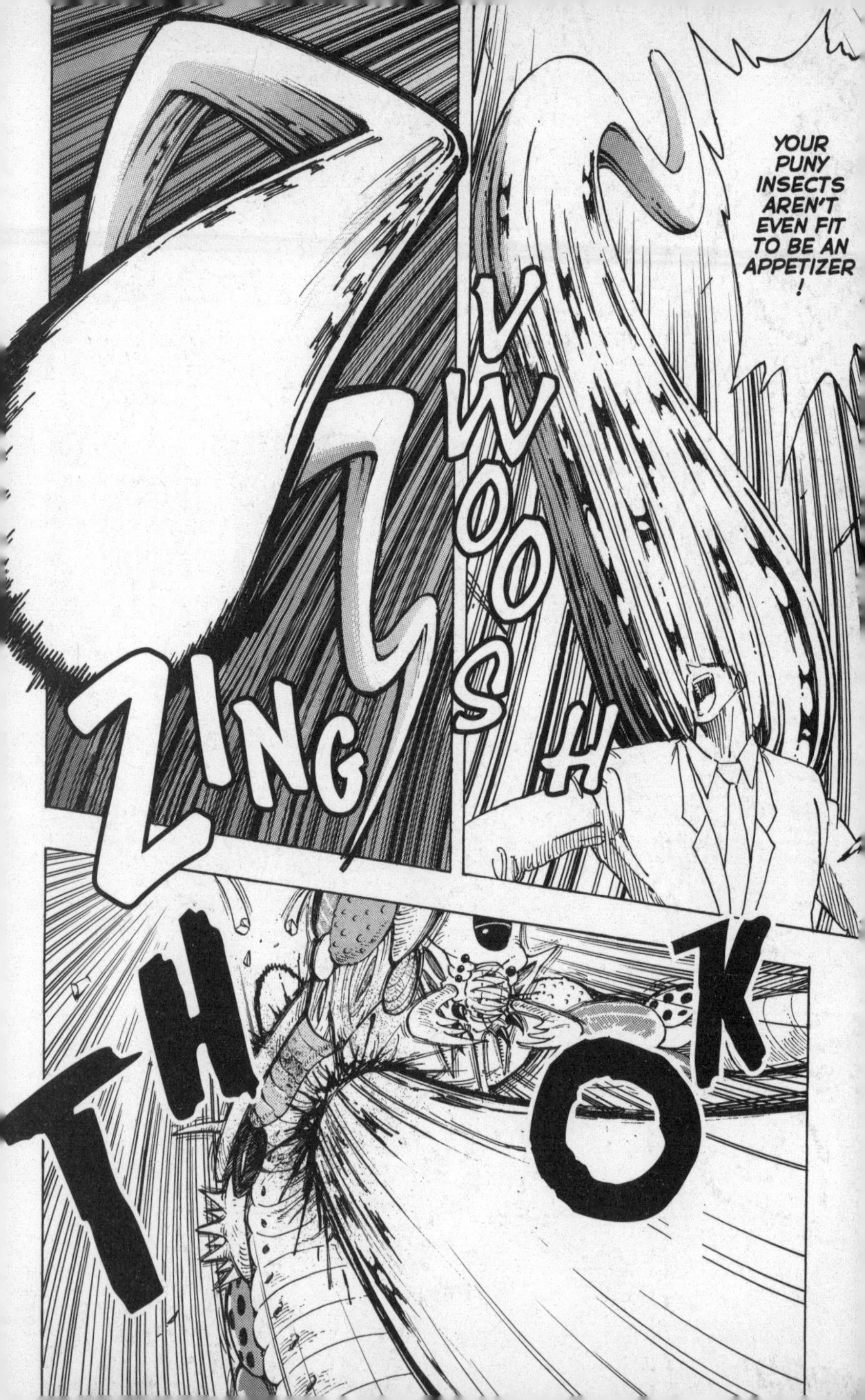
YOUR PUNY INSECTS AREN'T EVEN FIT TO BE AN APPETIZER!
VWOOSH
ZING
THOK

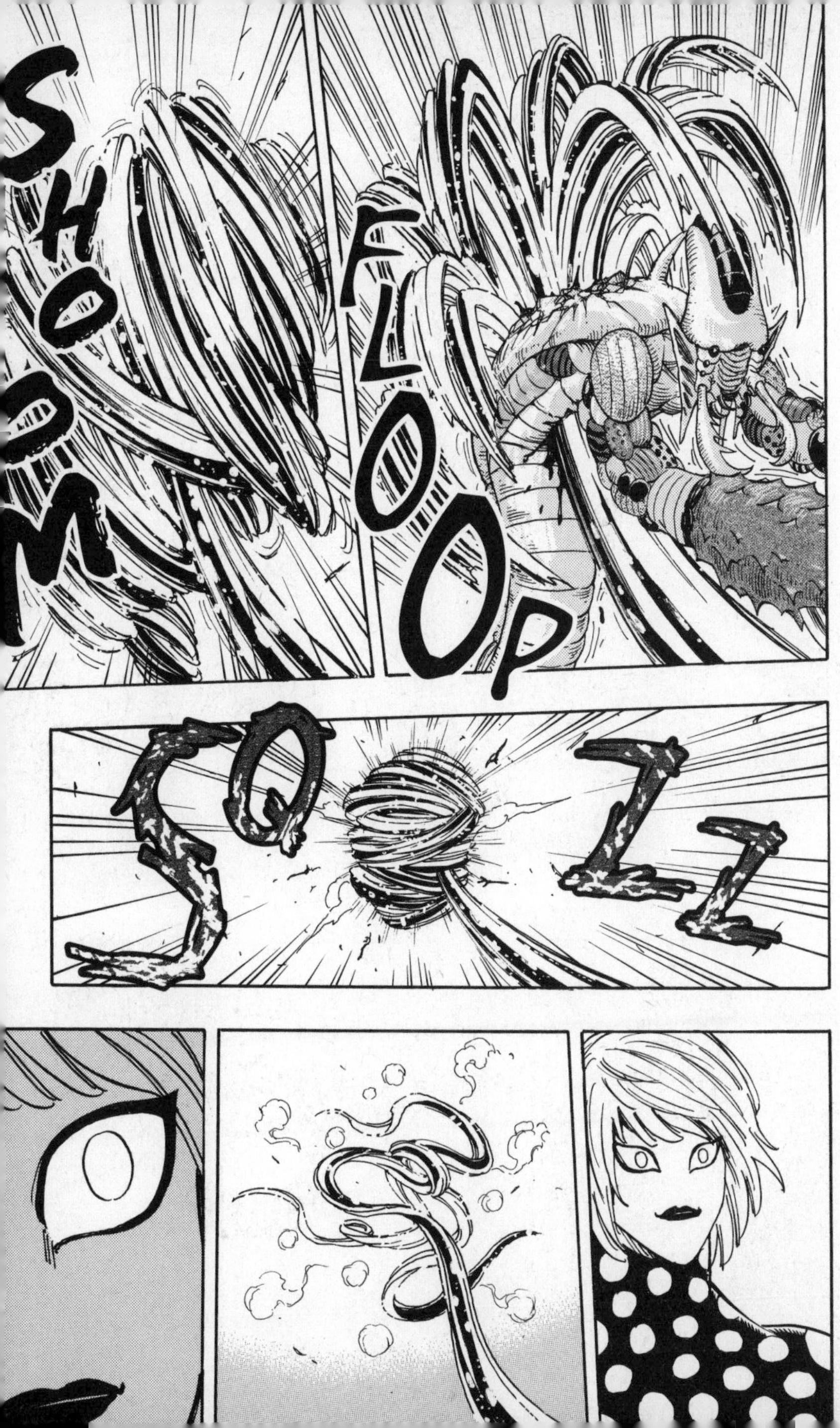
FLOOP
SHOOM
SQZZ

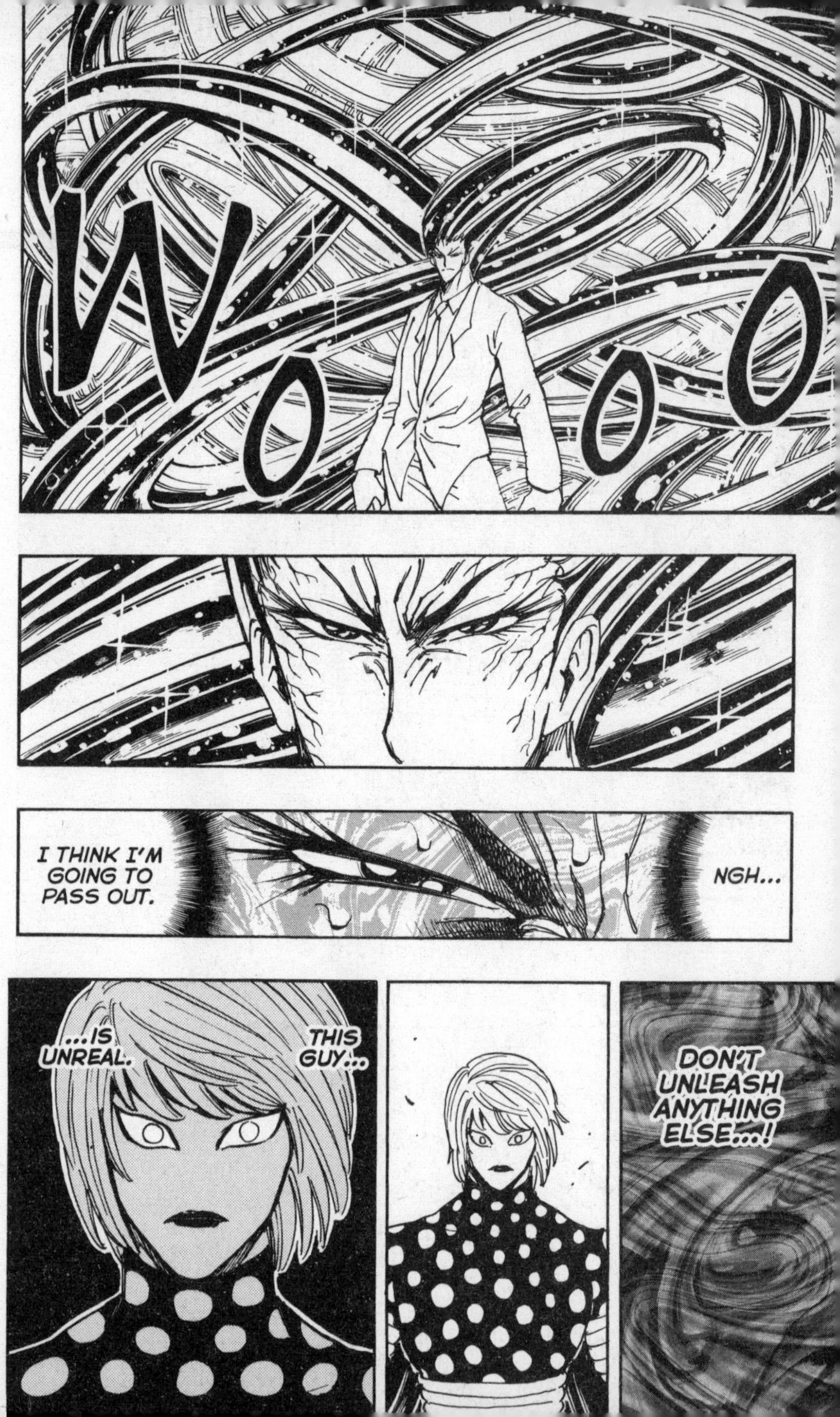
WOOOO
NGH...
I THINK I'M GOING TO PASS OUT.
DON'T UNLEASH ANYTHING ELSE...!
THIS GUY...
...IS UNREAL.

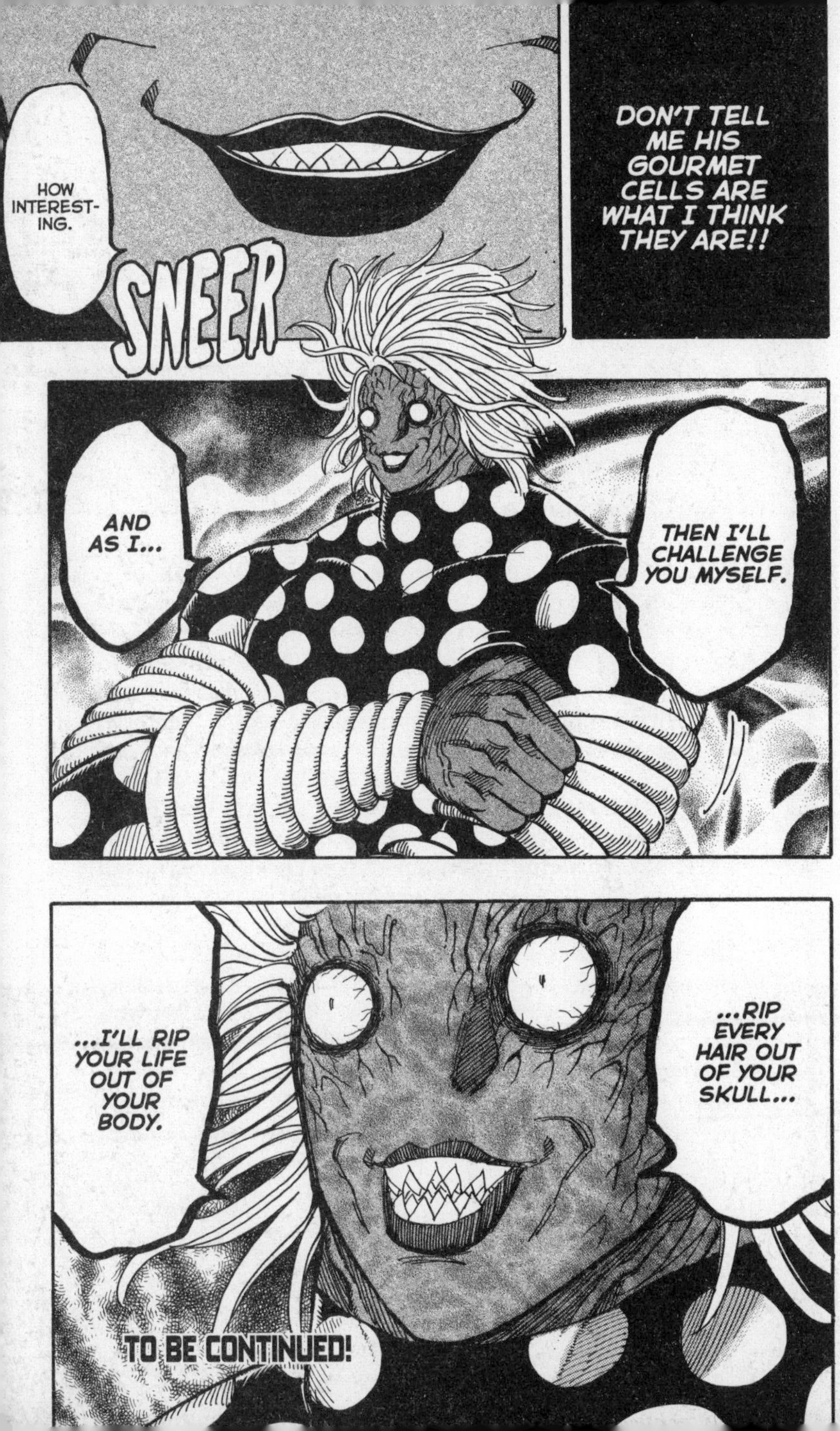
DON'T TELL ME HIS GOURMET CELLS ARE WHAT I THINK THEY ARE!!
HOW INTEREST-ING.
SNEER
THEN I'LL CHALLENGE YOU MYSELF.
AND AS I...
...RIP EVERY HAIR OUT OF YOUR SKULL...
...I'LL RIP YOUR LIFE OUT OF YOUR BODY.
TO BE CONTINUED!

SHIMABU SPEAKS

Well, I think I'd like to completely change the subject here and address the content of my author's comment: *Toriko*'s movie debut! Whoaaaa! The movie's been in the works for a while, and finally hits theaters the same month that this volume goes on sale in Japan, July 27th!

You know, to be completely honest, I was initially skeptical about *Toriko* becoming an animated film, and I think my editor told me a little lie to get me more jazzed about it. (What?!) But as the day draws nearer, everyone around me is getting more and more pumped and now I'm thinking "I can't believe this is happening!!" Will I be terribly shocked and disappointed?! Is Toriko seriously going to be screening in cinema multiplexes?! How about single-screen theaters?! Or in people's homes?! Will it be a home video?! The questions go on and on, and I'm a real wreck inside, but somehow it's still really happening. I never thought that *Toriko* would become an anime, and never in my wildest dreams did I think it'd hit the big screen, so now I'm all embarrassed and humbled thinking, "Is this really okay?"

This movie debut is thanks to so many people. Let me take this opportunity to say thank you to the staff, and especially to the kids who watch the show and all those readers who read the manga. Thank you so much, for everything. I'm looking forward to seeing it in theaters too. By all means, do yourself a favor and go to an air-conditioned theater, get yourself the biggest popcorn they have, and watch *Toriko*!

END

COMING NEXT VOLUME

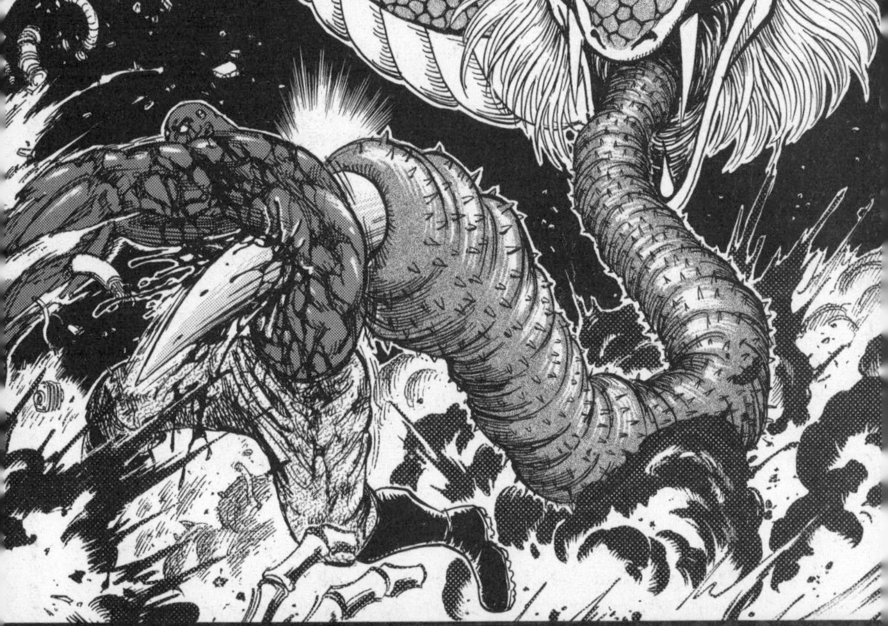

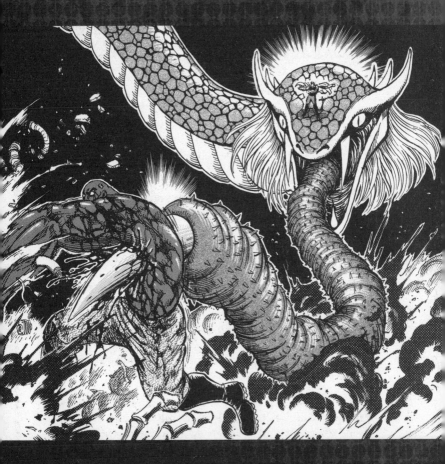

BEYOND THE LIMIT

When battle breaks out at the Cooking Festival, it's Toriko vs. Starjun, Sunny vs. Tommy and an assembly of world-class chefs and Gourmet Hunters against Gourmet Corp.'s vile monsters and souped-up villains. Then, Toriko stumbles during a battle to the death against Starjun, and Komatsu witnesses the unthinkable! Is this the end of Toriko?

AVAILABLE FEBRUARY 2015!

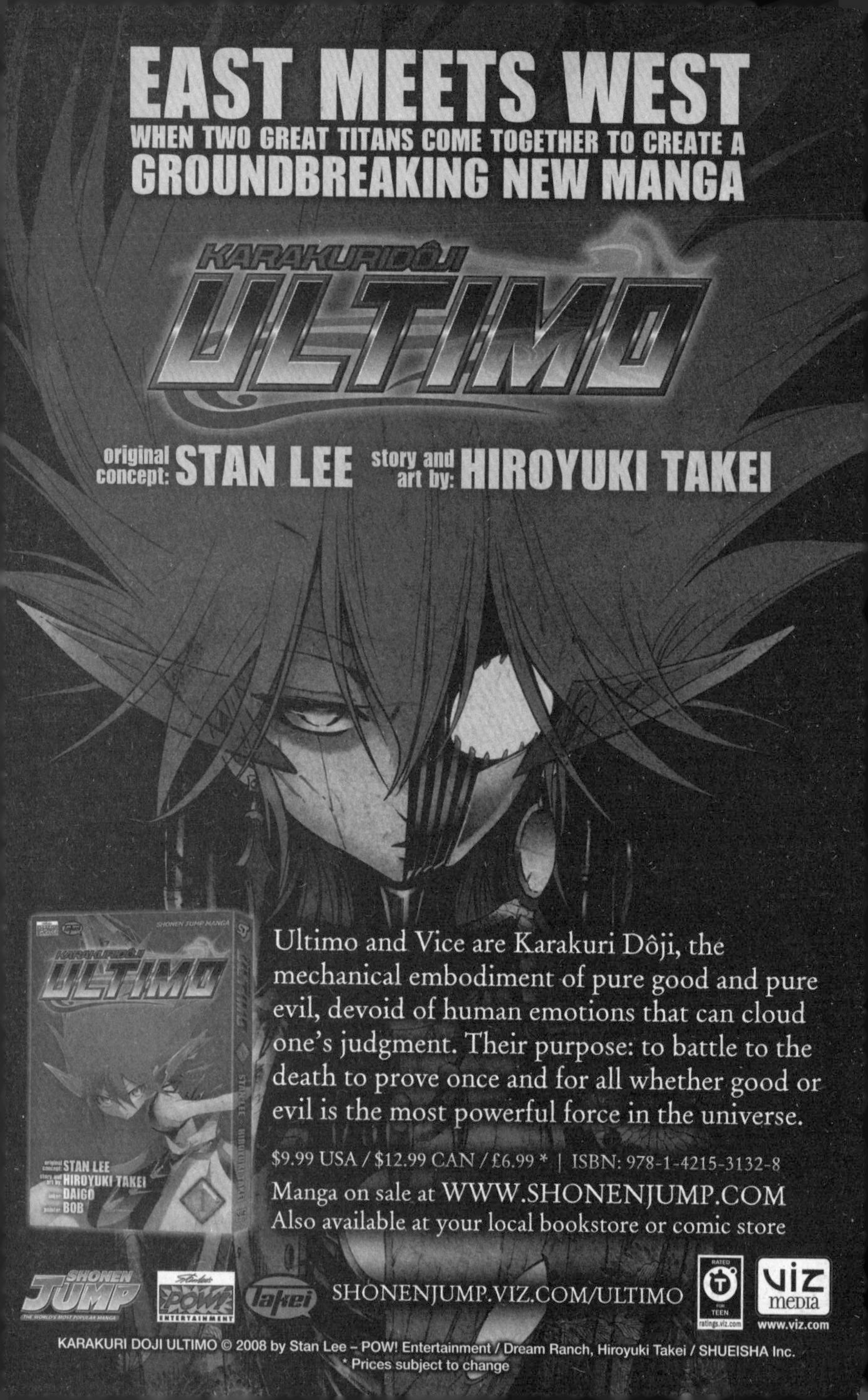
EAST MEETS WEST
WHEN TWO GREAT TITANS COME TOGETHER TO CREATE A GROUNDBREAKING NEW MANGA
KARAKURIDÔJI ULTIMO
original concept: STAN LEE story and art by: HIROYUKI TAKEI
Ultimo and Vice are Karakuri Dôji, the mechanical embodiment of pure good and pure evil, devoid of human emotions that can cloud one's judgment. Their purpose: to battle to the death to prove once and for all whether good or evil is the most powerful force in the universe.
$9.99 USA / $12.99 CAN / £6.99 * | ISBN: 978-1-4215-3132-8
Manga on sale at WWW.SHONENJUMP.COM
Also available at your local bookstore or comic store
SHONEN JUMP
POW! ENTERTAINMENT
Takei
SHONENJUMP.VIZ.COM/ULTIMO
RATED T FOR TEEN
ratings.viz.com
VIZ media
www.viz.com
KARAKURI DOJI ULTIMO © 2008 by Stan Lee – POW! Entertainment / Dream Ranch, Hiroyuki Takei / SHUEISHA Inc.
* Prices subject to change

You're R... the Wr... Direction!!

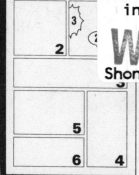

...ess from right to left, starting in the upper right corner.

Unlike English, which is read from left to right, Japanese is read from right to left, meaning that action, sound effects and word-balloon order are completely reversed... something which can make readers unfamiliar with Japanese feel pretty backwards themselves. For this reason, manga or Japanese comics published in the U.S. in English have sometimes been published "flopped"– that is, printed in exact reverse order, as though seen from the other side of a mirror.

By flopping pages, U.S. publishers can avoid confusing readers, but the compromise is not without its downside. For one thing, a character in a flopped manga series who once wore in the original Japanese version a T-shirt emblazoned with "M A Y" (as in "the merry month of") now wears one which reads "Y A M"! Additionally, many manga creators in Japan are themselves unhappy with the process, as some feel the mirror-imaging of their art skews their original intentions.

We are proud to bring you Mitsutoshi Shimabukuro's **Toriko** in the original unflopped format. For now, though, turn to the other side of the book and let the adventure begin...!

—Editor